Images of Disease

Science, Public Policy and Health in Post-war Europe

Edited by Ilana Löwy and John Krige

Barcelona, 25-28 November 1998

A great deal of additional information on the European Union is available on the Internet.
It can be accessed through the Europa server (http://europa.eu.int).

Cataloguing data can be found at the end of this publication.

Luxembourg: Office for Official Publications of the European Communities, 2001

ISBN 92-894-1146-5

Printed in Belgium

PRINTED ON WHITE CHLORINE-FREE PAPER

Table of Contents

Table of Contents

Editors' Note
Ilana Löwy and John Krige

Most of the material in this book originates from a conference held at the Universitat Autònoma de Barcelona in November 1998. We should like to thank the local organizers, the Centre d'Estudis d'Història de les Ciències (CEHIC) of the Free University for their invaluable help, and the Institucío Milà i Fontanals, CSIC, Barcelona for their support. A special word of thanks is due to Jon Arrizabalaga, José Pardo Tomás, Xavier Roqué, and Àlvar Martínez Vidal.

The organization of the conference and the preparation of the proceedings, was made possible thanks to the Fondation Maison des Sciences de l'Homme, within the framework of the project "Science, Public Policy and Health in Post-war Europe" of the European Science and Technology Forum of Research DG, European Commission, Brussels.

The Contributors

Olga Amsterdamska, Department of Science and Technology Dynamics, University of Amsterdam, The Netherlands.

Josep Bernabeu-Mestre, Unit of History of Medicine, Autonomous University of Barcelona, Spain.

Virginia Berridge, London School of Hygiene and Tropical Medicine, United Kingdom.

Danuta Duch-Krzystoszek, Institute of Philosophy and Sociology, Polish Academy of Science, Poland.

Dagmar Ellerbrock, Faculty of Science and Philosophy, University of Bielefeld, Germany.

Anna Firkowska-Mankiewicz, Institute of Philosophy and Sociology, Polish Academy of Science, Poland.

Jean-Paul Gaudillière, CERMES (INSERM, CNRS, EHESS), Paris, France.

Lyubov G. Gurjeva, CHSTM, University of Manchester, United Kingdom.

Barbara Gutmann Rosenkrantz, Harvard University, Boston, United States.

Nikolai Krementsov, Institute for the History of Science and Technology, St. Petersburg, Russia.

John Krige, Georgia Institute of Technology, Atlanta, United States.

Justyna Laskowska-Otwinowska, Department of Anthropology, Polish Academy of Science, Poland.

Ilana Löwy, CERMES (INSERM, CNRS, EHESS), Paris, France.

Barbara Markiewicz, Department of Philosophy, University of Warsaw, Poland.

Klim McPherson, London School of Hygiene and Tropical Medicine, United Kingdom.

Jorge Molero-Mesa, Unit of History of Medicine, Department of Philosophy, Autonomous University of Barcelona, Spain.

Sergei Orlov, Institute for the History of Science and Technology, St. Petersburg, Russia.

Paolo Palladino, Department of History, University of Lancaster, United Kingdom.

Enrique Perdiguero-Gil, Department of History of Science, School of Medicine, Miguel Hernández University, Valencia, Spain.

Esteban Rodríguez-Ocaña, Department of History of Science, University of Granada, Spain.

Images of Disease between Biomedicine and Politics
Ilana Löwy

In the second half of the twentieth century health-related preoccupations played an increasingly important role in the European political sphere. Health indicators, control of health-related risks, such as air and water pollution or food safety, and the availability of affordable and efficient health care for all, became important measures of success or failure of governmental policies. The statement that a poor health status of a given population is not merely the result of accidental circumstances, heredity, unusual activity of pathogenic agents, or plain bad luck, but is a straightforward political issue is not new. In 1847, a young Prussian physician, Rudolph Virchow was sent by his government to investigate a typhus epidemic in Upper Silesia. During his study Virchow became interested not only in the epidemic itself, but in its victims, principally Polish speaking peasants ruled by German speaking landlords and state administrators, who suffered harsh poverty and were denied rights to cultural autonomy and to self-organisation. His main conclusion was that while specific sanitary actions such as isolation of the sick may help to limit the spread of an existing epidemic, the best way to prevent such epidemics in the future was to raise the living standards and the education level of local populations. The later goal, he proposed, may be best achieved through a more liberal policy towards ethnic and linguistic minorities. The prevention of epidemics, Virchov concluded, cannot be dissociated from a wider socio-political context. Virchow's colleague and friend, Solomon Neumann, summed up the same idea in his well-known phrase: "medical science is intrinsically and essentially a social science"[1].

In the next 150 years, one may propose, Virchow's and Neuman's ideas were at the same time adopted and rejected. In the twentieth century, medicine became an increasingly technical endeavour, guided, in the main, by a reductionist perception of human pathologies. The leaders of the medical profession and key biomedical scientists stress the importance of new scientific knowledge and of new technical developments in the emergence of new ways to understand, to prevent and to cure disease. The bateriological era

---

[1] Rex Taylor and Annelie Rieger, "Rudolph Virchov on the typhus epidemics in upper Silesia: An introduction and translation", *Sociology of Health and Illness*, 1984, 36 (2), pp. 203-219.

in medicine was followed by the biochemical one, by spectacular development of new technologies such as medical imagery, and by the advent of molecular biology and the massive use of computers. In parallel, health, once mainly a private problem negotiatied in the interaction between a patient and a doctor, became increasingly viewed as public issue. Medicine is perhaps not seen as a straightforward social science, and doctors have a tendency to radically dissociate "hard" biomedical questions from "soft" psycho-social, cultural and ethical ones, but, on the other hand, management of health care is perceived as a key social and political problem.

In the nineteenth century, political intervention in health-related issues was limited to the control and the prevention of epidemic diseases. This problem was at the origin of the first municipal, national and international hygienic interventions[2]. The first International Sanitary Conference of 1851 dealt exclusively with a new major health threat in Europe – the Asiatic cholera. The subsequent conferences continued to discuss the cholera danger and added to their agenda the control of other epidemic diseases, especially those originating in remote geographic areas. Until the end of the 19th century, debates in Sanitary Conferences were focused on the relative virtues and drawbacks of quarantines, and on the efficiency of sanitary controls at the borders. The description (in the 1870s and 80s) of the role of bacteria in the transmission of infectious diseases did not lead immediately to important changes in medical practices. Traditional methods of prevention of epidemic diseases such as the isolation of the sick, quarantines for travellers from epidemic areas, the use of mosquito nets, the destruction of domestic "pests", the supervision of purity of drinking water, the promotion of personal cleanliness, or the elimination of sources of foul odours contuned to be viewed as valid. They were legitimated by the new microbiological knowledge, but their implementation did not depend on the diffusion of new scientific methods. The description of the plague baccillus confirmed the strongly suspected links between human and rodent disease, but anti-plague measures remained the same before and after the discovery of the bacillus: isolation of the sick and extermination of rats[3].

Bacteriological analyses were, by contrast, quickly adopted by municipal and governmental services which supervised the quality of drinking water and the safety of

---

[2] Anne Hardy, *The Epidemic Streets: Infectious Disease and the Rise of Preventive Medicine, 1856-1900*, Oxford, Clarendon Press, 1993; Charles Rosenberg, *The Cholera Years: The United States in 1832, 1849 and 1866*, Chicago, The University of Chicago Press, 1962; François Delaporte, *Disease and Civilisation*, Cambridge, Mas., MIT Press, 1987.

[3] Norman Howard Jones, *Les bases scientifiques des conférences sanitaires internationales, 1851-1938*, Genève, Organisation Mondiale de la Santé, 1975.

industrially produced foodstuffs. They were also introduced into epidemiological investigations. The rapid introduction of laboratory-based approaches into areas which are today gathered under the heading "public health", reflected probably not only their technical efficacy, but also the fact that bacteriological techniques promoted organisational innovation in areas at the cross-roads between political and administrative action[4]. Disease-inducing agents also rapidly penetrated the popular imagination. Images of health and disease became confounded in the late nineteenth century with the picture of the invisible threat of pathogenic micro-organisms[5]. On the other hand, the omnipresence of the bacterial threat, many experts had rapidly pointed out, limited the possiblity of its elimination. Aseptic environment can be achieved – at a great cost – in a small, well-defined spaces, such as an operating room or a segment of a production plant, but it is impossible to make aseptic the environment in which humans evolve. The view that "microbes are everywhere" was reinforced by the discovery of numerous "asymptomatic carriers" of infectious diseases, that is, individuals infected by a pathogenic micro-organism who are able to transmit the disease to others without being sick themselves[6]. The accent shifted from the elimination of microbes to actions aiming to protect humans from pathogens, such as vaccination and early detection. In parallel, isolation, and if applicable, cure of afflicted individuals who endanger the community was undertaken.

In the early 20th century, selected non-epidemic diseases, such as tuberculosis and syphilis became the target of governmental action[7]. State intervention in the broader domain of public health was intensified in the inter-war era. State intervention in health care, still mainly limited to areas such as the vaccination of children, health education and the supervision of safety of food and water was supplemented by activities of charities and of private foundations. The Rockefeller Foundation played an especially important role in the promotion of both biomedical research and of public

---

[4] Steve Sturdy and Roger Cooter, "Science, scientific management and the transformation of medicine in Britain, 1870-1950", *History of Science*, 1998, 36, pp. 421-466.

[5] Nancy Tomes, *The Microbe Gospel*, Cambridge, Mass, Harvard University Press, 1997.

[6] Andrew Mendelsohn, "The body between infection and disease: Heredity, etiology and constitution in European medicine, 1890-1940", in Jean-Paul Gaudillière and Ilana Löwy (eds.), *Transmission: Diseases Between Heredity and Infection*, Harwood Academic Publishers, in press.

[7] Lion Murard and Patrick Zylbermann, "Genève et la rationalisation des outils intellectuels de la coopération sanitaire, 1935-1939", in, *Le Ministère de l'Hygiène: création et action*, Paris, Convention MIRE-INSERM, 1996; Michael Worboys, "From heredity to infection? Tuberculosis 1870-1890", in Gaudillière and Löwy (eds.), *Transmission: Diseases Between Heredity and Infection, op. cit.*

health activities in interwar Europe[8]. Another important player in the public health domain in Europe was the Hygiène Bureau of the League of Nations. In the 1930s, this institution started to elaborate global "health indicators", an approach which, for the first time, attempted to bring together the multiple parameters able to affect health, from housing and employment to safety of childbirth and the prevalence of infectious diseases. This administrative innovation modified the way health was conceptualised by deciders, and later also by users, and it became a major tool of management of public health in the post World War II era[9].

After the Second World War, the generalisation of state-sponsored health care and the influx of public money to biomedical research radically modified the nature of interactions between medicine and politics in Europe. In Western Europe, health insurance regimes, which, in the previous era, were highly heterogeneous and often covered only a small fraction of the population, were homogenised and were extended to the great majority of the citizens. The state also considerably enlarged the scope of public health measures such as compulsory vaccination and the supervision of maternal and infantile health. In parallel, the highly visible success of antibiotics fuelled the hope that biomedical sciences would rapidly bring solutions to all the major medical problems, and stimulated governmental funding of basic and applied research. The important investment of governmental funds in medicine and in biomedical research increasingly submitted these areas to the public gaze. The gradual tightening of regulations on marketing of drugs and the spread of controlled clinical trials (presented as an objective and scientific method of evaluating the efficacy of therapies) can be seen as reflecting, among other things, the increased need to deflect suspicions that physicians as scientists promote corporate interests, and to neutralise possible accusations of a collusion between producers and prescribers of drugs[10].

Debates on health relates issues became important weapons in the Cold War. The communist regimes established in Eastern European countries after World War II gave a high priority to the development of health services. The improvement of the general health status of the population and the reduction of inequalities in access to health care were presented as unquestionable proofs of the superiority of the communist system

---

[8] Ilana Löwy and Patrick Zylberman, "Introduction: Medicine as a social tool", in *Studies in the History and Philosophy of Biology*, special issue, "Rockfeller Foundation and the Medical Sciences: 1913-1939", 2000, 31c, pp. 365-379.

[9] Lion Murard and Patrick Zylberman, *L'Hygiène dans la république*, Paris, Fayard, 1997.

[10] Theodore Porter, *Trust in Numbers*, Princeton, Princeton University Press, 1995; Harry Marks, *The Pursuit of Experiment: Science and the Therapeutic Reform in the USA, 1900-1990*, Cambridge, Cambridge University Press, 1997.

over the capitalist one. The official propaganda stressed that while in capitalist countries health was a luxury reserved for upper strata of society, socialist countries gave a high priority to workers' and peasants' health. Only socialist regimes (Soviet style), this argument went, are able to bring rapid and permanent improvement in health and in the general well-being of the previously neglected segments of population. These regimes were also presented as the only ones able to develop biomedical research free from commercial pressures and therefore truly attuned to people's needs. During the Cold War years Eastern Block countries, but also communist parties in Western countries extensively advertised East European achievements in the areas of health and biomedicine. Communism's opponents strove at the same time to demonstrate that claims concerning the superiority of the medical system in Eastern Europe were false, and that Western European democracies had more impressive achievements in the domain of health, and more efficiently improved the health of the underpriviledged strata of the population than Eastern Block countries. Capitalism and not communism, they affirmed, is the regime which holds the promise of better health care for all citizens and is more apt to provide freedom from suffering.

In democratic countries, the funding of health care and of medical research, the extent of government-sponsored health insurance, priorities in dealing with health-related problems, and the ways to deal with real and potential threats to health such as air pollution, toxic waste or the safety of food, became central issues in political debates. These subjects also played an important role in the transition to democracy in Eastern Europe and in Spain. The transformation of health into a major political issue was accelerated as the century came to its end. In the last analysis, many public debates in Europe are focused on health or on articulations between health and other elements of the "quality of life". The protection of the health of the present and the future generations is central to the debates on environmental issues or on energy policies, but also in discussions on the long-term effects of social problems such as unemployment, urban violence, or the widening of social inequalities.

The linking of health with broader social issues such as urbanisation and industrialisation is not new. It was one of the central topics of the hygienist discourse in the nineteenth century. The main innovation in the post World War Two era was the framing of the relationships between socio-economic change and health in terms of individual and collective risks, and in those of direct political choices[11]. Health-related issues

[11] Charles Rosenberg, "Pathologies of progress: The idea of civisilation as risk", *Bulletin of the History of Medicine*, 1998, 72, pp. 714-730; Ulrich Beck, "From industrial society to risk society", *Theory, Culture, Society*, 1992, 9, pp. 97-123.

tend to generate passionate public debates. Health is viewed as a priceless value, increasing the tensions over moves perceived as "selling out" health. The suspicion that an individuals' health is subordinated to financial interests of shareholders or becomes subject to power games between interest groups or between nations, may bring a prompt and sharp public reaction. The debates over the marketing of genetically modified crops in Europe, and the recent "sanitary alerts" on the safety and quality of food which peaked with the "mad cow disease" crisis of the late 1990s illustrate, one may propose, the increasingly tight feedback loop which links health, science and politics. This loop is at the centre of the studies presented in this volume.

•••

The aim of this book is to contribute to a better understanding of the multilevel articulations between scientific expertise, clinical practices, public health endeavours, and political action. It is focused on one of the main mechanisms which links biomedicine, public health and politics: images of health and disease. Such images are defined as conceptual frameworks which shape the lay but also the professional understanding of the normal and the pathological. Diseases, the historian of medicine Charles Rosenberg explains, do not exist in the void: our perception of a given pathology is always dependent on way this disease is "framed", that is, situated in a specific cognitive, social, cultural and political context[12]. Such frames, it is important to stress, are not devices which affect our perception of a natural entity which exists "out there" independently of its perception by humans, but they play a central role in the constitution of classificatory units named "diseases", that is, specific agregates of pathological phenomena.

The concept of the pathological, Georges Canguilhem explains, is always a normative one, because it is defined as a deviation from the normal, itself a socially constructed concept: "when we know that the word *norma* is the Latin word for T-square, and that *normalis* means perpendicular, we know almost all that must be known about area in which the meaning of the terms "norm" and "normal" originated, which have been taken to a great variety of other areas". Prominent among these areas, Canguilhem explains, was the establishement of sanitary norms. Such norms "determine the normal, starting from a normative decision", while the later is inseprably linked with specific social norms[13]. A

---

[12] Charles Rosenberg, "Framing disease: Illness society and history " in Charles E. Rosenberg and Janet Golden (eds.) *Framing Disease: Studies in Cultural History*, New Brunswick, NJ, Rutgers University Press, 1992, pp. xiii-xxvi.

[13] George Canguilhem, *The Normal and the Pathological* (transl. C. Fawcett), New York, Zone Books, 1991, p. 239, pp. 245-246.

human disease, defined against the norms of health, is therefore necessarily a biosocial phenomenon: the social, the cultural and the political shape the ways medical knowledge is generated, classified, diffused and employed, while this knowledge affects in turn culture, society, and politics[14].

This volume is focused on the multilevel interactions between biomedicine, culture and politics. While biomedicine, the cultural understanding of disease, and health policies are well-studied topics, their intertwining was more rarely the object of specific investigations. Researchers who study biomedical research, professional strategies of doctors and of scientists, or the links between science, medicine and industry seldom interact with those who are interested in the organisation of health care, public health arrangements, health and research budgets, and legislation related to health, or with those who investigate the understanding of health and illness in different cultures. The "intermediary zone" between biomedicine and politics, and the broader interplay between biomedicine, society and culture, frequently escapes the researchers' attention. In addition, a comparison among countries which have different cultural traditions, different histories of public health, and different political regimes may be especially efficient in bringing to light the role of cognitive and institutional "frames" in shaping the understanding of pathologies and of the policies elaborated to control them.

This volume brings together studies on Western Europe, Eastern Europe and on Franco's Spain. The comparison between national settings was organised around four major health issues: two well defined pathologies (tuberculosis and cancer) and two health issues which more directly incorporate social questions (addiction, and especially alcoholism, and the "production of healthy babies", that is, maternal and infantile health). Scholars who were invited to participate in this volume were asked to focus on one of these topics. It was hoped that mere juxtaposition of papers dealing with the same condition will be sufficient to provide abundant comparative material about the ways different societies deal with specific health problems. The original project underestimated, however, the extent of differences between East European, West European and Spanish traditions of articulation between biomedicine and politics.

---

[14] Robert A. Aronowitz, *Making Sense of Ilness: Science, Society and Disease*, Cambridge, Cambridge University Presss, 1999. Ludwik Fleck had already explained in 1935 that diseases are not natural classificatory units: their definition and their classification varies greatly in different places and periods, and reflects both professional and lay cultures. He also stress the stong interdependence and mutual shaping of lay and professional images of diseases. Ludwik Fleck, *Genesis and Development of a Scientific Fact*, transl. Frederick Bradley and Thaddeus J. Trenn, Chicago, University of Chicago Press, 1979 (1935).

The extent of regional differences is especially perceptible in studies originating from Eastern Europe. The topics and the approaches chosen by the authors of these studies vary widely, but all the East European studies stress the specificity of the communist regime and focus on the key role the state's ideology – and resistance to this ideology – played in attempts to frame and to control human diseases. Before 1989, the economy and nearly all the institutions of civil society in East European countries were tightly, if occasionally imperfectly, controlled by the state. In the absence of independent economic activity and other mediations between politics and society, ideological considerations were directly and overtly translated into policies. The only "legitimate" images of health and disease were those diffused by official organisations: the government and the communist party. Ideas which contrasted with the official views were frequently labelled "backward" and "reactionary", while the popular opposition to these views occasionally took the form of "asocial behaviour", "non-compliance", or alternatively, of spontaneous and organised attempts to elaborate purely technical solutions to concrete problems. Articles which discuss Eastern European countries focus frequently on the consequences of the extreme politization of health care and on attempts to escape this politization.

By contrast, in Western European countries the influence of an ideological component in health-related decisions was often masked by the existence of numerous mediations between ideological considerations and concrete actions. Studies dealing with Western Europe attempt therefore frequently to make visible values hidden in supposedly neutral and technical issues. To put it another way, "images of health and disease" in the West were frequently "under-politicised": their links with politics was often made invisible by their "technicization" and by professional rhetoric. Similar images were often "over-politized" in Eastern Europe where the extreme politicization of the discourse on health issues often blurred the role of professional groups and of the general culture in shaping the view of health and disease. Hence the important differences between "Western" and of "Eastern" papers. The first tend to focus mainly on institutions, structures and specific professional activities, and try to display the political background of these structures and activities. The second are frequently interested in culture, because in societies which banned practically all the structures of civil society, and in which a political ideology controlled (or at least aimed at controlling) practically all aspects of life, culture became one of the main areas for the expression of differences and of resistance.

Papers dealing with Spain are a specific case. During the Francoist era, Spain was a authoritarian regime with strong ideological underpinnings. However, unlike the East European countries, the influence of Francoist ideology was mainly limited to the political and cultural sphere, and was much less powerful in the economic sphere, because

Spain had remained, in the main, a free market economy. Individual doctors who worked within the framework of private medicine were allowed to develop independent professional views which often were not very different from the ones developed by their Western European colleagues. By contrast, public health, a domain directly related to the political sphere, was strongly influenced by the Francoist regime's ideological goals. Studies conducted by Spanish researchers tend therefore to focus on health policy, an area which makes especially visible the specific traits of Franco's regime. The papers originated in Poland, Russia and Spain illustrate also the influence of the specific history of each country on changes in the organization of health care during the transformation of the political (and, in Eastern Europe, also of economic) regime. These studies show how important modifications to the way health problems were dealt with in the 1980s and 1990s co-existed with equally important (and occasionally surprising) continuities with the previous era.

All the papers in this volume share a preoccupation with multiple "frames" which shape the understanding, the classification and the attempts to control a given pathology or condition. They vary, however, in their choice of a "frame" used as the main organising principle of a given study. Some papers (Ellenbrock, Gaudilliere, Krementsov, Löwy) accentuate the role of medical knowledge and of professional expertise, some (Amsterdamska, Duch and Firkowska, Mesa, Laskowska) focus mainly on society and culture, and some (Berridge, Orlov, Markiewicz, Molero, Paladino) focus principally on public health policies. It is not surprising to find that researchers interested in cancer tend to be more interested in biomedicine while those who investigate substance addiction or "the production of healthy children" often chose to focus on culture or on politics. This is, however, one should stress, a very rough classification. The majority of the papers have more than one focus, and some (eg., papers dealing with tuberculosis, often viewed simultaneously as a biomedical and a social problem) do not have a "main focus". Finally, the round table interventions (Berridge, Estaban, McPherson, Ronsenkrantz) discuss the general issue of the links between images of health and disease and public health policies.

•••

Although biomedicine may play a central role in understanding pathologies such as cancer, inborn genetic defects, or the infection by Koch's bacillus, and may guide interventions aiming at curing or preventing a given condition, biomedical practices seldom develops in the void. Krementsov's paper, and especially its first part which deals with the K-R affair, is a striking example of the ways political considerations – in this case, the shifts in desirable relationships between Soviet and Western scientists – shaped the perception of biomedical practices. On the other hand, one should be aware of a simplistic view of Soviet science as merely "subordinated" to politics, and of an equally sim-plistic perception of Western science as a "politics-free" enterprise. In some of their aspects, as Krementsov and Markiewicz convincingly show, activities of scientists working the Eastern Block countries were relatively free of political considerations. The professional standards used to evaluate cancer studies described by Krementsov were not very different from those used at the same period in Western countries. Conflicts about cancer cures (the K-R preparation, developed by Roskin and Kulieva, and, ten years later, a new anti-cancer drug proposed by Kachugin) usually reflected divergent professional interests, while political considerations (such as accusations to be manipulated by "enemies of the Soviet State") were mobilised later to promote such interests.

Similarly, Markiewicz recalls attempts to guide science by ideological considerations, such as those (made in the 1950s) to ground the view of tuberculosis in Mitchurin-Lysenko theories of heredity or in Pavolv's physiology. She indicates, however, that at the same time Polish specialists employed the same methods of diagnosis and of therapy of tuberculosis as their Western colleagues did, and that new anti-tuberculosis drugs (such as streptomycin and isoniazide) were introduced rapidly to Poland. Both Markiewicz and Krementsov stress the presence, in Eastern Europe, of an inseparable mixture of politics and science. However, while Markiewicz puts the accent on the particularities of the management of tuberculslosis by the Polish regime, Krementsov stresses the "nor-malcy" of Soviet science and medicine. He highlights the fact that scientists in the East, like their colleagues in the West, tried to use whatever resources at hand to promote their ideas and their specific interests. The main difference between Soviet scientists and their Western colleagues was the nature of the "resources at hand".

Visual materials, and especially scientific photographs are, Löwy argues, among the main resources used by the scientist and the physician. Infectious diseases are fre-quently depicted as a war between the organism and the invading pathogen (the wide-spread use of the expression "fight against tuberculosis", described by Markiewicz, alludes to this war image). By contrast, cancer is often presented as a "treason": nor-mal cells became "deviant", turn against the organism and destroy it from within. "Biological" therapies of cancerous organisms, which included treatments such as K-R therapy, the use of BCG, and more recently, of interferons and interleukins, were grounded in the principle of the stimulation of the "natural defences" of the organism and the increase of their capacity to eliminate the deviant growth. The development of these therapies was sustained, especially from the 1970s on, by a widespread diffu-sion of electron microscope images which show a cancer cell killed by white blood cells. These photographs, reproduced in numerous publications, both scientific and popular, strengthened the image of "cancer defeated by the organism". In France, such photographs, printed in semi-popular scientific publications, and in magazines destined to the general public, were employed to promote interferon and interleukin therapy. They were mobilised as a resource by scientists and by physicians who believed in the future of these therapies, and, in parallel, by industrialists who produced these substances and by cancer charities who funded research in this area. When initial expectations concerning the therapeutic value of these molecules were toned down, a different set of images was mobilised to stress the value of these molecules as a research tool.

While the images of cancer were, in the main, similar in all the European countries, those of inborn defects were, Gaudillière proposes, different in France and in the UK. Or to be more precise, the descriptions of these defects and of their consequences were akin in both countries, but UK and French physicians provided very different interpretations of the causes of inborn defects. The French doctors did not deny the importance of "heredity", but gave this term a very broad meaning. Every element which affected maternal health and general well-being was perceived as a contribution to the offspring "heredity", because, they explained, mothers who were sick, undernourished, or alcoholic gave birth to children with inborn defects. Better family-oriented programmes are the best way to prevent birth defects. The integration of the question of "production of healthy babies" in overall family-oriented policies was reinforced by the French tradition of pro-natalist governmental policies, and was further strengthened in the aftermath of World War II. When a French paediatrician, Jerome Lejeune first described a chromosomal defect (21 trisomy) as the main cause of the Down's Syndrome, his studies were integrated into a framework which included general supervision of maternal help and help to families with a Down's syndrome child. This approach was reinforced by the fact that Lejeune, a practising Catholic, strongly opposed abortion. He initially developed an interest in Down's syndrome babies because this abnormality was not seen as a classical "hereditary" defect (the great majority of "Down's syndrome" babies are born to non-affected mothers and there were no "Down's syndrome families"), but as a possibly enviromental one, the result of a defective "terrain". Lejeune was accordingly horrified to discover that his study, would, he hoped, would help to find a cure for children with 21 trisomy, was mainly used to test mothers at risk, and to abort trisomic foetuses.

By contrast, in the UK, physicians and scientists interested in inborn defects worked within in a conceptual framework which stressed the role of genes and Mendelian segregation of traits. They worked in genetics units, not in paediatric services, and had no direct contact with patients. Hence the important differences in the perception of trisomy – for UK experts such as Lionel Penrose, a cellular event, the duplication of chromosome 21, was the unique cause of the underlying pathology in children. By contrast, for French paediatricians the chromosomal aberration was a "passage point" connecting the constitution of the mother, the conditions of her pregnancy, and a child with Down's syndrome. The gap between the UK and the French perception of Down's syndrome was reduced in the 1970s, with the development of a new generation of French experts interested in medical genetics as such, and not only in relationships between "predispositions" and the child's well-being. In France too, trisomy 21 started to be perceived as a random accident of germinal cell division, especially in women over 40, and was dissociated from concrete events in the mother's life. This recognition led to the generalization of pre-natal tests for 21 trisomy in France.

Tuberculosis shared with genetic defects the dual property of being at the same time a well-defined pathology with a known cause, and one which can be interpreted in many ways. The occupation of Germany by the allies led to a confrontation, in the same geographical and cultural area, between contrasting perceptions of the correct way to treat tuberculosis patients developed by the Americans and the Soviets. The Americans believed in absolute bed rest and avoidance of sun, while the Soviet doctors favoured exercise and sunshine. They also objected to the use of lung collapse therapy by the Americans. No agreement could be found, and Soviet soldiers treated in the American zone were sent home as rapidly as possible.

While the Soviets and the Americans had contrasting views concerning the therapy of tuberculosis, German and Americans had contrasting views on the disease's etiology. American physicians, Ellenbrock explains, viewed tuberculosis mainly as a "dirt disease". Tuberculosis was connected with the image of the undisciplined patient who had to be taught to develop hygienic and socially acceptable behaviour. While harsh external conditions were seen as contributing to the development of tuberculosis, the accent was above all on individual responsibility, and on creating strong links between "tuberculosis" and "filth". By contrast, German medical officers viewed the various shortages of the post-war period as the main cause of the sharp increase in the incidence of tuberculosis, and believed that the occupation forces held the main responsibility for the development of such conditions. The "dirty tuberculosis sufferers", they affirmed, were not the cause of the epidemics, but were the victims of the inhuman treatment of Germans by the occupying forces. In addition, German experts presented tuberculosis as a serious public health problem, while the Americans at first believed that the Germans exaggerated the extent of this problem for political reasons. Circa 1947, when the Americans started to perceive tuberculosis as a serious threat, they transformed the efforts to control this pathology into a privileged domain of American-German cooperation and into a tool in the modernisation of Germany.

In Poland, anti-tuberculosis policies had at the same time a pragmatic and political dimension. One should distinguish, however, Markiewicz suggests, between two periods:

the early years of the communist regime (1948-1956) characterised by the predominance of ideological consideration and by an explicit reference to the Soviet model, and the post 1956 era, when communist ideology, while important, was not displayed as the unique organising principle of the society. In the first period, tuberculosis was simultaneously perceived as an important element of ideological struggle (the elimination of this poverty-linked pathology was to prove the superiority of communism over capitalism), as a major obstacle for the intensification of productivity, and as a straightforward medical problem. Thus the principle that workers should be given priority for sanatorium treatment was presented as a telling illustration of differences between health care in Poland and in the West (where, supposedly, only the rich can enjoy quality anti-tuberculosis treatment), and at the same time reflected the key importance of production workers for the reconstruction of Polish economy where no effort could be spared to allow a rapid return of a sick worker to the production line.

Ideology continued to be perceived as important in the post-1956 period too, but it coexisted then with more pragmatic considerations. The organisation of the prevention and the therapy of tuberculosis in the 1960s and 70s combined repressive elements (e.g., the control of compliance of patients by their workplace, or the right for medical personnel to inspect their houses) with a progressive anti-tuberculosis law which provided patients with free medical care and protected their employment. The control of tuberculosis was a successful public health campaign which led to significant reduction of the high incidence of tuberculosis in post-war Poland (although the indicence of this pathology remained well above Western European standards). This campaign was simultaneously used, Markiewicz proposes, to promote social control, that is, the subordination of the civil society to a regime's political and ideological goals. The latter, first defined as the "construction of socialism", became in the 1970s and 80s increasingly identified with the conservation of the existing socio-political structure and with the silencing of opposition.

The attempts to control tuberculosis in Spain were also inseparably linked with wider attempts to organise and to control the society and to promote the Franco's regime's goals such as patriotism and conservative social policy. The whole organisation of the Spanish health care in the early Francoist era, Ocana proposes, was articulated around the need to deal with the degradation of the health situation in the aftermath of the civil war, and around the parallel need to promote a minimal social cohesion. The phalangists developed, therefore, a "missionary" approach, which stressed conservative ideology, moral values, and the need to reconstruct the nation and to build a future "Empire". The government encouraged large families and promoted family values. It also initiated energetic campaigns against infectious diseases. This general structure was reflected in the organisation of anti-tuberculosis campaigns. The ideological role of these campaigns was especially visible, Mesa explains, during the early Francoist regime (1936-1951). At that time, the attempts to control this pathology were explicitly linked with a eugenic project of "bettering the nation". They were also linked with widespread efforts of sanitary education in the countryside. Such education, seen as the main weapon against tuberculosis, was directed in the main to women. It was diffused by visiting nurses and by the members of the specially created "Corps of Female Public Health Disseminators in Rural Areas". Their efforts did contribute to improvement of sanitary conditions in the countryside and increased the adhesion of the population to the new regime. Only later the government addressed the issue of prevention of tuberculosis through vaccination detection and treatment. These goals were first promoted by pathology-oriented insurance programs, and later through the development of centralised health care structures.

Child welfare programs in the first two decades of Franco's regime in Spain, Bernabeu-Mestre and Molero explain, were also multifunctional enterprises. They aimed at the same time to improve children's health (in the 1930s Spain had very high levels of child mortality, compared to West-European countries), to increase birth rates, to encourage women to dedicate themselves to motherhood, and to instil the love to the mother-country. Official propaganda presented a mother's ignorance as the main cause of children's morbidity and mortality. The main goal of the Child Hygiene Service was to educate and enlighten mothers. These services, which had a structure akin to the one of anti-tuberculosis services, worked mainly in the rural areas, where they effectively helped to reduce child mortality. They also contributed to the professionalization of child care and to the rapid growth in the number of experts in this area (both doctors, and intermediary professionals, such as visiting midwives, health educators and assistant child care nurses). These experts were assisted by a specific voluntary service which mobilised educated young women. A widespread education effort spread a sanitary gospel in the countryside, and at the same time acculturated women to their major task in life – to be good mothers.

In communist Poland at the other end of Europe and at the the other end of the political spectrum, the main message conveyed to women in the post-1956 period was surprisingly similar. By contrast, during the first "Stalinist" period (1948-1956), when the main societal goal was the "construction of socialism", and the official ideology glorified manual work in factories and in the field, the regime promoted the ideal of the working mother. Women were shown in posters and in official propaganda as happily combining vigorous physical labour and the joys of enlightened motherhood. Child rearing was presented as a joint enterprise between the mother and the state. The latter provided, in theory at least, efficient child care arrangements and quality medical services, and diffused knowledge about scientific principles of healthy child rearing.

Fathers and other family members such as grandparents or siblings were not presented as possible caregivers and, in fact, were hardly mentioned at all. Child education was presented as a joint effort of mothers and of the socialist motherland: no other participants were necessary. The state also used the important decrease in child mortality and morbidity in the post-war era as a key propaganda argument. The major improvements in children's health, the official publications claimed, was a inconstestable proof of the superiority of the communist regime.

In Poland, but also, according to Gurjeva, in the Soviet Union, attitudes to children in the 1940s and 50s were a mixture of sentimentalism, rationalism and instrumentalism (the healthy child was viewed as a future worker and "builder of socialism"). After 1956 Polish women were no longer presented as potential producers (of goods, of children), and the communist regime encouraged women to be above all mothers and homemakers. While the percentage of women in the work force remained high, women were then seen by professionals as the sole (or at least the main) providers of child care, and, especially in the 1970s, were strongly encouraged to stop working when their children were young. This attitude reflected, among other things, the paucity of quality day-care. Contrary to official propaganda, the communist regime was unable to solve the practical problem of care to young children, and the most prominent day-care institution in Poland was the grandmother. Her role as childminder was further stimulated by the frequent forced cohabitation of parents and grown-up children, the consequence of a severe shortage of flats.

The majority of the Poles were, to put it mildly, sceptical towards the regime's overt propaganda. From the late 1950s on, doctors and public health officials tried to find less simplistic and more subtle ways to promote their views. In some cases, such as the introduction of anti-tuberculosis measures, they could rely on the fear of disease, and on the aspiration of individuals infected with Koch bacillus to get well quickly. Alcoholism, unlike tuberculosis, was not viewed by the population as a health problem. The fight against alcoholism in Poland stumbled on the double obstacle of a long standing cultural tradition of the use of alcohol as a way to celebrate special occasions (often those with a religious content) and on a parallel tradition, alive among impoverished and often under-nourished peasant populations, to supplement their diet by a calorie intake from inexpensive alcohol drinks, such as vodka produced from potatoes. The latter role of alcohol in Poland diminished from the 1950s on thanks to the general improvement in the standard of living. In parallel, however, the cultural role of alcohol in Poland was enriched by its new role as an expression of opposition to the communist regime. Polish post-war literature, Amsterdamska explains, was soaked with alcohol. Numerous writers used drinking as a parody and a metaphor for Polish socio-political reality. The metaphor of "drunken motherland" which appeared first in the mid-1950s summed up all the wrongs of the social and political reality. In parallel, writers described alcohol – rather than the communist ideology – as the only device able to promote fraternity. The image of "drunken Poland" became even more prominent in the 1970s, a period of relative prosperity and political despair. Drinking was presented as a "normal" reaction to abnormal social reality and as a way to remain sane in an insane, absurd world.

On the other hand, the widespread abuse of alcohol in Poland was perceived by the party and the government as a major health issue, but, above all, an important problem for society. In the 1950s, Laskowska-Otwinowska explains, the regime put the accent on the disastrous effects of drinking on productivity. It presented the drunken person as an obstacle to the construction of socialism, and accused different enemies of the regime (the capitalists, the church) of encouraging alcoholism. From the late 1950s on, arguments against drinking had gradually shifted from harm to the collective ("drinking is bad for Poland/ socialism/ the working class") to harm to the individual ("drinking is bad for you"), and from a focus on repressive measures to the presentation of drinking, mainly as a psychosocial problem, and as a source of degradation of one's quality of life. The trend to analyse alcoholism in psychological terms was accentuated after the fall of the communist regime. Addiction, the new approach has proposed, is a personality disorder, and an afflicted individual should seek professional help – or, alternatively, should join a self-help group – in order to recover his/her free will, and thus to fully benefit from advantages offered by the post-communist society.

The attitudes to substance addiction in the UK also underwent changes in the post-war era. The career of Horace Joules, one of the pioneers of the British National Health Service who was very active in anti-tobacco campaigns in the early 1950's, Paladino explains, reflects the trend which viewed tobacco addiction as an asocial behaviour, harmful not only to the smoker but to others as well. Smoking, Joules and his friends argued, was a "social disease", an expression of the individual's lack of responsibility to the community. According to Berridge, before World War II the attitude of British officials towards alcohol abuse was similarly impregnated with moral undertones. However, in the post-war era, alcoholism was redefined as a true disease which may be cured by appropriate medication, by psychotherapy, or by a participation in activities of a self help group such as Alcoholics Anonymous. In the 1970s the dominant approach had changed to one which focused on alcohol as a social rather than an individual problem. The new approach stressed the social consequences of alcohol dependence, and its risks to the community. The solution was education and prevention rather than individualised treatment. The GP, rather than the addiction expert, was presented as the key person in dealing with alcohol abuse. In the late 1990s the focus of anti-alcohol activity seems to shift again. The most debated issue in the 1990s was not the excessive consumption of alcohol but high-risk drinking and policies aiming at the reduction of this risk.

In the Soviet Union too alcoholism was alternatively presented as an individual or as a collective problem, but both views were integrated within a larger framework in which the perception of alcoholism as a crime clearly predominated over its understanding as a medical or a psychosocial issue. Orlov's paper is focused on the history of a unique Soviet Institution: the medicalized sobering station. This Soviet invention was later transplanted to other countries in the Soviet Block as well (Amsterdamska's paper mentions police operated sobering stations in Poland) but only in the Soviet Union did the sobering station became a central social institution and an important tool for the control of individual and collective behaviour. At first (in the late 1920s) the sobering stations, established in all the major cities, were viewed as a place to provide immediate medical help for drunken people collected in the street. They rapidly became, however, predominantly repressive institutions, supervised by the militia and controlled by the Ministry of Internal Affairs. Persons brought to the station had to pay a fine, but, in addition, their workplace, and often also the "house council" of their apartment building, was automatically notified about the incident. "Comaradely courts" in the workplace or in the house councils were expected to react promptly to information provided by the sobering stations, and to initiate appropriate preventive and repressive steps.

In the 1970s, a step increase in the – already high – incidence of alcoholism in the Soviet Union led to intensification of repressive anti-alcoholism campaigns, and to the development of a network of "medicalized labour preventorium" which "treated" alcoholics by forced labour (in the peak period of their development, the mid-1980s, more than 300 such preventoria "treated" a quarter of a million individuals). While the scope of repressive anti-alcoholic actions was reduced after the disappearance of Soviet Union, the prevalence of alcoholism did not diminish. It may have even increased: excessive alcohol consumption is considered as one of the main reasons for the dramatic decrease in the average male life span in Russia in the 1980s and 90s. Sobering stations, with their unique mixture of criminalization and medicalization of alcohol abuse, continued to be perceived as useful social institutions. The main difference with the previous period is a greater involvement of physicians and of health administrators in the management of these stations.

•••

Historical studies display the great diversity of images of health and disease generated by the multiple ways of framing the biosocial phenomena named "diseases" by biomedical scientists, by health professionals and health administrators, by politicians, by the users of health services, and by the general public. Can we learn from such heterogeneous history? Can the study of the past help European countries to co-ordinate and harmonise the way they deal with major health issues and help to prevent crises (such as the "mad cow" one) rooted in differences in national policies and traditions of public health? Or perhaps the history of the interactions between health and politics in Europe is not so heterogeneous after all?

In the 20th century, Rosnekrantz explains, the responsibility for disease prevention shifted to a large extent from the individual to the state, perceived in all the European countries as responsible for fighting disease and for promoting health. The first task is often viewed as a relatively straightforward one. However, once the industrialised countries had eliminated the major threat of epidemic diseases and drastically reduced childhood mortality, the main issue had become the fight against chronic diseases, age-related pathologies or those perceived as "lifestyle related". This is a much more complex task, and one which, as McPherson eloquently argues, is often fraught with difficult choices.

The "promotion of health" is an even more complicated issue. In many European countries, especially in those under totalitarian regimes, Ocana proposes, health was instrumentalized to promote specific social, cultural, moral, political or economic values. But can one attain the ideal of fully non-instrumentalized health? The absence of democracy and of civil society institutions surely increases the danger of excessive use of health as a mere vehicle to promote other goals, some of which had little or no relation to the promotion of the well-being of the population. Even under the best of conditions "health" is, however, seldom a free standing, autonomous value. The understanding of health is always shaped by history and by local conditions. Health is perceived – as disease is – through the eyes of culture, society, economy and politics.

One should keep in mind, McPherson argues, the great majority of public health decisions are, above all, political decisions. It is thus impossible to have a truly non-instrumentalized public health. It is possible, by contrast, to enlarge greatly the scope of individuals and groups who actively participate in decisions about health policies and public health. A better understanding of the past can, one may hope, facilitate such participation and promote a collective elaboration of future decisions in this area. In the rapidly expanding European Union such decisions will have to be taken on an increasingly large scale. The passage to multinational decision-taking framework, Berridge stresses, does not abolish the importance of the local. Just the opposite may be true: with the growing internationalization of decisions concerning health protection and health care, the local level may become increasingly the locus where the issues of law, regulation and health are being brought together. Such a key role at the local level is, one may argue, embedded in the definition of public health. However universal biomedical science is, and however broad the scope is of collective interventions which aim to control and to prevent human pathologies, the final target of all these activities is – or at least should be – not disease but illness: the unique suffering of an unique individual.

Western Europe

Wars of State and the Disease of the Masses
Barbara Gutmann Rosenkrantz

1. Introduction

Historical demographers link tuberculosis and the industrial revolution in a complex pattern that identifies both rising and falling mortality with the urban proletariat that worked in factories and lived in city slums. Consumption was the most frequent cause of death recorded in the last half of the nineteenth-century, and most of its victims were working men and women between the ages of 15 and 25, identified by contemporaries as the "productive years". Nonetheless, TB mortality began to decline at the end of the century, before either the cause or cure of tuberculosis were known. While specific factors involved cannot be singled out credit is generally given to improved living standards that are also associated with the industrial revolution.

Tuberculosis remained, however, the great reaper, killing more people than all other diseases combined in 1900. Throughout the 20th century, despite brief interruptions associated with the two World Wars the decline in tuberculosis deaths in Europe persisted. Meanwhile, a rapid increase of TB mortality in Africa and Asia since 1950 eventually led leaders of the international health movement to identify a "global emergency". At the end of the 20th century it is estimated that there are 8 million new cases annually, with 80% of these in 22 countries located in South East Asia, sub-Saharan Africa and Eastern Europe. One quarter of all men, women and children diagnosed with TB will die of the disease, and case fatality rates are higher when there is co-infection with HIV[1].

Despite changes in the world wide distribution of TB one important characteristic remains, infection, disease and death continue to disproportionately ravage those peoples with the lowest living standards. Even as Robert Koch heralded the hope of controlling infection that was conceivable with the identification of the tuberculosis "germ" he also noted the obstacles to exploiting this knowledge without specific attention to the

---

[1] "Global Burden of Tuberculosis, Estimated Incidence, Prevalence, and Mortality by Country", Report from World Health Organization, Global Surveillance and Monitoring Project, published in *Journal of the American Medical Association*, 1999, 9 August.

greater impact of tuberculosis on the poor. "It appears to me not too early to proceed against tuberculosis with prophylactic measures", he wrote shortly after the announcement in 1882, "[B]ut owing to the great spread of this disease, all steps which are taken against the same will have to reckon with the social condition, and therefore, it must be carefully considered in what way and how far one may go on this road without prejudicing the advantages gained, by unavoidable disturbances and other disadvantages"[2].

The unequal impact of tuberculosis infection has only become more obvious in the 20th century as the association of poverty and disease are magnified in the aftermath of destructive civil and world wars and on an international scale. The multiple meanings of social inequities were underscored again after the discovery of effective drugs (the first streptomycin, in 1948) that fundamentally altered the chance of recovery. Effective interventions depended on large scale public health investments. At the end of the century, the organization of medical resources to bring treatment to those most frequently infected, particularly in war torn and impoverished nations, has not been forthcoming. Pleas for antibiotics to stem the epidemic have been caught in debates about how to raise funds and organize support for treatment. Further complicating the picture are scientific controversies over strategies of control. Dr. Gro Harlem Bruntland, director of the World Health Organization has called for money from government agencies and gifts from private organizations in Europe, America and Asia in the amount of $6 million dollars annually to assure the availability of drugs. While some tuberculosis experts champion a course of short term intensive treatment others advocate longer treatment with more drugs to check the development of antibiotic resistant strains of the tubercle bacillus. Experienced field workers predict that without massive support for public health systems in countries where disease is rampant no responsible course of treatment can be undertaken[3].

By contrast, the World Health Organization's successful Smallpox Eradication Campaign (1966-1977) is an example of international teamwork without parallel, but there are other precedents of collaborative campaigns that stanched outbreaks, for instance typhus fever in World War I, and more recently river blindness[4]. The inglorious

---

[2] Robert Koch, "Aetiology of Tuberculosis", Rev. F. Sause, tr. *American Veterinary Review*, 13: pp. 54-59, p. 106, p. 112, pp. 202-214, 1884.

[3] *New York Times*, "In Fight Against Tuberculosis, Experts Look for Private Help", 11/9/99. William Foege, MD a former public health official who advises the new Gates Foundation is quoted believing that negotiations have "moved the dialogue along so that people can stop fighting one another and start fighting the disease".

[4] See the WHO campaign against onchocerciasis (river blindness) supported by Merck and Company's contribution of the drug Mectizan. See also Hans Zinsser, *Rats, Lice and History*, 1935.

recent history of international campaigns against tuberculosis is undoubtedly entangled in characteristics of the infecting mycobacterium and the human immune system, but additionally this history illuminates the uneasy status of 20th-century public health. Under what conditions were international campaigns against tuberculosis initiated? More precisely, since both national and international response to dangerous disease have been oriented toward the exclusion or control of *epidemic* outbreaks, what conditions have brought tuberculosis under the shield of public health? My brief review separates these issues: first, a chronology of major international convocations oriented to aid the victims of tuberculosis, stem the spread of the disease and mitigate its impact, and second, some historically grounded observations on the obstacles that tuberculosis has presented, over time, to the realm of public health.

2. International health conferences

The genealogy of 19th-century international meetings on health has many branches, most of them characterized by a concern to guard the interests and borders of participating nations through protecting each state from contamination while somehow ensuring that commercial relations were not disrupted. Quarantines and isolation, the common product of these international conferences to promote health were therefore, somewhat paradoxically, the product of these collaborative ventures. Their connection with the first International Congress on Tuberculosis (1899) is less obvious than that of 19th-century conferences on hygiene and demography, in that the latter were self-consciously scientific meetings. In Berlin, not surprisingly the host for the initial meetings on TB, scientists from 24 countries exchanged papers about their work. The inaugural convocation, attended by official delegations and what amounted to a European press corps, heard an address by the German Emperor who simultaneously launched an educational "Exposition" for the public. The mixture of incentives for this display, as described by the correspondent from *La Presse Médicale*, included the promotion of German scientific knowledge, German instruments and German social policies. The address of Professor Brouardel, leader of the large and distinguished French scientific delegation that included Metchnikoff and Nocard, emphasized his conviction that a cure for tuberculosis was to be expected along the same lines of laboratory investigation that had already achieved success in the control of other pathogens. International meetings focused on conquering tuberculosis continued to bring together scientific delegations from participating nations, reconvening after a hiatus marked by World War I until September, 1936 when the 10th meeting scheduled for Lisbon was "postponed" because of difficulties in communication. These international gatherings were marked by persistent national disagreements as well as by accommodation in the interest of international collaboration. German and British delegates advocated far-reaching protection to control the spread of tuberculosis and its social dislocations; the French were less enthusiastic about such interventions as compulsory insurance or isolation of the sick which they considered extravagant and inexpedient. By 1924 the French delegation led by Albert Calmette, engaged the delegates in debate of the significance of variation in bacterial virulence. Soon after, the development of the Calmette-Guerin vaccine (BCG) led the British to persistent challenges of its safety and efficacy. When the Congress met in Rome (1928) Mussolini proposed that Italy would set a standard for public services, championing the importance of economic and social stability at a precarious moment when many Europeans admired his brand of socialist syndicalism. The differences in national policy and practice that were aired at these conferences forecast political and scientific tensions that would dominate popular and professional discourse throughout the 20th century[5].

After the second meeting of the International Congress which took place in London, differences in national policy and practice were partly muted in the International Bureau for the Campaign Against Tuberculosis (IBCAT) that was located in Berlin. The IBCAT was intended as a permanent resource and clearing house where information and advice might be available to the organizations of laymen that grew up within national borders in order to educate the public and support the fight of scientists and doctors against tuberculosis. These were societies dedicated to raising funds to further specific scientific and medical projects and, perhaps even more important, to spreading information where poverty and ignorance were barriers to the fight against tuberculosis. In most cases scientists also participated in the top councils of these national and local organizations, but programmatically these groups were organized to reach the public and reinforce popular understanding of the importance of combating tuberculosis as much as to provide a center for reporting scientific advance. While the IBCAT was a center of information there was emphasis on the importance of work at a national or local level where appropriate interventions would reflect specific cultural and political strengths. Consideration of "horizontal" and "vertical" interventions supported by the appropriate "infrastructure" were not part of contemporary discourse or practice. Instead, tradition and respect led to the assumption that knowledge produced by specialists was best put to work by men and women who knew where the trouble was.

Two world wars and the civic and economic disruptions that were suffered throughout the century by sectors of the population most vulnerable to tuberculosis, affected both the epidemiology of the disease and the formulation of campaigns for the control of tuberculosis. After the outbreak of fighting in 1914, tuberculosis temporarily

---

[5] See the bi-weekly *La Presse Médicale* published in Paris for detailed accounts of the International meetings.

shed its previous association with industrial work and city life and was, instead, connected with the trauma of war. As the International Committee of the Red Cross (ICRC) reorganized to meet the needs of contesting armies, national Red Cross groups developed programs that emphasized historic services to their own fighting men and tacitly neglected civilian needs, except where the health of the mothers of future soldiers were concerned[6]. Tuberculosis always presents itself in ways that embeds diagnosis and evaluation, let alone medical response to the sick, in the observers' expectations. Organizers of medical and humanitarian relief in both the Allied Nations and the Central Powers singled out the risk of breaking down with tuberculosis as the ever present danger to young men suffering from deprivation and stress.

The determination to convene a new organization, L'Union Internationale Contre la Tuberculose (UICT) in Paris after the war indicated a new twist to tuberculosis work in the aftermath of World War I. French military and civilians had suffered greatly during the war and were not about to yield leadership in a peacetime battle in which they had so much at risk and so much invested. Paris was already the headquarters of the Office International d'Hygiène Publique (OIHP), originally formed in 1907 to oversee containment of cholera and plague associated with world trade and expansion; the role of French social as well as medical scientists in establishing the UICT and assembling member nations reflected their claims to authority[7]. The continuity of tradition from pre-war years was exemplified through Leon Bernard, Professor of Tuberculosis Medicine. When finally representatives of 30 nations met at the Sorbonne in 1920 and UICT headquarters were established on the Boulevard Saint Michel (also the offices of the French National Committee) the durability of the non-government organizations represented was sufficient to hold out against the German Occupation in 1940. Unable to pry loose the UICT's records and treasury, the Nazis established their own "international" committee and a publication that made a brief appearance in Berlin and disappeared again[8].

The influence of the UICT on the League of Nations Health Organization (LNHO) investigation of tuberculosis (1930-31) is more difficult and more important to assess.

---

[6] John F. Hutchinson, "'Custodians of the Sacred Fire': the ICRC and the post-war reorganization of the International Red Cross," pp. 17-18, in Paul Weindling (ed.), *International Health Organizations and Movements 1918-1939*, Cambridge University Press, 1995.

[7] See Martin Davis Dubin, "The League of Nations Health Organization", pp. 56-58 in Weindling, *op. cit.*, for a brief summary of programmatic changes in the OIHP that reflected new scientific perspectives on disease control.

[8] "L'union internationale contre la tuberculose", *La Presse Médicale*, 12 October, 1935, pp. 1593-1596 and 22 April, 1950, p. 452.

Convenience as well as history supported the appointment of Leon Bernard to head the Reporting Committee and one of the four other members was also French; Bernard presided and the final communication was prepared by Etienne Burnet, Deputy Director of the Pasteur Institute in Tunis.

How can we assess the importance of the French connection with respect to the originality and boldness articulated in the "General Principles Governing the Prevention of Tuberculosis"? The request for the study came to the LNHO from national representatives to the League Assembly and the completed Report, based on research in eight European countries, was approved by the full LNHO. A recent study credits the cultural work of the biomedical sciences more generally for the authority of the LNHO and the support of League member nations for regulations to control disease and protect health[9]. When it came to the consideration of tuberculosis the special Committee Report boldly announced at the outset that tuberculosis was unlike all other contagious disease: "(A)like endemic and epidemic, [in that] it is more deeply embedded in the social body than any other infectious disease". The campaign against tuberculosis must be a work of "social hygiene", read the Report, explaining that hygiene that cannot be initiated personally, hygiene takes into account class differences and the unequal resources of the rich and the poor.

The Committee also took sober account of the decline in mortality over many decades while it rejected as unscientific the proposition that the bacillus lost virulence, it firmly noted unanticipated evidence that industrialization contributed to the decline in mortality. Although the Report attended to the contemporary persuasion, particularly prominent in Britain and the United States, that a population exposed to tuberculosis, might over time "naturally" acquire a degree of resistance or "tuberculization" that would assist programs of TB control it concluded that "… these views do not claim to reveal the cause of the decline in the death rate from tuberculosis, and, further, that tuberculization is a social fact"[10].

---

[9] Dubin, *op. cit.* "The LNHO's activities evolved, partly in response to external political, social and technological factors, but largely in response to changes in consensual scientific knowledge within the biomedical/public health episteme. This new knowledge also transformed state health agencies which were directed by members of the episteme" (p. 60). The dynamic and often controversial leadership of the Polish bacteriologist who was secretary of the LNHO, inspired significant support at the time and a record that included an epidemiologic data base and standard nomenclature of biologics handed on to the World Health Organization (WHO).

[10] Dr. E. Burnet, "General Principles Governing the Prevention of Tuberculosis", League of Nation, *Quarterly Bulletin of the Health Organization*, December 1932, pp. 497, 604.

Although there is ambiguity inherent in the Report's dismissal of tuberculization it never returns to the subject. Nor did it make other references to debate on the relation between mortality and morbidity, or on the longer lives of TB victims, questions that remained internationally on the agenda. These were otherwise considered challenging questions about the nature of resistance to tuberculosis infection and the breakdown to actual disease that, broadly speaking, complemented the practical concerns of all European nations especially during the Depression. National policy during the inter-war economic crises made it prudent to choose between support for hospitals to care for the seriously ill who were largely incurable but most contagious or treat those who endangered others less but could benefit most from treatment.

The Committee dodged these questions explaining that there was inadequate scientific evidence. Instead it took the opportunity to identify large scale causal agents that could neither be exactly measured or controlled and to indicate the significance of variables in epidemiologic analysis that identified tuberculosis as essentially a social disease. Outside of rest and lung collapse, the only specific medical intervention recommended in the Report was vaccination of children with BCG, a policy initiated in France but largely rejected in Britain [11].

In the absence of any compelling prophylaxis the Report concluded with 52 recommendations. First, in a brief review of "Practice and Scientific Research", it turned to the implementation of anti-tuberculosis campaigns and the status of public health administration in each country. Comparing the challenge that 19th-century cholera provided England in establishing "the impetus for modern public health" to the shock of 20th-century war the Committee proceeded with language reflecting the Report's opening thesis. "In no nation has the State directly and completely taken over the campaign against tuberculosis. Traditionally, it is concerned with medicine only in so far as it distributes diplomas, or if an epidemic occurs which is regarded as a social menace. Formerly, tuberculosis was not considered an epidemic. But nowhere was it a matter of indifference to the State. At present, the State is in the van rather than the rear of the movement. At a period when social health work is paramount, it remains the seat of the hygienic conscience and the source of power. Private initiative can never be sufficiently far-reaching, methodical or generous to conduct the campaign against tuberculosis single-handed" [12]. The Committee reached these conclusions

---

[11] *Ibid.*, pp. 588-96.
[12] *Ibid.*, p. 605.

seven years before the outbreak of World War II and the surge of tuberculosis associated with its massive displacement of civilians as well as soldiers. Public health and the control of tuberculosis were ideologically wedded although limited resources, as always, contested the union. Sixteen years after publication of the League of Nations Report, the first antibiotic that could effectively treat tuberculosis was discovered, and shortly clinical experience, epidemiologic experience and the development of effective medical treatment appeared to have decisively provided grounds for a divorce.

3. Public health and the control of tuberculosis in Europe

The last section of this paper turns briefly to the connections that 20th-century Europeans have made between public health and the control of tuberculosis in order to suggest some of the reasons that good will and modern science have not been enough to determine the best way to reduce the carnage of the disease and assure that the World Health Organization gets the help it needs to fight this modern plague[13]. What have been the foundations of our received picture of the relation of public health to tuberculosis? What persuaded the League of Nations Health Committee, in 1932, that the "anti-tuberculosis campaign is a specialized form, but not a separate form, of public health work, its local agents are, naturally, the officers of the general Public Health Department"? This did not reflect prior history at the time it was written and it unfortunately presented no guide to implementation. It does, however, provide an opportunity to identify some reasons no such history can be relied on and suggest some of the obstacles to bringing the anti-tuberculosis campaign into the realm of public health.

Many pleas for public health control of tuberculosis begin with Koch's discovery of the tubercle bacillus. This association is usually based on the assumption that discovery of the tubercle bacillus shaped medical and public health understanding and activity. A good deal has been written about the way that clinicians responded to these difficulties in both the 19th and 20th centuries, but for many reasons much less about the response of public health[14]. Indeed, as indicated earlier, the consequences of tuberculosis were beyond the scientific and programmatic resources of public health

---

[13] See footnote 3.

[14] Historians have not closely analyzed the elements of clinical concerns, but I recommend a new book that has a chapter on tuberculosis set in a larger framework of equal interest, see Michael Worboys, *Spreading Germs: Disease Theories and Medical Practice, Britain, 1860-1900*, Cambridge University Press, 2000, chapter 8, "From Heredity to Infection: Tuberculosis, Bacteriology and Medicine, 1870-1900".

and identification of the tubercle bacillus did nothing to place it in the realm of public health capacity to contain an epidemic.

The most important and instructive instances of public health response to tuberculosis among civilians before World War II came from European colonial contacts with Africa that were often represented as the initial exposure to TB of Africans and consequently to infection, disease and epidemic threats. Dr. Etienne Burnet and the LNHC believed that the growth of industry and life in cities had initially exposed the European population to risk of disease but eventually improved their lot through acquired resistance and immunity, reducing tuberculosis mortality if not its incidence. Out of the same material in different guise came a circumlocution for disease identified as "the price of civilization" native peoples faced. "Primitve" Africans were conceived by Europeans as immunologically innocent before colonial intrusion, the warrant of civilization meant either a high toll of tuberculosis mortality resulting from exposure of a "virgin" population, or more consonant with the development of colonial practice, an opportunity for public health essential to the civilizing mission. As Mark Harrison and Michael Worboys have written, this ultimately led to the "reframing of tuberculosis in Africa as an endemic disease made worse by the social and economic dislocation of imperialism..." leading to better health if not more wealth[15].

One element in the creation of an "epidemic" of tuberculosis, the crucial factor that has made it obligatory for the state and whichever office is made responsible for "public" health to take account of tuberculosis, has been, ironically, evidence of declining TB mortality and its irregular pattern. In Europe declining mortality was again interrupted by World War II and other social crises that evoked relief and refocused the image of susceptibility from the personal to the social circumstances that "produced" disease. But as both Dagmar Ellerbrock and Jorge Molero-Mesa have argued in papers included in this volume, the capacity of official campaigns against tuberculosis to fault personal hygiene and individual behavior has characterized late 20th-century response to TB much as heredity preoccupied physicians of the 19th-century. Although modern public health policy and practice has committed itself to detection, prevention and even care in ordinary times, when catastrophe overwhelms committed resources the image of tuberculosis as a disease of undue exposure through physical and social deprivation breaks down and the victim is blamed.

---

[15] Mark Harrison and Michael Worboys, "A Disease of Civilization, Tuberculosis in Britain, Africa and India, 1900-39", in Lara Marks and Michael Worboys (eds.), *Migrants, Minorities and Health*, Routledge, 1997.

Barbara Gutmann Rosenkrantz

Public health responsibility has grown strikingly in the 20th century, in part responsive to the underlying proposition that professional and social responsibility have been linked by scientific knowledge. But in the absence of a preventive vaccine the image of tuberculosis as the disease of the masses that was generated in the early 20th-century has remained intact despite fundamental change in the capacity to treat the disease. A paradox that has historical roots is evident in the paralysis that characterizes response to a disease once known as "the people's plague". Tuberculosis retains the capacity to ensnare its victims not only by infection, but somehow also in responsibility. Public health is once more responsible for scientific and social resources it cannot command.

Disease, Risk, Harm and Safety: Trends in Post-war British Alcohol Policy

Virginia Berridge

1. Introduction

The nineteenth century has received the lion's share of attention so far as the history of alcohol is concerned. The British and other temperance movements, the strong parliamentary and extra-parliamentary presence of the drink issue has attracted considerable historical research[1]. There is much less work on the twentieth century and especially the period since the Second World War, although there have been some notable contributions both from an historical and a policy science point of view[2].

The post-war period, both at the international level and so far as Britain was concerned, was a time of key scientific and policy developments which illuminate the overall theme of the complex relationship between the two and the nature of research. This is a story of discovery (or rediscovery) post-war; the emergence of a policy network; the development of a new paradigm in the 1970s; and now the signs of a further reordering of scientific concepts in the 1990s. The relationship with policy has been complex and often reciprocal.

This is also a history which has a strong international dimension. The role of international organisations and networks in the science/policy relationship is an important one. So, too, is the increased significance accorded research results. The post-war alcohol story is also one of the negotiations round the meaning of the term "public health". The changing ideology and policy implications of that concept are illuminated through the

---

[1] B. Harrison, *Drink and the Victorians. The Temperance Question in England, 1815-1872* (second edition), Keele University Press, 1994; J. Zimmerman, *Distilling Democracy. Alcohol Education in American Public Schools, 1880-1925*, Kansas University Press, 1999; see also issues of the *Social History of Alcohol Review* which provide valuable bibliographies; and e-mail networks maintained by the Alcohol and Temperance history group and the Kettil Bruun Society.

[2] R. Baggott, "Alcohol, Politics and Social Policy", *Journal of Social Policy* 15 (4), 1986, pp. 467-88; R. Baggott, *Alcohol, Politics and Social Policy*, Aldershot, Avebury, 1990; B. Thom and V. Berridge, "Special Units for Common Problems: the Birth of Alcohol Treatment Units in England", *Social History of Medicine*, 8 (1), 1995, pp. 75-93; B. Thom, *Dealing with Drink. Alcohol and Social Policy: From Treatment to Management*, London, Free Association Books, 1999.

alcohol story and its relation to other areas of substance use- smoking, illicit drugs- in the post-war period.

2. Pre-war context

Firstly, the pre World War II context so far as alcohol was concerned. How had the relationship between science, policy and health developed since the late nineteenth century?

The key issue for the nineteenth century had been the strong U.K. temperance movement[3]. Temperance originally meant not total abstinence, but the traditional humoral notion of moderate drinking. Both Benjamin Rush and John Coakley Lettsom with their "Moral and Physical Thermometers" put consuming small beer, cider, sherry, wine and port and even strong beer in moderate quantities on the right side of temperance, drawing the line at punch, toddy, grog, rum and whisky. Only fanatics wanted total abstinence.

In the nineteenth century temperance emerged as a movement, or rather movements, initially middle class and with a focus on spirits, later on a movement embodying working class "respectability" in the period between the end of Chartism and the emergence of mass political parties towards the end of the century. In its heyday it offered the model of a great public reforming movement with local as well as national political strength. By the end of the century, temperance had moved away from elimination of all drink to the aims of reduction of licences, local option, and temperance education. The alcohol question was part of turn of the century social hygiene.

Temperance was not autonomous. Movements are also a matter of alliances – and part of the picture towards the end of the century was the growing role for medicine in an anti-drink alliance. Certainly the belief was still strong in the profession that drink was good for you. Alcohol was itself still defined as a medicine which could be prescribed, as case notes demonstrate[4]. Pharmacists still held drink licences and there were blurred boundaries between what counted as a "medicine" and what was seen as a recreational substance – as was also the case with drugs[5].

---

[3] B. Harrison, *op. cit.*

[4] J. Harley Warner, "Physiological and Therapeutic Explanation in the 1860s: the British Debate on the Medical Use of Alcohol Theory", *Bulletin of the History of Medicine*, 55, 1980, pp. 235-57.

[5] S. Anderson, "The Role of the Pharmacist in the Sale of Tobacco and Alcohol", paper given at conference of the European Association for the History of Medicine and Health, Almuñecar, Spain, September, 1999; V. Berridge, "Changing Places: Illicit Drugs, Medicines, Tobacco and Nicotine in the 19th and 20th Centuries", in E. M. Tansey and M. Gijswijt-Hofstra (eds.), *Remedies and Healing Cultures in Britain and the Netherlands in the 20th Century* (forthcoming).

At same time medical opinion hostile to alcohol was also emerging. Here one can trace a genealogy back to Thomas Trotter and Benjamin Rush. Porter has argued that these writers with their theories of disease were crystallising ideas which were round in the eighteenth century. It was new circumstances such as the rise of Evangelism which gave them greater prominence[6]. It was at the end of the nineteenth century that the belief in illness coalesced into a scientific specialism. Through the activities of the Society for the Study of Inebriety (originally the Society for the Study and Cure of Inebriety), the notion of excessive drunkenness became identified as a suitable subject for medical intervention and for a role for the state. Both drink and drug taking, in liquid form, were subsumed under the concept of inebriety. The role of Norman Kerr, Society president, a strong temperance exponent and former Medical Officer of Health, was important. Inebriety drew on hereditarian concepts, in alliance with similar approaches in the world of insanity. There was a desire to have a state funded system offering compulsory treatment under the inebriates acts[7]. Here is a later president, Sir William Collins, speaking of the concept of what by then he called "addiction" during the First World War. It was, he said,

> "a disease of the will – if one may couple terms derived from the opposite poles of the material and the volitional – and assuredly a disease in which the individual possessed has in many instances a most essential cooperative influence in his own worsement or betterment"[8].

Collins, like many of the medical men involved in advancing disease and state-funded treatment, was also a strong temperance supporter. There was an intermingling of science and morality, but also a developing medical/ lay alliance. As MacLeod noted, the alcohol issue was not part of mainstream public health in the nineteenth century, because of temperance, but many temperance activists were Medical Officers of Health or asylum superintendents[9].

---

[6] R. Porter, "The Drinking Man's Disease: the pre-history of Alcoholism in Georgian Britain", *British Journal of Addiction*, 80, 1985, pp. 385-96.

[7] V. Berridge, *Opium and the People. Opiate Use and Drug Control Policy in Nineteenth and Early Twentieth Century England*, London, Free Association Books, expanded edition, 1999; V. Berridge, "The Society for the Study of Addiction,1884-1988", special issue of *British Journal of Addiction*, 85 (8), 1990.

[8] W.J. Collins, "An Address on the Institutional Treatment of Inebriety", *British Journal of Inebriety*, 1, 1904, pp. 97-115.

[9] R.M. Macleod, "The Edge of Hope: Social Policy and Chronic Alcoholism, 1870-1900", *Journal of the History of Medicine and Allied Sciences*, 22, 1967, pp. 215-45.

Such views were of less importance after the First World War. During the war a social rather than a medical form of control was adopted. The Central Control Board did not survive the war, although restrictions on licensing hours did, and alcohol was less of an issue. The interwar concerns, apart from licensing, were alcohol and industrial efficiency (in line with the heightened war-time role for psychological perspectives) and the road safety issue, where the 1930 Road Traffic Act created the new offence of being under the influence of drink and therefore unable to control a car. This in turn stimulated new forms of biochemical and physiological research, and the development of the blood alcohol test[10].

Treatment, so far as it can be ascertained, remained a mixture of occasional confinement in asylums, with no special provision, or in a private nursing home under medical care. To the moral treatment of the nineteenth century were added some new drug treatments, amongst which was apomorphine, advocated by Dr. John Yerbury Dent, Editor of the *British Journal of Inebriety*. Dent was a general practitioner with an interest in alcohol treatment, a clubbable character who occupied a middle class London Bohemia, with many society and other well known patients, the Macmillans, Macleans, William Burroughs among them. He was resolutely hostile to psychology. His view was that "there is also a danger of giving an overdose of most medicine; what is often overlooked is that there is also a danger of giving an overdose of analysis"[11]. The growing focus on "scientific treatment" and also on research marked a separation of the medico-scientific agenda from the temperance one. The temperance agenda in the interwar years was different. It focussed on availability, limitation of consumption, and connections with the "social problem" group, issues with a social rather than a scientific tinge.

3. Post World War II

The rediscovery of disease

This pre-history emphasises a policy alliance from the late nineteenth century (medicine and temperance) which had begun to unravel in the interwar period as new forms of research began to define a different role for medicine and science in relation to alcohol. Medicine was increasingly separate from temperance and was beginning to grope towards a scientific rationale for its approaches – which in themselves were hardly coherent. Research was beginning to play an important role in these relationships.

---

[10] See Berridge, "Society" history, *op. cit.*, note 7.
[11] Cited in *ibid.*, p. 1044.

How did these issues impact in the post World War II period? First came the discovery afresh (the rediscovery) of disease in relation to alcoholism. In part the story of this rediscovery lay outside the UK in the pre-war period, with developments in the United States. The development of Alcoholics Anonymous in the 1930's, along with what became the Yale Center on Alcohol (at Rutgers from late 1950's), the *Quarterly Journal of Studies on Alcohol*, and the Yale Summer School on Alcohol, together became the intellectual centre of what became known as the "alcoholism movement"[12].

In Britain, the rebirth of the disease concept came in the late 1940's, and with the new treatments such as Antabuse came the message that treatment and cure were indeed possible. This was a message of optimism and to some extent technological determinism, although not all agreed with excessive reliance on one mode or another. Lincoln Williams, an early post-war specialist, maintained the need for an alliance of different approaches. In 1954, he said, "it is surely high time we cease being fanatically intolerant of any approach other than the one which happens to take our particular fancy from among the five A's: Apomorphine, Aversion therapy, Antabuse, Analysis and Alcoholics Anonymous"[13].

What secured the legitimacy of the disease approach in the UK? The role of the newly established World Health Organisation was of key importance. Alcohol was included in the terms of reference of its expert committee on mental health which met for the first time in 1949. This period of early interest coincided with collaboration between the head of the WHO Mental Health Unit, Dr. Hargreaves, a British psychiatrist, and E.M. Jellinek, a scientist and scholar who had established his reputation in the field at Yale. This period of interest lasted until the mid 1950s when alcohol fell out of favour. Until the late 1960s, Jellinek acted as a kind of ambassador for alcoholism, through visits and reports and WHO European seminars in the 1950s, establishing the need for research on the extent of the problem, and interest in alcoholism as medical work and as a disease. The role of WHO was important also in establishing internationally recognized disease classifications for the condition of "addiction"[14].

This international dimension interacted with the domestic situation. Here the post-war period saw the growth of an initial (or rather, revived) "policy community" around alcohol, which resulted in 1962 in the memorandum issued by the Ministry of Health,

---

[12] See R. Roizen, *The American Discovery of Alcoholism 1933-1939*, PhD. Berkeley, Ca, 1991.

[13] L. Williams, "Discussion", *British Journal of Addiction*, 51, 1954, p. 50.

[14] R. Room, "The World Health Organisation and Alcohol Control", *British Journal of Addiction*, 79, 1984, pp. 85-92. Special historical issue edited by V. Berridge; B. Thom and V. Berridge, *Social History of Medicine, op. cit.*; B. Thom, *Dealing with Drink, op. cit.*

The Hospital Treatment of Alcoholism. This community was primarily hospital based, in particular through the specialist model developed by the psychiatrist Max Glatt at Warlingham Park Hospital in Surrey, where group therapy approaches developed into a separate group for alcoholics. Glatt, a German refugee and a relative outsider in policy terms, had influence through T.P. Rees, superintendent of Warlingham, who did sit on Ministry advisory committees and who promoted Glatt's membership of the BMA/Magistrates committee, which was credited with stirring the Ministry of Health into action. Within the Ministry, too, insider links were developing, in particular through Richard Philippson, a civil servant with special responsibility for alcohol (from the early 1960s). The Glatt specialist model, supported by research results from Warlingham, had policy influence over what might have been expected to be the more influential D.L Davies, Dean of the Institute of Psychiatry, a far more prestigious figure. But Davies thought alcoholics did not need separate treatment, and his research results were largely ignored. The specialist model offered, as Thom has argued, a means for the Ministry of being seen to take action-rather than the Davies model, which, while perhaps equally effective, simply offered "more of the same"[15].

Shifting paradigms: risk, population consumption and problem use

One piece of research evidence which was also ignored in the early 1960s was Sully Ledermann's statistical argument, first published in the 1950s, which suggested a relationship between average per capita alcohol consumption and levels of alcohol misuse in a population. Population approaches had temperance associations, and implied pressure for policy action in areas such as licensing or taxation (temperance economics). This did not fit with the specialist treatment option which stressed the 'cure' of a relatively few diseased individuals. But in the 1970s the population based scientific belief became central to what was termed a new public health approach to alcohol. It became the central tenet of an expanded "policy community" round alcohol which comprised psychiatrists, this time primarily based in the Institute of Psychiatry, which developed its networks, through its training of psychiatrists, across the UK; but it also took on board civil servants, the alcohol voluntary sector, the police and the law[16]. There was research evidence which suggested that limitation of availability and consequent harm was the problem to be addressed. Average alcohol consumption was to be lowered rather than just the high risk consumption of a few. Prevention, rather, or as well as, treatment and cure, moved centre stage.

---

[15] Thom and Berridge, *op. cit.*; Thom, *op. cit.*; V. Berridge, D.L. Davies's biography for New Dictionary of National Biography, (forthcoming).

[16] R. Baggott, *op. cit.* (article and book).

The means whereby this happened is a fascinating story, which can be only briefly surveyed here[17]. However, some key conceptual and policy events should be highlighted. An early forerunner of the widening policy community was indicated by the first AGM of the Camberwell Council on Alcoholism in 1963. The executive committee included representatives from psychiatry, general practice, preventive medicine (the local Medical Officer of Health), the churches, the probation service, professional and voluntary social work and prisoners' aid. Here in embryo was the emergent policy community. The 1970s however, was the key decade. Again the international context was important. The new scientific paradigm of "dependence" rather than addiction (incorporating both psychiatric and psychological perspectives) was established through the authority of WHO. The dissemination of research through networks at the international level gave scientific legitimacy to the new approach. A major product of this effort, supported by Kettil Bruun of the Finnish Foundation for Alcohol Studies and by the Addiction Research Foundation of Toronto was the famous "purple book", *Alcohol Control Policies in Public Health Perspective*, published in 1975, which gave scientific authority to new approaches. These stressed the impact of trade policies and the economics of alcohol supply. The text commented on the paradigm shift:

> There has so far been little published scientific work in this area and it may be that one reason is the obvious sensitivity of the issues involved and the research worker's fear that his scientific intentions will draw him into an ideological arena. Those who have been trying to give alcohol studies a scientific basis have of course been much concerned to shake off the contentious moral overtones which have traditionally surrounded the subject of drinking and to suggest that "the trade" should now be an object of study may seem to carry the danger of reawakening all sorts of confusions and the accusation that the research worker has surrendered his impartiality...[18] [19]

The group, however, considered that these supply issues were a legitimate subject for scientific enquiry, because changes in overall consumption had an important bearing on the health of the population. Control measures and their impact were therefore public health issues. At the national level a group developed dedicated to transmitting

---

[17] The relationship between research and policy embodied in these developments is considered as one of several case studies in V. Berridge and B. Thom, "Research and Policy: What Determines the Relationship?", *Policy Studies,* 17 (1), 1996, pp. 23-34.

[18] K. Bruun, M. Lumio, K. Makela, L. Pan, R. Popham, R. Room, W. Schmidt, O. Skog, P. Sulkunnen and E. Osterberg, "Alcohol Control Policies in Public Health Perspective", Finnish Foundation for Alcohol Studies, 6.

[19] See Edward's evidence, "Minutes of Evidence taken before the Expenditure Committee" (Social Services and Employment sub committee), 28/1/76, pp. 56-62.

this message. Amongst them was a pupil of D.L. Davies, Griffith Edwards, a charismatic proponent of the new orthodoxy. He was able, through social background and interests, as well as positioning in the Institute, the powerhouse of British psychiatry, to cross boundaries between voluntary and statutory sectors, between upper class interest in this "social problem" and the involvement of the state and of politicians. Take, for example, his evidence to the Commons Expenditure Committee's enquiry into Prevention in 1976. This was a model of the new research based policy strategy. Edwards' ideological model at that stage was the recently defined WHO concepts (Edwards had a key role in the definition) on alcohol which linked "dependence" with what were then termed "alcohol related disabilities", a medicalised term which was later to transmute into "problem alcohol use". Epidemiological enumeration of "what counts as a problem" was central to these new definitions and Edwards' evidence was notable by its reference to statistics, surveys and subsamples. Some had been conducted locally in Camberwell by the Addiction Research Unit at the Institute of Psychiatry which was established in the late 1960s; national surveys came in the 70s. The efficacy or appropriateness of treatment for all cases was given less of a role[20]. Responses directed at the population were central. This was not mass persuasion through health education, although the importance of changing the terms of the debate was recognised, but rather measures affecting the general availability of alcohol.

> "It seems likely that the general availability of alcohol bears on prevalence of disabilities- the more a country or a segment of a population drinks, the greater the prevalence of problems. Such a position is of course quite contrary to more traditional wisdom which saw 'alcoholism' as a disease of a few unfortunates possessed of innate propensities, while the rest of the population drank 'normally' with the social pleasures of the many in no way related to the disease of the few. Any measures affecting general population consumption of alcohol are therefore potentially instruments of public health; such measures include pricing and licensing".

Such an approach was of course in tune with the general rise of the 'preventive paradigm' within government policy in the 1970s, which stressed epidemiologically defined population levels of risk while focussing on the responsibility of individuals to safeguard their own health. For alcohol, the 'field' expanded (this period saw the foundation of the National Council on Alcoholism, the Medical Council on Alcoholism, and local Councils on Alcoholism), and the treatment paradigm changed. An emphasis on community services rather than specialist treatment became the norm through a tranche of reports and circulars. A key arena of activity was the newly established Advisory

---

[20] The Advisory Council on the Misuse of Drugs was another.

Committee on Alcoholism, one of a range of new advisory committees established by government during the 1970s[21]. This, in its short life (1975-78) produced three reports, on *The Pattern and Range of Services for Problem Drinkers, Prevention, and Education and Training* which epitomised the new approach. The report on services changed its terminology to problem drinking from alcoholics during the course of its work. It proposed locally based services with a co-ordinated response from statutory and voluntary services. Research evidence supporting the value of 'brief intervention' from a G.P. rather than more intensive care brought that section of primary care into the new public health ambitions at the end of the decade. At the Institute of Psychiatry, D.L. Davies, a convert to Ledermann, was holding Alcohol Summer Schools which brought together medical and voluntary interests in the arena, and which served to propagate the consumption/harm theory, in conjunction with the newly established Alcohol Education Centre at the Institute[22].

Towards the end of the 1970s, the wider aspects of consumption/harm came to the fore. The most eloquent call for the new focus of policy came in 1979 with the Royal College of Psychiatrists report on *Alcohol and Alcoholism*, which gave central medical acceptance to the consumption theory. The main emphasis was not on treatment but on prevention through extensive health education, the explicit use of taxation to influence the price of drink and a moratorium on plans to relax the licensing laws. But the Report which attracted most attention was an initially unpublished one: the report on alcohol by the Central Policy Review Staff, also compiled in 1979. It was not published until 1982, and then in Finland. The main recommendations were for a co-ordinated alcohol policy based on the Royal College of Psychiatrists' recommendations, with a central body within government to monitor and co-ordinate policy. Politicians like Sir George Young and Patrick Jenkin as Health Ministers argued within the Conservative government for a concerted response. But the ultimate response was not the one hoped for. It was a milder document entitled *Drinking Sensibly*, published officially in 1981. This sequence of events has often been discussed, in part because of the parallels with the Black Report on inequalities, and later with regard to the NACNE report on nutrition – other reports which found publication difficult, or where there were rival reports, for political reasons. Its interest from our point of view lies in the fact that government itself also accepted the consumption/harm thesis. In fact it rejected control policies precisely because of their likely effect on consumption and the economic consequences. So the new alcohol science to some extent had permeated government circles as well. The establishment of this new 'scientific orthodoxy' was underlined by

[21] See Thom, *op. cit.*
[22] See Baggott, *op. cit.* and Thom, *op. cit.*

the hostile reception given to an official report which questioned its credentials, Mary Tuck's 1980 report for the Home Office, *Alcoholism and Social Policy: Are we on the Right Lines?* This advanced many of the ideas which were to be accepted in the 1990s, but which were outside the new scientific orthodoxy in 1980[23].

Although the overall policy wanted by the Think Tank report was never put in place, consumption/ harm did come to play an important role in prevention strategies, in particular through the 'drink unit' focus, which has been a matter of recent controversy. Originally the unit policy, which came to form the basis of policy advocacy and government prevention initiatives (for example *The Health of the Nation* alcohol targets), was a telling example of the interpenetration of policy and science. As Betsy Thom points out, the idea of a unit policy arose out of scientific imperatives, principally the standardisation of measurements of alcohol consumption for the assignment of individuals to drinking categories in epidemiological surveys. The three reports by the different Royal Colleges produced in the mid-1980s all used this concept identically, but with no clear description of the scientific basis. Later Richard Smith, now editor of the *British Medical Journal* and one of the people involved in defining the unit categories at this time, commented,

> "the public really wanted to know how much was safe… The answer is, of course, that we don't know. One strand of thought on the committee said that we should say so and another strand said that we shouldn't confuse people. So we plucked a figure out of the air… "[24].

This way of establishing an orthodoxy in science through the medium of an expert committee recalls the negotiations around dietary advice which David Smith followed in the 1930s[25]. But the important point is that the unit policy gave scientific legitimacy to the consumption/harm whole population approach: it was outstandingly successful as a marketing concept.

4. Harm and safety

Recently there are signs of an emergent reconceptualisation of alcohol issues. Just as consumption/harm and problems were the post-addiction model, so a new post-problem

---

[23] Quoted in Thom, *op. cit.*, p. 201.

[24] D. Smith, "The Social Construction of Dietry Standards: The British Medical Association, Ministry of Health Advisory Committee on Nutrition Report of 1934", in D. Maurer and J. Sobal (eds.), *Eating Agendas. Food and Nutrition and Social Problems*, New York, Aldine de Gruyter, 1996.

[25] G. Edwards *et al.*, *Alcohol Policy and the Public Good*, Oxford University Press, 1994.

model seems to be struggling to be born. *Alcohol and the Public Good* (1994), with its re-interpretation of the older public health case was recognisably a successor to the original purple book and conceived as such[26]. It was also of course, a neo-temperance approach, for which it has attracted criticism. But a newer consensus is now stressing, not general population consumption, but rather the impact of high-risk drinking, and its more visible aspects, such as public drunkenness. Reducing alcohol-related harm, rather than reducing consumption overall, has acquired greater policy salience. Predominantly social- psychological models of intervention and the focus on individual behaviour and lifestyles are yielding to a new interest in "community" and community-development theories and a basis for achieving changes at the community level in norms and structures[27]. The controversial Department of Health report of 1995, *Sensible Drinking*, which introduced changes in unit levels, as well as the concept of light drinking for older people for health reasons, also suggested the need to encourage harm reduction approaches at the local level. Unlike drugs and harm reduction, where there was a consistent policy community round the concept, it is difficult to see who will carry forward this new aim of policy outside government. A reordering of alliances is taking place.

5. A new public health paradigm?

The standard way of talking about alcohol policy, as with smoking policy, is in terms of 'industry influence', yet this has largely been absent from the analysis in this paper. The alcohol industry's role in the science/policy relationship through players such as the Portman Group, should not be forgotten. Industry also funds research. But in terms of dominant paradigms which all in the field have come to accept (even if they argue against them), the main issue is the growing interpenetration in the post-war period of research (epidemiological and psychological for much of this period) with policy networks and communities. For much of the post-war period these networks have been psychiatric led, but drawing in a wide range of players in the alcohol field.

Disease and treatment initially, and consumption/harm latterly since the 1970s, have been the science/policy banners under which this community has operated. For the consumption/harm approach, Bruun *et als* purple book in 1975 and Edwards *et als* successor in 1994 may be seen as the beginning and the end of an era. But it is important

---

[26] See, for example E. Single, "The Concept of Harm Reduction and its Application to Alcohol: The 6th Dorothy Black Lecture", *Drugs: Education, Prevention and Policy,* 4 (1), 1997, pp. 7-22.
[27] K. Middleton Fillmore, R. Roizen, A. Bostrom and W. Kerr, "Musing Cirrhosis", paper given at the Society for the Study of Addiction, Annual Conference, November, 1998, York, and subsequent discussion.

not to overemphasise clear boundaries between different approaches and their supportive communities. There are degrees of overlap and internal controversies, for example over controlled drinking. Kaye Middleton Fillmore has written of what she calls 'cross paradigm conceptual borrowing', in relation to the role of cirrhosis as a marker for both disease and consumption/harm. Fillmore's US group have been reinterpreting the role of cirrhosis in line with the newer high risk emphases, but this has brought hostility from publication outlets which wished to safeguard consumption/ harm orthodoxies[28]. Such recent episodes illustrate the reciprocity of relationships between paradigm shifts and policy imperatives.

The story of those relationships in the post-war period has been an international one. The role of the WHO has been emphasised in this paper and research networks internationally have been crucial in marketing concepts and approaches. Key charismatic individuals have been important, as have sites of expertise, in particular the Institute of Psychiatry in England. Marketing concepts brought the science to the public and to policy makers (in line with the mass media marketing approach of the new public health), in particular the unit strategy. There has also been a strong local dimension to policy since the 1970s.

At the end of the century, cross-substance similarities under the public health umbrella are increasingly apparent. The focus is on the individual in the environment, which in a paper on passive smoking, I have called environmental individualism[29]. For alcohol, smoking and drugs, there are cross-substance similarities in the new policy focus on harm reduction, on local strategies of control, on the role of the local environment (illustrated by controls on public drinking, public smoking, and the community safety concept for alcohol and drugs). Risk-based public health established in the 1970s is giving way to a public health based on safety and harm and the role of alcohol in that redefinition is again significant.

Acknowledgements

I am grateful to the Wellcome Trust for funding the "Science Speaks to Policy programme" at the London School of Hygiene and Tropical Medicine. My thanks are also due to Ingrid James for secretarial assistance.

---

[28] V. Berridge, "Passive Smoking: Policy Speaks to Science?", *Social Science and Medicine*, 49 (9), 1999, pp. 1183-1195.

[29] V. Berridge, paper given to conference on *Public Health: Past, Present and Future*, LSHTM, June, 1998.

On Smoking, Socialism and the Health of the British Nation
Paolo Palladino

1. Introduction

In September 1997, the recently elected Labour government sought to block a plan by the European Union to ban the advertising of tobacco during sporting events. The British press quickly linked this effort to a pre-electoral donation from Bernie Ecclestone, the wealthy head of the Formula One Constructors' Association and former supporter of the Conservative Party. Ecclestone had built his fortune by transforming car-racing during the preceding 20 years into a major form of popular entertainment, which had become especially visible following Damon Hill's conquest of the world title. His donation was particularly gratifying because he exemplified the new entrepreneurial spirit promoted by the Conservative Party, which the Labour Party now also wished to advance. This new spirit was to be translated by the Labour Party, under the banner of the 'third way' between capitalism and socialism, into benefits for all rather than the few. Unfortunately, the Labour Party had committed itself before the election to decisive action against smoking, especially among the young who might be inspired by Hill's achievement or Ecclestone's entrepreneurship. This did not fit well with Ecclestone's close connection with tobacco manufacturers, who are the main sponsors of car-racing. Not surprisingly, the news of Ecclestone's donation rapidly eroded the high standing of the government. It was now accused of reneging on its promises to cleanse government of political corruption and build a fairer, healthier nation. A few commentators observed, however, that this controversial donation was only one in a series from even more influential corporate organisations than the Formula One Constructors' Association, such as Sainsbury's, British Telecom, British Gas and British Airways. They argued that all these donations called for a more incisive discussion of the modernisation of socialism being pressed by the Labour Party. These commentators also felt that the morally charged rhetoric that characterized this modernisation was no longer acceptable. What was needed was hard questioning and answering[1].

---

[1] For a summary of these events and their repercussions, see, "Suddenly the Red Rose Doesn't Smell so Sweet", *Guardian*, 12/11/1997 and "The Prime Minister Regards the Lobby Boys as Little Monsters", *Observer*, 12/7/1998. On the modernisation of British socialism see Michael Gove, "War on the Vague: Towards the New Tories", in Anne Coddington and Mark Perryman (eds.), *The Moderniser's Dilemma: Radical Politics in the Age of Blair*, London, Lawrence & Wishart, 1998, pp. 244-261.

In this paper, I want to contribute to this critical exercise by turning to an earlier episode in the history of smoking, socialism and the health of the nation. More specifically, I want to focus on the work of Horace Joules, the former medical director of the Central Middlesex Hospital, who was remembered on his death in 1975 as a combative socialist and an influential, if aggravating, figure in the establishment of that signal achievement of British socialism that is the National Health Service[2]. Thus, the author of one obituary wrote that:

'Horace was a many-sided person, a great humanist, a committed socialist, an outstanding physician and an exciting teacher. But I will always think of Horace as a fighter'[3].

The author of another obituary wrote rather less flatteringly that Joules had been:

'one of the stormy petrels of the early years of the National Health Service. An enthusiast for whole-time service in it, he never pulled his punches and he showed scant mercy for any critics of the Service. His pen and his voice, both of which he could use with facility and an abrasiveness… were well to the fore throughout the first two decades of the National Health Service'[4].

While Joules's socialism and involvement in the establishment of the National Health Service are very important to the overall structure of my argument, I want to begin by focusing on his role in the modern campaign against smoking, a role that has recently earned him an entry in the *New Dictionary of National Biography* and a place in more conventional forms of historical recollection[5]. I will then return to Joules's socialism and his involvement in the establishment of the National Health Service, hoping to explain thereby why Ecclestone's donation triggered so effectively the public debate about the contemporary modernisation of British socialism.

2. Taking action against smoking

In 1948, when the National Health Service had just been established, Joules was a member of three advisory committees to the Ministry of Health, namely the Standing Medical

[2] For the role of socialism in the establishment of the National Health Service, see Charles Webster, "Conflict and Consensus: Explaining the British Health Service", *Twentieth Century British History*, 1, 1990, pp. 115-151.

[3] Papers in Keith P. Ball's possession: "Horace Joules and the Central", manuscript, 27/1/1978.

[4] "Dr. Horace Joules", *Times*, 28/1/1977.

[5] See also Keith Ball, "Horace Joules's Role in the Control of Cigarette Smoking", in Stephen Lock *et al.* (eds.), *Ashes to Ashes: The History of Smoking and Health*, Amsterdam, Editions Rodopi, 1998, pp. 214-215.

Advisory Committee, the Standing Advisory Committee on Cancer, and the Central Health Services Council. It was he who first brought to these committees' attention Austin Bradford Hill and Richard Doll's now famous epidemiological study of lung cancer[6]. He argued immediately that their claim that tobacco, especially when smoked in the form of cigarettes, rather than pipes or cigars, was the principal cause of lung cancer called for a national campaign to warn the public about the danger. The failure of other researchers to find any pathological evidence to support Hill and Doll's claim resulted, however, in a recommendation to the Ministry that such publicity was undesirable and that more research was needed instead. Moreover, it was argued that such research should look into other possible causes of lung cancer besides smoking, including the more widely suspected atmospheric emissions of motor vehicles and power plants[7].

Joules, however, having foreseen that the ministerial committees would disagree with him, had begun to circumvent them by taking the case directly to Hilary Marquand, the Labour Minister of Health. He did so by approaching Barnet Stross, Member of Parliament for the Labour Party, Parliamentary Secretary to the Minister of Health, and a fellow member of the Socialist Medical Association, which had advised the Labour Party on the organisation of the National Health Service. He convinced him to place a Parliamentary Question regarding Doll and Hill's finding and the need for a national publicity campaign to warn the British public against the dangers of smoking[8]. This set off a series of further questions from other Members of Parliament, Labour and Conservative. Marquand responded to them all by repeating the recommendations of his advisory committees. While Sir Harold Himsworth, the Secretary of the Medical Research Council, which had commissioned Hill and Doll's study, was as convinced as Joules about the link between smoking and lung cancer, he was not 'too pleased' with this situation, especially since he was advised that:

> 'Dr. Joules will not let us go… He is, as you know, the main protagonist against smoking, on the [advisory committees to the Ministry of Health] and in the press'[9].

In fact, from this time onward, Joules was either quoted in, or writing to, the *Times, Lancet* and *British Medical Journal* on smoking and its dangers. He began by discussing

---

[6] See R. Doll and A.B. Hill, "Smoking and Carcinoma of the Lung", *British Medical Journal*, 1950, vol. II, pp. 739-748. For a parallel account of British governmental responses to this study, see Charles Webster, "Tobacco Smoking Addiction: a Challenge to the National Health Service", British Journal of Addiction, 79, 1984, pp. 7-16.

[7] Meeting of Standing Advisory Committee on Cancer, 18/1/1951; and 20: Central Health Services Council; Chairman, 22/9/1951 (Public Record Office, henceforth PRO, MH133/ 453).

[8] Stross to Marquand, 28/6/1951 (PRO- MH55/1011).

[9] Cancer of the lung investigation; note, 27/2/1952 (PRO- MH55/ 1011).

the more incisive actions taken in socialist countries. Thus, in 1951, on his return from a trip to the Soviet Union, he was cited by the *Times* as complaining that:

'at the All-Union Research Institute for Sanitary Instruction the woman director said that Russian doctors had been convinced by the statistical evidence compiled by doctors in Great Britain and America that smoking was the major cause of cancer of the lung. Without conducting any research of their own, they began to publicise this fact a year ago and there had already been a 10%. fall in the consumption of tobacco throughout Russia. Dr. Joules said that, in this country, where the number of deaths from this disease now exceeded those caused by tuberculosis, he had little success in publicising this fact'[10].

Joules also described at length the alliances that resisted any attempt to warn the British public, writing in the *British Medical Journal* that:

'[M]any powerful bodies have a vested interest in playing down such publicity. The Treasury is foremost in this respect because it receives £610 million yearly from the tobacco tax. The national press is interested in revenue from advertisement and the cinemas are also recipients of advertising revenue from the tobacco companies'[11].

He then argued in the *Lancet* that the medical profession had to take the lead and do what the government was so unwilling to do:

'The profession itself must now meet a very personal responsibility in preventive medicine. For years clinicians have tended to pay lip service to the wider aspects of prevention of disease. If we continue to smoke, our patients will follow our example. Are we justified in encouraging them to take this risk? Whatever decision we make about our own health we must tell them of their risk. Doctors who see men slowly dying of this unpleasant and painful death must feel impelled to prevent such death in the future. The general public will respond if they are given a sufficiently bold lead. The nation cannot afford to lose many of its most able and industrious men at the peak of their careers'[12].

By 1959, however, he was convinced that little could be expected from the medical profession because the 'medical men and women' who spoke on 'the great sociomedical problems' of the day were not just 'holders of professorial chairs and other important

---

[10] "Scientists' Visit to Russia", *Times*, 15/8/1951.

[11] Horace Joules, "Cure of Tobacco-Smoking", *Lancet*, 1952, vol. II, p. 781.

[12] Horace Joules, "Smoking and Cancer of the Lung", *British Medical Journal*, 1953, vol. I, pp. 161-162.

positions in the medical world [but] also act[ed] as expert advisers to industrial concerns'[13]. In other words, everyone was beholden to tobacco manufacturers and the nation was suffering as a consequence.

3. Smoking and Socialism

Significantly, however, Joules' relentless campaigning was easily tarred by many of his opponents as motivated, first and foremost, by his desire to transform the political organisation of the nation. Thus, a Conservative medical commentator complained in the *Times* about Joules's view that the link between smoking and lung cancer was incontestable, that the 'figures' were beyond doubt. He argued that, in fact, 'there can be, and there is, a good argument all about the figures and what they mean'. He then asked sarcastically:

> '[A]re we expected at this stage of our knowledge to take seriously the proposition that the enlightened government of the U.S.S.R. has immediately informed its people of a new development in preventive medicine, and that they have as a result responded at once by cutting their tobacco consumption by 10%? Is it not conceivable that, in a planned economy, a decision to reduce the amount of tobacco grown or imported may have been supported by a propaganda campaign for economic rather than medical purposes? Is this sufficient cause for blame at home and commendation abroad'[14]?

Iain McLeod, Marquand's successor when the Conservative Party returned to power in 1951 was far more explicit about the grander political motivations of the incessant demand for public action against smoking when he pointed out that the situation was being exploited by,

> 'a man of extremely advanced left wing opinions… who will… not hesitate to embarrass the government'[15].

This man was, of course, Joules himself.

Paradoxically, many of Joules's colleagues in the Socialist Medical Association were no more sympathetic to his campaign against smoking than his Conservative critics. In 1954, as vice-president of the Association, Joules had established a special committee on

---

[13] Horace Joules, "Associations with Commerce", *Lancet*, 1959, vol. I, p. 585.

[14] D.W. Smithers, "Diseases of the Lung", *Times*, 16/8/1951.

[15] McLeod to Boyd-Carpenter, 29/1/1954 (PRO- MH55/1011).

'Clean Air and Diseases of the Lung', which drew together medical experts on industrial diseases, and representatives of the engineering, mining, and tobacco workers unions[16]. The committee's terms of reference did not mention smoking, and focused instead on industrial air pollution. Joules, the committee's chairman, seemed to follow this line. Thus, he was very active in moving Sir Hugh Beaver, chairman of Guinness Brewers and member of the management committee of the Central Middlesex Hospital, to lead a parliamentary inquiry into the problem, which eventually resulted in the *Clean Air Act* of 1956[17]. Moreover, the pamphlet issued by Joules's committee, which was effectively the Association's official response to Beaver's report, suggested, in the midst of intense debates over the relationship between smoking and lung cancer, that 'pollution of the atmosphere may be a factor in the production of cancer of the lung'[18].

Notwithstanding the emphasis the Socialist Medical Association then seemed to place on air pollution as an important cause of lung cancer, the former president of the Association and Member of Parliament for the Labour Party, Somerville Hastings, was at the very same time pressing the Minister of Health to take a more decisive line on smoking[19]. Joules himself was pursuing this alternative line within the Association itself, by suggesting that it should organise a conference so that it might 'define its policy on tobacco'[20]. Eventually, Joules's and Hastings' efforts moved the secretary of the Association to write to the Minister of Health and protest against his failure to take any concerted action against smoking, stressing that 'the government must now agree to a countrywide educational campaign to warn the people of this peril'[21]. This victory notwithstanding, Hastings, Joules, and Norman Macdonald, another colleague of Joules at the Central Middlesex Hospital, found the pace of the Association's response frustratingly slow[22]. In fact, it was not until 1957 that Macdonald and Doll, who, besides being the author of the seminal report on smoking and lung cancer, was a long-standing member of the Association, were asked to prepare a pamphlet on smoking. Moreover, in September of the same year, the representative of the Tobacco Workers' Union on the Clean Air and Healthy Lungs Committee insisted that the pamphlet should mention not just smoking but the other causes of lung cancer identified by the

---

[16] Clean Air: Minutes of meeting, 26/6/1954, Archives of the Socialist Medical Association (University of Hull), henceforth SMA; DSM 2/10.

[17] See D. Allan Gray, *The Central Middlesex Hospital,* London, Pitman, 1963.

[18] Clean Air: Draft leaflet, 1955 (SMA-DSM 2/10).

[19] Gregson, 7/5/1955 (PRO- MH55/2220).

[20] Clean Air: Minutes of meeting, n.d. and 26/4/1956 (SMA-DSM 2/10).

[21] Jupp to Turton, 9/11/1956 (PRO-MH55/2221).

[22] Clean Air: Minutes of meeting, 27/2/1958 (SMA-DSM 2/10).

committee as well. Joules objected to this qualification by stressing the unimportance of any other causes, but his unrelenting conviction that smoking was the single culpable agent was as ignored by his socialist colleagues as it was by his opponents in the Ministry of Health[23]. It took another full year before the Association agreed to take a more definite position on smoking, but, very importantly, it now stressed the need to emphasise the political and social aspects of why people smoked, not just the dangers of smoking[24]. In other words, members of the Association, other than Joules and his allies, thought that understanding why people chose to smoke was just as important as emphasising the inherent dangers.

Once again, Hastings ignored the reservations of the Socialist Medical Association and called on the Minister of Health to appoint a Royal Commission to investigate the public danger presented by smoking. The Minister replied, just as his predecessors had done in all their public statements since 1954, that the problem was a matter for further scientific investigation, rather than for any commission. For Hastings, this could only mean that the Minister was taking his advice from the tobacco industry rather than the medical profession. That the cause might be unpopular with the public, especially one bombarded by very contradictory reports from inside and outside the medical profession and increasingly sceptical about all claims regarding smoking, never crossed his mind[25]. Similarly, Joules pursued the case in the press, arguing in the *Times* that such inaction could only mean that:

> 'We have become a nation of tobacco addicts. I wonder if there is any other drug addiction that the world has ever known that has produced such a pathetic harvest of disease'[26].

Interestingly, while I have found little contemporary material to elaborate on the reasons for the reluctance of the Socialist Medical Association to follow Joules and his allies, Elizabeth Hilliard, a leading figure in the Association, recalls that she and many of her colleagues objected to Joules's unrelenting efforts, which they apparently compared to those of a 'preacher', because:

> The main objective of the Socialist Medical Association was to get a fair distribution of health services, and the campaign against smoking was not part of this objective. We did all agree that we disapproved of smoking, but it was *not* a *political* matter to us, whereas

---

[23] Clean Air: Minutes of meeting, 31/1 and 19/9/1957 (SMA-DSM 2/10).

[24] File of minutes of Executive Committee: Minutes of meeting, 15/10/1958 (SMA- DSM 1/13).

[25] Archives of the British Medical Association: Record B/120/1/39/1958-9, Sc31A.

[26] "Call for Royal Commission on Chest Disease", *Times*, 21/5/1959.

the campaign for a health service "free to all at the time of need", our slogan then, was clearly political and as such our main interest.' (emphasis in the original)[27].

This divergence of goals among socialists was also evident at the annual meeting of the Trade Unions Congress in 1956. On this occasion, the very radical Medical Practitioners' Union and the Association of Scientific Workers called on the government to take action against smoking. The motion was blocked by the interventions of the Tobacco Workers' Union and the General and Municipal Workers' Union, who, like the Ministry of Health before them, drew attention to the contradictory evidence about the link between smoking and lung cancer. The motion was eventually amended and reduced to the usual call for more research into the causes of lung cancer[28].

4. Smoking and social responsibility

Unlike Hilliard, Joules and his allies seemed to think that the Socialist Medical Association should become actively involved in the debates over smoking, but what exactly was the connection they made between smoking and socialism?

Joules found it infuriating that his patients should suffer 'needlessly from their... own habits'[29]. Smoking was, for him, a form of intolerable escapism, which he decried by writing that:

> 'Too often energetic trade union officials and other left wing workers smoke excessively. The resultant disease and death from this must be made clear. *There is no magic in a cigarette that can compensate for the harm it does to our society*.' (emphasis in the original)[30].

Strikingly, smoking was socially injurious because:

> 'some, otherwise courteous and well-mannered, become completely indifferent to the nuisance they cause to others by their smoking... it should be emphasised that it is in the confirmed chain-smoker that this level of behaviour is reached, but it is in this direction that

---

[27] Elizabeth Hilliard to Paolo Palladino, 11/5/1996.

[28] "Discouragement of Smoking", *Times*, 8/9/1956.

[29] "Ball, Horace Joules and the Central", see note 3.

[30] Horace Joules, "Clearing the Air", in Socialist Medical Association, *Danger: Dust at Work*, London, Today and Tomorrow, n.d., pp. 2-4, on p. 4.

too many unknowingly drift, away from the higher standards of social behaviour, of tolerance, consideration and fair play'[31].

Apparently reflecting on his own efforts to stop smoking, Joules wrote that all that was needed to defeat such antisocial behaviour was 'quiet determination to abstain, associated with having a cigarette available in the pocket to avoid a panic search throughout the house… in the early days of complete abstention'[32]. In other words, smoking was an objectionable 'bad habit' with grievous 'physical and moral' consequences for those who did not enjoy Joules's 'self-control' and sense of 'fair play' in their engagement with the rest of society.

This morally charged language, which echoed the concerns of 19th century political reformers over the social costs of alcohol, was even more evident in the pamphlet that Doll and Macdonald prepared for the Socialist Medical Association[33]. They wrote, in a peculiarly gendered fashion, which I am unable to explain other than in terms of their overwhelming concern for masculine industrial welfare, that:

'There is no working-class household where both husband and wife are real addicts which can afford the expenditure such smoking demands… the heavy smoker may cut down on essential food requirements to maintain his supply of cigarettes; heavy smokers, too, may also be immoderate in other respects, with regard to alcohol, for example. Also, many itinerant males and those with an unstable social background are cigarette addicts; many such show great laxity in matters of personal care and hygiene. In their relationship to the rest of society they are misfits'[34].

It is perhaps unsurprising then that Joules addressed popular audiences on the dangers of smoking in conjunction with the Temperance Union, and that he linked alcohol and tobacco in his call upon the 'Royal College of Physicians [to] re-enact history, and help to revivify itself by giving advice comparable to that given in respect to alcohol 200 years ago'[35]. Importantly, this pathologised moral condemnation of smoking was not confined to Joules, Macdonald, and Doll, but extended to very influential

[31] Norman Macdonald, *Your Chest Could be Healthy: Smoking and Lung Diseases*, London, Today and Tomorrow, n.d., pp. 5-6.
[32] Horace Joules, "Cure of Tobacco Smoking", *Lancet*, 1952, vol. II, p. 781.
[33] On alcohol and 19th century political reform, see Brian Harrison, *Drink and the Victorians: The Temperance Question in England*, 1815-1872 [2nd ed.], Keele, Keele University Press, 1994.
[34] Macdonald, *Your Chest could be Healthy*, pp. 1-12.
[35] "Ball, Horace Joules and the Central", see note 3.

members of the Labour Party and Socialist Medical Association, such as Baroness Summerskill. Thus, in 1962, the Royal College of Physicians decided to disregard the absence of pathological evidence and throw its weight behind the epidemiological claim that smoking was the principal cause of lung cancer by issuing its famous report on *Smoking and Health*[36]. During the ensuing debate in the House of Lords, Summerskill condemned smoking by appealing to images of smokers as men of weak will, prepared to sacrifice their families to satisfy their craving for nicotine, and needing secretive visits to special clinics, comparable to clinics for venereal disease, to overcome their socially destructive addiction[37].

In sum, Joules and his allies were not prepared to accept any opposition to public action against smoking, especially from within socialist circles, because smoking was a 'social disease' and therefore such action was necessarily important to the socialist cause[38]. The roots of their peculiar merger of medical, political, and moral concerns can be examined very fruitfully by considering Joules's biography.

5. The making of a socialist doctor?

Joules was born in 1902, one of ten children of grocers in a small rural village in the English Midlands[39]. His family adhered to strict Primitive Methodism and, like most adherents to this religious denomination, his father was both politically radical and a vehement teetotaller[40].

For Joules and four of his ten siblings, professional caring for others provided a very suitable way of rising above their modest circumstances. Thus Joules began medical studies at the University College in Cardiff and eventually graduated very successfully from Middlesex Hospital in 1925. He was then appointed as house physician in the Middlesex and Brompton Hospitals, where he is said to have learnt from Sir Robert

---

[36] Royal College of Physicians, *Smoking and Health*, London, Pitman Medical, 1962. See also Virginia Berridge, "Science and Policy: The Case of Post-war British Smoking Policy", in Lock, *Ashes to Ashes*, pp. 143-162.

[37] See House of Lords, "Smoking and Health", 22/3/1962, col. 646-647.

[38] Horace Joules, *Stop that Cough!*, London, Today and Tomorrow, n.d., p. 6.

[39] This section is based largely on information from Joules' sister, Margaret; David Joules to Paolo Palladino, 13/9 and 23/9/1996.

[40] On Primitive Methodism and political radicalism, see E.P. Thompson, *The Making of the English Working Class* [1963], London, Penguin, 1980; and Peter d'A. Jones, *The Christian Revival, 1877-1914: Religion, Class, and Social Conscience in Late-Victorian Britain,* Princeton, Princeton University Press, 1968.

Arthur Young about the importance of specialisation[41]. He then moved as medical officer and registrar to the Ancoats, City of London and Middlesex Hospitals[42]. Eventually, he obtained the more secure post of resident physician in the Selly Oak Hospital, recently built in one of the more heavily industrialised areas of Birmingham as one of the first municipal hospitals in the country. He remained at Selly Oak Hospital from 1931 to 1935, maintaining contact with the metropolitan medical community by frequently attending meetings of the Royal Society of Medicine and by beginning his association with the Socialist Medical Association. In 1935, he returned to London, to work as senior resident physician in the Central Middlesex Hospital, another municipal hospital just established by the Middlesex County Council, outside Park Royal, one of London's largest industrial estates. Joules eventually became the medical director of the Central Middlesex Hospital, and remained there until his early retirement in 1962.

Joules's lifelong involvement with municipal hospitals coincided with a strong commitment to a social function for medicine. These municipal hospitals had been established in the name of greater social efficiency under the authority of the *Local Government Act* of 1929. This legislation transferred to the municipalities the medical facilities previously provided under the *Poor Law*, with strengthened finances and improved access (the Central Middlesex Hospital had once been the Willesden Workhouse Infirmary). Inevitably, this extension of state involvement in the provision of medical care was opposed by voluntary hospitals and their associated consultants, such as Geoffrey Evans from the very prestigious St. Bartholomew's Hospital[43]. Joules responded to Evans's opposition by linking medical care and the moral welfare of the nation in ways that presaged his later condemnation of smoking. He wrote in the *Lancet* that:

> 'We must, I think, in attempting to formulate schemes for the future of the profession, bear in mind the fact that unless we are prepared to study and provide personal treatment for the relatively poor… we shall accelerate [their] physical and mental, and consequently [their] moral, degradation'[44].

---

[41] Papers in Keith P. Ball's possession: Dr. Horace Joules, manuscript, n.d. On Young, see "Young, Sir Robert Arthur, 1871-1959", in Richard R. Trail (ed.) *Lives of the Fellows of the Royal of Physicians*, London, Royal College of Physicians of London, 1968, pp. 467-468.

[42] Roger Cooter and John Pickstone have argued that small urban hospitals in the midst of poor neighbourhoods, such as the Ancoats Hospital, were sometimes very attractive to aspiring consultants developing new medical specialisations. This may be quite important for an understanding of Joules's later career; see Cooter and Pickstone, "From Dispensary to Hospital: Medicine, Community and Workplace in Ancoats, 1828-1948", *Manchester Region History Review*, 7, 1993, pp. 73-84.

[43] Geoffrey Evans, "A Medical Service for the Nation", *Lancet*, 1930, vol. II, pp. 872-873.

[44] Horace Joules, "A Medical Service for the Nation", *Lancet*, 1930, vol. II, p. 935.

Importantly, Joules believed that the increasing importance of municipal hospitals, which motivated Evans's criticism, was changing the understanding of disease and its causes. Beginning with his earliest clinical training at the Brompton Hospital, which is historically associated with tuberculosis, he dedicated himself to diseases of the chest, especially chronic bronchitis, and not long after joining the staff at the Selly Oak Hospital he was writing in the *British Medical Journal* that 'the profession seems to be awakening belatedly to the immense problem of pneumonia'. This, he continued, was due 'to some realisation of the great number of cases treated in municipal hospitals', concluding that the disease was often due to 'devitalising social factors'[45]. Joules's interest in these factors continued uninterrupted throughout his career. Thus, in 1953, he precipitated a controversy in the pages of the *Lancet* over the persistence of tuberculosis in Glasgow, by arguing that it was due to inadequate housing. He concluded his contribution to the controversy by arguing that: 'Tuberculosis in Glasgow will not be eradicated until a fully staffed medical and nursing service is associated with a radical approach to re-housing'[46].

Like most members of the Socialist Medical Association, Joules believed that medicine would not serve the needs of the nation until it became more 'democratic', ie, until private practice was completely eliminated and replaced with a salaried, medically trained civil service. Thus, in the words of a member of the King Edward's Hospital Fund, the leading coordinators of voluntary medical services, he was never 'slow to point out the deficiencies of voluntary hospitals or of those still run on more or less voluntary lines'[47]. Not surprisingly he relished the electoral victory of the Labour Party in 1945 and the prospect of a complete elimination of private medical practice under the promised National Health Service[48]. Soon thereafter he became embroiled in the attempt by the Willesden Borough Council to unionise the medical and nursing staff in its employment, including those working in the Central Middlesex Hospital[49]. However, the much more pragmatic Minister of Health, Nye Bevan, condemned the attempt and agreed with the medical profession that the Council, and all other local authorities, had no right to determine which associations should represent

---

[45] Horace Joules, "Primary Pneumonia: A Two Year Survey of Cases Treated Non-Specifically", *British Medical Journal,* 1933, vol. I, pp. 455-457, p. 455.

[46] Horace Joules, "Tuberculosis in Glasgow", *Lancet*, 1953, vol. II, p. 1152.

[47] King Edward's Hospital Fund, Visitors, Central Middlesex Group Hospital Management Committee: Report, 9/1951 (Greater London Record Office, henceforth GRO, A/KE/735/10/1).

[48] Somerville Hastings and Horace Joules, "The Labour Party and a National Health Service", *Lancet*, 1945, vol. II, p. 479.

[49] "An Indefensible Doctrine", *Times*, 4/12/1945.

their employees (in this particular case, the British Medical Association or the Royal College of Nursing, as desired by the medical and nursing staff; or the National Association of Local Government Officers, as desired by the Council)[50]. This pattern was repeated when Bevan disregarded the Socialist Medical Association's advice and decided to allow the continuation of private practice under the National Health Service. Joules was thoroughly disappointed. Such disappointment with one of the greatest achievements of British socialism must raise questions about what meaning Joules gave to socialism.

6. Romantic rage and technocratic answers

Charles Fletcher, a leading figure in the modern campaign against smoking, once wrote that he found it 'odd that in spite of his concern with the injustices of the under-privileged... Joules... did not emphasise poverty and social deprivation as a cause of chronic bronchitis'[51]. I think that the explanation of this paradoxical statement lies in Joules's link to a form of radical social criticism that stopped short of any analysis in terms of class, but has nonetheless played an important role in the history of British socialism.

Many of Joules's obituaries drew attention to his love for walks in the countryside and reading the works of John Clare[52]. Perhaps Joules was following Clare and other Romantic critics of modern society when he wrote that there had been a time when the British nation had some respect for the health of its people and that this respect 'was lost in the industrial revolution'[53]. Furthermore, after visiting Sheffield in 1953, he contrasted almost elegiacally the corrupt landscape and atmosphere of the industrial revolution with a purer countryside, writing in the *British Medical Journal* that:

'Not long ago I sat in a churchyard not far from a maternity hospital in that city. In the countryside it was a beautiful spring morning, but in Sheffield the sun showed through a haze of smoke and dirt. I held out a hand and smuts almost a centimetre in diameter fell on it. I wondered how many children being born in the hospital would die, victims of the atmosphere'[54].

[50] "Willesden Nurses", *Times*, 6/12/1946.

[51] C.M. Fletcher, "The Prevention of Chronic Bronchitis", *British Journal of Diseases of the Chest*, 73, 1979, pp. 48-50, on p. 49. On Fletcher's role in the campaign, see Charles Fletcher, "The Story of the Reports on Smoking and Health by the Royal College of Physicians", in Lock, *Ashes to Ashes*, pp. 202-205.

[52] On Clare, see Raymond Williams, *The Country and the City*, London, Hogarth Press, 1985.

[53] Joules, "Prevention of Dust Disease".

[54] "Horace Joules and the Central".

Paradoxically, while Joules suggested sometimes that opening the countryside to more than just the fortunate few was the solution to this tragedy, the more general rationalisation of modern society was for him the real solution[55]. Thus, he wrote that:

> 'Mental health, in an acquisitive and densely crowded society, can only come from a wise education by which endeavour is canalised along routes likely to bring harmony rather than internecine competition'[56].

This education of the British public, including its education into ways of coping with the psychological stresses of the new salutary regime, which compelled them to avoid that other corrupter of the air we breathe and paragon of the acquisitive society, the cigarette, was to be accomplished, of course, by Joules's salaried, medically trained civil service[57].

Like many medical planners before the war, Joules believed that hospitals should act as coordinating centres in the provision of medical care. As he explained in 1948, at the annual meeting of the British Medical Association, 'The district hospital should be a common meeting-ground for all health workers in the area, with responsibility for the postgraduate instruction of the practitioners who would ultimately serve in the health centre practices'[58]. However, just as he had discovered with the relationship between municipal hospitals and pneumonia, this institutional reorganisation of medicine entailed a conceptual reorganisation as well. These hospitals had to become centres for the development of the new, social medicine advocated by Joules's more famous friend and holder of the chair in social medicine at the University of Oxford, John Ryle[59]. Thus, in 1938, Joules segregated 50 beds for research into gastroenterology and dietetics, offering the post of researcher to the young, talented, and, most importantly, politically conservative, Francis Avery-Jones[60]. Significantly, while the Central Middlesex was viewed by many of Avery-Jones's fellow students in the prestigious St. Bartholomew's Hospital as a 'dump', he accepted Joules's offer because he

---

[55] "Call for Royal Commission on Chest Disease", *Times*, 21/4/1959.

[56] Joules, "Health from the Health Service", 1172.

[57] On cigarettes and the culture of consumption, see Matthew Hilton, "Smoking in British Popular Culture, 1800-2000", Manchester, Manchester University Press, 2000.

[58] "Preventive Medicine under the National Health Service Act", *British Medical Journal*, 1948, vol. II, p. 97.

[59] Horace Joules, "Potentialities of Municipal Medicine", *Lancet*, 1942, vol. II, pp. 396-397; on Ryle, see Dorothy Porter, "Changing Disciplines: John Ryle and the Making of Social Medicine in Britain in the 1940s", *History of Science*, 30, 1992, pp. 137-164.

[60] M.J.S. Langman, "Sir Francis Avery Jones", *Guardian*, 18 /5/1998.

thought that it was on the 'up and up' and sympathetic to 'younger men' with very different ideas about the future of medicine[61]. In fact, the beds he came to control became a crucial resource for Doll and Avery-Jones's epidemiological study of the peptic ulcer and its relationship to occupational background, a study that for David Armstrong epitomises the emergence of the new discourse of social medicine and its attendant social body[62]. In line with this grander transformation of medicine, Joules was not interested in just the intellectual development of social medicine and its cognate sciences, most notably epidemiology and medical sociology, but in it widest extension possible. The project of social medicine was for Joules a truly all-encompassing project of social reconstruction.

He began this project in 1939, by linking the Central Middlesex with the Middlesex Hospital Medical School, establishing the former as a centre for training in social medicine. As Joules's colleague and other influential figure in the modern campaign against smoking, Keith Ball, once recalled about Joules' teaching:

> 'Woe betide those students who did not know the occupation and social background of their patients!'[63]

More importantly yet, Joules aimed to translate such research and education into new forms of medical provision. Thus, soon after the war, he began to displace general practitioners by transforming the Central Middlesex into a base from which to despatch hospital consultants on visits to the home and the workplace. By 1956 he was able to establish a department of occupational health and the associated Central Middlesex Industrial Health Service Ltd to provide health services to employees of local manufacturers such as Guinness Brewers, Heinz and Walls[64]. Those visited by these specialists also obtained from them a dose of the education in proper social behaviour given in the first ever publicly funded clinic for smokers, which Joules helped to establish within the hospital[65]. The Central Middlesex was becoming an institution that extended the domain of social medicine well beyond the ambitions of

---

[61] Sir Francis Avery-Jones, personal communication, 20/6/1996; and Keith Ball, personal communication, 3/5/1996.

[62] See David Armstrong, *Political Anatomy of the Body: Medical Knowledge in Britain in the Twentieth Century*, Cambridge, Cambridge University Press, 1983.

[63] Papers in Keith P. Ball's possession: Maurice Orbach, *Dr. Horace Joules - A profile*, n.d.

[64] Allan Gray, *Central Middlesex Hospital*.

[65] Cancer: General: Smoking and Lung Cancer: Anti-smoking clinics, 10/3/1963 (PRO-MH55/2233).

pioneering 19th century reformers of medicine and the state, such as John Snow, Edwin Chadwick and John Simon[66]. Not surprisingly, Joules wrote in the *British Medical Journal* that:

> 'We shall not progress in the prevention of… chest diseases until we regard a persistent cough as seriously as persistent vomiting… The air we breathe as important as the water we drink. It must be uninfected and unpolluted. A sanitary revolution started 100 years ago has done much to eliminate water-borne disease. We should work towards the elimination of bronchitis and other air-borne disease'[67].

He also admitted to a special attraction to Chadwick's 'projected pure air company to suck down pure air from especially constructed towers into the dwellings and work-shops of city populations'[68].

From this perspective, it is more understandable why some of Joules' conservative critics were far more worried by his extension of the consultant's domain than by his call for an end to private practice. Thus, James Brailsford, a radiologist at the Queen's Hospital in Birmingham, condemned Joules's involvement in the controversy over the persistence of tuberculosis in Glasgow as self-serving. Brailsford asked why:

> 'with the terrible conditions such as Dr. Joules describes in Glasgow, and such as I have seen in this and many other countries,… we waste our slender resources on less profitable specialist propaganda and activity? It is little less than humbug to take, at great expense, infected persons from these breeding-grounds to elaborate chest hospitals… to 'profit' by the skill of specialists and nurses, and then return them to these breeding grounds for further infection. As demonstrated by Sir John Robertson many years ago, the home could be the best place for the treatment of tuberculosis. Home treatment is the least expensive, the most pleasant and stimulating for the patient, and the most expeditious and lasting. In the hands of the general practitioner, now provided with more effective medication, success would be achieved. But the homes must be improved to permit such treatment. The evidence is that good housing and a good standard of living will eradicate the disease, and leave the people contented with their desirable happy homes; yet modern specialist propaganda

---

[66] Dorothy Porter and Roy Porter, "What was Social Medicine? An Historiographical Essay", *Journal of Historical Sociology*, 1, 1988, pp. 90-106.

[67] Horace Joules, "Chronic Bronchitis", *British Medical Journal*, 1953, vol. II, pp. 440-441, p. 441.

[68] Horace Joules, "A Preventive Approach to Common Diseases of the Lung", *British Medical Journal*, 1954, vol. II, pp. 1259-1263, p. 1259.

demands the use of many of our slender resources for an ever-increasing build-up of an elaborate chest-hospital system with its ever-increasing staff. In them there is little indication of achieving or even wishing to achieve, the desired eradication; for, as the death-rate diminishes, the propaganda increases and the techniques for treatment are elaborated, and these call for more and more personnel, and the concerted demands of these exhibit a group selfishness that would not be tolerated in any voluntary organisation with limited funds'[69].

For Brailsford, Joules was part of the medical élite who facilitated the establishment of National Health Service because it promised to consolidate their power over the organisation of medical care, at the expense of general practitioners. Brailsford's suspicions were not far off the mark. Joules had been a member of the special committee organised by the Royal College of Physicians to consider the effects of the planned National Health Service on consultant and specialist services[70]. Furthermore, in 1947, he was elected unanimously to the newly established North West Regional Hospital Board and to the Ministry of Health's Standing Medical Advisory Committee and Standing Advisory Committee on Cancer soon thereafter[71]. All these organisations were controlled by medical consultants in the leading hospitals of the nation.

It is then very unclear what exactly Joules meant by the democratic organisation of medicine, other than the redistribution of power to specialists more committed to insuring the health of the nation than to their own financial gain. Nevertheless, this commitment meant that the proponents of social medicine, regardless of whether they were drawn from the left or right of the political spectrum, would also be supported in their search for greater institutional power by the labour movement. Thus, in 1954, trade unions protested against the Conservative government's dismissal of Joules, Hastings, and David Stark Murray, the editor of the Socialist Medical Association's preferred outlet, *Medicine Today and Tomorrow*, from the influential Central Health Services Council of the Ministry of Health, and they protested especially strongly against Joules's dismissal[72]. It is also less surprising that Joules's friend Ryle was sometimes exasperated by foreign colleagues' confusion between social and socialist medicine: the relationship between the two was far from straightforward and

---

[69] James F. Brailsford, "Tuberculosis in Glasgow", *Lancet*, 1953, vol. I, p. 951.

[70] See C. Allan Birch *et al.* "Meeting of Whole-Time Specialists", *British Medical Journal,* 1944, vol. II, p. 479.

[71] North West Regional Hospital Board Committee, 1947-49: Minutes of Establishment Committee, first meeting, 5/12/1947 (GRO-HA/NW/A3/1).

[72] Cancer Standing Advisory Committee: Watkins to Ministry of Health, 15/6/1954 (PRO-MH133/449).

this was no more evident than in Joules's campaign against tobacco[73]. Caring for the social body and socialism are not quite the same thing, even if the current Labour government seems to believe that the evolution of socialism depends on our adoption of a healthier 'lifestyle'.

7. Conclusion

I have been puzzled recently by the conjunction between debates over the proper attitude of government toward smoking and the redefinition of socialism pressed by the current Labour government. I thought that examining Joules's biography might help to understand how these disparate discourses fit together. Joules's case seemed promising because, immediately after the release of Hill and Doll's first and controversial findings on the relationship between smoking and lung cancer, he called for a national campaign against tobacco. While this call was viewed by some of his most influential opponents as motivated by 'extremely advanced left wing opinions', a number of Joules's equally radical colleagues in the Socialist Medical Association did not believe that eliminating tobacco from the British people's shopping list was important to their cause, which was instead to 'get a fair distribution of the health services'. What then did socialism mean to Joules and why was smoking so important for his socialism?

Starting from Joules's opposition to smoking, I have tried to show how his plans to reorganise medicine in the name of socialism were rooted in a morally impassioned critique of modern society, which stopped short of any systematic inquiry into its political legitimacy. His fervent belief in the individual citizen's responsibility to the community, a responsibility eroded by their addiction to smoking and especially by their addiction to the politically pernicious cigarette, echoes instead a powerful strain of Christian radicalism. This had once viewed addiction to alcohol as a major hurdle to the construction of a fairer world for all, but this was eventually rejected by many, but not all, socialists for its blindness to the class relations shaping public appetite for alcohol. Importantly, Joules's language was that of the medical expert rather than Christian pastor[74]. It was the responsibility of medicine, and social medicine in particular, rather than Christianity, to bring about the world in which individual citizens could live out the fairer and morally uplifted life Joules envisioned for them. Thus, the seemingly ineradicable popular appetite for tobacco, sustained by personal choices in

---

[73] Porter, "Changing Disciplines".

[74] For a particularly apposite discussion of the importance of Christianity in the formation of the British socialist movement, see Stephen Yeo, "A New Life: The Religion of Socialism in Britain, 1883-1896", *History Workshop Journal*, 4, 1977, pp. 1-56.

a world of ambiguous and contradictory information about its dangers, was transformed from sinfulness into physiological addiction. Salvation from such addiction, then, was no longer a task for the chapel, but for the similarly all-encompassing hospital. It seems to have totally escaped Joules's attention that the Christian technocracy he proposed completely undermined his professed commitment to a more democratic organisation of medicine and society more generally. It is perhaps not coincidental that William Morris, one of the most famous figures in the history of British socialism, sometimes criticised the undemocratic tendencies of equally famous socialist reformers, such as Sidney and Beatrice Webb, by focusing on their 'selfish' attitudes toward both alcohol and tobacco[75].

Returning to the opening of this paper, it seems to me that Joules's paradoxical merger of moral condemnation of modern society with the belief that its problems could be solved by the systematic application of medical expertise to establish a community of socially responsible citizens echoes the views of those seeking today to modernise the Labour Party[76]. They are seeking to merge, equally paradoxically, the old, Christian aspiration to a 'fair' society with the new practices of corporate management and the support of corporate donors who have advanced these practices most vigorously. The contradictions of this merger became evident when Ecclestone and his own corporate allies, tobacco manufacturers, appeared on the scene. One commentator, asked about the increasing sense that there was something wrong with this closeness between the government and corporate donors, said:

> 'What gave these arrogant and avaricious strutters the impression that government was a commodity to be bought and sold? Perhaps it was the practice, now so well established that no one bothers querying its probity anymore, of selling businessmen dinner places next to Cabinet Ministers. Perhaps it was the striking correlation between the names on Labour's honours lists and the list of donors to party funds. Or perhaps their inspiration was the red carpet rolled out by Number 10 for Bernie Ecclestone'[77].

While this commentator overlooked the fact that Ecclestone's donation was in fact only the last in a problematic series, there is something very special about this particular

---

[75] See Harrison, *Drink and the Victorians*; and William Morris, "News from Nowhere", in Clive Wilmer (ed.), *News from Nowhere and Other Writings*, London, Penguin, 1993.

[76] For a sustained discussion on the parallel, see Paolo Palladino, "Discourses of Smoking, Health and the Just Society: Yesterday, Today and the Return of the Same?", Social History of Medecine, (in press).

[77] "The Prime Minister Regards the Lobby Boys as Little Monsters".

donation. Consuming tobacco, with its implicit rejection of conventional notions of utility and responsibility to the social body, which has now replaced the community of Christian believers, was and continues to be viewed as a matter of dangerous addiction rather than a matter of choice. The advice of Richard Branson, the charismatic chairman of the Virgin Group and former supporter of the Conservative Party, was considered particularly important to the formulation of the governmental response to this problem. This was presumably because the reduced longevity of smokers meant that they would have less time to consume the products of the Virgin Group and thus build a more vigorous consumer economy[78]. Smoking, in sum, is a matter of addiction to, rather than personal choice to consume, the ultimate consumer good, the cigarette. It is an addiction that contributes nothing to the growth and reproduction of the social body[79]. It is thus especially abhorrent to many British socialists, old and new, and will always reveal the paradoxes of their politics.

---

[78] Department of Health "Anti-Smoking Summit, Dying for a Fag", 14/7/1997.

[79] See Fred Botting, "The Art of Smoking in an Age of Techno-Moral Consumption", *New Formations*, 38, 1999, pp. 78-97.

Images of New Cancer Therapies
Ilana Löwy

1. The definition of cancer as a cell's disease

From the mid-19th century on, cancer, previously a mysterious pathology characterised by tumefaction and inflammation was redefined as a disease of "deviant cells". This new view of cancer was grounded in new developments in the laboratory and in the oncology clinics:

1. Pathology and cytology became decisive elements in the diagnosis of cancer. From the 1870s until today, a diagnosis of malignancy and the staging of tumours is based on the cytological studies of cells taken from a suspected growth (or, in case of haematological tumours, on the identification of abnormal cells in the blood). All the other tests – from biochemical to genetic, are secondary to cytological analysis, and a person cannot be declared as "having a malignant tumour" without the cytologist's verdict. The controversies, in Britain, around what was described as erroneous reading of PAP smears by cytologists, and a consequent under-evaluation of the number of women suffering from cervical cancer or pre-cancerous condition, highlight the central importance of cytologists – experts of the cell – in cancer diagnosis.

2. Anti-cancer therapies introduced in the twentieth century, first radiotherapy and then chemotherapy, were based on the principle of a selective destruction of rapidly multiplying cells. The logical conclusion was that if cancer can be brought to a halt and occasionally cured by the elimination of rapidly proliferating cells, the uncontorolled proliferation of these cells *is* the malignant disease.

3. The development of multicentre clinical trials of cancer drugs in the 1950s and 60s, led to elaboration of standardised, quantifiable criteria for the evaluation of the efficacy of anti-cancer therapies. The universally adopted criterion of decrease of the tri-dimensional size of solid tumours (or, for haematological tumours, of the number of malignant cells in the blood and in bone marrow) further strengthened the identification of malignant *disease* with malignant *cells*.

4. From the 1920s on, studies of cancer in the laboratory were linked with studies of mechanisms which regulate cell division[1]. The normal, scientists argued, will be understood through the study of the pathological. In addition, the fact that mammalian malignant cells – but not normal cells – can be grown indefinitely in a test tube, increased the interest in these cells. Researchers who studied cellular mechanisms and who, for technical reasons, employed malignant cells, were able to claim (and to sincerely believe) that they investigated cancer – and to benefit from earmarked funds for cancer research.

The definition of cancer as a "disease of the cell" (and, in the 1990s, increasingly, as a genetic disease) was not, however, the only possible interpretation of malignancies. Some unorthodox oncologists proposed that cancer is a systemic pathology characterised mainly by cachesis and wasting; some viewed cancer as a disease which originates in an exaggerated reaction of the body to a localised dysfunction; others stressed that the problem of cancer is not the one of development of an initial cluster of abnormal cells, but of the ability of these cells to form metastases, and stressed that, in the majority of cancer-associated deaths, people do not die because of their primary tumour, but as a consequence of its metastases, and that tumours which are slow to form metastases are much easier to cure or to control.

Oncologists which put the accent on the systemic aspects of cancer remained, however, marginal. The tendency to identify the disease cancer with the transformed cell, prominent in twentieth century oncology, was further strengthened by the development of molecular biology, and by the description of mutations seen as responsible for the cancerous transformation. From the 1980s on, fundamental oncological research is increasingly centred on the genome, and the description of mutation shared by several types of cancerous cells consolidated the definition of "cancer" as a single disease (or, for some, a family of closely related diseases), and as pathology grounded in a defective transcription of DNA. The focus on "oncogenes" and on "predisposition genes" – genes active in the malignant transformation of the cell – consolidated the links between changes of DNA in a single cell (or a group of cells) and the disease "cancer". The definition of this disease as a cellular aberration favoured the development of anti-cancer therapies focused exclusively on the destruction of malignant cells. Until the 1960s, three methods were employed to get rid of malignant cells: surgery, radiotherapy, and chemotherapy. All were perceived as violent and unnatural: "cutting, burning and poisoning". In addition, radiotherapy and chemotherapy

---

[1] James B. Murphy, "Certain etiological factors in the causation and trasmission of malignant tumors", *American Naturalist*, 1926, 60, pp. 227-236.

are based on the principle of the elimination of all the rapidly mutiplying cells: malignant cells but also normal cells with a rapid rate of duplication such as bone marow cells, cells which line the digestive tract, or cells responsible for hair growth. They induce therefore a vast array of severe "side effects". A more "natural" way of eliminating deviant cells, some experts proposed in the 1960s, will be the stimulation of the "defence mechanisms" of the body to selectively eliminate cancerous cells.

2. "Killer lymphocytes" as soldiers in the "war against cancer"

The term "defence mechanisms of the body" was first introduced in the context of early bacteriological studies. Bacteriology was, from its very beginning, associated with war metaphors. In the late 19th century bacteriologists and immunologists promoted the image of an army of white blood cells fighting an external invader, the bacteria. This image, and the parallel representation of antibodies as "magic bullets" (an expression first introduced by a German pioneer of immunology, Paul Ehrlich), permeated expert and lay perceptions of infectious diseases. Early immunological studies focused on the role of macrophages – a sub-group of white blood cells able to engulf and destroy pathogenic micro-organisms. Macrophages were, however, difficult to study in controlled conditions, mainly because their non-specific bactericidal action is dificult to quantify. In the inter-war period, immunological studies were therefore focused mainly on specific antibodies in the serum, entities which can be studied by quantitative methods, and which were important as diagnostic and therapeutic tools (serodiagnosis and serotherapy).

The importance of serotherapy of bacterial diseases decreased greatly after World War II following the introduction of antibiotics. In parallel, the development of transplantation of organs (at first, of kidneys), a highly visible medical activity (a "medical miracle") from the mid-1950s on, led to a renewed interest in the role of cells in immune reactions. The surgical problems of kidney transplantation were solved as early as 1910, but the feasibility of such transplants in humans depended on finding a way to prevent the "biological reaction" which led to the rejection of the grafted tissue[2]. Some investigators suspected that such rejection was mediated by an immune mechanism, but they were unable to demonstrate the presence of specific anti-graft antibodies[3]. In the 1940s a British researcher, Peter Medawar, had shown that the

---

[2] Alexis Carrel, 'Remote results of the transplantation of the kidney and the spleen', *Journal of Experimental Medicine*, 1910, 12, pp. 146-150.

[3] James B. Murphy, *The Lymphocyte in Resistance to Tissue Grafting, Malignant Disease and Tuberculous Infection: An Experimental Study*, Rockefeller Institute, Monograph no. 21, New York, 1926.

rejection of a skin graft is highly specific, and therefore is probably an immune phenomenon[4]. At first Medawar and his colleagues believed that anti-graft immunity was induced by antibodies, but faced with repeated failure to uncover such antibodies they linked graft rejection to previously described cell-mediated immunological phenomena such as "delayed hypersensitivity".

In the 1950s pathologists who studied abnormal tissue reactions independently proposed that a specific category of white blood cells, the lymphocytes, may play a role in both graft rejection and in delayed hypersensitivity. This proposal was not new. It was made by James Murphy from the Rockefeller Institute, New York, in the 1910s, but it was never convincingly proven, and was forgotten later[5]. In contrast, in the 1950s the idea that lymphocytes are directly involved in graft rejection was accepted rapidly, mainly, one may propose, following studies of the graft versus host (GVH) reaction. The GVH reaction was first observed accidentally when new-born animals were injected with white blood cells of a genetically different individual in an attempt to induce tolerance to foreign tissues, that is, to "teach" an animal not to reject tissues of the same genetic makeup that injected white cells (an approach which, the scientists hoped, could be used to prevent the rejection of grafts in humans). However, instead of becoming tolerant, recipients of foreign lymphocytes often became very sick and died, displaying characteristic symptoms of wasting and a very enlarged spleen (the so-called "runt disease")[6]. The disease was then ascribed to the reaction of the grafted lymphocytes against the host's body. The GVH was literally the killing of a new-born animal by foreign white blood cells. It was therefore a powerful demonstration of the capacity of lymphocytes to kill. The white blood cells of the donor involved in the GVH reaction were named "cytotoxic" (that is, cell-killing) lymphocytes. GVH was rapidly introduced to studies of cellular immune reactions, and its diffusion popularised the concept of the "killer lymphocyte", able to eliminate "undesirable" cells.

---

[4] Thomas Gibson and Peter B. Medawar, 'The fate of skin homografts in man', *Journal of Anatomy*, 1943, 77, p. 299; P.B. Medawar, 'The behaviour and fate of skin homografts in rabbits', *Journal of Anatomy*, 1944, 78, p. 176.

[5] Ilana Löwy, ''Biomedical research and the constraints of medical practice: James Bumgardner Murphy and the early discovery of the role of lymphocytes in immune reactions', *Bulletin of the History of Medicine*, 1989, 63, pp. 356-391.

[6] Morten Simonsen, 'The impact on the developing embryo and newborn animal of adult homologous cells', *Acta Pathol. Microbiol. Scand,* 1957, 40, p. 480; R. Billingham and L. Brent, 'Quantitative studies on tissue transplantation immunity. IV. Induction of tolerance in newborn mice and studies on the phenomenon of runt disease', *Phil. Trans. Roy. Soc. London*, series B, 1959, 242, p. 439.

In the 1960s, transplanters found that the rejection of a grafted kidney was not an "all or nothing" reaction, but was dependent on the degree of similarity between the tissues of the donor and the recipient of the kidney. If the tissues were sufficiently similar, the recipient developed a milder rejection reaction which could be reversed by immunosuppressive drugs[7]. Transplanters then started to look for ways to evaluate the degree of compatibility between the tissues of the recipient and the potential donor of a kidney graft (histocompatibility), in order to minimise the strength of rejection. They drew on laboratory studies of GVH to devise tests for the selection of the best kidney donor among the family members of the recipient. At first, lymphocytes from potential donors were injected intradermally into the recipient, and doctors measured the intensity of skin reaction to these lymphocytes[8]. Later, the same test was made in the test-tube[9]. In the 1960s scientists also elaborated a technique of measuring cytotoxic activity of lymphocytes based on the labelling of target cells (often malignant cells grown in a test tube) with radioactive chrome, incubation of these cells with putative "killer lymphocytes", and the measurement of radioactive substance liberated from the destroyed target cells into the culture medium. Thanks to the simplicity and the rapidity of the chromium release test, scientists were able to multiply experiments which studied the destruction of "foreign" cells by white blood cells[10]. This test was also rapidly applied to the studies of anti-tumour immunity[11].

Researchers who looked for links between immunity, or, in an earlier period, "the body defences" and cancer, followed two distinctive pathways. Investigators who assumed that cancers (or at least some cancers) were induced by infectious agents

---

[7] John P. Merrill *et al.*, 'Successful homotransplantation of the kidney between non-identical twins', *New England Journal of Medicine*, 1960, 242, p. 1251.

[8] F.T. Rapaport, L. Thomas, I.M. Converse, and H.S. Lawrence, 'The specificity of skin homograft rejection in man', *Annals of the N.Y. Academy of Sciences*, 1960, 87, p. 217; R.E. Wilson, L. Henry and J.R.E. Wilson, L. Henry and J.P. Merrill, 'A model system for determining histocompatibility in man', *Journal of Clinical Investigations*, 1963, 42, p. 1497.

[9] K. Hirschhorn, F.H. Bach, F.T. Rapaport and J.M. Converse, *Annals of the N.Y. Academy of Sciences*, 1964, 120, pp. 303-306; The relationships of *in vitro* lymphocyte compatibility to homograft sensitivity in man', K. Hirschhorn, I.L. Firschein and F.H. Bach, 'Immune response of human peripheral blood lyphocytes in vitro', *Histocompatibility Testing*, 1964, Washington D.C., National Academy of Sciences Publication, 1965, pp. 131-139.

[10] A.R. Sanderson, 'Application of isoimmunocytolysis using radiolabeled target cells', *Nature*, 1964, 204, p. 250; Hans Wigzell, 'Quantitative titration of mouse H-2 antibodies using 51 Cr labelled target cells', *Transplantation*, 1965, 3, p. 423; Ivan Roitt, *Essential Immunology*, London & Oxford, Blackwell Scientific Publications, 1977, pp. 177-180.

[11] Karl Eric Helström and Ingrid Helström, "Immunologic defences against cancer", in Robert. Good and David Fisher (eds.) *Immunobiology*, Stanford, Ca: Sinauer Associeted, Ltd., 1971, pp. 209-218.

such as viruses, looked for the putative role of immune mechanisms in the elimination of these putative agents. Other researchers focused on the deviant – thus presumably structurally different – aspect of cancer cells, and looked for immune mechanisms able to selectively destroy transformed cells. The first direct relationship between transplantation studies and cancer research was established in the early twentieth century. Before scientists learned (in the 1920s) to induce tumours in laboratory animals by the application of chemical irritants or by X-ray radiation, the only way to study cancer in the laboratory was to graft tumours from one animal into another. Researchers noticed then that such grafts were very often rejected, an observation which led to investigations of the conditions that allow for "resistance" to grafted tumours. A better understanding of the mechanism of such resistance, the specialists hoped, might contribute to the development of a cure for cancer. Studies of "resistance" to grafted tumours became an important branch of experimental cancer studies in the 1910s[12]. Their importance decreased, however, in the 1920s, when scientists found that such "resistance" was usually a reaction to any grafted foreign tissue and not specifically to malignant tissue[13].

In 1953 Medawar's student Avrion Mitchison drew on the long-standing tradition of the use of tumours in transplantation studies, and showed that an acquired capacity to reject a grafted tumour was transferred by lymph-node cells, but not by the serum[14]. Consequently, tumours became an interesting object of study for the cellular immunologist. In the late 1950s and early 1960s, scientists immunised mice with BCG (Bacillus Calmette Guérin, an attenuated strain of the tuberculosis bacillus) and observed that the immunised mice rejected more rapidly both skin grafts and transplanted tumours[15]. This observation was the basis for a therapy of leukaemia by BCG injections, developed in France by Georges Mathé and his collaborators[16]. The claim

---

[12] E.F. Bashford, J.A. Murray and W. Cramer, 'The natural and induced resistance of mice to the growth of cancer, *Third Scientific Report of the Imperial Cancer Research Fund*, 1908, 3, p. 315; William H. Woglom, *Study of Experimental Cancer: A Review*, New York: Columbia University Press, 1913.

[13] William H. Woglom, 'Immunity to transplanted tumors', *The Cancer Review*, 1929, 4, pp. 129-214; Ilana Löwy and Jean-Paul Gaudillière, 'Disciplining cancer: Mice and the practice of genetic purity', in J-P. Gaudillière and I. Lowy, (eds.) *Invisible Industrialist: Manufactures and the Production of Scientific Knowledge*: London, Macmillan, 1998, pp. 209-249.

[14] N. Avrion Mitchison, 'Passive transfer of transplantation immunity', *Nature,* 1953, 178, pp. 267-268.

[15] Lloyd J. Old, Donald A. Clarke and Baruj Benacerraf, 'Effects of Bacillus Calmette Guérin infection on transplanted tumors in the mouse', *Nature*, 1959, 184, pp. 291-292.

[16] Georges Mathé, J.A. Amiel, L Schwartzenberf *et al.*, 'Active immunotherapy of acute immunoblastic leukemia', *Lancet*, 1969, i, 697. For summary of these studies c.f., summary cf. Helström and Helström, "Immunologic defences against cancer", *op. cit.*

that BCG therapy prolonged disease-free survival in leukaemia patients opened an era of enthusiasm for the immunotherapy of cancer, reflected in a wave of publication of popular books on this topic. These publications often combined two powerful images: the "war against cancer", propagated by cancer charities, and the "body is the hero", diffused in popularised accounts of immunity[17]. The immune system was presented in such accounts as "a sophisticated, integrated army, that for most of us performs splendidly for seventy years or more", and describes "killer" T cells as especially efficient soldiers in this army: "they move up to an enemy, say a cancer cell, and attach themselves leech like to the abnormal cell. From a repertoire of more than a hundred poisons stored in their cytoplasm they secrete chemicals that will kill it"[18].

In the late 1970s it became evident that BCG and other bacterial vaccines used to stimulate the immune mechanisms of cancer patients had at best marginal clinical efficacy[19]. From the late-1970s on, the promoters of immunotherapy of cancer focused therefore on a different family of potential therapeutic agents – the cytokines. Cytokines (interferons, interleukins) are a family of natural molecules credited with the ability to stimulate growth and activity of cells of the immune system. In the late 1970s and early 1980s cytokines became one of the main targets of the biotechnology industry. The race to clone and produce these molecules – first interferon, then interleukin-2 and other interleukins – was fuelled by the hope that these substances would rapidly become important anti-cancer drugs. The anti-tumour activity of interleukins in humans was attributed mainly to their ability to stimulate cytotoxic lymphocytes able to eliminate cancer cells. "Biological therapies of cancer", presented as a highly promising new approach to cancer cure, were able to benefit from widespread publicity in the media, and from an important influx of public and private funds[20]. Clinical studies conducted in the 1980s did not confirm, however, high hopes attached to these molecules. The new therapies worked in selected patients, but they were far from becoming "a penicillin of cancer". Moreover, their anti-tumour effects, if present, could not be correlated to specific changes in the activity of cytotoxic lymphocytes[21].

---

[17] E.g., Ronald Glaser, *The Body is the Hero*, New York, Random House, 1976; Harold M. Schmeek, *Immunology: The Many Edged Sword*, New York; George Brazillier, 1974.

[18] John Dwyer, *The Body at War: The Story of Our Immune System*, London, Sydney, Wellington: Unwin Hyman, 1988, p. 38; p. 52.; see also Glaser, *op cit.*

[19] There was one notable exception to this rule. BCG was found to be effective in the treatment of the superficial cancer of the bladder. But, with the exception of the therapy of this rare cancer, BCG practically disappeared from the therapeutic arsenal of the oncologist.

[20] Robert K. Oldham and Richard V. Smalley, 'Immunotherapy: The old and the new', *Journal of Biological Response Modifiers*, 1983, 2, pp. 1-37.

[21] Eli Kedar and Eva Klein, 'Cancer imunothrapy. Are the results discouraging? Can they be improved?', *Advances in Cancer Research*, 1992, 59, pp. 245-322.

The difficulties in transferring observations on cytokines made in the laboratory to the clinics may recall similar difficulties during the first wave of enthusiasm for BCG therapy of cancer in the 1970s[22]. The fate of cytokines was however very different from that of the BCG. The BCG – an attenuated bacterial strain developed in the 1920s – was a "low tech" biomedical innovation. By contrast, interferons and interelukins were "high tech" products of the biotechnology industry. The heavy investments (in time, and above all in money) in the manufacture of these molecules prompted important efforts to find clinical uses for the new products. These efforts were mostly successful. In the 1980s and 90s interferon and interleukin-2 were introduced to cancer therapy, while other cytokines became important research and diagnostic tools for oncologists, an additional, and highly efficient way to link the immunology laboratory, the cancer ward and the production plant.

The first wave of immunotherapy of cancer in the 1970s contributed to popularisation of the idea that immune mechanisms participate in the elimination of malignant cells. In the 1980s the conviction that such mechanisms, and above all cytotoxic "killer cells", play an important role in the elimination of malignant tumours in humans was (partly) stabilised through a move from the domain of highly specialised immunological knowledge to its popular representations. In the 1980s such a move was strongly encouraged by the "cancer immunotherapy coalition" which included scientists and clinicians who promoted interferon and interleukin therapies, health administrators and politicians interested in new developments in this area, and biotechnology and pharamaceutic firms which produced and marketed interleukins. The efforts of the "cancer immunotherapy coalition" were sustained through enthusiastic presentations of the new cancer therapies in popular publications, destined to the lay public. These publications not only presented in glowing terms the new approaches to cancer cure, but, more importantly, were literally able to show their efficacy by providing highly persuasive photographic evidence.

---

[22] Some cancer experts attributed these difficulties to the excessive artificiality of laboratory models of cancer. David W. Weiss, 'Animal models of cancer immunotherapy', in R.L. Clark, R.C. Hickey and E.M. Hersh, *Immunotherapy of Cancer: Present Status of Trials in Man*, New York, Raven Press, 1978, pp. 101-109.

3. Visual display of new cancer therapies in a non-professional press

In his book, *Genesis and Development of a Scientific Fact* (written in 1935), Ludwik Fleck explains that scientific concepts and scientific facts are translated into more popular terms during their migration from the inner, "esoteric" circle of experts to a wider "exoteric" circle of lay persons. Such translation, Fleck explains, is not merely a simplification and a reduction of the original message. Some things are lost, but others are found in translation. For example, scientific concepts often gain "vividness" when popularised[23]. Such "vivid" – and thus often more robust – concepts may in turn influence the way of thinking of members of the "esoteric" circle of experts. "Killer lymphocytes" – the valiant fighters against malignant cells – became an especially "vivid" entity through an extensive use of war metaphors, through the presentation of simplified graphic representations of the interactions between tumour cells and lymphocytes, through photographs which dramatised new cancer therapies, and, above all, through a widespread diffusion of highly suggestive scanning electron microscope photographs.

Electron microscope photographs represent the end product of a complicated processing of cells. In order to obtain a scanning microscope image, cells are fixed with chemical substances (usually glutaraldehyde, then osmium tetroxide), dehydrated through gradual passages in increasing concentrations of ethanol, dried in a special apparatus by the critical point drying method, coated, in another apparatus, with a thin coat of carbon, then of gold-palladium mixture, and finally photographed throughout the electron microscope[24]. In addition, the black-and-white scanning electron microscope photographs are often artificially coloured to enhance the dramatic aspect. Small changes in the technique of fixation of cells and then in the preparation of the photographs may lead to a great variability of the final images, and may therefore hamper a stabilisation of the "right view" of a studied phenomenon. However, the great majority of the publications on biotherapies of cancer – both those directed to lay public, and those addressed to doctors – showed remarkable uniformity, for a very simple reason: they were illustrated with pictures originated in the same series of photographs representing "killer lymphocytes" attacking and destroying a tumour cell, first published by the pharmaceutical firm Bohringer. A repeated reproduction of the same set of "telling" (and technically excellent) photographs in different publications contributed to the stabilisation of the "typical" representations of the body fighting an "enemy from within". These dramatic photographs visualised and made

---

[23] Ludwik Fleck, *Genesis and Development of a Scientific Fact* (transl. F. Bradley & T. Trenn), Chicago & London, Chicago University Press, 1979 (1935).

[24] Richard G. Kessel and Ching Y. Shich, *Scanning Electron Microscopy in Biology*, Berlin, Heidelberg and New York, Springer-Verlag, 1976, pp. 8-15; pp. 63-66.

perceptible hopes of a "victory over malignancy". They became the iconic images of "the body is the hero", in the same way the celebrated *Time/Life* photographs of the embryo as a miniature cosmonaut floating in bluish amniotic liquid became the iconic images of life before birth, and contributed to a shift of the public's attention from the pregnant woman to the foetus alone[25]. Thus, for example, when "Bohringer" images showing the killing of cancer cells were used in a leaflet published in 1991 by the Cancer Research Institute, (a New York charity founded in 1953 to promote the development of cancer immunology), they were accompanied by a text which explained that these photographs, "show something most people will never see or even imagined was possible: the destruction of a human cancer cell by a human immune cell. The depiction is proof positive of the powerful cancer-fighting potential of the human immune system"[26].

Microscopic images of the killing of cancer cells were used in France to illustrate magazine articles which enthusiastically greeted the introduction of cytokine therapy to cancer therapy in France[27]. *Le Figaro Magazine* published in its May 5, 1990 issue an article entitled "A photographic feat. Interleukin's incredible journey. Beating cancer through natural defence". The article is illustrated by a series of colour pictures, showing the uneven and dramatic struggle between a huge, highly asymmetrical tumour cell, and several small round lymphocytes. The first photograph shown presents the protagonists: the "killer" lymphocytes and the tumour cell. In subsequent photographs, several lymphocytes are shown in the vicinity of a tumour cell, in an arrangement which recalls chase scenes in which several hounds are surrounding a deer or a boar. The article ends with a picture of a cancer cell with an lymphocyte attached to it, bearing a legend: "The death kiss. One can see here a lymphocyte armed by interleukin-2 which is killing a tumour cell by sticking to it. This attack will end in the death of the tumour cell which will be progressively emptied of its content"[28]. There is no mention of the fact that all the photographs represent an activity observed and recorded in a test tube. The strength of the argument developed in this article derives from the combination of an attractive intellectual schema – the extension, to cancer, of the documented role of immune system cells in elimination of infectious agents in the body ("we can understand why it works"), of a reference to the curative effects of "biological response modifiers"

---

[25] On the social role of photographs representing foetuses, see Rosalind Petchesky,"Foetal images: The power of visual culture in the politics of reproduction", *Feminist Studies*, 1987, 13 (2), pp. 263-292.

[26] *Cancer and the Immune System*, The Cancer Research Institute, NY, 1991, p. 5.

[27] Ilana Löwy, *Between Bench and Bedside: Science, Healing and Interleukin-2 in a Cancer Ward*, Cambridge, Mass., Harvard University Press, 1996.

[28] Yves Christen, "Un exploit photographique. Le merveilleux voyage de l'interleukine. Le cancer combattu par l'autodéfense", *Le Figaro Magazine*, 5 May, 1990, pp. 87-94.

(interferons, interleukin-2), attributed by the promoters of biotherapies of cancer to the stimulation of "killer cells" by cytokines ("we have proven that is works"), and of highly suggestive electron-microscope photographs ("we can see how it works")[29].

In a different category of pictures, the message of innovation and salvation was provided by graphic representations which associated the new therapies with more traditional symbols of scientific progress. One of the first papers on the use of interelukin in cancer therapy in France, published in *Le Nouvel Observateur* in January, 1989, under the heading "Interleukin-the hope" was announced on the

magazine's cover by a rather stereotyped image of a bright yellow sun in a blue sky. An article published by *Le Figaro Magazine* of December 5, 1992, and which described

the use of TIL (Tumour Infiltrating Lymphocytes, another kind of interleukin activated killer T-cells) in cancer biotheraphy, employed a more subtle combination of special photographic effects and of quasi-religious symbolism to transmit a similar message. The article is illustrated by photographs of researchers who prepare the TIL cells who will be injected to patients. The centrefold picture shows a young man and a young woman holding a plastic pouch in which they cultivate TILs. The pouch, like a holy relic, irradiates bright yellow light which

---

[29] Steven A. Rosenberg, Michael A. Lotze, Susan Leitman *et al.*, 'Observations on the systemic administration of autologous lymphokin-activated killer cells and recombinant interleukin-2 to patients with metastatic cancer', *New England Journal of Medecine*, 1985, 313, pp. 1485-1492; Steven A. Rosenberg, 'Adoptive immunotherapy for cancer', *Scientific American*, May 1990, pp. 34-41.

illuminates the faces of the two researchers The legend reads: "a dose of hope. One billion cells in a bag. Four weeks ago at the Cochin hospital Nicolas Thiun and Nicole Joyeux cultivated these lymphocytes. In a few hours they will be injected into a patient to break down his tumours". Another photograph shows two senior investigators involved in the TIL project standing behind a graph drawn on a transparent board, and which indicates the distribution of surface markers of cytotoxic T cells. In this photograph, the signs that represent the cytotoxic T-cells rather than the cells themselves, are the source of an intense green light, reflected on the faces of the two reserchers. Each cluster of cells is represented by a luminous dot. The scientists gaze is fixed on constellations of these star-like dots, strongly conveying the impression of communion with a mystery.

In their analysis of the rhetoric of French popular articles on immunotherapy of cancer, Daniel Jacobi and Bernard Schele stress the central role of images and metaphors and then notice that these metaphors have not been invented by the journalists but have been proposed by the scientists themselves, and are either a direct part of the style of the language of specialists or are borrowed from analogous models frequently used for heuristic purposes by scholars[30]. The metaphoric language, which represents the immune system's reaction to cancer as a "self defence" of the body fighting against a treacherous and sneaky enemy, and as forces of light struggling against dark powers of malignancy, is indeed frequently present – although in an attenuated form – in scientific publications[31]. The concept of tumour specific "killer lymphocyte", first developed by cellular immunologists, was rapidly adopted by distinct (to borrow from Fleck) "thought collectives" (or "social worlds", or "professional cultures"). On the other hand, the power of the image of the body "fighting back" against malignant cells may account for the persistence of the efforts to look for anti-tumour "killer cells" and to demonstrate their role in cancer cure, the difficulties of stabilizing this concept by scientists notwithstanding. This idea was attractive not only to the lay public but to professionals as well. Journalists who explained that lymphocytes have an important role in eliminating cancerous growths, and photographers whose work illustrated and strengthened the journalists' claims, were not merely passively translating the scientists' vocabulary into a more popular idiom. By propagating and making visible the concept of "tumour killing lymphocyte" they also contributed to the continuation of the use of this concept by scientists and by policy makers.

---

[30] Daniel Jacobi and Bernard Schiele, 'Science in magazines, and its readers', *Public Understanding of Science*, 1993, 2, pp. 3-20, p. 17.

[31] The image of the hidden enemy which kills by felony and in a treacherous way is borrowed from a book written by the pioneer of interleukin-2 therapy, Steven Rosenberg. S. Rosenberg and J. Barry, *The Transformed Cell*, New York, G.P. Putnam's Sons, 1992.

4. Cancer therapies and images of malignancy

The development of immunotherapies of cancer in the 1970s was promoted as a rad-ically different, natural way to cure malignant disease. The powerful metaphor "the body is the hero" was backed with no less powerful microscopic images. The destruc-tion of cancer cells by the defence mechanisms of the body was not an esoteric phe-nomenon observed by scientists who follow lines on cathodic screens or made complicated calculations on their computers. It could be made plainly visible for everybody. It was not necessary to trust blindly scientists who explain that this phe-nomenon existed: it was sufficient to trust one's own eyes.

Popular publications on interleukins were grounded in this reservoir of widely shared signs and symbols. Pictures of lymphocytes attacking a cancer cell became an easily accessible symbol of the triumph of the body over malignancy, and of order, repre-sented by "police forces" composed from leukocytes, over disorder, represented by the malignant cells. A popular book on the immunotherapy of cancer explained in 1972 that, "the comparison with a police or a counter-espionage system is unmistakable. The criminal or a traitor has to be defeated and rendered inoffensive by the police before his activities can become a menace to the whole community. This has to be done, how-ever, without disrupting the activities of normal, law-abiding citizens"[32]. The image – prominent in 1990 *Le Figaro Magazine* article, of the small but brave attackers of the giant, and then of the emptied shell of a cancer cell, the skeleton of a Goliath defeated by a valiant and obstinate David, was a powerful icon. The frequent use of a cancer metaphor to describe groups or organisations perceived as able to undermine social order (a cancerous growth on the healthy body of the society) reinforced also the belief in the possibility to uncover healthy forces of the body.

Images of biotherapies of cancer aimed at to health professionals (or, to be more accu-rate at individuals, such as physicians who treat cancer patients, who mediate between the inner circle of the experts and the outer circle of the lay public) presented cytokines simultaneously as "natural substances" and as "high tech" products. The cloning, then the mass production of interferons and interleukins with genetic engi-neering methods were important technological achievements: their "high-tech" aspect was therefore self-explanatory. Their "natural" aspect – reflected in the name "bio-therapy" – was less obvious. Interferon therapy, and later interleukin therapy were found to generate severe side effects such as fever, chills, nausea, digestive troubles,

---

[32] David Wilson, *Body and Antibody: A Report on the New Immmunology*, New York, Alfred A. Knopf, 1972, p. 220.

muscle pain and dizziness. These effects are quite similar in intensity and in scope to those induced by radiotherapy and chemotherapy. In addition, interelukin-2 induced capillary leak which occasionally led to sever oedema and heart troubles, and provoked temporary dementia in some patients. In some cases, deaths of cancer patients were attributed to the consequences of a treatment with interferon or with interleukin. The presence of severe side effects of a treatment with a "natural substance", is, by itself, not surprising. Doctors are familiar with violent reactions to high doses of substances already present in the body such as hormones, and authors of detective stories like to describe a murder through an injection of a natural substance, like insulin, which can be more easily disguised as a natural death. The description of important toxic effects of cytokine therapy contrasted, however, with the public image of new therapies of cancer which combined the images of cutting edge technology with the recent fascination with "natural" therapies, reinforced, in the 1980s, by images of nature (mountains, trees and flowers) which became a constant feature of publicity for cytokines[33].

In the 1990s, with the generalisation of knowledge about severe side effects of cytokines, their presentation as a "natural treatment" became more problematic. Promoters of cytokines focused instead on their "power", their "sophistication", and, above all, their "precision"[34]. The physiological role of cytokines in the regulation of cellular interactions was put to the fore to promote the claim that these substances, when used as drugs, are able to reach well defined targets. In 1975, the historian of science June Goodfield explained that "of all scientists working on cancer, the immunologists gave me the strongest impression (…) of being able to focus precisely on a series of intellectual and therapeutic targets. Here I finally sensed just where T.H. Huxley's physician, "the blind man hitting out with a club" will metamorphose into the sniper picking out intruders with lethal accuracy"[35]. The accuracy of the snipers, it was hinted in the late 1990s, does not depend on their individual skills, but on the fact that they are able to use "magic bullets" which hit their targets with great precision[36]. The new image which accentuates the specific activity of cytokines was

---

[33] E.g. Leaflet published be Cetus to promote its interleukin-2 in 1988; advertisement of Immunogenetics, *Cytokine*, 1993, 5 (2).

[34] E.g. advertisement of Endogen, *Cytokine*, 1996, 8 (10).

[35] June Goodfield, *The Siege of Cancer*, New York: Random House, 1975, p. 113.

[36] This specificity was however, mainly demonstrated in the test-tube. By contrast, when cytokines are used as drugs they induce numerous "side effects", that is, non-specific physiological reactions. This is not surprising. Cytokines, powerful modulators of cellular reactions, are administered to patients in doses which greatly exceed their physiological concentrations. Scientists have proposed to develop cytokine inhibitors – small molecules which will specifically inhibit the binding of cytokines to their target cells – in order to refine the biological effects of cytokines. Steven Gillis and Douglas E. Williams, "Cytokine therapy: lessons learned and future challenges", *Current Opinion in Immunology*, 1998, 10 (5), 5°1-504.

reflected in a few advertisements for these substances[37]. In the 1990s, such advertisements for cytokines continued, however, to be dominated by images of nature (flowers, leafs, trees, fields)[38]. These images may be related to the new therapies of cancer in two distinct ways. They may serve as an increasingly vague reminder that those are "natural" (and not "chemical") treatments of cancer – a reminder increasingly necessary in an era in which these molecules are employed in combination with other anti-tumour drugs and are administered in the same way as more traditional chemotherapies. They may also stand not only for "biotherapy" but, more broadly, for "life" as opposed to "death" which is identified with cancer.

Cancer continues to be perceived as a "dread disease" and its popular images still represent a body "eaten from within" by its own treacherous cells. It is possible that this image will be modified in the future. Some scientists attempt to develop cytostatic anti-tumour drugs which do not destroy the cancer cells but inhibit their multiplication. Others try to find ways to prevent the development of metastases, the main reason for cancer-associated mortality and morbidity. If these or akin therapeutic approaches are to be successful, the accent in oncology may shift from the search for a cure to a lifelong management of malignancies, and from the view of cancerous growth as a cruel enemy which must be exterminated before it kills its carrier, to its perception as a diseased part of the organism which needs to be treated in order to prevent a further degradation. But until this happens – if this will happen – lay and expert views of cancer and attempts to control this disease will continue to be dominated by war images.

---

[37] E.g. advertisement for Genzyme "Rapid, reliable, sensitive", *Cytokine*, 1998, 10 (3).

[38] E.g. advertisement for PeproTech, "The seeds of the future", *Cytokine*, 1998, 10 (8); advertisement for PeproTech, "One breakthrough at a time", *Cytokine*, 1998, 10 (3).

Bettering Babies: Down's Syndrome, Heredity and Public Health in Post-war France and Britain

Jean-Paul Gaudillière

The first decade after the Second World War was a time of tremendous change both in France and Britain. The end of the war was widely viewed as an opportunity to build up new societies. In the discourses of many politicians, administrators, union representatives and social experts the necessities of "reconstruction" were intertwined with ideas of modernisation, rational organisation, and social progress. The state was at the very centre of this perspective. Moreover, in both countries, the political climate favoured social commitments: the Labour party was in charge in Britain while members of the Communist Party participated in the French government. Similar paths of action were therefore often taken. The years 1946-1947 thus led on both sides of the Channel to the nationalisation of important sectors of the economy, to the development of new public services, and to the establishment of advisory planning bodies.

From this viewpoint, health is a domain of critical importance. By 1950, both countries had reorganised their medical services. True the British National Health Service and the French Sécurité Sociale were built on radically different assumptions[1]. The former emerged out of the nationalisation of a majority of medical institutions transforming physicians into members of a salaried profession. The latter was in the first place a financial administration covering medical costs while playing little role in the organisation of services. Nonetheless both systems were taken as a form of recognition of the people's rights to health and described as a major step towards a more social medicine.

Building on this background, historians of medicine have pointed to major changes in public health notions and practices during the post-war era. The vision and treatment of hereditary diseases was no exception to this pattern. Observers of eugenics have accordingly stressed the decline of most eugenic movements[2]. This decline has usually

---

[1] C. Webster, *The National Health Service,* Oxford, Oxford University Press, 1998; P. Laroque, *Succès et faiblesse de l'effort social français*, Paris, Armand Colin, 1961.

[2] On Britain: D. Kevles, *In the Name of Eugenics,* San Francisco, University of California Press, 1985; on France: W. Schneider, *Quality and Quantity*, Cambridge, Cambridge University Press, 1990.

been interpreted as a mere consequence of the close relationship between eugenics policies and "Nazi excesses" (as one member of the French eugenics society once put it). In the context of rapidly changing political, ideological and scientific contexts most specialists of hereditary disorders in Britain and France followed a path which consisted in advancing medical genetics as a clinical alternative to eugenics.

This new form of medicine was viewed as opposing global and coercive public health measures by combining medical research on familial disorders with genetic counselling, presented as being simply an informational practice focusing on the definition of genetic risk. This realignment of medicine and genetics is usually illustrated with the career of Lionel Penrose. Renowned for his study of hereditary mental disorders in the 1930s, Penrose was nominated in 1946 Galton professor of eugenics at University College, London. He was to replace an increasingly embarrassing individual: Ronald Fisher, a bold and outspoken leader of the British Eugenic Society[3].

In his first lecture, Penrose carefully redefined eugenics in his own terms[4]. He focused on a Mendelian disorder he had recently studied, phenylketonuria, taking this peculiar form of inborn mental disease as an exemplary target for "reformed" eugenics. At the time Penrose was not thinking of a biochemical cure for phenylketonuria which is now known. He emphasised the diagnostic value of genetic knowledge and the notion of computable risk. Reproductive advice based on probabilities of transmission was envisioned as the natural medical outcome of the science of heredity. The betterment of babies should not be based on sterilisation policies as the old eugenicists thought but on voluntary birth control. The program was taken up by British physicians like J.F. Roberts, C.O. Carter or E. Slatter who established active research units and genetic clinics in the early 1950s[5].

The counterpart of this British-centred narrative on the origin of medical genetics is usually that the same process took place in France too. The old eugenics disappeared. It was replaced by the same sort of Mendelian medical genetics. Change just took a little longer in coming due to the low level of genetics in the country[6]. At a general level, this story of medical progress inspired by the science of human genetics is quite

---

[3] P. Mazumdar, *Eugenics, Human Genetics and Human Failings*, London, Routledge, 1992.

[4] L. Penrose, "Phenylketonuria", *Lancet*, 1946, ii: pp. 950-956.

[5] P. Mazumdar, *op. cit.*, chapter 5.

[6] For a testimony on this renewal: M. Lamy, "Le conseil génétique" *Bulletin national de l'Académie de médecine*, 1970, 154: pp. 175-178. J. Frezal, "La responsabilité eugénique du pédiatre", *La Presse Médicale,* 27 mai 1967. On the status of genetic research: J.P. Gaudillière, "Les raçines de l'exception française", *La Recherche*, 1998, n° 311, pp. 89-93.

satisfactory. Viewed from the perspective of medical practices and public health debates it is misleading since: a) it does not take into account the continuities between the 1930s and the post-war era; b) it undermines the differences between national configurations by postulating a rapid trans-Channel alignment.

In actual fact, medical policies for bettering babies and taking care of pathological heredity differed in both countries for a long time after the war. In 1944, the French paediatrician Robert Debré, then head of the medical committee of the Resistance National Council – a quasi-Parliament established by clandestine resistance movements – wrote a general report on the future of public health and population issues[7]. In this well known piece on medical policy Debré pointed to the catastrophic state of public health in the country. He systematically compared French and British medical statistics to point out pressing needs. France had a higher rate of tuberculosis, a higher incidence of diseases caused by alcoholism, higher figures for infant mortality and child diseases. The latter issue was thought to be of peculiar importance due to the on-going demographic decline in the country.

Debré was a hospital practitioner with an interest in social medicine. To his mind, the betterment of French babies was not only a matter of concern for caring mothers and wise doctors. It was also a duty of the state. The most important recommendation of the report was a plea for the establishment of a large and influential ministry of public health. The aims of this administration would include, as concerns babies and children, the establishment of a comprehensive system of public paediatric services (les Centres de Protection Maternelle et Infantile) whose mission would be the medical surveillance of pregnant mothers, newborn babies and youngsters. The medical targets of these centres were classical infectious scourges: tuberculosis, missals, or viral infections. Heredity was not mentioned, not even by alluding to the impact of mental defects or malformations. This position was by no means exceptional. After 1945, French debates on the part played by inheritance in human suffering were dominated by the contrast between the low visibility of inherited disorders and the advancement of medical genetics at the local level.

This paper focuses on these different national agendas taking Down's syndrome as an exemplary case. This disease became, in the late 1960s, the most important target of genetic screening. The first part of the paper briefly comments on the pre-war status of eugenics in both countries and on the early images of Down's syndrome. The second part contrasts the post-war reconstruction of pathological inheritance by looking

---

[7] R. Debré and A. Sauvy, *Médecine, Santé, Population*, Paris, Editions médicales, 1944.

more closely at the work done in a few settings where most of the genetic research was done on this disease in both countries. Finally, the third part of the paper introduces the transformation of Down's syndrome into a target for public health intervention, in the 1960s and 1970s, within the context of acrimonious debates over abortion and birth control.

1. Down's syndrome, eugenics and public health between the world wars

One may summarise the historiography on the development of eugenics in Britain and France between the two world wars with three general claims:

1. In France, eugenics was a medical issue. A majority of the members of the French Eugenics Society (Société Française d'Eugénique, SFE) were physicians. Among them, paediatricians, and obstetricians played a prominent role. In contrast, the British Eugenics Education Society was dominated by academics and civil servants.

2. French eugenics was part of a large constellation of organisations active in hygiene. Physicians participating in the SFE were often members of medical foundations involved in the fight against syphilis, tuberculosis, or alcoholism. In contrast, British eugenicists opposed many claims made by the public health advocates leading the campaigns against these very same diseases. In other words, in Britain mental illnesses and hereditary disorders did not belong to the world inhabited by cholera and tuberculosis.

3. French eugenicists were "natalists" convinced that depopulation was the most urgent medical problem the country was facing. They opposed attempts at legalising birth control and favoured policies aimed at increasing the number of babies rather than selecting the fittest. Quantity rather than quality was their target. In contrast to their British colleagues, members of SFE did not press for sterilisation laws but lobbied for clinical premarital examination.

The close relationship between eugenics and population debates calls for comment since depopulation was an issue in both countries[8]. In Britain the decline in the birth rate became a matter of concern after the Boer War in the context of discussing the poor health status of British soldiers[9]. Discussions on depopulation and degeneration

---

[8] J.P. Gaudillière, "Le syndrome nataliste, étude de l'hérédité en France et en Grande-Bretagne" in J. Gayon (ed.), *Les eugénismes après 1945*, forthcoming.

[9] R.A. Saloway, *Demography and Degeneration. Eugenics and the Declining Birth Rate in Twentieth- century Britain,* Reilegh, The University of North-Carolina Press, 1990.

were led by eugenicists like Karl Pearson who focused on the rapidly declining birth rate among the intellectual middle class. In 1914, an official "Birth Rate Commission" took up the issue recommending measures to advance birth rate among the most desirable classes. This class-based framing of the depopulation issue dominated the 1920s and 1930s with the construction of an "anti-natalist" alliance opposing general family allowances which linked feminists, union members, and eugenicists.

The French depopulation issue was different. It was a national problem of a very general nature. Debates linking national decline, degeneration and demography surfaced at the end of the 19th century too. The *Alliance Nationale pour l'Accroissement de la Population Française* was established in 1896. It gathered social reformers, physicians, and policy makers. Their audience expanded tremendously in the 1920s as World War I resulted in the premature death of millions of young men. Demography was then viewed as a national disaster. Family associations campaigned for increased state support for large and healthy families. A widely accepted ideological complex then linked high birth rate, good health, family values, national spirit and a critique of industrial modernity. This strong "natalist" movement was highly successful. In 1920, a national law banned abortion and any form of advertisement for contraceptive means. In the 1930s, a very comprehensive system of family allowances depending on the number of children rather than revenues was established. In contrast to what happened in Britain, French eugenicists shared the natalist perspective but they never shaped the population debate.

Other contrasting elements have to do with the fate of public health. Current historiography has it that public health in France was a field with a bad reputation and little power[10]. The French state did not built a significant public health administration in the 19th century. A law was passed in 1902 to mandate the creation by local authorities of "bureaux d'hygiene" and to specify policies against infectious diseases. However in practice little was done. As documented by Lion Murard and Patrick Zylberman, the city councils which nominated and paid municipal hygiene officers had all sorts of good reasons not to act "unwisely" and most of them did not even create the requested services. Tuberculosis may be viewed as the one exception. In 1916, another law established " dispensaries " as local centres for the prevention, diagnosis and support of individuals and families affected with the disease. Associated with preventoria and sanatoria these centres played a significant role in the management of patients as well as in the advancement of hygiene education. Their operations were however often plagued by the lack of personnel and funds. The absence of a professional body of

---

[10] L. Murard and P. Zylberman, *L'hygiène dans la République*, Paris, Fayard, 1997.

public health officers impaired the development of epidemiology as a medical science though not as a suitable subject for the laboratory study of disease causation. As a matter of fact, in the 1920s, the official body in charge of all statistical inquiries for public purposes – *la Statistique Générale de la France* – did not try to collect and count death certificates[11].

What was the place of Down's syndrome, or as it was labelled at the time, of mongolism within these contrasted configurations of heredity, hygiene, and public health?

Mongolism surfaced in the medical literature in 1862 when John Langdon Down, physician to the asylum for idiots at Earlswood, published a report on idiocy[12]. The paper focused on various conditions of the mouth. On that basis Down's described a special group of patients exhibiting deep transverse furrows and closely resembling one another. A few years later, Down's advanced an ethnic classification of idiots in which the same group of patients was referred to as typical 'Mongols'. As the historian Lilian Zihni has argued, Down's' depiction of the "mongolian idiot" as racially degenerate reflected a widely shared anthropological hierarchy of racial differences[13].

In the following decades, the clinical images of mongolism crystallised around morphological traits and idiocy with less emphasis on the ethnic terminology. Mongol patients were then consistently viewed as forming an homogenous group and attributed common mental characteristics like remarkable imitativeness, a taste for musical rhythm, and a placid disposition. Paediatricians and psychiatrists thought that mongolism could not be mistaken for long by experienced practitioners. Diagnosis was usually based on physical examination, i.e. the search for hypotonia, epicanthus, abnormal palm lines including the famous "four-fingers line", and furrowed tongue. Photographs of typical mongols were used as reference material. From the 1920s on, morphological analysis was complemented by intelligence testing (Down's patients normally showed IQ values ranging from 50 to 75). Variability of association of these signs was, however, significant. One or two of the so-called mongolian traits could be found in many normal individuals. As a French psychiatrist phrased the rule of thumb: an individual

---

[11] P.G. Marietti, *La Statistique Générale de la France*, Paris, Rufisque, 1947; A. Desrosières, "Official Statistics and Medicine in Nineteenth-Century France: The SGF as a Case Study" *Social History of Medicine*, 1991, 4: pp. 515-537.

[12] On the early history of mongolism see: M. Jackson, "Changing Depictions of Disease: Race, Representation and the History of 'Mongolism'", forthcoming.

[13] L. Zhini, "The History of the Relationship between the Concept and Treatment of People with Down's syndome in Britain and America from 1866 to 1967", PhD thesis, University of London, 1989.

would qualify as "Mongolian" as soon as he would show "both mental deficiency (IQ below 65) and at least half the signs included in the Mongolian series."[14]

In Britain, mongolism was situated within the context of lively public debates over the classification and management of mental disorders. On the policy side, the scene was dominated by the eugenicists' attempt to have a sterilization law passed by the Houses. The sterilisation coalition was far from being marginal since it linked the Eugenics Society and a wide range of social and medical organisations including the Royal College of Physicians, the Mental Hospital Association, the County Medical Officers of Health, the National Council of Women and the Blind Association[15]. The final failure was contingent, a by-product of the declaration of war. Mongolism was then listed among the forms of mental disorders with a strong hereditary component which would qualify for eugenic sterilisation[16].

The scientific side of these debates was the quest for a precise, scientific classification scheme which would ensure an accurate diagnosis of hereditary forms of mental illnesses. The resulting research dynamics is well illustrated by the Colchester survey as part of which Penrose did his first study of mental disorders and identified "phenylketonuria" as a peculiar biochemical disorder[17]. Before taking any action, public health authorities asked for reliable numbers of mentally retarded people in order to evaluate the percentage of hereditary forms of what eugenicists thought to be an increasingly important scourge. Accordingly, the study of all inmates at the Colchester asylum (for which the young L. Penrose was paid) aimed at re-evaluating the old classification opposing mental illnesses to inborn mental retardation. Within this context, Penrose's work was clinical rather than genetic. Another goal of the survey was to produce means of medical testing that could complement or supersede the use of the Binet IQ test. Chemical testing of urine and blood was part of this approach. Once linked to a peculiar group of patient, this practice gained a momentum of its own, leading to the definition of an autonomous clinical entity "phenylketonuria" with simple familial transmission as a recessive Mendelian trait. Mongolism was however not reduced to the same sort of biochemical logic, thus remaining a mere clinical entity[18].

---

[14] R. Mallet, "Aspect clinique et diagnostic du mongolisme", *Revue du praticien*, 1964, 14: pp. 7-18.

[15] J. Macnicol, "Eugenics and the Campaign for Coluntary Sterilization in Britain Between the Wars", *Social History of Medicine*, 1989, 2: pp. 147-169.

[16] C.P. Blacker, *Voluntary Sterilisation*, London, The Eugenics Society, 1934.

[17] D. Kevles, *op. cit.* chapter 5. For a re-examination of this period: P. Ricard, PhD thesis, Université Paris 7, in preparation.

[18] L. Penrose, *The Biology of Mental Defect*, London, Sidgwick and Jackson, 1949.

In France, early studies of Down's syndrome as an inherited problem can be traced back to the late 1930s when Raymond Turpin published a few papers on the topic. Turpin was a paediatrician at the Hopital Trousseau in Paris, and active in the French Eugenics Society. Interestingly enough, his work on Down's syndrome juxtaposed two approaches revealing a combination of degeneration theory and Mendelism which was not rare among French baby doctors[19]. Turpin was, on the one hand, examining kin of Down's patients in order to find pathological signs associated with the disease. Signs of a weak constitution within the family were carefully recorded: tuberculosis, malformations, other forms of mental retardation[20]. Turpin thus built on a putative high incidence of neurological disorders to advocate familial change of the hereditary make-up. Mothers, their life habits and bodily conditions, were the key target. One major result Turpin stressed was the relationship between the age of the mother and the incidence of the disease. Convinced that mongolism was related to the deterioration of the germ substance, Turpin was on the other hand looking for Mendelian abnormal traits transmitted within the families of Down's patients which could be taken as predisposing factors. He found one: the furrowed tongue was part of the mongolian series and the trait was transmitted as a Mendelian dominant factor.

The juxtaposition of these approaches should not be viewed as a sign of tension between old-style hereditarism and modern Mendelian genetics. Tensions were actually smoothed in Turpin's integrated vision of "morbid inheritance". Turpin took Mendelian patterns of transmission to be theoretically important. But he considered them to be the tip of the iceberg rather than a universal clue to the familial transmission of disease. Inherited predisposition was a more diffuse but more general feature. Moreover, Turpin considered heredity as a component in a broader system of vertical transmission which included gene transmission, infection, intoxication, and other biological relationships between parents and children[21]. This reproductive vision of heredity was legitimated and reinforced by Turpin's public health commitments. Turpin – like his fellow eugenicists – was more concerned by the declining French birth rate than interested in the inheritance of insanity or criminality. He viewed eugenics as a branch of social medicine focusing on the family as living unit and aiming at the production of healthy babies by healthy mothers. Accordingly, as a medical expert to the Vichy regime, Turpin was active in the preparation of a law on premarital examination which was eventually

---

[19] J.P. Gaudillière, "Etude de l'hérédité, pédiatrie et eugénisme en France", *Médecine/Sciences*, 1997, 13: pp. 1165-1171.

[20] R. Turpin and A. Caratzali, "Remarques sur les ascendants et les collatéraux des sujets atteints de mongolisme", *La Presse Médicale*, 25 juillet 1934.

[21] R. Turpin, "De l'importance médicale des phénomènes héréditaires", *Le Progrès Médical*, 21 juin 1941.

passed in 1942. It is emblematic of French eugenics that this law did not establish pre-marital examination as a system for controlling inheritance but as a secret medical examination focusing on "heredo-infectious" disorders: syphilis and tuberculosis.

2. Changing images: Scientific Down's and the Reconstruction era

In 1956, two Swedish geneticists, J.H. Tjio and A. Levan, published an article on the number of chromosomes in normal human cells[22]. Tjio and Levan opposed the then prevailing view that the correct chromosome count was forty-eight, and claimed the proper number to be forty-six. Three years later, Jérome Lejeune, Marthe Gauthier and Raymond Turpin, a team working at the Hôpital Trousseau in Paris announced that cells from nine Down's patients contained forty-seven chromosomes. Although a priority dispute later surfaced, the discovery that Down's syndrome is caused by trisomy-21 has usually been dated back to this paper.

Following these developments, in the 1960s, innovations in cell studies and karyotyping techniques were used to turn Down's syndrome into a special form of cellular disease, i.e. a disease directly related to impaired genetic material and an exemplar of a whole category of pathological events which fell under the umbrella of "chromosomal abnormalities".

The rewriting of Down's syndrome as a major genetic abnormality was no mere laboratory curiosity. The status of Down's patients was then rapidly changing. Generalised antibiotherapy resulted in expanded life expectancy. It was no longer rare to see Down's patients aged 15 years and older. As parents argued for the specificity of the disease which was not to be confused with other, more frightening, mental disorders, this enlarged population was increasingly taken care of in specialised home institutions. Early chromosomal diagnosis could therefore mean that issues like who should be insitutionalised, and how and when, would fall under the jurisdiction of medical geneticists. Alternatively, the domination of a clinical diagnosis of the disease would keep its management in the hands of family paediatricians. The future status of Down's syndrome was therefore linked to the future of karyotyping practices. This proved quite similar on both side of the Channel in spite of contrasted ways of making a genetic Down's syndrome.

In the early 1960s, as karyotyping of Down's patients became more frequent, troublesome findings emerged and reinforced etiological uncertainties. A few months

---

[22] D. Kevles, *op. cit.*, chapter 16.

after the publication of Lejeune's analysis of nine "mongols" showing forty-seven chromosomes, oral claims were made that if many Down's patients have forty-seven chromosomes, others have only forty-six. As Penrose put it: "Just now there is an epidemic of mongols with chromosomes stuck together in the wrong way. I suppose this phenomenon will become elucidated eventually. Ford has one, Fraccaro has one and we have one"[23]. Other cases soon followed. The causal relationship between abnormal chromosomal number and the disease seemed to fall apart.

In theory this could result either in changes in the definition of the disease, or in changes in the karyotyping procedures. One possibility was to play down the notion that the forty-seven-count was the cause of Down's syndrome. Accordingly, alternative origins of the disease should be investigated and the karyotyping technique ought not be employed in clinical practice as the reference tool for making a diagnosis. The alternative route was to retain the genetic explanation, either by considering that the troublesome patients had been misdiagnosed, or by looking for unnoticed alterations of the chromosomes. Commenting on the case of "a mongol girl with 46 chromosomes," the British cytogeneticists P.E. Polani and C.E. Ford, who had both confirmed Lejeune's conclusion, thus wrote: "On present knowledge it is difficult to believe that there might be a genetic mechanism causing mongolism that did not involve the presence in triplicate of at least part of chromosome 22. The clinical diagnosis of mongolism in the present case is undoubted... The most likely interpretation of the finding is an unequal reciprocal translocation"[24]. Difficulties were also raised by clinically-diagnosed Down's patients showing variable numbers of chromosomes. Swedish paediatricians discussing the "provocative" case of a "Down's syndrome with normal chromosomes" put the problem in the following terms: "The finding of a normal karyotype in a typical case may be explained in several ways... The possibility exists that the whole or part of the Down's syndrome chromosome is hidden somewhere in the karyotype. Nor is another possibility precluded – namely that a genic mutation may have the same final effect as the extra chromosome 21. The vast majority of cases with Down's syndrome, in which the chromosomes have been analysed, have been trisomic for chromosome 21. For practical purposes this establishes its usefulness as a diagnostic sign for the syndrome. That the correlation, and possibly the aetiology, may not be an absolute one is demonstrated by the present case"[25].

[23] L. Penrose to J. Frézal, 21 January 1960, Penrose papers, University College, folder 133/1.
[24] P.E. Polani et al, "A Mongol Girl with 46 Chromosomes", *Lancet*, 1960, i, pp. 721-723.
[25] B. Hall, "Down's Syndrome with Normal Chromosomes", *Lancet*, 1962, ii: pp. 1026-1027.

In January 1961, Lionel Penrose was lecturing on Down's anomaly at a British Medical Association gathering in Cambridge[26]. Penrose began his talk with photographs (unfortunately not preserved) of a group of mongols at the Royal Albert Institution in Lancaster. His aim was to show that the "disease can be recognised at birth". The talk then tackled the epidemiological problem and Penrose used maternal age to distinguish two groups of patients. In group A, the incidence was related to the age of the mother. In group B, maternal age played no role. Group B gathered "familial cases" meaning families with an accumulation of cases or instances of an affected mother giving birth to an affected child. Penrose's conclusion dealt in two lines with the causation in group A "an event related to the age of the mother". But he discussed at length the genetic mechanisms responsible for the transmission of Down's in group B: "the mother may possess a chromosomal anomaly or a predisposing gene". Thus Down's patients with normal chromosome counts were referred to events translocating chromosomal segments. To the geneticist's eye, group B, although rare, was of greater scientific interest because it revealed a quasi-mendelian Down's syndrome for which some form of probabilistic computation could be done.

Growing interest in these peculiar forms of familial chromosomal abnormalities is well documented in Penrose's correspondence. Based on the new karyotyping techniques, the geneticist at University College looked for new cases of mental disorders correlating with some chromosomal abnormalities. In the following decade Penrose and his colleagues within a handful of medical genetics research units turned half a dozen syndromes like Turner syndrome, and Klinefelter mongols, into chromosomal disorders[27]. One may say that the main outcome of their research was changing aetiological images of these disorders along the Down's line.

One aspect of this search for genetic curiosity which is worth mentioning was its weak relationship with clinical work and caring. Although Penrose regularly made pleas for the development of genetic counselling he did not invest many resources into it himself. One obvious reason was that University College was not a hospital. But Penrose was a physician and his strong clinical connections would have facilitated the opening of a consulting service in a nearby medical institution. No such service ever materialised. This inevitably raised the problem of the collection of interesting patients. The local response was a dense network of medical correspondents in paediatric and psychiatric services. Examples of these are Valerie Cowie at the Maudsley Hospital in

---

[26] Penrose papers, folder 62/4, notebook "Mongolism, The Langdon Down's Anomaly, Cambridge British Medical Association".

[27] R. Turpin and J. Lejeune, *Les chromosomes humains*, Paris, Gauthier-Villars, 1965; M. Lamy, *Génétique médicale*, Paris, Masson, 1975.

London, Hans Frossman at the Psychiatric Research Center in Uppsala. Operating in the context of a rapidly expanding biomedical research complex exemplified by the growth of the Medical Research Council, Penrose could develop "pure" genetic research without much insight into medical innovations.

The most important and most paradoxical feature in the discussion of Down's karyotypes is therefore that the process neither led to changes in clinical work nor jeopardized the use of karyotypes. Clinically-defined Down's patients remained Down's patients while the genetic aetiology was accepted. Most cases were linked to chromosomal abnormalities, either as trisomy-21, or as translocations and mosaics which were frequent in cases of "familial" mongolism. A reasonably small number of typical Down's syndromes remained problematic but they quietly disappeared from the scene. The association between genotypes and medical phenotypes which was finally attained in the early 1960s rested on the following claims: 1) Down's syndrome is usually a disease of chromosomal origin; 2) karyotypes generally provide a useful sign for paediatricians; 3) if clinical and laboratory criteria conflate, the former prevail for all medical purposes. In other words, the counterweight to Penrose's biomedical autonomy was the clinician's independent work.

This may be illustrated with the most widely used textbook on Down's syndrome published in the late 1960s by the American specialist Clemens Benda[28]. The chapter on diagnosis was entirely devoted to the description of clinical signs beginning with a classical trilogy: hypotonia, epicanthus, and the "four finger line" in the palm print. One sentence only dealt with karyotypes: "In all cases where there is a question with Down's syndrome, a chromosomal test can dispel all doubts". Benda further added: "If the stigmatisation is very conspicuous and yet the chromosomal analysis negative, one has spoken of paramongolism." By virtue of the bio/medical division of labour, whatever the fine-grained genetic aetiology a rightly assessed clinical Down's patient was a Down's patient.

The French context proved more amenable to the blending of genetics and paediatrics. But this in turn left Down's syndrome half geneticised only, as revealed by Jérome Lejeune's career.

In the late 1950s, Lejeune was working in a small laboratory at the Paris Medical School with Turpin at the head. Given the specificity of eugenics in France, one may understand why, in contrast to the classical chronology of medical genetics, World

---

[28] C. Benda, *Down's Syndrome, Mongolism and Its Management*, New York, Grune and Stratton, 1969.

War II and the decreasing legitimacy of racial and authoritative eugenics made little impact on the images of heredity that paediatricians like Turpin supported. After 1945, Turpin's continued commitment to the betterment of the constitution of French babies is illustrated by his establishment of the "Centre de Progénèse". One aim of this small but publicly supported foundation was to promote research and conferences on the medical control of human reproduction. Generation, not heredity, was the problem of interest. Turpin distinguished between hereditary and environmental factors controlling human generation but his ambition was to advance a unified science of all the forces influencing reproduction taken as a single process ranging from the production of gametes to the raising of children.

Continuity prevailed in the analysis of hereditary disorders too. Turpin's main textbook, *L'Hérédité des prédispositions morbides*, published in 1951, was typical[29]. Turpin contrasted biochemical diseases like Penrose's phenylketonuria that could be described with simple Mendelian patterns with the complex relations between genetic factors (*la constitution*) and environmental factors (*l'ambiance*) that characterized medically important diseases. The book focused on the discussion of hereditary predispositions to allergy, infectious disorders, cancer, congenital malformations, and mental retardation.

Research on Down's syndrome resumed when Lejeune joined Turpin's medical unit. Lejeune's status was then at odd with his colleagues. He was a general practitioner who couldn't pass the internship examination. Thus he could not hope for a position at the Paris Medical School. Lejeune was nonetheless nominated local resident by virtue of Turpin's support. This promotion meant that working in the hospital as a paediatrician would for ever depend on special protection by Turpin or another medical patron. Administratively, Lejeune was left no choice other than to apply for a position at the Centre National de la Recherche Scientifique, the state research agency.

Taking advantage of a decline in the incidence of congenital syphilis in the country, Lejeune gradually transformed the Trousseau Hospital's consulting room for venereal diseases into a place for the examination of Down's patients. Beginning with Turpin's pre-war survey of "mongoliens," he started to gather data about features such as sex-ratio or palm prints that he thought could be characteristic of families having a mongoloid child[30]. In 1954, Turpin and Lejeune reported that palm lines of normal human

---

[29] R. Turpin, *L'hérédité des prédispositions morbides*, Paris, Presses Universitaires de France, 1951.

[30] Lejeune to Penrose, January 19, 1953. Penrose collection, file 174/4. University College London.

beings did not resemble those of inferior monkeys like macaques, while the palm lines of Down's patients did. To the authors, this fact of "regressive evolution" was a new argument in favor of the genetic causation of the disease.

While following this morphological track, Lejeune established a second line of inquiry which linked Turpin's interest in the environmental factors affecting human reproductive ability with opportunities originating in the development of collaborative research on the effects of radiation. In the late 1950s Lejeune was receiving funds from the American NIH and the French equivalent of the Medical Research Council (the Institut National d'Hygiène) for investigating the medical consequences of X-ray exposure. The introduction of cytogenetics into the laboratory was part of this program[31].

In the early 1960s, Lejeune's scientific credentials were based on the forty-seven chromosome hypothesis and on his participation in the emerging international network of medical (cyto)geneticists. Yet the peculiar cognitive and administrative niche Lejeune had found for himself and his work made medical practices more influential than they were in other research settings. Lejeune was eager to show the medical utility of his work. Like Turpin, he viewed medical genetics as a form of "preventive medicine" concerned with pregnant women, newborns and young children. In other words, it was a form of medicine that would pay sufficient attention to the environmental and hereditary factors which influence human generation. Genetic counselling was not viewed as a mere assessment of computed risks. It was seen as a clinical examination taking into account pedigrees but focusing on the sick individual, leading to some form of treatment.

Within this perspective, Down's syndrome remained associated with progénèse. Rather than being the first cause leading to illness, chromosomal abnormalities were viewed as "passage points" connecting the constitution of the mother, the conditions of pregnancy, and the abnormal child. In contrast to Penrose, Lejeune focused on the most abundant type of Down's syndrome: the patients showing a trisomy-21 and no familial transmission. He thought that mutations whose frequency increased with age were not hazardous accidents but outcomes triggered by specific circumstances, like chemical mutagens or hormonal imbalance, and linked to unknown predispositions[32].

---

[31] Dossier R. Turpin, Archives de l'INH, AN versement 771535.

[32] "All statements about the effect of heredo-syphilis and fetal trauma have been proved wrong. The incidence of the disease, however, dramatically increases with the age of the mother. Similar features have been observed with dominant mutations. In the latter cases, however, the magnitude of the phenomenon was much smaller. Peculiar mechanisms must account for the mutation causing mongolism." J. Lejeune 1960, "Le mongolisme, trisomie dégressive", *Annales de génétique*, 1960, 2, pp. 1-34, quote p. 11.

The mechanism could barely be specific, but Lejeune kept mentioning the signs for the disease which had been noticed by Turpin among the unaffected relatives of Down's patients already in the 1930s.

In terms of medical practice, the paediatric context in which Lejeune was evolving meant particular attention was given to the fate of families affected with the disease. Lejeune was given the responsibility for the "consultation des mongoliens". Consequently, he had to advise the families about care and institutionalisation. Since the use of antibiotics had radically altered prognosis, parents of French Down's patients then fought for the creation of new institutions and opposed institutionalisation in general asylums. During the decade which followed the end of the war, the number of Down's patients living in these specialised centres increased from a few thousand to roughly one hundred fifty thousand[33]. The main role of paediatricians was therefore to help families provide care. Lejeune responded to this issue not only by enlarging the "consultation des mongoliens" but also by establishing early links with the Union Nationale des Associations de Parents d'Enfants Inadaptés which was established by the families of French mentally retarded patients[34].

Lejeune's work as a geneticist was directly affected by this supremacy of clinical aims. First, karyotyping analysis led to few changes in clinical practices. As a French specialist in mongolism put it: "it is exceedingly rare that one hesitates to give a clinical diagnosis of mongolism. If it happens to be that the first examination raises some doubts, then further examination, a few weeks later will make the case"[35]. Cell culture and microscopic examination could be helpful when assessing rare clinical puzzles, for instance that of "mongoloid blacks," but they would not matter much for normal clinical work. Even in Turpin's service, where Lejeune researched chromosomal abnormalities, the practice of routine karyotyping did not change the clinical status of the patients. Lejeune did not try to correlate the description of different chromosomal abnormalities with variable clinical symptoms. In contrast to Penrose, who described different forms of the disease and even looked for correlation between genotypes and palm prints, Lejeune did not challenge the homogeneity of Down's syndrome. In a similar way, he did not lean toward the description of "fascinating" cases which would shed light on chromosomal dynamics, but he rapidly focused on therapeutic issues.

---

[33] P. Pinell and M. Zafiropoulos, *Un siècle d'échec scolaire (1882-1982)*, Paris, Editions Ouvrières, 1983.

[34] Mme Lejeune, interview with the author, January 1996.

[35] "Il est bien rare que l'on se méprenne longtemps sur le diagnostic de mongolisme, avec cette réserve qu'un doute léger peut subsister à un premier examen, qui ne résistera pas si on prend la précaution de revoir l'enfant au bout de quelques semaines". R. Mallet, *op. cit.*

From 1960 onwards Lejeune advocated a treatment of Down's syndrome based on his discovery of an anomaly of the amino-acid metabolism which he viewed as a metabolic characteristic of the syndrome.

3. Down's syndrome as a target for medical intervention: the 1970s

In the late 1960s, the meaning of karyotyping was altered by technical developments originating in a medical arena unrelated to medical genetics. Amniocentesis as a means for obtaining foetal tissues originated in obstetrics. By the mid 1950s, the amniotic tap had become a routine procedure to relieve patients with hydroamnios or permit biochemical tests of rhesus incompatibility [36]. In 1960, the procedure was first employed to predict the sex of a human foetus whose mother was a carrier of haemophilia. The positive result led to abortion [37]. The procedure however remained rare. It was generalised to hereditary diseases unrelated to sex by the mid-1960s when techniques for the culture of foetal cells were developed [38]. Two years later, abortions following prenatal diagnosis of Down's syndrome were reported by British practitioners [39]. Within a few years time the putative generalisation of the procedure to pregnant women at significant risk of carrying a foetus affected with Down's syndrome was a topic of open talk among medical geneticists. Age was the main criteria for advising amniocentesis and chromosomal analysis [40].

This new form of medical intervention was rapidly taken over by genetic counsellors. Cooperative registries to ascertain the safety and accuracy of the procedure were started both in Britain and in the United States. By the mid-1970s, in Britain, the procedure was performed by the thousands every year. Physicians talked about a possible "elimination" of Down's syndrome by means of extended prenatal diagnosis. Massive screening was on the agenda raising new questions about the meaning and impact of genetic counselling: what was the impact of prenatal diagnosis on family reproductive choices? What were the psychological consequences of a positive diagnosis? How should positive results be announced? What safeguards were there for permitting the consulting pregnant woman to make a free choice? Surveys were

[36] R. Schwartz Cowan, "Aspects of the History of Prenatal Diagnosis", *Fetal Diagnosis and Therapy* 1993, 8: pp. 10-17.

[37] P. Riss and F. Fuchs, "Antenatal Determination of Fetal Sex in Prevention of Hereditary Disease", *Lancet* 1960, ii: p. 180.

[38] M.W. Steele and W.R. Breg, "Chromosome Analysis of Human Amniotic Fluids", *Lancet*, 1966, ii: p. 383.

[39] C. Valenti, E.J. Schutta and T. Kehaty, "Prenatal Diagnosis of Down's Syndrome", *Lancet*, 1968, ii: p. 220.

[40] A. Dorfman *et al.*, (eds.) *Antenatal Diagnosis,* The University of Chicago Press, 1972.

organised by geneticists, psychologists, and social scientists[41]. Down's syndrome thus played a critical role in the shaping and regulation of genetic counselling as a new medical speciality based on prenatal diagnosis and abortion.

From the NHS perspective, professional evaluation and guidelines were not enough. Cost/benefit analysis was started to complement the doctors' surveys. By the late 1970s, the consensus was that risks of killing a foetus by performing amniocentesis were greater than the incidence of Down's syndrome for women under 40. Thus led to proposals for mandatory screening for women over 40. The work of health planners encouraged the tendency to extend the screened population, by arguing for a 35 year old boundary on the basis of economic costs[42]. The period remains to be properly investigated by historians of medicine but a reasonable hypothesis is that the widening scope of intervention was enhanced by the conjunction of professional interests in growing genetic services, the demands of women, and pressure from the NHS authorities toward a nation-wide economically-sound policy.

Once again, developments in France took a different path. It is not that prenatal diagnosis of Down's syndrome did not exist. But it did so on a much smaller scale without the strong support of the health authorities. In the mid-1970s, five centres in the country were offering prenatal diagnosis with less than a hundred amniocentesis performed each year[43]. Simultaneously, Down's syndrome was enrolled in a major battle over the legalisation of abortion which was waged within the medical community. Lejeune played a central role in the French abortion debate and he is the one who brought the Down's patients in.

In 1972 as pressure from feminists'organisations and from the left mounted to obtain a change of the 1920 law prohibiting abortion, Lejeune created *"Laissez-les-Vivre"*. The aim of this voluntary organisation was to fight against freedom of choice. It was strongly supported by catholic circles and French conservatives. The cause was well received in the medical profession. In 1973 the government started to discuss a change of the 1920 abortion law. Lejeune wrote a petition circulated by Laissez-les-Vivre among French practitioners. It was endorsed by 10,000 French physicians, one out of

---

[41] R. Antley and L.C. Hartlage, "Psychological Responses to Genetic Counseling for Down's Syndrome", *Clinical Genetics*, 1976, 9: pp. 257-265; G. Zorzi et al, "Importance and Adequacy of Genetic Counseling Information: Impressions of Parents with Down's Syndrome Children", *Mental Retardation*, 1980, 18: pp. 255-257.

[42] S. Hagard and F. Carter, "Preventing the Birth of Infants with Down's Syndrome: A Cost-benefit Analysis", *British Medical Journal*, 1976, 1: pp. 753-756.

[43] J. Feingold, A. Boué and J. Boué, conférence de presse, INSERM, 23 février 1976.

six. Much has been written about the catholic roots of this attitude and about Lejeune's commitment to a conservative form of catholicism. One may argue however that the motives for Lejeune's anti-abortion militancy were also medical, originating in the blending of paediatrics and genetics which dominated his work and more generally the early development of French genetic counselling. In this respect, Lejeune's rhetoric about Down's syndrome, prenatal diagnosis, and abortion is suggestive.

In June 1973 Lejeune appeared on TV with another paediatrician Prof. J. Milliez who favoured the government's law proposal. During the discussion, Lejeune suddenly faced the camera, urging the Down's patients listening to the show to cry out in rage at the abortion propagandists who "think that they should be dead"[44]. Down's patients, their life and their parents were key assets in the campaign against abortion but also Lejeune's major motive for opposing the transformation of medical genetics and the emerging form of preventive counselling. Arguing that he should not have discovered trisomy 21 if it was to turn karyotyping into a death sentence, Lejeune reputedly gave up practising amniocentesis in his service at the Sick Children's Hospital. Again and again he explained that he was a doctor, that his duty was to take care of Down's patients, to help them live a more dignified life, to search for a cure which he thought he had almost discovered.

> "Pour une certaine catégorie de personne je représente quelque chose par nécessité. Il s'agit des enfants handicapés. Car je m'occupe d'eux, je reçois les familles, je soigne ces enfants. Et lorsque l'on me traite de menteur quand je me présente comme médecin, je veux bien passer sur l'injure, on est fort loin de la réalité. Il se trouve en effet que j'ai la plus grosse consultation du monde pour les enfants trisomiques 21… Il y en a à peu près 5000 que nous suivons régulièrement, que nous connaissons individuellement. Alors nous dire que nous ne savons pas ce que sont les détresses dans les famille, et que nous ne soignons pas ces malades, alors qu'il en passe 70 par semaine à la consultation, plus 40 au laboratoire…"[45]

In spite of *Laissez-les-Vivre*'s campagning, the abortion law was passed by the French parliament in the Spring 1974. As such the legal change did not produce a consensus

[44] J.V. Manevy, "Le Prof. Lejeune sonne le tocsin", *L'Express*, 11 juin 1973.

[45] Entretien avec le professeur Lejeune, *La Croix*, 29 juin 1973. "There is a special group people for whom I represent something simply because they need me. They are the handicapped children. I take care of them. I see the families. I provide treatment. If one accuses me of lying, of not being a doctor then this far from being the truth to put it mildly. I have the world's largest consulting room for Down's patients. I know personally 5,000 of them. It is absurd to say that we don't know how these families suffer, that we don't take care of them. I see 70 of them in the consulting room every week. And 40 more in the laboratory". (Translated by the author)

about prenatal diagnosis and the abortion of foetuses showing trisomy 21, but it did create a space for medical geneticists who were ready to provide this form of service and who were already advocating a screening program[46]. The change also opened a space for feminist pressure on hospitals, gynaecologists and obstetricians. By 1983, the Ministry of Health made amniocentesis free for all women "at risk", meaning pregnant women of 39 and older. In spite of a bitter public controversy, Down's syndrome thus became in France too a topic for preventive medical policy, a disease diagnosed in utero, and a motive for almost sytematic therapeutic abortion.

4. Conclusion

This paper has argued that the post-war redefinition of Down's syndrome as a chromosomal disorder amenable to early diagnosis based on karyotyping techniques followed contrasted paths in Britain and in France. The "terrain" for these paths was provided by peculiar configurations of eugenics and public health which developed in both countries during the 1930s and 1940s.

In France where eugenics had been a medical movement mobilising paediatricians attracted by theories of heredo-infection, by hygiene, and by natalist policy, the geneticisation of Down's syndrome emerged out of studies of human reproduction and mother/infant relationships. The disease thus remained a clinical entity; karyotyping developed as a laboratory curiosity without much impact on the actual practice of diagnosis; paediatricians building clinical genetics paid special attention to the fate and care of the bulk of Down's patients, i.e. those affected with a non-familial form of the syndrome. In terms of health policy, Down's syndrome was a target for state intervention aiming at the development of specialised home institutions.

In Britain, eugenics had been a movement without many links to hygiene-oriented public health, dominated by a professional middle class which advocated birth control. In the 1950s, studies of Down's syndrome were part of the making of medical genetics as a "reformed eugenics" focusing on Mendelian disorders and on the practice of genetic counselling, i.e. the probabilistic assessment of hereditary risk. The British geneticists building up human genetics envisioned a new form of intervention based on risk, probability calculus, early detection. Within this context, Down's syndrome was a research target with a strong emphasis on the transmission of chromosomal abnormalities.

---

[46] A. Boué, interview with A. Jallon, March 1996.

The 1960s thus echoed the pre-war contrast between policies aiming at bettering babies either by eliminating or by educating the unfit. Given this "longue durée" of the cultures of heredity, one may wonder what triggered the alignment of the 1970s since amniocentesis, genetic counselling, prenatal diagnosis and abortion were, in both countries, increasingly practised to prevent the "risk" of Down's syndrome. The convergence was to a large extent a political product. As exemplified by Lejeune's trajectory, debates about Down's patients were tightly related to the French abortion debate. By the mid 1970s, a legal reframing which made abortion possible had been imposed on a reluctant medical profession by the pressure of women organisations and family planning advocates. As a consequence, prenatal diagnosis as a form of preventive medicine became technically, socially and legally doable. The alignment on British practices was however never complete. In France, genetic prevention of Down's syndrome developed later than in Britain. It was less organised and it was not evaluated on the basis of health management criteria. Notwithstanding the general reference to risk and risk management, professional autonomy dominated the French scene, while cost-benefit analysis, systematic screening, and public health administration remained British habits.

Between Fear, National Pride and Democracy: Images of Tuberculosis in the American Zone of Occupation, 1945-1949

Dagmar Ellerbrock

1. Preliminary theoretical statement

The area under examination: health policies

Since the turn of the century tuberculosis has been a classic area of intervention for health authorities, and historians as well as doctors have paid great attention to the period of the Empire and the Weimar Republic[1]. With regard to the period of occupation, however, the historiography of the fight against tuberculosis has been treated as having no great significance although it played a considerable role in discourse at the time. With the discovery of the tubercle bacillus, the establishment of a far-reaching system of care for those with tuberculosis in the Weimar Republic and the development of technically more reliable means of diagnosis in the form of X-ray

---

[1] See also, from the large body of writing, e.g. Gerd Göckenjan, *Tuberkulose – Prävention und Spuckverhalten. Bedingungen, Ziele und Maßnahmen einer historischen Kampagne zur Einstellungs- und Verhaltensänderung,* Berlin, 1989; Sylvely Hähner-Rombach, "Künstlerlos and Armenschicksal. Von den unterschiedlichen Wahrnehmungen der Tuberkulose", in Hans Wilderitter, assisted by Michael Dorrmann (eds.), *Das große Sterben. Seuchen machen Geschichte,* Berlin, 1995; Kristin Kelting, *Das Tuberkuloseproblem im Nationalsozialismus,* Diss. Univ. Kiel 1974; Andrea Öhring, *Tuberkulose: Krankheitsbegriff,* Diss. med. Univ. Freiburg i. Br. 1981; Peter Reinicke, *Tuberkulosefürsorge. Der Kampf gegen eine Geißel der Menschheit. Dargestellt am Beispiel Berlins 1895-1945,* Weinheim, 1988; Wolfgang Seeliger, *Die Volksheilstätten-bewegung in Deutschland um 1900. Zur Ideengeschichte der Sanatoriumstherapie für Tuberkulöse,* Münster Diss. med. 1987; René and Jean Dubos, *Tuberculosis, Man, and Society*; Barbara G. Rosenkrantz (ed.), New Brunswick, 1992; Georgina Feldberg, *Disease and Class. Tuberculosis and the Shaping of Modern North American Society,* New Brunswick, 1995; John E. Murray, "The White Plague in Utopia: Tuberculosis in Nineteenth-century Shaker Communities", *Bulletin of the History of Medicine,* 1994, vol. 68, pp. 278-306; Sheila M. Rothman, *Living in the Shadow of Death. Tuberculosis and the Social Experience of Illness in American History,* Baltimore/London, 1994; Frank Ryan, *The Forgotten Plague. How the Battle against Tuberculosis was Won - and Lost,* Boston, 1993; F.B. Smith, *The Retreat of Tuberculosis 1850-1950,* London, 1988; M.E. Teller, *The Tuberculosis Movement: a Public Health Campaign in the Progressive Era,* New York, 1988; Leonard G. Wilson, "The Rise and Fall of Tuberculosis in Minnesota: The Role of Infection", *Bulletin of the History of Medicine,* 1992, vol. 66, no. 1; Leonard G. Wilson, "The Historical Decline of Tuberculosis in Europe and America: its Causes and Significance", *Journal of the History of Medicine and Allied Sciences,* 1990, vol. 45, pp. 366-396.

examinations[2], tuberculosis no longer appeared to be a subject worthy of investigation. Later outbreaks were thus implicitly interpreted as a repetition of situations that had been known of for a long time and as new versions of familiar control strategies. Health policies between 1945 and 1949 were considered to have no creative potential and to simply involve the administration of shortages and a concentration on stemming the spread of epidemics. As such they could only be used for solving the most urgent problems, and this appeared to speak against dealing with the problem of tuberculosis itself. Tuberculosis, however, was one of the serious epidemics of the period and was given serious consideration by American and German health politicians. Tuberculosis and health were not just topics in health reports but also subjects included in the situation and morale reports that the German police chiefs supplied to the CIC. This underlines the significance that the American occupation forces placed on the health situation with a view, too, to the contentment and political accessibility of the Germans. Furthermore, it emphasises the relevance that German public officials assigned to the topic of health. Health was of such central importance to them that this subject was raised week after week, thus confronting the occupation forces with this issue.

Occupying American officers linked health policies with clear political ambitions[3] and worked on the assumption that "there is no function of government that is not related to the health function…"[4]. Thus the question of how ensuring health was influenced by the political ambitions of the Military Government will be looked at in more detail. Above all, the concrete aims of the American occupying forces' medical mission need to be pinned down in order to follow how, and with what degree of success, it was carried out. In the process, it will be seen that the fight against tuberculosis was much more than simply subsistence safeguarding or the pure administration of shortages. The principal political aim of the occupation forces, namely reorientation, made the fight against tuberculosis part of a framework based upon the American model of democracy and thus gave it strong contextual, cultural and traditional bonds. This link with American attempts at democratisation raises the question of the legitimating function of health policies in the new German society that was to be created. The relationship between the occupiers' political intentions and the continuity, resilience and power of the German health system must be explained, taking this background into account.

---

[2] This method of diagnosis came about as a result of the development of the Coolidge tube in 1913 by the American physicist Coolidge. See Jens Ruhbach, *Die Anfänge der Radiologie in der Inneren Medizin von 1986 bis 1900*, Diss. med. Univ. Würzburg 1995, p. 102.

[3] OMGUS RG 5/332-1/14.

[4] RG 260: 5/332-1/14, Resumé of Problems and Accomplishment in the Public Health Branch May 1945 - Nov. 1947, enclosure: Memorandum for: Chief, 'Public-Health and Welfare Branch', Subject: Health Organization in the German Civil Government, p. 1.

The fight against tuberculosis was more than functional problem-solving, and not just from the point of view of the tasks and aims it set itself. Because 'health' and 'illness' ultimately affect the highly significant, personal and emotional feelings of people, the safeguarding of health embodies a political field whose range does not solely consist of the prevention of illness. Illness was always seen as both a potential and very real danger that concerned both groups involved: the occupying forces and those that were occupied. No hierarchical or factual distinction, that is found when considering many other problems, could be made when considering illness. Immediate existential involvement meant that illness was not just discussed by medical experts but became a daily topic for the Military Government, the German administration, the press and the general population. Information provided by the occupying power on the danger of epidemics, water quality, infection risks, and the danger posed by tuberculosis, affected everyone: women and men, young and old, German and American. Thus mental patterns during the years following the war were influenced as much by fears of becoming ill as by the daily confrontation with food rationing[5]. This far-reaching penetration of everyday experience and collective consciousness points the way for the question of the social, political, cultural, gender-specific and national implications of safeguarding health.

Mary Douglas writes that "the body as a social structure… (controls) the way the body is perceived as a physical structure and, on the other hand, … a particular social conception is manifest in the perception of the body"[6]. This means that the underlying political model, that reflects concepts of society and expectations of the future that extend far beyond the emergency situation in existence at the time, has to be reconstructed.

The conception of illness involves an immediate relationship with collective anxieties and feelings of being threatened, and society's definition of risk is not only expressed in social security programmes but also in its handling of the risks of becoming ill. The subject of illness therefore promises the closest possible approach to central patterns of perception that, in turn, should be related back to political intentions. Apart from institutional and administrative arrangements, this process is carried out above all through discursive patterns of understanding of the body. Cultural ideas and aims are thus carried directly into bodies and inscribed through health norms. In this connection, two

---

[5] For the dominance of the latter in everyday experience compare: Rainer Gries, *Die Rationen-Gesellschaft. Versorgungskampf und Vergleichsmentalität – Leipzig, München und Köln nach dem Kriege,* Münster, 1991.

[6] Mary Douglas, *Ritual, Tabu und Körpersymbolik. Sozialanthropologische Studien in Industriegesellschaft und Stammeskultur*, Frankfurt/M., 1986, p. 99.

aspects are of particular interest: firstly the roles of 'illness', 'health' and 'body' as supporting social concepts with whose help values and patterns of interpretation are constructed[7], and secondly the "hypothesis,… that control of the body is an expression of social control, that… in certain rituals correspond to the requirements of… social experience"[8].

It thus becomes evident that in this case the politics of tuberculosis cannot be reduced to institutional politics, but should be investigated in its social form[9] and symbolic content. This expansion of social and political history to a 'cultural approach' is to be used here on the politics of health to expand the models created during previous studies of the politics of occupation that assumed a rational political process, whereby aims and interests were plainly formulated and rationally implemented. Emotions, experiences and the values and preferences brought about by socialisation, that are non-intentional or above the level of individuals, were not included in such treatments. Individual's imaginations and their way of seeing the world, their patterns of perception and interpretation, have a fundamental significance of decisive importance[10] on the sub-political level and above all, in the fight against illness[11].

Political terms and political field analysis

The classic Anglo-Saxon term 'policy analysis' and its German counterpart, *Politikfeldanalyse*, are mainly concerned with administrative aspects of problem-solving taking a functional political term as a basis[12]. Politics is made up of three levels according to this model: the institutional system (polity), public-political dealings (policy), and political processes (politics). The institutional dimension is embodied by the system

---

[7] For concepts on constructing support systems see Peter L. Berger and Thomas Luckmann, *The Social Construction of Reality*, pp. 115-120; 124; For interdependence between social experience and the perception of body, Douglas, p. 103f.

[8] Douglas, p. 106; For linkage of health and morality see: Manuel Frey, *Der reinliche Bürger. Entstehung und Verbreitung bürgerlicher Tugenden in Deutschland, 1760-1860*, Göttingen, 1997, p. 84/85, and also Alfons Labisch, *Homo Hygienicus. Gesundheit und Medizin in der Neuzeit*, Frankfurt/New York, 1992, p. 105f.

[9] For construction of public health by "differing perceptions, interests and politics" see Labisch, 1992, p. 58f.

[10] For the pre-rational content of ideas of illness see Jutta Dornheim, "Verweisungszusammenhänge als kulturelle und sozialhistorische Prämissen von Krankheitsdiskursen", in Rolf Rosenbrock and Andreas Salmen (eds.), *AIDS-Prävention*, Berlin, 1990.

[11] For the influencing role of health perceptions on politics see Labisch, 1992, p. 60.

[12] T.R. Dye, *Policy Analysis. What Governments Do, Why They Do It, and What Difference It Makes*, Alabama, 1978.

of laws, public officials, institutions, etc. The normative substance of politics is acquired through its content, duties, subjects and aims. The procedural dimension means the course of political dealing, the bringing about of an exchange of interests, the mediation of conflicts by a political process[13].

The political terms that I use are linked to this conception and expand them in two ways: the phases of political planning and the actions directed at institutional preconditions can be included in the above model and shown in their historical context. In the following, however, the normative and procedural levels should be understood in a much wider sense. Political aims, content and their implementation should be looked at from the point of view of how they were perceived, the reasoning behind them, their tradition and their degrees of internalisation. As a result they will, at least to some extent, be dragged out of their direct everyday political framework and considered on a deeper cultural level. As a result, the analytical level includes individuals and social groupings in addition to institutions and bureaucracies, so that the cultural interpretations, practices, social norms, and values, that are the foundations of a political process and thus the basis of every rational political formulation, can be tracked down. This approach will break down the hierarchical (from the top downwards) policy-analysis model[14]. The clear causal relationship, that subordinates the political process to the formulation of aims and the institutional dimension, is thus revoked. On the contrary, it is assumed that local communities have an effect on the political planning of aims and the perception of problems "through pre-political connections and communication networks"[15]. This understanding tallies with the opinion of the US secret service at the time, who assumed that in the main, most people let themselves be directed by local conditions"[16]. This understanding has led to a theoretically expanded policy analysis. Previous policy analysis, according to the main point of criticism, "fails to capture... the essence of policy-making in political communities: the struggle over ideas. Ideas are a medium of exchange and a mode of

---

[13] Compare D. Sternberger, *Drei Wurzeln der Politik,* Frankfurt/M., 1978 and K. Rohe, *Politik. Begriffe und Wirklichkeiten*, Stuttgart, 1994 (2).

[14] In this sense see also Paul Sabatier, "Advocacy-Koalitionen, Policy-Wandel and Policy-Lernen: Eine Alternative zur Phasenheuristik", in Adrienne Hértier (ed.), *Policy-Analyse. Kritik und Neuorientierung*, Opladen, 1993, pp. 116-148, who no longer conceptualises the policy process hierachically from above downwards, but as influenced by multiple, interacting policy cycles, cf. p. 143.

[15] Eberhard Holtmann, *Politik und Nichtpolitik. Lokale Erscheinungsformen politischer Kultur im frühen Nachkriegsdeutschland. Das Beispiel Unna und Kamen*, Opladen, 1989, p. 26, and also Gries, p. 12.

[16] OMGBY 10/65-1/11, ICD Augsburg, German Attitudes Towards Occupation Forces, 21. July 1947, quoted according to Gries, p. 12.

influence even more powerful than money and votes and guns.[17]" In an extended policy understanding this led to the "calculable, economically rational person"[18] being replaced by one that is also directed by ideas and orientations[19] that were compiled in a concept of "belief systems"[20].

In this way the definition of political problems is made dependent on underlying value judgements[21]. The patterns of interpretation to be researched are thus conceptualised, by investigating communication situations, particularly in policy sub-systems[22]. The perspectives of the examination are thus opened up, allowing local and pre-political[23] fields to be reached alongside the administrative level. The presumption of the underlying communication model consists in the assumption that "dealings are persuasively oriented", and their intention is to convince a potential public or political counterpart of one's own ideas and value judgements and the resulting preferences regarding political activity[24]. This analytical point of view brings about a negation of motivation which is based on a rational weighing up of dealings. Instead the actors are conceived to be tied up in plans, strategies and interests, as well as nets of metaphors, symbols and norms that makes up such a complex view that a reduction of the political decisions and expectations of the future to a purely workable maximum is no longer possible[25].

Policy change, in the model of analysis sketched out here, is above all contingent on "fluctuations in the dominant belief system"[26]. The question is: How are political problems constructed and how are relevance criteria developed? Values, norms and

---

[17] Deborah A. Stone, *Policy Paradox and Political Reason*, Glenview, 1988, p. 7.

[18] Adrienne Hértier, "Policy-Analyse. Elemente der Kritik und Perspektiven der Neuorientierung", in Hértier, *op. cit.* pp. 9-38, at p. 15.

[19] *Ibid.*, p. 16.

[20] "Belief system" understood as both "a set of value priorities" and tallying assumptions. Compare with this definition Sabatier, 1993, p. 120; Hértier, 1993, p. 17.

[21] *Ibid.*, p. 22.

[22] Sabatier defines a field of research that is constituted by a subject area or subject question in which actors of various institutions, interested organisations, journalists, researchers, etc. are involved as a policy sub-system, 1993, p. 120. In this sense, health policies will now be considered as a field of politics and discussion of individual health policy measures as sub-systems.

[23] For an understanding of pre-political connections in the local context see Holtmann, 1989, pp. 25-30, and p. 52ff and pp. 121-138.

[24] Frank Nullmeier, "Wissen und Policy-Forschung. Wissenspolitologie und rhetorisch-dialektisches Handlungsmodell", in Hértier, *op. cit.*, pp. 175-198, p. 191.

[25] Nullmeier, p. 191.

[26] Nullmeier p. 179, and Paul A. Sabatier, "An Advocacy Coalition Framework of Policy Change and the Role of Policy-orientated Learning Therein", in *Policy Science*, 1988, vol. 21, p. 158.

114

interpretations, as driving forces for the perception of problems of health policy, and models of medical/hygienic processing should therefore be set in relation to the policies drafted.

The concept of 'body' and discourse on illness

As a result of these considerations, 'body' and 'corporeality'[27] can neither be understood to be antithetical, the opposite of rationality and rationalisation, nor can they any longer be defined as a biological constant, a substance that stays the same forever. The critical studies of civilisation that took place in the 1980s[28] examined 'body' as a resource of a "new authentic experience"[29] or as "resistance potential"[30] against an instrumentalising, disciplining society, and thus simply continued the western division of 'mind and body', of 'body and soul' the other way round. The idea of a natural "raw corporeality"[31] was also raised again. Instead of this onotological continuity of 'corporeality' I assume a historification, an ever-changing re-shaping of corporeality in different epochs, cultures, forms of society, etc. The culturalisation[32] of the body is thus not exclusively considered from the point of view of disciplining[33] and norming[34], but rather as the penetration of corporeality by the most varied of values, norms and interpretations. A non-disciplined, in effect 'pre-modern', 'pure' body is inconceivable in this setting, as every form of corporeality remains linked to the dominant belief system of each particular society. The debate on how the 'body' is to be evaluated is thus provided with no new variant[35]. Instead of a judgement on what the body is, we should follow what descriptions it attracts, what it 'incorporates' symbolically, to which mechanisms of effect it is bound and what role the properties ascribed to it

---

[27] 'Corporeality' understood as the specific form of experience of bodies in their particular society. Compare Utz Jeggele, "Im Schatten des Körpers: Vorüberlegungen zu einer Volkskunde der Körperlichkeit", in *Zeitschrift für Volkskunde*, 1980, 76, (2), p. 172.

[28] See the overview in Dietmar Kamper and Christoph Wulf, *Die Parabel der Wiederkehr*. For an introduction see Dietmar Kamper and Christoph Wulf (eds.), *Die Wiederkehr des Körpers*, pp. 9-21, Frankfurt, 1982, and Jakob Tanner, "Körpererfahrung, Schmerz und die Konstruktion des Kulturellen", *Historische Anthropologie*, 1994, vol. 3, pp. 489-491.

[29] Kamper and Wulf, *op. cit.*, 1982, p. 9.

[30] Kamper and Wulf, *op. cit.,* 1982, p.10.

[31] Barbara Duden, *Geschichte unter der Haut*, Stuttgart, 1987, p. 10.

[32] The empirical analysis of the "lack of history of the body" in its biological conditions, initially in Duden, *op. cit.*

[33] This historisation process took place initially during critical questioning of civilisation in an essay by Foucault, that represents the first culturation of "body" and "sexuality".

[34] Compare the overview in Duden, *op. cit.*, pp. 26-46.

[35] For the variations in evaluation see, among others, Kamper and Wulf, *op. cit.,* 1982, p. 18.

play in the political process. The term 'corporeality', used here as a basis, is not, however, completely expended in discourse[36], even if the experience of corporeality can only ever be communicated discursively.

This form of historisation of the 'body' is above all a challenge to the medical historians, because it qualifies biological/medical categories considered to be constant[37]. The conception of the 'body' as a symbolic medium of expression that possesses an immediate reference to political transformations, allows the analysis of political processes through the examination of change, or the symbolic re-evaluation of concepts of body[38]. The expressive function of the body in bourgeois society is not only linked to long-examined forms of distinction such as, for example, hygienic practices[39], fashion[40], sport[41], politics[42], but is also given representative, because changeable, meaning in the linkage to 'health' and 'illness'. Thus the explicitly 'healthy' or 'ill' body is a body extending beyond the 'class body' and reflects not just social distinctions[43] but a variety of diverse sub-systems with their particular values and hierarchies. The symbolic

---

[36] For a complete resolution of all the biological corporeal pre-conditions see, e.g., Joan W. Scott, "Gender: A Useful Category of Historical Analysis", in Joan W. Scott, *Gender and the Politics of History*, pp. 28-50, New York, 1988, and also Judith Butler, *Das Unbehagen der Geschlechter,* Frankfurt, 1991.

[37] For research originally concerned with corporeality and thus simultaneously with phenomena such as hunger, pain, etc. that are understood to be constants compare, e.g. Elaine Scarry, *Der Körper im Schmerz. Die Chiffren der Verletzlichkeit und die Erfindung der Kultur,* Frankfurt/M., 1992.

[38] Compare Gunter Gebauer, "Ausdruck und Einbildung. Zur symbolischen Funktion des Körpers", in Kamper and Wulf, *op. cit.*, 1982, pp. 313-329.

[39] Klaus Mönkemeyer, *Sauberkeit, Schmutz und Körper. Zur Sozial- und Kulturgeschichte der Sauberkeit zwischen Reichsgründung und Erstem Weltkrieg*, Diss. Marburg, 1988.

[40] Compare, e.g. Anne Hollander, *Seeing Through Clothes*, New York, 1978.

[41] See G. Hauk, "Kollektive Symbole, Mythen und Körperbilder in Filmen und Festern der Arbeiterkultur- und Sportbewegung", in H.J. Teichler (ed.), *Arbeiterkultur und Arbeitersport,* Clausthal-Zellerfeld, 1985; Thomas Alkemeyer, *Körper, Kult und Politik. Von der Muskelreligion Pierre de Coubertins zur Inszenierung von Macht in den Olympischen Spielen von 1936,* Frankfurt, 1996; U. Müller, *Die Politisierung der Körper. Der Zusammenhang von Körperübung und Herrschaft,* Diss. Hannover, 1986.

[42] Inge Baxmann, "Der Körper der Nation", in E. Francois, H. Siegrist, and J. Vogel (eds.), *Nation und Emotion,* Göttingen, 1995; A. Richartz, *Körper - Gesundheit - Nation. Tiefenhermen-eutische Analysen zur bürgerlichen Körperkultur in Deutschland in der ersten Hälfte des 19. Jahrhunderts*, Diss. Freie Univ. Berlin, 1992.

[43] For the structure of the 'class body' that reproduces the social sphere by means of cultural distinctions concerning taste compare Pierre Bourdieu, *La distinciton. Critique sociale du jugement*, Paris, 1979, p. 215f.

significance of corporeality increases in discourses about illness[44], as the approach to illness reveals social norms and patterns of interpretation[45] particularly clearly. Illness, as a fundamental component of everyday culture, thus includes not only diffuse tendencies towards anxiety, ideas of somatic and social infection and transmission, and social relegation, but also wide-ranging symbolic forms of representation, particularly as references to opinions on guilt, punishment and morals[46]. When this is taken as a basis, the connections and symbolic forms of representation of tuberculosis and what led to the mystification of this disease during the years of occupation require clarification. In this sense, a 'concept of illness' is not just a "thought-out, systematically formulated and reasoned theory about the appearance of illness, its character, causes and regularity"[47], but an idea that also encompasses interpretations, associations and symbols on a pre-rational level and includes all the elements of significance that are relevant in the context of the discourse on illness. Concepts of illness thus imply not only ideas based on natural sciences but interact with, and are dependent on, conceptions of body, conceptions of society, and self-images and are therefore central to the creation of a social and individual meaning[48]. Conversely, concepts of illness are not expended in the cultural reshaping of corporeality, but extend beyond the insular biological causes of the illness, and the medical description of the course and development of the illness, in spheres of corporeality considered more or less unchanging, and thus produce an immediate connection between 'society', 'culture' and 'body' that were originally conceived as independent entities. Illnesses thus incorporate social interpretations at the same time as they transfer practices, interpretations of meaning, agreement, and protest back to society. This

---

[44] For the social construction of illness see introduction in Jens Lachmund and Gunnar Stollberg (eds.), *The Social Construction of Illness,* Stuttgart, MedGG-Beihefte 1, 1992, pp. 9-19. There is also an overview of international discussions of research on different disciplinary approaches used by medical sociology, medical anthropology and social history; also Martin Dinges, "Neue Wege in der Seuchengeschichte?", in Martin Dinges and Thomas Schlich (eds.), *Neue Wege in der Seuchengeschichte*, Stuttgart, MedGG-Beihefte 6, 1995, pp. 7-24. Dinges drafts an interesting model of actors that illustrates the varied interdependencies in the construction process of illness. However, he too assumes that actors only deal rationally and he thus fails to concentrate on the pre-rational levels and interpretations that are so relevant to the interpretation and understanding of illness.

[45] Compare Jutta Dornheim, "Verweisungszusammenhänge als kulturelle und sozialhistorische Prämissen von Krankheitsdiskursen" in Rolf Rosenbrock and Andreas Salmen (eds.), *AIDS-Prävention*, Berlin, 1990, p. 197f.

[46] See Dornheim, 1990, pp. 198-200.

[47] Definition according to R. Rothschuh, *Konzepte der Medizin in Vergangenheit und Gegenwart*, Stuttgart, 1978, p. 8.

[48] In this sense see also Dornheim, 1990, p. 197.

relationship intensifies itself in the state of the illness. Communication and representation have an immediate effect on illness as a medium of expression, more varied and effective, as there is an interaction that can be expressed on the unspoken, pre-rational level. Medically, in a modern setting, illness can be universally experienced as an egalitarian body concept. In the western, natural sciences body model, experiences of illness are no longer fragmented along social, religious, gender or regional lines. This potential, that anyone can be affected, makes illness the ideal medium between body and society.

An analysis dealing with patterns of interpretation, symbolic practices and social interaction processes cannot pursue current debates on medical differences. The resolution of causal arguments from a quasi-objective historical standpoint is not the subject under consideration, but rather the discourse itself. In the process, health statistics, for example, are understood as a symbol, as an element of the social practice of the perception of illness, and not interpreted as the supposed beginning of a causal chain. The objection that the actual existence of tuberculosis patients makes a symbolic interpretation of the tuberculosis discourse impossible, as the illness 'actually existed' is too superficial. It is not the presence or accuracy of statistical values that is being questioned or confirmed, but the interpretations implicit in them that need to be brought to light. The production of statistics is thus a component of illness as a social field, whose meaning and interpretative content is to be unravelled here. The representation of 'self' and 'society' contained in the concept of illness is to be analysed from the point of view of the form of the debate, the methods of treatment and the group represented by those affected.

Both 'body' and 'illness' are socially constructed phenomena whose meaning is only derived through an interactive process. 'Tuberculosis' is the object of individual experience, collective perception, Allied health policies, medical intervention and communal health care within a network of interpersonal relationships, symbols and interpretations, that are now to be untangled for the period of the occupation.

Occupation politics as interaction politics

With reference to the period of occupation this means that the demands of the problem must be resolved again. The question is therefore: Why did tuberculosis become a central theme in health policy discourse during the years of occupation at all? Firstly, the perception of tuberculosis will be examined, i.e. the recognition and definition of an existing problem. In this sense I understand the occupation period as a coming together of German and Allied traditions and 'belief systems'. Individual measures were therefore not just negotiated or decreed; value judgements that had evolved over time were also involved.

Tradition and values did not, then, come together independently of substance and body, but found an actor, a face, in their respective historical representatives. The history of the occupation should, therefore, be seen as the history of the interaction between Germans and Americans. Building on daily contacts, the interdependence or history of the effect of this contact must be followed. Thus we are not looking for institutional or personal divisions from 1945 onwards, but changes and challenges arising from the contact between the occupiers and the occupied. During these contacts previous political, social, and cultural interpretations were condemned, taken to absurd levels, called insignificant, not perceived as being at all relevant, or simply confirmed.

According to Berger and Luckmann's sociological model concerning knowledge the "appearance of an alternative symbolic world of meaning" represents a "danger because its mere existence demonstrates empirically that one's own world of meaning is not without alternative"[49]. This was precisely the situation that could be observed in occupied Germany from May 1945 onwards. Not only had a war, with all the expectations and interpretations of reality that came with it, been lost, but all four occupying powers had also started off with the declared aim of wanting to change German society by eliminating the dominant ideology. I will not, however, examine the de-Nazification process in its strictest sense, but rather the much more far-reaching conflict between two different 'worlds of meaning'. In other words the subject of this examination is the confrontation between different patterns of perception, interpretation, and legitimisation that encompassed the total social reality, symbolically encoded it and, in this way, structured and meaningfully shaped experience, dealings, communication, and knowledge in the everyday life of individuals. Thus political culture will be 'dissected out' of everyday interactions and interpretations and not reduced to the results of opinion polls. In addition, this approach makes it possible to explain the oft-described missionary zeal[50] of American occupation policies that would be incomprehensible in a purely rational political model. This motivation, considered missionary at the time, can only be understood after the political aims of the occupiers have been explained and linked to elementary sets of fundamental values.

This process of negotiation, and the controls that resulted from it, are the important aspects to be looked at. Both levels will be communicated using convictions of legitimacy.

---

[49] Berger and Luckmann, 1980, p. 116.
[50] According to, among many others, Rupieper, p. 27.

2. Case study on tuberculosis during the period of occupation 1945-1949

Tuberculosis as a 'disease of conflict'

a) Perceptions of tuberculosis and traditional patterns of interpretation

"Public Health in general, throughout the area occupied during the past week… is in a good state with no serious epidemics reported"[51], the reports repeated with similar formulations, with relief and disbelief that the worst health fears had not been realised. In view of this positive evaluation of the health situation, tuberculosis played no role in American health reports, or in their health planning, during the first few weeks of the occupation. If it was mentioned, then it was only as an illness of prisoners of war, DPs, and former concentration camp inmates. Tuberculosis thus appeared to be group-specific and limited in terms of the country[52], and represented no danger, in the estimation of army physicians, either for American soldiers or for the American occupation bureaucracy.

Tuberculosis as a 'city disease'

That the fight against tuberculosis received little attention from the Americans is all the more astonishing because after 1945 American health policies concentrated on German cities, and tuberculosis was anyway considered to be a "city disease". The interpretation of tuberculosis as an urban illness was, however, surprisingly absent from both German and American reports of the post-war period. This is remarkable, as tuberculosis established itself during the occupation as a platform for German criticism of the occupying power. Therefore what could have been more obvious than to refer to the prevalence of tuberculosis in the cities, and thus place particular stress on German complaints. The presentation of tuberculosis as a 'city disease' would have meant that American health policies, which laid emphasis on the cities, could have placed it at the centre of their efforts. Why, then, did German medical officers not try to establish this context?

---

[51] RG 331 SHAEF, Historical Sect. entry 54, Box 169, G-5 Section, 7th Army Group, Weekly Report for week ending 31. March 1945, p. 9.

[52] RG 260: 8/59-1/3, Monthly Narrative Report of Public Health (Medical Department Report for Month of August 1945), to Commanding Officer, MG det. E-6, p. 2.

Abandoning the urban frame of reference made tuberculosis ubiquitous. It was no longer limited to certain suburbs, particular social classes or exceptionally exposed people, but metamorphosed into an omnipresent disease, whereby its potential threat – at least discursively – reached unlimited heights. The removal of regional limits led to a removal of structural limits in addition to the removal of social limits, in other words led to the abandonment of analytical limiting categories. The fact that the whole German population could be affected prevented a scientific narrowing down of how, and in what situations, tuberculosis was spread, and made an accurate statistical description of its frequency difficult. This re-evaluation of tuberculosis by German medical officers would initially have provided an opportunity for exerting great political pressure on the occupying power, but at the same time concealed the risk that the Germans would be criticised for being unscientific and acting improperly. The Americans would underline this connection by heavily criticising German tuberculosis statistics in 1947/48.

Tuberculosis as a 'dirty disease'

Tuberculosis finally came to the attention of American medical officers in a context that had played absolutely no role whatsoever in their health policy planning. The concentration camp inmates and DPs often proved to be seriously ill with tuberculosis and had to be treated by American army doctors: "The health of a number of displaced persons and many allied prisoners of war – especially of the Russians – was seriously affected by the presence of tuberculosis. Serious nutritional and vitamin deficiencies were believed to be the contributing causes. The Russian prisoners in particular told the story of having been shifted from camp to camp, finally winding up in the coal mines and heavy industries of the Ruhr, and having been worked twelve hours a day with one day off a month when the coal quota was filled. Diets were seriously deficient. Barracks were crowded"[53]. Although the military doctors knew why the prisoners had contracted tuberculosis[54], they defined it as an illness caused by poor hygiene among Russian prisoners of war and eastern forced labourers: "It was difficult to teach these men, however, the principles of hygiene; they had lived for years under prisoner-of-war camp conditions"[55]. This is all the more astonishing as American treatment of tuberculosis concentrated on the improvement of diet and this treatment

---

[53] *Medical Policies*, 1947, p. 156.

[54] The reports of the G-5 army staff also quote as the reason for contracting tubersulosis: "The bad housing conditions to which the forced laborers had been subjected by the Germans, and… malnutrition." RG 331 SHAEF, Historical Sect. entry 54, Box 170, Historical Report G-5 Section, 6th Army Group for Period 1 through 31 May 1945, p. 20.

[55] *Medical Policies*, 1947, p. 157.

had also proved successful: "When American forces liberated these prisoners and displaced persons all efforts were directed at improving their diet qualitatively. Soon patients… improved clinically"[56]. Concrete measures for fighting the disease and the interpretation of tuberculosis were therefore incongruent. While dietary deficiencies, forced labour and life in the concentration camps were recognised as causes, and compensated for by careful nursing, the idea of the figure of the "unclean tubercular"[57], who "polluted the world" through his indiscipline and who must be taught to develop hygienic and socially acceptable behaviour[58] persisted.

The campaigns against spitting and poor hygiene, raising awareness about tuberculosis, were disciplinary measures aimed at controlling individual behaviour. The 'dirty patient' was tubercular as a result of individual behavioural failings and not because of any external conditions. This pattern of interpretation was also repeated by American medical officers, despite their better knowledge about the actual cause, with the Russian tuberculosis sufferers in mind. The simple mention, in American health reports, of tuberculosis in the form of its being linked to typhoid, reactivated the traditional 'dirty disease' frame of reference. Medically, the connection between typhoid and tuberculosis made little sense because typhoid as an infection, the profiles of those contracting it, and the measures used to fight it, demonstrated that they were dealing with two completely different illnesses. Typhoid and tuberculosis were connected together in the reports and in their actual presentation by the groups of carriers involved. These had a supposed affinity to both diseases as a result of their dirty nature. Thus dirt represented the actual bond between tuberculosis and typhoid. The first mention of tuberculosis in connection with typhoid underlined the component of meaning 'dirt' in an effective form, without ever having to mention it directly. The Americans referred this level of meaning to their Russian patients. Political opportuneness could hardly weaken this pattern of meaning. The Russian tuberculosis sufferers were considered – despite being partners in a military alliance – members of an alien country and, as such, dirty tuberculosis sufferers. If American officers used this interpretation to refer to their Russian allies, what could have been more natural than to extrapolate this interpretation to explain the high rate of tuberculosis among the German population, considering that the living conditions during the first few

---

[56] *Medical Policies*, 1947, p. 157.

[57] For the symbol field 'cleanliness' in the battle against tuberculosis see Gerd Göckenjan, "Über den Schmutz - Überlegungen zur Konzeption von Gesundheitsgefahren", in Jürgen Reulecke and Adelheid Gräfin zu Castell Rüdenhausen (eds.), *Stadt und Gesundheit, Zum Wandel von 'Volksgesundheit' und kommunaler Gesundheitspolitik im 19. und frühen 20. Jahrhundert*, Stuttgart, 1991, p. 125.

[58] Compare Göckenjan, 1991, pp. 125-127.

post-war years really did make German tuberculosis cases not just symbolically, but also in reality, dirty sufferers. Why, then, does one seek the semiotic pair 'tuberculosis' – 'dirt' in vain in the American files?

'Dirt' and 'tuberculosis' did indeed form a pair in post-war Germany. Not in American files but in those of the Germans instead. After 1945, German medical officers were sure that it was the various shortages of the post-war period that led to infection, and not an unhygienic relationship to dirt among certain individuals: shortages of soap, clothing, accommodation and opportunities to wash. The occupying forces were also held responsible for these shortages. Not only did they have these things, but they also kept them away from the Germans or removed the little that remained, even by means of dismantling them. "A clean, washed people is really no danger to the world!"[59] as Stuttgart's Chief of Police hurled at the American secret service in November 1947, in criticism of the supposed absurdity of the Americans' dismantling plans. "The publication of the dismantling lists... resulted... in a psychic shock among all sections of the population[60]. "This "psychic shock" was repeatedly mentioned by the Germans as the cause of contracting tuberculosis. Thus 'dismantling', 'tuberculosis' and 'dirt' became directly connected to one another. "Soap is probably more important than any other means of bringing an epidemic to a stop. These unhealthy conditions have already made a great contribution to increasing epidemics and mortality in Germany. ... The destruction of an industry of great importance for the hygiene and health of a people (could) hardly be justified under the pretext of disarmament, but rather, this destruction really is intended to destroy German competition on the world market. ... In addition, one feels that if there is a policy behind it then it cannot be a humane one, because it is being applied to a helpless people and, not least, to their children"[61]. The 'dirty tuberculosis sufferers' were thus converted from the accused to the accusers. Illness was no longer a sign of failure but a sign of being disadvantaged. In this function it was the only way that Germans could express criticism of the occupying power.

b) National interpretations of tuberculosis

The therapy that the American military doctors used for treating former Russian forced labourers provoked the first conflict about an appropriate fight against tuberculosis in

---

[59] Stuttgart state archives, Hauptaktei Gruppe 0, Bestand 14, Nr. 27, Berichte Polizeipräsident Schumm an CIC, Situationsbericht Nr. 104, 10. Nov. 1947, p. 5.

[60] Stuttgart state archives, Hauptaktei Gruppe 0, Bestand 14, Nr. 27, Berichte Polizeipräsident Schumm an CIC, Situationsbericht Nr. 101, 20. Okt. 1947, p. 1.

[61] Stuttgart state archives, Hauptaktei Gruppe 0, Bestand 14, Nr. 32, Tagesberichte Kripo an CIC Juli 1945 - März 1950, Situationsbericht Nr. 112, pp. 3-4.

the US occupation zone. As a result, American doctors were initially at odds with their Russian colleagues, and not German health officers.

American - Russian differences: "the best of American methods"
or "Russian-type food"?

Doctors in the American armed forces prescribed the measures that were familiar to them in order to cure the former forced labourers of their tuberculosis as quickly as possible: "Attempts were made to establish absolute bed rest – attempts that failed, for the simple reason that bed rest in the treatment of tuberculosis was unknown to the.e persons, particularly to the nationals of the Soviet Union. With the latter, it was against their established principles of treatment of tuberculosis, which commended exercise and sunshine"[62]. Despite the scepticism of the Russian patients, American doctors carried out the therapy as they thought best and proved successful: "Nonetheless, the men who had not died of the disease improved soon after treatment was instituted"[63]. Disregarding this recovery, the conflict over the treatment of Russian patients was not laid to rest, on the contrary it continued to grow: "In spite of this, Russian medical officers criticised American medical methods…" As a result, the Americans authorised the head of their tuberculosis staff to inform the Soviet doctors about the tuberculosis therapies that had been carried out and to convince them of the efficacy of these American measures. However, the reservations of the Russian doctors did not evaporate. On the contrary, the more they knew of the measures being carried out, the more new objections they raised: "On an inspection tour of the hospital with the Chief of the Division of Tuberculosis in the Surgeon General's Office, War Department, a Soviet Army medical officer objected strongly because the patients had not been fed Russian-type food and sufficient bread, even though they had, on the average, gained twenty-five pounds in weight." It was, therefore, not the success of the measures that was decisive in a therapy being accepted. Conforming to national customs and traditions was just as important. Behind the doubts was the suspicion that deviation from tried-and-tested measures would mean that the Russians were getting worse treatment. The awkward constellation of 'trans-national treatment' of Russian patients by American doctors encouraged the hypothesis that patients were being given different, i.e. inferior, treatment because their nationality was different. The Americans immediately reacted to this implied reproach by pointing out that their own soldiers had also received this treatment, which they backed up with the whole

---

[62] *Medical Policies*, 1947, p. 157.
[63] *Medical Policies*, 1947, p. 157.

authority of American science. "Objection was taken also to the prohibition against physical exercise and sunshine, although the best of American methods of treatment called for absolute bed rest and avoidance of sunshine. Soviet authorities objected also to the use of collapse therapy. It proved extraordinarily difficult to convince the Russians of the fact that the best and latest methods of treatment were being given their men – the same treatment that American soldiers were receiving…" American efforts to resolve this conflict ended, however, when fundamental therapeutic views were questioned. "… every effort was made to comply with their wishes, insofar as they were compatible with fundamental precepts of treatment of the disease. There was no other course left open but to return the Soviet nationals to their homeland at the earliest opportunity"[64]. The retention of elementary medical practices was thus deemed more important than any political strategic considerations.

Of central importance was the confirmation of predominant images of illness against the background of varying national opinions. A compromise in fundamental interpretations of illness would have meant giving up national convictions, which is why neither Russian nor American doctors were prepared to do so. Even "scientific methods and proofs" failed to form a bridge by which these basic differences in interpretation could be set aside. The repudiation of accepted methods of treatment by doctors of another nationality would obviously imply a low opinion of the particular 'other patient' involved. The Russian doctors did not intervene because the American doctors were obviously mistreating Russian men, but because they treated them differently. 'Differently' here implied potentially 'worse'. This suspicion was not even contradicted by the obvious recovery of the Russian patients.

The national component in the differences in the interpretation of illness made this conflict so delicate that it could not be resolved, but simply avoided by a transfer of Russian tuberculosis sufferers to the USSR and their continued treatment by doctors of their own nationality. The transfer of Russian patients for the reason of national differences in conceptions of illness was the result of a conflict *inter pares*. But how did one deal with differing interpretations of illness that arose between unequal partners and that could not, as in the above case, be avoided but had to be settled? Did the hierarchy of power, that existed between German and American medical officers, have any influence of the handling of similar conflicts?

---

[64] All quotations from *Medical Policies*, 1947, p. 158.

The feebleness of German ideas of democracy

At the turn of the century tuberculosis was already the most important widespread disease in Germany. Prophylactic efforts during the time of the Empire were only temporarily successful because the First World War drove tuberculosis statistics up to the same level as in 1897, when it was at its most widespread[65]. The loss of this war by Germany and the widespread incidence of tuberculosis throughout all social classes and age groups, led to the illness being increasingly seen as a threat to the whole nation and not just the working classes[66]. The war transformed tuberculosis into a disease that could potentially infect anyone[67]. Workers still caught the disease more often but this was no longer primarily attributed to poor individual hygiene but to the stresses of war and defeat that had brought distress, poverty, illness and democracy to the people. The nationalisation of the German interpretation of tuberculosis was thus also loaded with democratic theory. It was not the success of Weimar tuberculosis prevention that was noticed but the problematic pressure caused by the high number of sufferers. The stronger feelings of being threatened led, in 1923, to the introduction of compulsory registration for tuberculosis cases in Prussia. The unwavering social and hygienic battle against tuberculosis did not assert itself when the illness was at its peak, during the time of the Empire, but during the Republic. The increased attention that tuberculosis now received, its ubiquitous presence in Weimar health policy discourse, paradoxically allowed democracy to appear responsible for the high tuberculosis infection rate. According to this interpretation, the World War was only seen as a peripheral cause of the high rate of infection, it acted principally as a switch for a now altered perception of tuberculosis as a 'widespread disease'. The intense concentration of Weimar health care on the problem of tuberculosis, and the presence of tuberculosis in political, social, economic and health discourse it brought about in the first German democracy, had made tuberculosis into a German symbol of world economic crisis, hunger and unemployment. The various critics of the new German Republic were pleased to adopt tuberculosis as a symbol. In the use of this easily understood representation system it was irrelevant that democracy was busy trying to heal the damage caused by the Empire and the World War. Despite the numerous tuberculosis care centres democracy appeared consumptive and feeble. The linkage between criticism of democracy, national defeat, distress, poverty, and anxiety about

---

[65] Sachße and Tennstedt, 1988, p. 115.

[66] Sachße and Tennstedt, 1988, p. 117.

[67] Compare e.g. Karl Ernst Ranke, *Richtlinien der Tuberculosisbekämpfung nach dem Krieg*, Würzburg, Würzburger Abhandlungen aus dem Gesamtgebiet der praktischen Medizin, 1919, XIX. Band.

the future had become so deeply ingrained in the German interpretation of tuberculosis that these linkages were immediately reactivated after 1945.

Consequently as early as September 1945 German health officials introduced their tuberculosis report with the observation that: "The fight against tuberculosis has always been a very urgent problem for the German Public Health Office"[68]. Health statistics were not employed in the main argument for dealing with tuberculosis. Instead this reference to a traditional field of activity for German health officials was used.

Weimar health politicians had turned the successful fight of the shortage-based disease, tuberculosis, into a yardstick of the equal opportunities, integration, and options for the future brought about by democracy, an aim that was only partially achieved. Thus, after 1945, the rising tuberculosis rates again became a symbol for the inadequacy of a democratic system in the eyes of the German people. Tuberculosis became the medium whereby the constant shortages were indivisibly linked to the genesis of the German democratic administrative system. This made the "consumptive appearance of the German democratic model" appear constitutional, ontological. It was communicated through the Germans' "weakness", the "physical and spiritual decay of past accomplishments", the "loss of courage to face life and lack of *joie de vivre*"[69] brought about by tuberculosis. "Exhaustion and despondency, obsession with criticism and argument, bitterness, and hate dictate the lethargic mood of the people." The 'difference' of this disease brought about the formulation of the implicit reference that no democratic state could be created with these ill people. There was only one way to remedy the deterioration in the constitution of both people and the democratic idea: the deficient nutritional situation would have to be improved with the help of the Americans. Thus, at the end of 1947, the tuberculosis debate became increasingly concentrated on the theme of nutrition[70]. The American food requested by the Germans was to restore those with tuberculosis to health and thus simultaneously 'feed' the new German democracy.

German tuberculosis discourse during the years of occupation had a double significance: it stood for a retreat from political events, apathy and criticism of American concepts and, simultaneously, it was an appeal for assistance. Thus on the one hand tuberculosis

---

[68] RG 260: 8/59-1/1, General Food Condition for TBC Hospitals, original text in German, translation of a German letter.

[69] Stuttgart state archives, Hauptaktei Gruppe 0, Bestand 14, Nr. 27, Berichte Polizeipräsident Schumm an CIC, Situationsbericht Nr. 101, 20. Oct. 1947, p. 2.

[70] Compare, among many others, e.g. Stuttgart state archives, Hauptaktei Gruppe 0, Bestand 14, Nr. 27, Berichte Polizeipräsident Schumm an CIC, Situationsbericht Nr. 82, June 1947, p. 3; Stuttgart state archives, Hauptaktei Gruppe 0, Bestand 14, Nr. 27, Berichte Polizeipräsident Schumm an CIC, Situationsbericht Nr. 97, 22. Sept. 1947, p. 1.

represented German democratic reservations and the fear that this form of state would bring with it shortages and disease, and so fail, while on the other hand German medical officers and police officials oscillated between concern and hope that the American occupation forces, that were so determinedly committed to a comprehensive democratisation, would also fight tuberculosis energetically and help eradicate it.

The reference to a health emergency had a further function regarding this democratisation. A sick German population, German politicians never tired of mentioning, would not only be incapable of constructing a democratic form of government. They could not either be made responsible for this failure that would have been the result of illness. "The three post-war years up to now have brought about a considerable reduction in the spiritual and physical strength of the German people. A country where hunger, misery, social need and economic chaos continue to rule, can never take its place as an active component in the defensive front against Communism"[71]. Thus, responsibilities were suddenly turned upside down. In this setting, it was not the Germans that were responsible for the success of the young democracy but the USA. Building on this argument a demand for assistance, and not a request, could now be made to the occupying power. "Great concern is being expressed over the unstoppable spread of tuberculosis. The conditions under which the people have to live have become a veritable breeding ground for tuberculosis. This disease, resulting from poor diet, housing, and living conditions, would never have become so widespread during the time of good working and living conditions. … If the spread of tuberculosis continues as at present than at least 2.2 million Germans will be seriously ill with tuberculosis by 1950. This horrifying prospect faces every single German. This argument is supported by the overexploitation of the body and health forced on the undernourished population just to keep going. The people are of one opinion: that the occupying power is in a position to relieve this great poverty of a nation that is being helplessly sucked down to the depths, by delivering medicines, by helpful support, and by the building of hospitals and convalescence homes"[72]. For the failed Weimar democracy tuberculosis implied, as a metaphor, not only the innocence of the Germans regarding the collapse of the democratic state system, but also their inability to build a democratic administration of society using their own resources. The reference system 'tuberculosis', 'defeat' and 'shortages', that had already dominated the years since the First World War, were immediately reactivated after 1945 and applied to the political system of administration.

---

[71] Stuttgart state archives, Hauptaktei Gruppe 0, Bestand 14, Nr. 32, Tagesberichte Kripo an CIC Juli 1945 - März 1950, Situationsbericht Nr. 17, 30.03.1948, pp. 1-2.

[72] Stuttgart state archives, Hauptaktei Gruppe 0, Bestand 14, Nr. 27, Tagesberichte Kripo an CIC Juli 1945 - März 1950, Situationsbericht Nr. 109, Feb. 1948, pp. 4-5.

The close linkage that existed between health and civil administrations was clearly revealed in the personified consideration of Germany in German reports: "If the world, and in particular the large western nations, are interested in a political and economic recovery in Germany, then they should really start doing something and not just keep on debating and discussing, because otherwise 'the patient will die before the deliberating doctors can bring about a cure through the administering of fortifying medicine'"[73]. It was not only the Germans themselves that were ill and feeble – efforts towards democratisation were also ailing. As long as the Germans were tormented by the consumptive and tubercular decay of their constitutions, democratic ideas would simply remain an ideology and thus verbally equated with communist models of administration: "Doctors, in particular, refer with serious concern to the advancing decay in the constitution of the working population. ... The trust placed in democratic development by the larger part of the willing population is increasingly in *decline* and is making room for a growing distrust in democratic ideology. Those circles that desire a quiet transition to a new democracy hope that the American occupying forces also recognise this growing danger for the future political development of Germany deriving from the spread of poverty. They see that it is only by ensuring adequate supplies of food... that the German people can be freed of the creeping poisons of nihilism and radicalism with which every day new segments of the population are being infected"[74]. The metaphor of illness used here contains a further reference to tuberculosis. Tuberculosis was subsumed under harmful toxins in medical literature[75], the tuberculous body was considered to be poisoned by toxins[76]. If a German model of democracy was to be successful in the future then this poisoning had to be brought to a stop. In this sense, the tuberculosis metaphor included the urgent appeal to the occupying power for substantial help in the detoxification of society and in the democratisation process.

It was not any acute illness that became the form of expression for German difficulties during their democratisation but the creeping, not always fatal, tuberculosis. The chronic 'people's disease', tuberculosis, was the ideal embodiment of the structural problems to be solved during the de-Nazification of German society. In the successful construction of this new form of state it was less a matter of dealing with an acute crisis than the alteration of fundamental structural preconditions. In the same way that those

---

[73] Stuttgart state archives, Hauptaktei Gruppe 0, Bestand 14, Nr. 32, Berichte Polizeipräsident Schumm an CIC, Situationsbericht Nr. 119, April 1948, p. 3.

[74] Stuttgart city archive, Hauptaktei Gruppe 0, Bestand 14, Nr. 27, Berichte Polizeipräsident Schumm an CIC, Situationsbericht Nr. 85, 28. June 1947, pp. 1-2.

[75] Compare Öhring (1981), pp. 85-86, reference there to Emil Kraeplin, *Compendium der Psychiatrie*, Leipzig: 1883, p. 26f., and W. Hollmann, "Zur klinischen Psychologie des Tuberculosiskranken", *Der Tuberculosisarzt*, Stuttgart, 1948, p. 558.

[76] For method of action of 'tuberculosis toxins' Öhring, p. 87.

who had tuberculosis required lessons on their behaviour, economic support, security and a sunny, clean environment, it seemed that German democratisation was also in need of reasonable economic preconditions, functional institutions and political optimism. In this sense, the discourse on tuberculosis contained features of simultaneous criticism and acceptance of American policies of de-Nazification and democratisation. Germans and Americans differed, above all, in their confidence in a successful outcome to the fight against tuberculosis. German anxieties about tuberculosis had been, as it turned out in 1948, exaggerated[77]. This exaggerated German anxiety was also motivated by the fear that the democratisation project was, from the start, endangered by the rising incidence of tuberculosis. American doctors, on the other hand, assessed the tuberculosis situation from 1945 to autumn of 1947 as a threat to health hardly worthy of consideration. The vitality of American ideas of democracy did not, at first, allow them to take a consumptive democracy seriously. Against this background, the American interpretation of tuberculosis should be seen as a weakening of the German pattern of interpretation. The stubborn refusal of American doctors to see any comprehensive threat in the form of tuberculosis split the semiotic pair 'democracy' – 'tuberculosis' apart. The occupation force that clearly characterised itself as democratic saw no threat to democracy, the future, or the nation from the number of cases of tuberculosis, and simply got on with the pragmatic and calm preparation and equipping of more tuberculosis hospitals. They were totally convinced that the fight against tuberculosis would be successful, and that the dominant German patterns of perception, equating tuberculosis with economic crisis, political radicalism, and the failure of democratisation, would be repudiated as a result.

3. Tuberculosis as a 'consensual disease'

Thus from 1947 onwards, tuberculosis gained increasing importance in the eyes of American medical officers. They now agreed with German medical officers that the rising numbers of tuberculosis patients was a health problem that should be taken seriously and required intervention. The "slow disease", tuberculosis, was only able to jump the sensibility barrier of American health politicians after it had been present for many years. From 1946 onwards, tuberculosis rates came closer and closer to the American health policy's limit of perception until in 1947 it finally passed it with rates

---

[77] "According to this we have a tuberculosis mortality rate that… is much lower than we expected" in report by Dr. Schrag, Senior Medical Council, Social Department, Stuttgart city administration. Stuttgart state archives, Hauptaktei Gruppe 5, Reg. Nr. 5052-0, laufende Nr. 150, Die Tuberculosis und ihre Bekämpfung in Stuttgart, nach dem Stand vom 1. Jan. 1948, Sitzung der Sozialabteilung of 2. Feb. 1948, p. 1.

of up to 60%. When, finally, both German and American doctors agreed on the significance of tuberculosis as a widespread disease, they continued to be divided over the strategies that needed to be employed in the fight against it.

a) Tuberculosis as an area of competence

Tuberculosis was obviously underestimated by the Americans because it is almost always a latent disease initially, with a long incubation period. Meanwhile, German anxieties proved to be at least partially justified. In this process, German fears were to a large extent founded on developments after the First World War: "The whole dreadful tragedy that we experienced during and after the First World War is repeating itself now to a considerably amplified extent. In Württemberg, war losses resulting from tuberculosis in the first four years of the war just ended are higher in absolute terms, and relatively very much higher, than during the same period of the First World War, judging from the tuberculosis mortality curves…"[78] reported Dr. Schrag, *Obermedizinalrat* (Senior Medical Officer), in October 1946 in a report to the Ministry of the Interior. The experiences of the First World War proved to be an advantage, in terms of competence, enjoyed by the German health politicians over their American counterparts. However, after the American officers had finally recognised the seriousness of the tuberculosis problem in the summer of 1947, they hardly lost any time at all analysing the false assessment they had made in the past, but immediately concentrated on the newly recognised danger posed by tuberculosis.

German criticism of the occupying power had, since 1946, covered up the rising tuberculosis statistics, and these statistics now became the subject of longer and more heated arguments between the Germans and the Americans. Communication about the disease intensified with the increasing involvement of the Americans in the tuberculosis question whereby inferior German reporting soon came to light. The health administrators of the Military Government now began to pay more attention to German tuberculosis reports and soon discovered that German statistics were so full of mistakes that they could not be used as a basis for discussion. German statistics showed a reduction in the mortality rate in the first quarter of 1948 of 2.3% compared to 1947, though the rate of new infections showed a 49% increase since December 1947. This caused American public health officers to remark that: "The extreme suddenness of this

---

[78] Stuttgart main state archives, EA 2/009 Innenministerium, Abt. Gesundheitswesen 1945-1973, Bü. 2310, Bericht über Tuberculosissituation nach dem Krieg, Obermed.-Rat Schrag an Innenministerium, p. 1, translated.

reported increase in new cases led OMGH public health officials to re-examine the bases upon which tuberculosis statistics were founded, and this led, through the remainder of the year, to constant skirmishes with German public health authorities as to the validity of their statistics. The first investigation concerning TB statistics initiated by OMGH concerned suspected irregularities in the number of active closed tuberculosis cases reported for children "[79]. The conflict intensified over the years. After lengthy argument lasting the whole year, a rapprochement was finally reached at the end of 1948[80]. Tuberculosis statistics were in need of correction mainly because many Germans were reporting themselves to be ill with tuberculosis in the hope of receiving larger food rations.

"During the last quarter of 1948 'Military Government' won a significant battle with German public health officials when they were persuaded to revise their old reports and initiate new ones in the interests of accurate information on tuberculosis[81]" was the summary of American health officers at the end of 1948. A report by a tuberculosis investigating committee, sent to Germany by the American army in February 1948 to compile their own useable figures and estimates, played a substantial role in this success. Under the chairmanship of Dr. E. Long, since 1945 advisor to the American armed forces on questions of tuberculosis and chairman of the National Tuberculosis Association[82], the commission came to the conclusion that tuberculosis mortality rates, after an increase due to the war, were already falling again and had almost reached pre-war levels throughout the whole zone. The total tuberculosis infection rate in Germany was about as high as in Great Britain and far lower than in France or other parts of Europe. The number of officially reported cases was rising and German doctors – according to Long – still continued to emphasise this as evidence for the seriousness of the situation. All the same the commission had come to the conclusion that this increase was primarily a statistical phenomenon caused by improved recording techniques and more self-reporting by those affected, triggered by increased food rations for those with tuberculosis. "The tuberculosis problem appears

[79] RG 260: 8/189-2/6, Hessian main state archives, Wiesbaden, dept. 649, OMG-Hessen, Historical Division, Historical report 1948 by William R. Karsteter, Historian, OMGH, Chap. III, Public Health, p. 477.

[80] RG 260: 8/189-2/6, Hessian main state archives, Wiesbaden, Abt. 649, OMG-Hessen, Historical Division, Historical report 1948 by William R. Karsteter, Historian, OMGH, Chap. III, Public Health, p. 479.

[81] RG 260: 8/189-2/6, Hessian main state archives, Wiesbaden, Abt. 649, OMG-Hessen, Historical Division, Historical report 1948 by William R. Karsteter, Historian, OMGH, Chap. III, Public Health, p. 479.

[82] Esmond Long and Virginia Cameron (eds.), *National Tuberculosis Association* 1904-1955, New York, 1959.

well in hand[83]" is how Esmond Long concluded his report. The "tuberculosis argument" was thus robbed of its statistical basis[84].

The significance of tuberculosis in German-American interactions grew with the numerical reduction. This paradoxical effect was based on the proof of American competence provided by this statistical re-evaluation. This made it possible to continue the tuberculosis discourse using an altered allocation of roles. "The recommendations of specialists in the epidemiology and control of tuberculosis will undoubtedly be of value to the German health authorities"[85]. Tuberculosis therefore no longer functioned as the Germans' basis of need for the American occupation force, but confirmed America's leading health policy role.

b) Tuberculosis as an area of co-operation

In addition to German statistics, the measures the Germans had undertaken to fight tuberculosis were also evaluated as unsatisfactory and inadequate by the Military Government. How did this exchange of roles, whereby American officers criticised the inefficiency of the Germans' fight against tuberculosis although for over two years it had been the Germans themselves that had repeatedly emphasised the need for intensive tuberculosis control, come about?

Since the middle of 1946, American health policies had focused, once the first phase emphasizing the rebuilding of the German health system and controlling infectious diseases was over, on reforming German health administration. The German health bureaucracy was repeatedly criticised for organisational deficiencies and inefficiency[86]. From the American perspective, what could be more reasonable than to link

---

[83] RG 260, 5/333-1/4, OMGUS, Tuberculosis in Germany, Summary Draft, Dr. E. Long to OMGUS, Commanding General, Tuberculosis in U.S. Zone, Germany, p. 2.

[84] RG 260, 5/333-1/4, OMGUS, CAD- PHBr, TB Statistics for Department of Army TB Mission; and: RG 260, 5/333-1/4, OMG-Hessen, CAD, Tuberculosis in the German Population, US Zone Germany, by Sartwell, Moseley, and Long. RG 260, 5/333-1/7, Office of the United States High Commissioner for Germany, Office of Public Affairs, Education & Cultural Relation Div., Tuberculosis death rate in Germany.

[85] RG 260 5/333-1/6, 390/42/33/4-5; Tuberculosis-correspondence, OMG-Hessen, Public Health and Welfare Branch, Department of the Army, Tuberculosis Mission, p. 1.

[86] See e.g. RG 260, 5/331-1/11, Office of Military Government Land Württemberg-Baden, Weakness of the Public Health System of Land Württemberg-Baden, Letter Office of Military Government Land Württemberg-Baden to Minister President, Dr. Reinhod Maier; 390/49/31/5-6, Box 222, Militärregierung-WB: Central Records, Personnel & Administration Div. 1945-49, Deficiencies of Baden Public Health System; RG 260: 12/75-2/5, 390/49-50/35-1/6-1 Box: 231, Militärregierung-WB: Records of the PH-Advisor, Deficiencies of Baden Public Health System.

this criticism to a reference to a health problem that had also been given top priority by German health politicians. The need for re-organisation must have appeared totally logical for German politicians if it was accompanied by an improvement in the fight against tuberculosis.

Furthermore, the new attention that American medical officers paid to bringing tuberculosis under control was not only based on the varying tolerance thresholds of the Military Government's public health teams on the one hand, and the German health authorities on the other hand, but was founded on the clear drop in the infection rates for sexually transmitted diseases [87]. Venereal diseases had, up to then, been the main focus of attention of American medical officers. The reduction in the number of patients with venereal diseases resulted in an increase in American capacity that they could now be brought to bear on the fight against tuberculosis [88].

In concrete terms, the increasing similarity between German and American perceptions of tuberculosis was brought about by intensive co-operation, argument and discussion between German and American medical officers that finally led to an alignment of perspectives. Furthermore, the transfer of responsibility for tuberculosis questions to the Germans made it easier for the Americans to accept that a tuberculosis problem did indeed exist, as now it was no longer the Military Government but the German health administrations that would be responsible for increasing rates of infection.

The new American attention to tuberculosis was an offer to the Germans in many different ways. Dr. Long had indeed emphasised in his tuberculosis report that he saw no uncontrollable health problem in the tuberculosis situation in Germany. At the same time, however, he offered comprehensive ideas on what means could be used to support the fight against tuberculosis in Germany both materially and financially [89]. The Germans had repeatedly received instructions to produce detailed lists that would be needed to improve the fight against tuberculosis. This brought about an end to the undifferentiated complaints about "general shortages" as the cause of the high

---

[87] Compare RG 260: 8/59-1/9, Summary of Public Health Activities in Land Hessen, for Feb. 1948, p. 1: "Increase of venereal diseases during the past two years".

[88] Venereal diseases were also considered more important than tuberculosis even after 1948. This can be seen from, among others, the fact that responsibility for venereal diseases stayed with the Military Government, while all other areas of health were transferred to German authorities. RG 260: 8/59-1/9, OMG-Hessen, Abt. 649, Public Health Division, Summary of Public Health Activities in Land Hessen, 1. Jan. 1948 - 31. March 1948, p. 1.

[89] RG 260, 5/333-1/4, OMGUS, Tuberculosis in Germany Summary Draft, Dr. E. Long to OMGUS, Commanding General, Tuberculosis in U.S. Zone, Germany.

tuberculosis infection rate, and these lists became an expression of the real and pragmatic support provided by the American army and occupation administration. Making
lists of the X-ray film, medicines, hospital beds, blankets, laboratory materials, etc. that
were required, forced the Germans to be more aware of the capacities that were available and to provide concrete lists of requirements instead of the unfocused complaints
that they had been making up to then. In this way, the diffuse feelings of powerlessness
and of being threatened dissolved into easily comprehensible lists. The creation of these
lists of German requirements brought about a new conceptualisation of the perception
of tuberculosis – as a conquerable problem that could be handled. The sheets and X-ray
film handed over to the Germans from American army stocks, the medicines and vaccines donated by private organisations, and the buildings, fuel and transport provided
by OMGUS, were both a symbol for the "active help of the Military Government[90]" in
the fight against tuberculosis and an empirical de-mythologising of tuberculosis. The
American occupation power's pragmatic campaign strategy stripped tuberculosis of its
historical significance and reduced it to an illness that was unspectacular because it
could be conquered. In this sense American tuberculosis policies in Germany from
1947 onwards led to an immediate reshaping of the Germans' perception of tuberculosis. The help offered resulted in direct material assistance and simultaneously
implied an conceptual re-interpretation.

c) Tuberculosis as an area of modernisation

As, in the opinion of the American army's tuberculosis mission, the tuberculosis problem was being controlled well by the German tuberculosis care system, the American
officers no longer saw any actual, compelling reasons for remaining active in the fight
against tuberculosis. Despite this, the American occupation officers applied considerable money, time and energy to providing information on the latest results of
research. The aim of this activity was obviously not to avert a threatening health danger but to provide persuasive orientation on the methods available. The intention of
the American medical officers was to convince German medical officers of their own
ideas and value judgements and the resulting preferred political methods of getting
things done[91].

---

[90] Stuttgart main state archives, EA 2/009 Innenministerium, Abt. Gesundheitswesen 1945-1973,
Bü. 2310, Mängel in der Tuberculosisbekämpfung in Württemberg, p. 1, translated.

[91] Nullmeier, Frank, "Wissen und Policy-Forschung. Wissenspolitologie und rhetorisch-
dialektisches Handlungsmodell", Hértier, *op. cit.*, 1993, pp. 175-198, at p. 191.

That health policy had, in the meantime, become a political field in which the Americans used communication and interaction as the central pattern of behaviour in a democracy, and linked modernisation, self-reflection and the development of adequate health care with political ambitions, can be seen from their activities in spring 1949. At this time they were still trying to make the German tuberculosis solution more modern and media-friendly: "In an effort to develop an informed public and medical profession, news releases and a radio script concerning tuberculosis in Land Hessen was prepared to factually present this subject. Military Government prepared these items because German officials, even though they concur in the contents of the story, are hesitant to make initial releases of this type "[92]. Such late action would have had little sense if it were only to do with tuberculosis prophylaxis in its narrowest sense. Such emphatic involvement by the American medical officers as late as March 1949, in other words at a time when the end of the occupation was in sight and the fight against tuberculosis had long been in German hands, cannot be explained using the reductive model of a functional health policy. "… bringing (the public health) department(s) up to standards in line with those of the most modern Western ideas[93]" had become the aim of American efforts. Thus American tuberculosis policy now acted in the service of Americanisation, a functionalisation, that was only made possible at all in this form thanks to the effective tuberculosis control that had gone before. The disappearance of tuberculosis as a danger to health enabled this disease, so central for German health politicians, to serve the purposes of the democratisation of the Germans and their assimilation into western interpretations of illness and methods of treatment. What is remarkable is that the American occupation officers pursued this adaptation to western standards in the case of the fight against tuberculosis in an area where the actual measures used for treatment exhibited great similarities. How then could one's sights be set on the political aim of 'Americanisation' in a sector of health care where there were hardly any practical differences? The project of Americanisation gains plausibility when it is referred to the symbolic significance of tuberculosis. The Weimar Republic gradually lost its relevance as a yardstick and starting point for the German fight against tuberculosis during the dispute with the American doctors and officers. The new yardstick was the "most modern western ideas", that were being practised in the USA. Scientifically, increasing reference was made to American

---

[92] RG 260: 8/62-2/3, Hessisches Hauptstaatsarchiv Wiesbaden, Abt. 649, OMG-Hessen, Public Health and Welfare Branch, Summary of Public Health Activites in Land Hessen for February, 1949, p. 1.

[93] RG 260: 8/62-2/3, Hessisches Hauptstaatsarchiv Wiesbaden, Abt. 649, OMG-Hessen, Public Health Division, Summary of Public Health Activites in Land Hessen for the Second Half of 1949.

capacities and American specialist publications, initially in the occupation zone and later in the young Republic. It was not so much the practice of the fight against tuberculosis that changed as a result, rather its derivation and legitimisation was altered.

Tuberculosis was not just a political field on which the convergence of Germans and Americans was successfully practised. In the following period it also functioned as a marker for effective German-American co-operation.

Both partners weaved 'tuberculosis' into a branched network of significance that strongly coloured their perceptions of the disease. These different patterns of perception initially divided the Germans and the Americans, but simultaneously, however, offered an opportunity for reconciliation. Perceptions of illness can be given a new accent more rapidly (by the acceptance of new interpretations), and images of illness can be aligned more quickly, than the actual statistics on the illness. In the case of tuberculosis the reconciliation of the two perceptions of the disease was thus made easier because tuberculosis no longer played a role as a threatening disease and therefore, in effect, all methods and traditions of treatment could be declared to be successful while statistics were improving. This, however, also means that the arduous process of evaluating the particular patterns of interpretation relevant to tuberculosis and deliberately referring them to social, political and cultural processes did not take place.

Esmond Long, tuberculosis consultant to OMGUS and HICOG, summed up as follows in September 1950: "The Western Zone of Germany has experienced a remarkable and in the case of Berlin, an extraordinary decline in tuberculosis mortality in the last two years. … Great credit is due to the German Public Health authorities for this remarkable achievement. The public health officials of the occupying powers, also, are entitled to credit, for they have stimulated the antituberculosis campaign constantly for five years"[94].

Thus, at the end of the occupation period, the shared fight against tuberculosis turned out to the complete satisfaction of both parties. The American approach, the careful, step-by-step implementation of their perception, and the constant offer of certain preferred treatment strategies without any binding patterns, allowed the Germans to retain their identity despite having to give up their traditional points of reference. The

---

[94] RG 260, 5/333-1/5, Office of the United States High Commissioner for Germany, Office of Public Affairs, Education & Cultural Relation Div., Report of Consultant on Tuberculosis Problems, p. 1.

decoupling of the interpretation of tuberculosis from national feelings of identity was fundamental to this. The relatively great similarity between the two 'catalogues' of measures provided German doctors and health politicians with a supportive continuity, on the basis of which they could reformulate the justification and aim of their fight against tuberculosis and slowly adapt to the patterns of the occupying power. Tuberculosis, in new frames of reference, no longer functioned as a symbol of national defeat and the isolation of the German people, but symbolised their international re-integration.

The Americans considered health policy to be a sensitive political field and, as such, put it into German hands only very late. The varied functionalisation of health themes by German medical officers and health politicians also illustrates their multiple linkages. From this position, tuberculosis could become a paradigm for the intentions and course of American occupation policy, and later consolidate itself into a symbol of a successful German-American co-operation by cutting out, or suppressing, all dissonances and conflicts.

Spain

Health and Public Policy in Spain during the Early Francoist Regime (1936-1951): the Tuberculosis Problem [1]

Jorge Molero-Mesa[*]

1. Introduction

From the late 19th century to the middle of the 20th, tuberculosis was regarded as the 'social disease' *par excellence* throughout the Western world[2]. Its high morbidity, specific mortality and lack of an effective treatment added to its tendency to attack principally society's productive members – 80% of its victims were workers between the ages of 15 and 35 – made it 'disastrous' for the economic development and national efficiency of industrialised countries, and it played a big part in the gradual degeneration of the race[3].

In addition, medico-social studies of tuberculosis in Spain revealed a disease directly related to the poverty in which the proletariat lived. As well as poor living conditions – manifest in malnutrition, foul and overcrowded living quarters lacking water, electrical

---

[*] This work forms part of Research Project PS91-0178 (DGICT).

[1] An early version of this paper was published in Jorge Molero-Mesa, "Enfermedad y Previsión Social en España bajo el Primer Franquismo (1936-1951). El frustrado Seguro Obligatorio contra la Tuberculosis", *Dynamis*, 14, 1994, pp. 199-225.

[2] Barbara Bates, *Bargaining for Life. A Social History of Tuberculosis, 1876-1938*, Philadelphia, University of Pennsylvania Press, 1992; M. Caldwell, *The Last Crusade: The War on Consumption, 1862-1954*, New York, Atheneum, 1988; Sheila M. Rothman, *Living in the Shadow of Death. Tuberculosis and the Social Experience of Illness in American History*, New York, Basic Books, 1994; Dominique Dessertine and Olivier Faure, *Combattre la tuberculose. 1900-1940*, Lyon, Presses Universitaires de Lyon, 1988; P. Guillaume, *Du désespoir au salut: les tuberculeux aux XIXe et XXe siècles*, Aris, Aubier, 1986; William Johnston, *The Modern Epidemic. A History of Tuberculosis in Japan*, Cambridge, Massachusetts, Harvard University Press, 1995; Peter Reinicke, *Tuberkulosefürsorge. Der Kampf gegen eine Geissel der Menschheit. Dargestellt am Beispiel Berlins 1895-1945*, Weinheim, Deutscher Studien Verlag, 1988; Wolfgang Seeliger, *Die "Volksheilstätten-Bewegung" in Deutschland um 1900: zur Ideengeschichte der Sanatoriumstherapie für Tuberkulöse*, München, Profil, 1988; Smith, F.B., *The Retreat of Tuberculosis, 1850-1950*, London, Croom Helm, 1988; Michael E. Teller, *The Tuberculosis Movement. A Public Health Campaign in the Progressive Era*, New York, Greenwood Press, 1988.

[3] Linda Bryder, *Below the Magic Mountain. A Social History of Tuberculosis in Twentieth-Century Britain*, Oxford, Clarendon Press, 1988; Jorge Molero Mesa, *Estudios Medicosociales sobre la Tuberculosis en la España de la Restauración*, Madrid, Mº de Sanidad y Consumo, 1987, pp. 28-36; Jorge Molero-Mesa, "Fundamentos sociopolíticos de la prevención de la enfermedad en la primera mitad del siglo XX español", *Trabajo Social y Salud*, nº 32, 1999, pp. 19-59.

light or drainage, and long working hours in appalling conditions – there were also cultural aspects conducive to the spread of the disease. Among such 'popular habits', sexual promiscuity, onanism and alcoholism stood out as weakeners of the body. Also, the lack of personal and domestic hygiene together with the habit of spitting favoured the spread of Koch's bacillus. Finally, illiteracy, rebelliousness, superstition and fatalism, all of them traits pointed to by hygienists as being characteristic of the working class, hindered the acceptance of advice on how to avoid the disease[4].

In spite of scientific acknowledgement of all the aforementioned factors in the origin of tuberculosis, the anti-tuberculosis campaigns organised throughout the Western world, as a key part of the new Social Medicine, failed to base their strategies on the improvement of the awful living conditions of workers. Instead they concentrated their efforts on modifying the 'consumption habits' of the popular classes. The alibi offered for this approach was that it was for the purposes of bacteriological science – the breaking of the epidemiological chain of tuberculosis[5].

According to Alfons Labisch[6], this cultural habit-changing offensive launched by Social Medicine, together with the implementation of Compulsory Health Insurance, played a very important role in the process of civilisation, rationalisation and social disciplining of the working classes. In the final extreme, these health campaigns contributed to the proletariat's permanent internalisation of the bourgeois ideal of life based on the attainment of health.

Following this line of thought, we have focused our study on the tuberculosis problem in an especially significant period for the recent history of Spanish public health. Indeed, from 1936 to 1951, the various public health policies emanating from the new totalitarian State defined a special model of healthcare, the consequences of which were felt in Spanish society until the proclamation of the *Ley General de Sanidad (General Law on Public Health)* of 1984. Even today, many of the problems posed in

---

[4] Jorge Molero-Mesa, "La tuberculosis como enfermedad social en los estudios epidemiológicos españoles anteriores a la Guerra Civil", *Dynamis*, 9, 1989, pp. 185-224.

[5] Michael Worboys, "The Sanatorium Treatment for Consumption in Britain 1890-1914", in John V. Pickstone, (ed.) *Medical Innovation in Historical Perspective*, London, Macmillan, 1992, pp. 47-71.

[6] Alfons Labisch, "Doctors, Workers and the Scientific Cosmology of the Industrial World: The Social Construction of 'Health' and the 'Homo Hygienicus'", *Journal of Contemporary History*, 20, 1985, pp. 599-615; Alfons Labisch, *Homo Hygienicus. Gesundheit und Medizin in der Neuzeit,* Frankfurt, Campus Verlag, 1992.

public health have their origins in the early part of the Spanish post-war period. In the construction of this healthcare model, the tuberculosis problem became the catalyst that brought existing differences between the power groups of the new regime to the surface, and unmasked the monopolistic aspirations of the Falangist Party over all the new regime's social policy.

In this study, we shall first analyse the characteristics of the anti-tuberculosis campaign launched by the Francoist regime, as well as the underlying justification for its development, which acted as the driving force behind the public authorities' decision-making. Secondly, we will study the part played by the post-war political situation in the construction of the healthcare model and social welfare, which culminated in the division of powers between the different factions of Franco's regime. We shall also look at some of the problems that this power-sharing brought with it, which proved to be a real hindrance to a definitive establishment of a true welfare state in Spain.

2. The Francoist regime and the tuberculosis problem

One of the first steps taken by the rebel side after the armed uprising was the creation of the Patronato Nacional Antituberculoso (National Tuberculosis Foundation) in December 1936[7]. This meant, in Nationalist territory, a return to the situation prior to 1931 with the creation, once again, of an autonomous body, which, despite coming under the auspices of the State and having links with the Dirección General de Sanidad (State Office of Public Health), recreated the structure and charitable nature that Republican nationalisation had tried to eliminate[8].

The creation of the Anti-tuberculosis Foundation under the slogan, "Healthy Spain will have to make sacrifices for sick Spain" was a propaganda ploy that the new regime exploited to the full to justify the armed uprising against the Republic. Its main aim, namely to hospitalise every tuberculosis sufferer, was materially impossible

---

[7] Decreto-Ley 20-XII-1936.

[8] The first Republican Government nationalised the fight against this plague in 1931, following the dissolution of the Royal Foundation for the Fight Against Tuberculosis, a private institution created by Primo de Rivera in 1924. It also provided the campaign, for the first time, with a big enough budget to start on the construction of clinics and sanatoriums, and to incorporate, after public examinations, personnel qualified in consumption in the National Body of Public Health. Molero-Mesa, Jorge, "Clase obrera, Medicina y Estado en la España del Siglo XX. Bases sociopolíticas de las campañas antituberculosas entre 1889 y 1950", in Jesús Castellanos, Isabel Jiménez Lucena, Mª José Ruiz Somavilla and Pilar Gardeta, *La medicina en el siglo XX. Estudios Históricos sobre Medicina, Sociedad y Estado*, Málaga, Sociedad Española de Historia de la Medicina, 1998, pp. 221-228.

to achieve, but it presented the rebels as being the only side capable of bringing "true social justice" to Spain[9]. One way of spreading this propaganda was in the interviews Franco gave to both the foreign and domestic media at the height of the civil war. In them, the future dictator highlighted the large number of sanatoriums being set up[10] and his project's underlying demographic objective: to reach, in the long term, a Spanish population of 40 million people[11]. The fight against the premature loss of lives, brought about mainly by tuberculosis and infant mortality, was to be completed by the Francoist policy of promoting family life, and the role to be played by women in the new State[12].

However, to achieve this objective, as was again pointed out in 1950, the fight against infectious disease in general and against tuberculosis in particular, depended on the qualitative enhancement of the population, in other words, the 'improvement of the race'[13]. The conditions in which the Spanish post-war population found themselves,

---

[9] This unrealistic goal was rectified the following year by the Foundation, as the number of tuberculosis sufferers had been put at 300,000 (not counting those who would join these ranks after the ravages of the civil war). This figure would mean providing a budget, just for maintaining beds, of almost 800 million pesetas a year. *Anteproyecto de Lucha Antituberculosa,* Valladolid, Imp. Castellana, 1937, pp. 7-8.

[10] Franco highlighted the fact that in just eight months of conflict, 37 sanatoriums had been created. These centres, which in reality were converted halls in premises that had been given up or confiscated after military occupation, had mostly to be dismantled or returned to their owners at the end of the war. Bartolomé Benítez Franco, M. Oñorbe and E. Ripollés, *Informe técnico al proyecto de organización sanatorial*, Madrid, PNA, 1944, pp. 4-5.

[11] Francisco Franco, *Palabras del Caudillo, 19 de abril 1937-7 de diciembre 1942*, Madrid, Ed. Vicesecretaría de Educación Popular, 1943, p. 389. Mª Carmen García Nieto and Javier Mª Donezar, "La España de Franco 1939-1975", in *Bases documentales de la Historia de España Contemporánea*, vol. 11, Madrid, Guadiana, 1975, p. 49; Jesús de Miguel, *La sociedad enferma: las bases sociales de la política sanitaria española*, Madrid, Akal, 1979, pp. 36-40. For more on fascism and population, see Paul Weindling, "Fascism and Population in Comparative European Perspective" in Michael S. Teitelbaum and Jay M. Winter (eds.), *Population and Resources in Western Intellectual Traditions*, Cambridge, Cambridge University Press, 1989, pp. 102-121.

[12] Rosario Sánchez has pointed out the pro-active role of the Women's Section in this undertaking, as well as the laws proclaimed to this end. Among these, we could single out those referring to: Prizes for Motherhood; Family Benefit; prohibition on divorce (retrospective in nature); harsh penalties for abortion, adultery and illicit union; supplementary taxation for bachelors; and a prohibition on women working. Rosario Sánchez López, *Mujer española, una sombra de destino en lo universal. Trayectoria histórica de la Sección Femenina de Falange (1934-1977)*, Murcia, Universidad de Murcia, 1990, pp. 25-26. On the same theme, see also Pedro Carasa, "La revolución nacional-asistencial durante el primer franquismo (1936-1940)", *Historia Contemporánea*, nº 16, 1977, pp. 89-140.

[13] Bartolomé Benítez Franco, *La tuberculosis. Estudio de la lucha contra esta enfermedad en España (1939-1949)*, Madrid, PNA, 1950, p. 64.

brought to light by various studies of its state of nourishment[14], did not exactly lend themselves to the fulfilment of such an aim. The new regime's answer, after starting a war for the very reason of safeguarding the interests of the ruling class and so avoiding a more equitable distribution of wealth, was to put the blame on the population and their health-related habits (a claim tantamount to blaming the victim)[15]. The campaign, as it was conceived, touched upon, as it had done before, changing the 'consumption' practices of the working classes, such as spitting, sexual abuse (masturbation, promiscuity), poor diet, insufficient personal and domestic hygiene or the lack of precautions, among other things.

In this context, we must situate all the actions which, from diverse quarters, were designed by Franco's regime to fight tuberculosis. The propaganda-education network was supplemented by various nursing home institutions. The Instructoras sanitarias (Female Public Health Instructors) (visiting nurses), in the employ of either the Foundation or the Cuerpo de Puericultores del Estado (State Corps of Paediatricians), were soon aided by the work of the Women's Section of the Falange through the Cuerpo de Divulgadoras Sanitario-Rurales (Corps of Female Public Health Disseminators in Rural Areas), created by law in June, 1941[16]. All of this was supported by the indoctrination of women in a compulsory form of Social Service, in which they were taught a series of hygiene rules as well as the 'art of cookery', in other words, how to prepare calorific diets using the scarce food available. The Frente de Juventudes (Falange Youth Front), with the organisation of camps, youth hostels and school holiday camps, was responsible for improving children's physical development. The resulting doses of fresh air coincided with an early contact with political orientation[17]. For those children in "delicate physical condition", this

---

[14] Carlos Jiménez Díaz, "Memoria sobre el estado nutritivo de la población madrileña (1941-1943)", *Estudios de Historia Social*, n° 5, 1978, pp. 409-465. It is worth highlighting that the Francoist regime never accepted responsibility for the result of the surveys on nutrition in Madrid. In 1940, Benítez Franco pointed out that one of the factors that had brought about the increase in the number of tuberculosis sufferers after the war was the "starvation diet" to which the Republican zone was "exclusively" subjected. Bartolomé Benítez Franco, *El problema social de la tuberculosis*, Madrid, Gráf. Afrodisio Aguado, 1940, p. 24.

[15] This strategy, implicit in previous anti-tuberculosis campaigns in Spain and other countries, could be carried out by Franco's regime with all the coercive rigour that its laws allowed. See for example the institutional response to the problem caused by spotted fever, after 1941 in Málaga: Isabel Jiménez Lucena, *El tifus en la Málaga de la postguerra. Un estudio historicomédico en torno a una enfermedad colectiva*, Málaga, Universidad de Málaga, 1990, pp. 44-70.

[16] For details of the latter's functions, see Mª Teresa Gallego Méndez, *Mujer, Falange y franquismo*, Madrid, Taurus, 1983, pp. 124-126.

[17] Cfr. Juan Sáez Marín, *El Frente de Juventudes. Política de juventud en la España de la postguerra (1937-1960)*, Madrid, Siglo XXI, 1988.

organisation had special preventive sanatoriums. In the words of one of the officials in charge in 1942, their establishment was designed to "considerably reduce the number of disabled people and so raise the average strength and capacity of all Spaniards"[18].

The aim of this habit-changing offensive, together with the introduction of social insurance schemes, was, in the final analysis, that the proletariat should permanently internalise the bourgeois ideal of life based on the attainment of good health[19]. The development of the health campaigns of the first third of the present century had played a key role in this process, which stripped disease of its political connotations[20]. In our country, they led part of the proletarian movement to include public health policies in their political programmes, without waiting for a political revolution to put social classes on an equal footing in other aspects[21]. In the period that concerns us, this process of social formation received a big boost from the introduction of insurance against illness, by offering the proletariat a small measure of hope of improving their life expectancy without fear of misfortune[22]. The importance that Franco's regime attached to the concepts of disease and health insurance – which was most clearly exemplified in tuberculosis and the planned insurance against it – is reflected throughout the present study in the struggle between the various Francoist factions to control these aspects of social policy.

3. The Falangist Party and the Compulsory Insurance against Tuberculosis

From its creation in 1936 until 1943, the composition of the anti-tuberculosis Foundation was characterised by the total absence of consumption specialists. The structure of the Central Committee was a copy of that of the Real Patronato de Lucha Antituberculosa (Royal Foundation for the Fight against Tuberculosis), organised under Primo de Rivera's dictatorship, with heavy monarchic representation. Its members included

---

[18] Fernández Cabezas, "Las Estaciones Preventoriales del Frente de Juventudes", *Ser*, n° 6, 1942, pp. 111-116, p. 116.

[19] Labisch, 1985, *op. cit.* in footnote 6.

[20] Esteban Rodríguez-Ocaña and Jorge Molero-Mesa, "La cruzada por la salud. Las campañas sanitarias del primer tercio del siglo XX en la construcción de la cultura de la salud", in: Montiel, L. (ed.) *La salud en el estado de bienestar. Análisis histórico*, Madrid, Editorial Complutense Cuadernos Complutenses de Historia de la Medicina y de la Ciencia, n° 2, 1993, pp. 133-148.

[21] Molero-Mesa, 1998, *op. cit.* in footnote 8 and Molero-Mesa, 1999, *op. cit.* in footnote 3.

[22] Esteban Rodríguez-Ocaña, *La constitución de la Medicina Social como disciplina en España (1882-1923)*, Madrid, M° de Sanidad y Consumo, 1987, p. 28.

several high office-holders in the dictator's administration: its President, General Martínez Anido[23], was Minister of the Interior with Primo de Rivera and, therefore, statutory President of the old Royal Foundation for the Fight against Tuberculosis; the spokesman for the Foundation, Conde de Casal, had been its delegate President; while another spokesman, Antonio Horcada Mateos, had been Director General of Public Health from 1928 to 1930. Furthermore, José Palanca, who was an *ex officio* member because he was Director General of Public Health, had already held this last post in the two governments preceding the exile of Alfonso XIII[24]. Also, among the members appointed for 'their zeal in the fight against tuberculosis' figured a duchess, a marchioness and Irene Rojí Acuña, the wife of Martínez Anido[25]. The Comités Delegados Provinciales (Provincial Delegate Committees) had a similar structure. Despite this considerable monarchic presence, the technical leadership was taken over by the Falangist Party. Their doctors were responsible for elaborating healthcare plans and future projects for anti-tuberculosis policies[26], guided by reports that they solicited from medical specialists, but did not always act upon[27].

---

[23] This military man held the ministerial post for Public Order in Franco's first government. After his death in December 1938, this post was taken up by the Falangist, Ramón Serrano Suñer, the Minister of the Interior. In the second government (August 1939), this Ministry adopted the definitive name of Ministerio de Gobernación (Ministry of the Interior), to which the State Office of Public Health was added.

[24] This was not an isolated phenomenon as many other of Primo de Rivera's collaborators were recruited by the various Francoist departments. José Antonio Biescas and Manuel Tuñón de Lara, *España bajo la dictadura franquista (1939-1975)* 2nd ed., Madrid, Labor, 1981, see the appendix on pp. 574-575.

[25] Patronato Nacional Antituberculoso, *Revista Española de Tuberculosis*, 9, n° 60, 1940, inside cover.

[26] José Ramón de Castro, *Resumen de la Obra y espíritu del Patronato Nacional Antituberculoso desde su creación hasta la promulgación de la Ley de Bases*, Vigo, Imp. 'La Competidora', ca 1941. From the Falangist doctor José Ramón de Castro, Advisor to the Presidency of the Foundation and until that moment removed from anti-tuberculosis questions, came the "Blueprint for the Anti-Tuberculosis Fight", some "Notes on an Organisation of the National School of Consumption", "Scripts for a Spanish Anti-tuberculosis Fight", and "General Regulations of Health Sanatoriums" and, very probably, the text of the *Bases Law* of 1939.

[27] See for example, José Merino Hompanera, *Algunos rasgos sobre cómo debiera organizarse la Lucha Antituberculosa en el Nuevo Estado Español Nacional Sindicalista*, Cáceres, Tip. "La Minerva Cacereña", 1938. This study was commissioned by the National Delegation of Public Health of FET and the JONS. José Merino, Director of the Central Antituberculosis Clinic of Cáceres, proposed a campaign based on the multiplication of these centres as a means of fighting tuberculosis. He also argued that the organisation should be put in the hands of specialist doctors from National Public Health, under the leadership of the State Office of Public Health. This opinion went against the aspirations of the Falange at that time.

One such project, in 1937, was the creation of a Compulsory Insurance against Tuberculosis, just like that which had been established by the fascists in Italy in 1927[28]. The influence of Italian fascism in the configuration of the insurance against tuberculosis was clearly revealed in its guiding philosophy and ultimate aim. According to José Ramón de Castro, "in order to fulfil a doctrine of a pure National Syndicalist revolution, the personality of the Fight against Tuberculosis initiated by the people must return to the people through the State". Such an approach started from the supposed "minority of the people", meaning that, in the first stage, the State would come to their aid, digging into its own funds. Later on, the State would "consent to" the creation of an Instituto Nacional del Seguro Antituberculoso (National Institute of the Anti-tuberculosis Insurance), within the Foundation, to channel the contributions of each citizen (insurance policy-holders), and so finance the fight against tuberculosis. The next stage would see the emergence of "satellite" institutions entrusted with the effective management of actions against disease (provincial commissions, schools for the study of consumption and the fight against tuberculosis in the armed forces). Finally, the Foundation would become financially independent of the State and the fight against tuberculosis would be directed towards "autarchy", constituting a "power in its own right". In this way, the hygiene question would be treated as a "pure social instrument" rather than "charity towards tuberculosis sufferers"[29]. In accordance with these approaches, the insurance against tuberculosis was presented as an alternative to the concept of 'Marxist nationalisation', which had been dominant in the Republican era, according to the accusations made to this effect in 1935[30] (at the height of the civil war)[31].

---

[28] *Anteproyecto de Lucha Antituberculosa (1937), op. cit.* in footnote 9, pp. 4 and 7. It should, however, be stressed that that the issues raised by this disease were key topics in the debate in Spain over the introduction of an insurance against disease until 1936. Thus, the introduction of a specific insurance scheme against tuberculosis had already been called for in the various scientific meetings of consumption specialists, which had been held in our country since 1924. It was seen as an alternative to the budget deficits that burdened the fight against this plague. Cfr. Jorge Molero-Mesa and Esteban Rodríguez-Ocaña, "Tuberculosis y previsión. Influencia de la enfermedad social modelo en el desarrollo de las ideas médicas españolas sobre el seguro de enfermedad", in M. Valera, Mª. A. Egea, Mª. D. Blázquez (eds.) *Libro de Actas del VIII Congreso Nacional de Historia de la Medicina. Murcia-Cartagena 18-21 diciembre 1986.* Murcia, Cátedra de Historia de la Medicina. Universidad de Murcia, 1988, vol. 1, pp. 502-513.

[29] Castro (ca. 1941) *op. cit.* in footnote 26, pp. 28-32.

[30] José Alberto Palanca, *Discurso de contestación. In: Verdes Montenegro, J. Deficiencias de nuestra organización antituberculosa. Discurso en la RANM*, Madrid, Imp. Augusto Boué, 1935, pp. 21-59, p. 47.

[31] José Blasco Reta, "Sobre la lucha antituberculosa en Granada", *Actualidad Médica*, 23, 1937, pp. 266-275.

Just one year later, in 1938, the *Fuero del Trabajo (Employment Charter)* was proclaimed. It literally copied the contents of the Italian Fascists' Employment Charter, which included this same insurance, along with the rest of the declarations[32]. The tenth declaration of this new Fundamental Law included the task of creating a Compulsory Insurance against Tuberculosis along with insurance against old age, disability, maternity, work accidents, professional illnesses and redundancy[33]. Its confirmation came in August 1939 with the law that regulated and established the Foundation. In its seventh clause, the setting up of a 'National Savings Bank for Compulsory Aid Against Tuberculosis in Conjunction with the National Insurance System' was outlined, the Foundation itself being designated the task of preparing the project[34]. Consequently, the Delegación Nacional de Sindicatos (National Delegation of Unions), responsible for the Obra Asistencial 18 de julio (Welfare Project 18th July), reached an agreement with the Foundation on the provision of 4,000 beds to put the introduction of the insurance scheme on a firm footing.

In order to ensure its control over anti-tuberculosis welfare work in those zones still to be occupied, the Falangist Party planned the creation of Anti-tuberculosis Technical Commissions, which would take immediate charge of the campaign against tuberculosis, especially in the most populated cities like Madrid, Barcelona and Valencia. The Falangists supposed that the anti-tuberculosis centres – almost all of them in Republican territory at the beginning of the war – would be abandoned by their staff (health officials during the Republic) after the final victory[35]. This idea was reinforced by the fact that a large part of Republican anti-tuberculosis officials were accused of collaboration with the socialist Marcelino Pascua (Director General de Sanidad – Director General of Public Health – from 1931 to 1933) in the expulsion of doctors belonging to the monarchic Royal Foundation after the service's nationalisation. This would explain the absence of medical specialists on the Central Committee of the Foundation until the appropriate purges were made after the war.

---

[32] The 27th declaration of this charter included the improvement of insurance against accident, the extension of maternity insurance and the establishment of insurance against professional illnesses and tuberculosis as a starting point for the institution of a general insurance. Fernando Gazzetti, *Asistencia y previsión en Italia* (Roma: Societá Editrice di Novissima, 1937). In this monograph, which was edited in Castilian and must have circulated in the Rebel zone, all the social achievements of Italian fascism were related, the tuberculosis insurance figuring among them.

[33] *Fundamentos del Nuevo Estado*, Madrid, Ed. Vicesecretaría de Educación Popular, 1943, p. 179.

[34] Benítez Franco (1940) *op. cit.* in footnote 14, p. 181.

[35] *Anteproyecto de Lucha Antituberculosa* (1937) *op. cit.* in footnote 9, p. 9.

4. Post-war power-sharing: public health versus health insurance

However, the panorama at the end of the war differed hugely from that which the Falangists had anticipated: the sanatoriums were nearly all destroyed, but the majority of doctors and health workers employed by the State in the fight against tuberculosis had not abandoned their posts. Indeed, although the number of exiled doctors after the war was far greater than in any other scientific field[36], this was not so in the case of specialists in consumption. Thus, together with health officials, the Foundation ended up accepting those doctors struck off by the Republic in 1931, as well as those who had been appointed by official bodies, such as town and county councils. In order to build up personnel, public examinations were held in 1940 for the incorporation of those who had collaborated with the new regime[37]. According to the provisional payroll of 1944, the Foundation consisted of 187 doctors in total, including directors, assistants and specialists, of whom 109 (58.3%) had been appointed before 1936[38].

Along with anti-tuberculosis officials, most of the doctors belonging to the Cuerpo de Sanidad Nacional (National Public Health body) also kept their posts, something that damaged Falangist hopes of monopolising (possibly through a Ministry of Employment and Public Health) all aspects of health and welfare. Alfonso de la Fuente Chaos (1908-1988), a surgeon and National Secretary of the Falangist Party[39],

---

[36] Ernesto García Camarero, "La ciencia española en el exilio de 1939", in Abellán, José Luís (ed.) *El exilio español de 1939*, Madrid, Taurus, 1978, vol. 5, pp. 191-243. This author points out that 500 medical professionals sought exile in Mexico alone, in 1939. For his part, González Duro highlights the dismantling of psychiatry after the civil war, owing to the exile, purges and ostracism to which its most representative figures were subjected. Enrique González Duro, *Psiquiatría y sociedad autoritaria: España: 1939-1975*, Madrid, Akal, 1978, p. 5.

[37] At the end of 1938, the Foundation had 84 doctors, 72 medical assistants, 144 nurses, six school mistresses, 16 chaplains and 164 nuns who, together with auxiliaries and administrators, formed a staff of 922 people.

[38] The specific proportion of the official doctors employed by the Foundation is made clear by comparing it with the number of practitioners that made up the National Body of Public Health in 1943, which included, together with health inspectors, doctors involved in various health campaigns (malaria, spotted fever and poliomyelitis). They totalled, in the same year, 199. Apart from them, there was the State Body of Paediatricians. *Cuerpo Médico de Sanidad Nacional. Puericultores del Estado. Tisiólogos Españoles. Primeras reuniones anuales. Conclusiones*, Madrid, PNA, p. 20.

[39] He was also National Leader of the Project '18th July', and founder of the journal Ser, the mouthpiece of the National Delegation of Public Health of FET and the JONS (Spanish Traditionalist Falange and of the Committees for the National Syndicalist Offensive). Among the posts he occupied throughout the Franco period were the Presidencies of the Spanish Football Federation (1956) and the General Council of Medical Associations (1963)."Sesión Necrológica en memoria del Excmo. Sr. D. Alfonso de la Fuente Chaos. Comunicación a la Real Academia de Medicina el día 13 de diciembre de 1988", *Anales de la Real Academia Nacional de Medicina*, 105, 1988, pp. 531-553.

put it clearly when confessing that 'the fundamental thing in social security is Public Health, economic considerations are auxiliary'. According to this surgeon, in a National Syndicalist State, both elements had necessarily to be unified under a 'National Authority', and in the charge of the Syndicates[40].

The distribution of the power centres within the different groups that made up the wartime rebel side assigned to the Falange mainly those within the socio-political domain[41]. In 1938, however, the Government of Burgos gave provisional control of the Dirección General de Sanidad (State Office of Public Health) to José Alberto Palanca y Martínez Fortún (1888-1973)[42], medical Commander and a member of Catholic army circles of monarchic persuasion[43], this despite the fact that this body formed part of the Ministry of the Interior, whose head was the Falangist, Serrano Suñer.

At the end of the war, the political factions making up the Francoist organisation engaged in bitter power struggles within the State apparatus. The State Office of Public Health was fought over by medical associations (close to the army) and the Falangist Party[44], which still had the advantage of controlling the Ministry of the Interior. As part of this political struggle, and in a final attempt to take over the domain of public health, the Falange tried to remove anyone they accused of being 'leftist' or 'an enemy of the regime' from the National Public Health body. After this purge, which affected all public workers, the vast majority of health officials kept their jobs[45]. The solution that the regime came up with was to share out the various Ministries and the fields that each one had assigned to it. In May 1941, General Valentín Galarza took over from Serrano Suñer as head of the Ministry of the Interior, which still incorporated the State Office of Public Health. At the same time, the Ministry of Employment,

---

[40] Alfonso de la Fuente Chaos, *Política sanitaria. Madrid, Delegación Nacional de Sanidad,* 1943, p. 94.

[41] Sheelag Ellwood, *Prietas las filas. Historia de la Falange Española, 1933-1983*, Barcelona, Ed. Crítica, 1984, p. 113; y Carasa, 1997, *op. cit.* in footnote 12.

[42] This doctor was also Professor of Hygiene and ex-deputy of the CEDA (Spanish Confederation of Autonomous Right-wingers). In 1934, he had actively participated in the transfer of the State Office of Public Health to the Ministry of Employment, against Socialist proposals that it should remain in the Ministry of the Interior. José Alberto Palanca, *Medio siglo al servicio de la Sanidad Pública*, Madrid, Ed. 'Cultura Clásica y Moderna', 1963, p. 99.

[43] *Ibid.* p. 104; Miguel Jerez Mir, *Elites políticas y centros de extracción en España: 1938-1957*, Madrid, Centro de Investigaciones Sociológicas, 1982, p. 224. He was to occupy this post without interruption until 1957, when he was substituted by Jesús García Orcoyen (b. 1903).

[44] This is according to José Palanca in an interview with the journalist, Gómez-Santos. The Falangists had Tomás Rodríguez as their candidate. Marino Gómez-Santos, *Médicos que dejan huella*, Madrid, Organización Sala, 1973, p. 430.

[45] Jorge Molero-Mesa and Isabel Jiménez Lucena, "Salud y burocracia en España. Los Cuerpos de Sanidad Nacional (1855-1951)", *Revista Española de Salud Pública*, 74, 2000, pp. 45-79.

which incorporated the Instituto Nacional de Previsión (National Welfare Institute), was assigned to the Falange, with Girón de Velasco at its head[46].

The problem posed by this distribution of power soon became apparent with the beginning of the debate over the model of health insurance to be set up in Spain. On the one hand, legislation favoured the anti-tuberculosis Foundation, the Presidency of which fell to the Director General of Public Health. As we have just seen, however, the body responsible for initiating all social welfare policy was part of the Ministry of Employment.

The alternative to the Compulsory Insurance against Tuberculosis proposed by the Falangist Party was a global insurance against illness, bearing more similarities with the German model than the Italian one[47]. Its legislative arguments were based on the final sentence of the tenth statement in the Employment Charter, which outlined a tendency towards the introduction of a comprehensive insurance scheme. A specially appointed commission was given the task of studying which insurance model was to be adopted[48].

Apart from these talks, 'experts' hitherto uninvolved in the official anti-tuberculosis organisation, and in league with the State Office of Public Health, began planning a future insurance against tuberculosis. The main justification was that, without such an insurance, the objectives of a fight against tuberculosis could not be met, not to mention the cost of the provision of 20,000 beds decreed by law in 1940.

The person responsible for the implementation of the project was Bartolomé Benítez Franco (b. 1909), editor of the *Revista Española de Tuberculosis (Spanish Journal of Tuberculosis)*, a publication that had become the official mouthpiece of the Foundation

---

[46] General Valentín Galarza, considered by the single party to be anti-falangist (Ellwood, 1984, *op. cit.*, in footnote 41, p. 127), was replaced in September 1942 by Blas Pérez González, a specialist of no specific political affiliation, according to Ramón Tamames, who devoted himself efficiently to the work of 'political policing'. Ramón Tamames, *La República. La era de Franco*, Madrid, Alianza Ed., 1986, p. 308.

[47] José Palanca highlighted this controversy in a speech made before the Chief of Public Health of the Reich, Dr. Conti, on the occasion of the International Tuberculosis Congress, organised by the Germans in November 1941, in Berlin: "Some prefer your system, a totalitarian insurance which covers all risk of disease. Others are inclined towards Italian methods, an insurance just for tuberculosis, which is the most common disease and the one which brings most expense, *but* which is also easier to organise". José Alberto Palanca, "Los servicios sanitarios españoles a través de nuestra guerra de liberación", *Actualidad Médica*, 18, 1942, pp. 1-12, p. 9.

[48] It should be emphasised that in the debate over the introduction of these insurance schemes, doctors were excluded as a pressure group. In December 1942, the Zaragoza-based journal *La Opinión Médica*, was closed by order of the Government for its opposition to the introduction of the SOE. Mariano Gastón Barcos, *'Clínica y Laboratorio'. Análisis de una institución cientificomédica aragonesa*. Doctoral Thesis, 1992, MSS. p. 99.

since its relaunch in January 1940. This doctor, who had been made unofficial General Secretary of the Foundation while its restructuration was being planned, was also a member of the aforementioned commission, which was to report on insurance. The project was presented at the first National Congress of Practical Medicine (Madrid, May 1941)[49]. It was, according to its author, an improved version of the Italian welfare model, which had introduced compulsory insurance against tuberculosis in 1927, and which he had studied during a previous visit to Italy[50].

The insurance against tuberculosis was to be compulsory for those earning less than 600 or 700 pesetas a month, and was independent of, and prior to, general insurance against illness. The running of the scheme was to be shared, after an agreement with the National Welfare Institute. This body would collect premiums and pay out benefits. The Caja de Asistencia Obligatoria (National Savings Bank for Compulsory Aid) was set up within the Foundation to administer funds for the construction and maintenance of sanatoriums, and the provision of aid to those insured. Such an arrangement would, according to the speaker, unite "the activity of the two bodies, which would come together in the fight against tuberculosis: the Foundation taking care of propaganda work, prevention and aid to poor tuberculosis victims; the National Welfare Institute collecting insurance premiums, paying out benefits and contributing to the success of the National Savings Bank for Aid".

In other works, Benítez Franco extended the list of advantages of tuberculosis insurance over general illness cover. Thus, in the face of the traditional opposition of the medical profession[51], insurance against tuberculosis was more readily accepted by medical professionals as it was limited to the disease most common among those living on charity. He also affirmed that the tuberculosis sufferer, due to the nature of her or his illness, neither believed in the doctor nor even gave him "the intimate satisfaction of doing his duty"[52].

---

[49] Bartolomé Benítez Franco, "El seguro social contra la tuberculosis", in *Movilización Cultural Médico-Práctica. Madrid 1941. III Ponencia. Tuberculosis en la postguerra, desarrollada por el PNA*, Madrid, Gráf. Uguina, 1941, pp. 234-241.

[50] Bartolomé Benítez Franco, "El seguro social contra la tuberculosis en Italia. Notas y comentarios (Memoria presentada al PNA)", *Revista Española de Tuberculosis*, 10, n° 74, mayo 1941, pp. 199-217.

[51] Esteban Rodríguez-Ocaña and Teresa Ortiz Gómez, "Los médicos españoles y la idea del seguro obligatorio de enfermedad durante el primer tercio del siglo XX", in M. Valera, Mª. A. Egea, Mª. D. Blázquez (eds.) *Actas del VIII Congreso Nacional de Historia de la Medicina. Murcia-Cartagena 18-21 diciembre 1986*, Murcia, Cátedra de Historia de la Medicina. Universidad de Murcia, 1988, vol. 1, pp. 488-501.

[52] Bartolomé Benítez Franco, "Contribución al estudio de los seguros sociales de enfermedad", *Revista Española de Tuberculosis*, 10, 1940, pp. 452-461, p. 459.

To finance this scheme, this consumption specialist proposed adding a few minutes to the working day, dedicating the resulting effort to the insurance against tuberculosis, and so neutralising the opposition of the sponsors. He summed up the numerous advantages of the insurance in the following way: "The insurance against tuberculosis will save thousands of workers from death; it will spare many families from misery; sponsors will accept it without protest; doctors will serve it with enthusiasm; and its benefits to both the physical and economic health of Spain will be incalculable"[53].

5. Compulsory health insurance and the national anti-tuberculosis foundation: an impossible partnership

At the end of 1941, the creation of the Seguro Obligatorio de Enfermedad (SOE) (Compulsory Health Insurance) was decided upon, while that of tuberculosis was finally rejected. The debate, however, was centred on the control of medical affairs among the various pressure groups involved (the Falange, Medical Associations and the State Office of Public Health). In February 1942, José Palanca took advantage of the launch of the journal *Ser* (the official mouthpiece of the National Delegation of Public Health of the Falange) and warned of the impossibility of waging a campaign against tuberculosis without the SOE. At the same time, he questioned the wisdom of fighting tuberculosis on two different fronts and warned of the need for collaboration between the State Office of Public Health, the Foundation and the medical profession in the introduction of the new insurance scheme[54].

The reaction from Falangist circles was not long in coming. At a conference at the Madrid Faculty of Medicine one month after the proclamation of the *Compulsory Health Insurance Law* (December 14, 1942), Alfonso de la Fuente Chaos did not put forward technical justifications for the monopolisation of this body, but instead adopted a posture of force legitimised by victory in the civil war. On the one hand, the medical associations had been discredited for not using their position to prevent the regime's enemies from filling official posts in Public Health, "but also, and this is the saddest part, in three years of forgiveness they have not shown the slightest hint of repentance"[55]. The same doctor also reminded them of their obligation to join the union, as was demanded in a National Syndicalist State.

[53] *Ibid.*, p. 461.

[54] José Palanca, "La sanidad oficial y el Seguro de enfermedad", *Ser*, nº 1, 1942, pp. 60-61, p. 61.

[55] Fuente Chaos, 1943, *op. cit.* in footnote 40, p. 161.

In the face of the wish of both the State Office of Public Health and the Foundation that the insurance should use public services, Alfonso de la Fuente was even more emphatic: "If the State claims the means of production as its own (clinics, sanatoriums, material) and makes doctors mere employees, it has carried out a total socialisation of medicine, and Spain could not send 15,000 men to fight in the snows of Russia for an article of law and then cruelly to ridicule their death"[56]. At the same time he described the State Office of Public Health's work as 'charitable', while the insurance was a social project. From this viewpoint, the State Office of Public Health should stand aside and limit itself to preventive campaigns that would benefit the insurance by reducing morbidity: "Let the fight against tuberculosis, with its wonderful possibilities, go on. Take up the fight against cancer and rheumatism, and see how, with all of this, you can do great things without our function taking any of the credit away from you"[57].

According to the Falange, the only possible alternative was, therefore, that the SOE should lend its assistance through the 'Project 18th July', dependent on the National Delegation of Syndicates of Falange, and on the medical centres set up with the creation of the Insurance against Disease, as stipulated in the *Compulsory Health Insurance Law*. If this approach was not adopted, it would give rise to the paradoxical situation of the economically weak having to maintain with their premiums the services that the State had previously provided free.

From this moment on, the Foundation sought coordination with the SOE in both preventive and healthcare material for tuberculosis sufferers and professional material for its specialists. On the occasion of the First Annual Meeting of Spanish Consumption Specialists held in Madrid in May 1943, the Foundation claimed sole legal jurisdiction over the fight against tuberculosis, with the aim of avoiding the dichotomy that had arisen in Italy. Here, the Welfare Institute provided its insurance holders with direct healthcare, while the provincial associations and the National Fascist Federation against Tuberculosis (the equivalent of the Spanish Foundation) went on operating independently. The *Compulsory Health Insurance Law* already made it clear that the rules of the State Office of Public Health should be observed in preventive matters. Another of the Foundation's demands was the establishment of a disability insurance, as the maximum of 26 weeks for medical and financial help was insufficient for chronic diseases like tuberculosis. It was even dangerous to reintroduce somebody carrying germs into society. As for the Foundation's consumption specialists who would treat

---

[56] *Ibid.*, p. 163.
[57] *Ibid.*, p. 165.

insurance holders, it was argued that they should receive the same consideration as insurance specialists. Also, a total separation of administrative and health services lent to the Foundation should be maintained within the organisation[58].

The proclamation of the *Compulsory Health Insurance* regulations (November 11, 1943) confirmed the fears expressed by consumption experts with regard to jurisdiction in the area of tuberculosis. Indeed, article 35 of the regulations created the Tuberculosis Service of the SOE[59], and although it stated that maximum cooperation with "specially commissioned institutions from the areas of preventive medicine and social hygiene" would be established, it only served to complicate even further the jurisdictional network between the various health bodies.

The definitive restructuration of the Foundation

After the meeting of medical specialists, the Foundation was reorganised through a new *Law of Bases* (December 1943). As already planned, the membership of the Central Committee was cut to 17, and it became more technical than political in nature. Of the ten doctors who formed part of the committee, five had direct links with the fight against tuberculosis, including its new General Secretary, Bartolomé Benítez Franco. The Delegate President continued to be the Director General of Public Health, José Palanca. Only two representatives of the Falange remained on this committee (National Delegation of Public Health and Project '18th July'), while the aristocratic female presence was eliminated. Irene Rojí, Martínez Anido's widow, was retained as a member[60].

This new *Law of Bases* was the Ministry of the Interior's response to its legislative 'battle' with the Ministry of Employment, and represented official recognition of the Foundation's anti-tuberculosis monopoly. Nevertheless, the "organisation and control of medical insurance against tuberculosis" was to be managed, according to the new law, "in agreement with the Law of December 14, 1942, and in collaboration with the organs of the SOE".

---

[58] Bartolomé Benítez Franco, "Estudios. IV. Coordinación de la lucha antituberculosa con el seguro de enfermedad", *Revista Española de Tuberculosis*, 12, nº 97, 1943, pp. 235-244.

[59] The services of Venereology, Psychiatric Care, Infectious Diseases and Preventive Medicine were also created. *Recopilación legislativa del Seguro de Enfermedad*, Madrid, INP, 1947, p. 86.

[60] Among the non-medical personnel were a representative of the State Office of Welfare, Salvador Criado del Rey; the General Director of Architecture, Pedro Muguruza and the Higher Attorney of Housing, Blas Sierra, all of them being members. The Treasurer was Juan Oller Piñol. Bartolomé Benítez Franco, *Información sobre la Lucha Antituberculosa en España y Memoria correspondiente al año 1944*, Madrid, PNA, 1945, p. 14.

Apart from legal sources and other statements of intent, the annual budgets of the Foundation are available to us as indicators of the general direction of insurance discussions. The budget allowances were substantially increased on two key dates: in 1941, when the decision not to create an insurance against tuberculosis had already been taken, and in 1944, with the definitive setting up of the SOE by the Ministry of Employment. In 1945, the controversial street collection called the Festival of the Flower was resorted to once again[61]. It had been heavily criticised by workers groups in the two previous regimes for its charitable nature. These funds were to top up those coming from the compulsory Christmas postal surcharge and the special October lottery, both in operation since the beginning of the decade. These funds represented the biggest contribution to the rise in income above budget levels[62]. Help was also provided in the construction of sanatoriums. In 1943, a decree signed by Franco declared that the building work for the Foundation was "urgent and preferential", mainly because of the difficulty of obtaining building material[63]. Thus, in 1952, the Foundation already had 14,000 beds available and those needed to reach the new target of 25,000 were on their way[64].

Duplication in the health services

The 'trial of strength' between the State Office of Public Health, the anti-tuberculosis Foundation and the SOE went on at a legislative level. In this way, the *Ley de Bases de Sanidad Nacional (National Healthcare Bases Law)* of November 25, 1944 was seen as a manoeuvre against the Falange[65]. This law sanctioned those functions of the Foundation included in the Bases Law and obliged it to reach an agreement with the SOE on aid to its beneficiaries and any preventive campaigns the latter might organise. The 30th base, which imposed a series of duties on the SOE with regard to the

---

[61] In 1946, the provincial organisations were asked to complement the collection with other fund-raising activities, such as tombolas, parties or other shows. "PNA. Circular n° 1 sobre organización de la Fiesta de la Flor", *Revista Española de Tuberculosis*, 15, n°132, pp. 226-228.

[62] Between 1939 and 1949, 103 million stamps were issued, which earned 8,263,347 pesetas for the Foundation. These stamps had to be added as a supplement to the normal postal charges at Christmas time. Spain was the only European country where this postal surcharge was compulsory. Benítez Franco, 1950, *op. cit.* in footnote 13, p. 253.

[63] Decree of November 11, 1943. Blas Pérez, *Discurso pronunciado el día 15 de abril de 1944, con motivo de la inauguración del edificio central de este Patronato*, Madrid, PNA, 1944, p. 5.

[64] José F. Fernández Turégano, *Patronato Nacional Antituberculoso. Dos años de labor 1951-1952*, Madrid, PNA, 1953, p. 178.

[65] Palanca, 1963, *op. cit.* in footnote 42, p. 184.

State Office of Public Health, such as the inspection of its premises or the prohibition on duplicating services in places where they already existed (sanatoriums, clinics and other state bodies), was never respected[66]. Eventually, the Falange saw to it that a new Fundamental State Law, the *Fuero de los Españoles* (Spaniards' Charter of Rights) of July 17, 1945 would definitively sanction the insurance against disease. Thus, the article in the Employment Charter referring to the insurance scheme against tuberculosis became obsolete.

The second half of the decade witnessed constant criticism of the SOE by state health organisations. In 1947, after a speech in which the need to study social factors in the origin of disease was defended, the general report of the Second Meeting of the National Public Health Body (Barcelona-Madrid April) denounced the medical policy of the SOE on the grounds that it was ignoring the prophylactic fight against diseases and, in doing so, was harming the economic stability of the insurance scheme itself. The alternative put forward was the implementation of a healthcare plan, based on a detailed epidemiological study of the aforementioned factors. Such a plan, among other things, would have the advantage of "sparing the country unnecessary duplication of services and expenditure". Although not directly named, the creation of a Ministry of Public Health ("a powerful directing body") was called for, to coordinate all public health centers[67].

In 1947, the Director General of Public Health used arguments along these lines, related to the economy and the defence of social order, to involve the insurance scheme in health campaigns throughout the population. In the first place, to show that infectious diseases were more common among the poor, he stated: "Go round the Foundation's sanatoriums and you'll see that for every patient who does not come from Welfare Charity, six do". From this reservoir, he said, germs were passed on to all social classes, including those of insurance holders: "If we reduced tuberculosis in the poor, we would reduce the opportunities for contagion in the well-off, and we would be doing important prophylactic work". By way of example, he cited American insurance

---

[66] José Palanca, *Sociología sanitaria y medicina social en España. Discurso correspondiente a la apertura del curso académico 1958-1959*, Madrid, Estades, 1958, p. 58. In this speech, Palanca claimed that, with the exception of the Ministry of the Interior, the remaining departments acted as if this law did not exist, "doing whatever suited them" (p. 55). He also recognised that the State Office of Public Health had played no part in the implantation of the SOE (p. 116).
[67] Enrique Bardají López, Ciriaco Laguna, José Fernández Turégano, and Bartolomé Benítez Franco, *II Reunión Nacional de Sanitarios Españoles. Ponencia General. Perspectivas de la Sanidad en España*, Madrid, Imp. Sáez, 1947, 16 pp., p. 13.

companies that understood perfectly that the reduction of general mortality effected that of their clients, and the economic benefits that this brought[68].

Criticism from the Foundation grew when the SOE put into practice medical specialities. In 1948, clinic heads denounced the fact that the queues of patients at their centres had shrunk alarmingly and, in consequence, so had proposals for admission to sanatoriums. The cause, they argued, was that these patients were receiving treatment in the surgeries of the insurance scheme's specialists. This phenomenon would, in the long term, lead to an involuntary rise in patients with serious cases of tuberculosis as they were slipping through the clinics' net[69]. This problem also led, for the first time since 1949, to the establishment of a minimum cooperation between both bodies. Patients detected by the insurance scheme had to be sent to a clinic, where they were given a free check-up (including laboratory tests and X-rays). Surgical operations were also financed by the Foundation, but not medication. So insurance holders didn't have to wait, they were given different visiting hours to other clinic patients. As for the SOE, it was to be responsible for discharging patients and declaring them ill. The rewards for the Foundation's doctors were very clear, as any services rendered would be favourably considered when it came to applying for admission to the ranks of the SOE Heart and Lung specialists[70]. In spite of these timid attempts at coordination, however, the outcome of the battle was already decided. In 1950, José benítez Franco denounced the duplication of services that the SOE was operating throughout Spain. The paradoxical situation arose that in many places, such as Oviedo and Guipuzcoa, the county councils were having trouble finishing their health centres, whereas the insurance scheme was building its residences, of similar characteristics, in such a way that "The differences can only be found in the nomenclature and administration: what some call sanatoriums or hospitals, others call residences; instead of clinics or health centres, these are called health service hospitals; some depend on the Ministry of the Interior and others on Employment, through the insurance scheme's Savings Bank"[71]. Finally, the Foundation's Secretary accused the insurance scheme of not conforming to the technical criteria of the Official Health

---

[68] José Palanca, "Los seguros sociales sanitarios", in J. Palanca, G. Clavero, E. Zapatero and L. Nájera Angulo, *Orientaciones actuales de Sanidad Pública (un esquema de Medicina Preventiva,* Madrid, s.i., 1947, p. 557.

[69] "Reunión de Directores de Dispensarios", *Revista Española de Tuberculosis*, 17, nº 164, 1948, pp. 776-784, p. 776.

[70] "Legislación", *Revista Española de Tuberculosis*, 18, nº 172, 1949, pp. 499-502.

[71] Bénitez Franco, 1950, *op. cit.* in footnote 13, p. 74.

Service for setting up its centres as, although the fountain of resources "is channelled through one pipeline or another, it is still the same"[72].

Benítez Franco's constant criticism of the SOE led to his punishment in 1950. He was substituted as head of the General Secretariat of the Foundation by José Fernández Turégano (b.1908), until then Director of the Escuela de Instructoras Sanitarias (School of Female Public Health Instructors). Significantly, he was not long after awarded the Medal of Honour by the French Committee for the Fight against Tuberculosis. This event was also an expression of the shift in relations between the democratic countries and Spain since the UN had revoked its diplomatic boycott of the latter in November 1950[73]. Despite his dismissal, in his new post as Counsellor of the National Welfare Institute, Benítez Franco continued to denounce the separation between Public Health and the Insurance against Disease. One consequence of this, he claimed, was the call for the creation of a Ministry of Public Health during the Third Meeting of National Public Health body, held in April 1951[74].

6. Conclusions

As this study has shown, research into the tuberculosis problem during the Francoist regime is both a valid and privileged route to the discovery of some of the sociopolitical keys to general sociomedical questions, as well as the late introduction in our country of a ' welfare state'.

The fight against tuberculosis waged by the regime after the civil war was essentially based on healthcare and charity, and in the field of prevention was limited to modifying the customs of the classes at the lower end of the social scale. In this sense, the work carried out by medicosocial experts contributed to the integration and adhesion

---

[72] *Ibid.* (p. 75). These opinions cast doubt on the hypothesis that the insurance scheme started building its own hospitals in 1948, owing to the shortage of existing hospital installations, as Felíp Soler Sabaris claims. The matter will undoubtedly be cleared up when historical research into the SOE is carried out with the depth and rigour it deserves. Felíp Soler Sabaris, "Alternativas de la Seguridad Social en un Plan de Reforma Sanitaria" in Jesús M. de Miguel, (Comp.) *Planificación y Reforma Sanitaria*, Madrid, Centro de Investigaciones Sociológicas, 1978, pp. 195-220. This claim is made on p. 210.

[73] "Condecoración al Dr. Benítez Franco", *Revista Española de Tuberculosis*, 20, nº 191, 1951, p. 142. In 1951 Spain was also admitted to the World Health Organisation, along with Japan and Germany.

[74] Bartolomé Benítez Franco, "Sobre la inclusión de la Sanidad Pública en los programas de Seguridad Social", in *Primer Congreso Iberoamericano de Seguridad Social*, Madrid-Barcelona, Ediciones Cultura Hispánica, 1951, vol. 2, pp. 671-676, p. 675.

of the population to the new regime, which used the tuberculosis problem to justify the rising against the Republic. Also underlying the campaign was the ultimate demographic aim of achieving a population of 40 million people. In the debate over the establishment of compulsory insurance against tuberculosis, and later in debates about disease in Spain, the influence of Italian fascism can be seen in the new regime's medicosocial statements. The Italian model was adopted by both Catholic-military circles and the Falangist Party even though, for reasons of political strategy, they ended up introducing an insurance scheme that bore more resemblance to the German model.

At the same time, we can observe the effect of power-sharing between the different factions of the Francoist regime on the definitive split between national Public Health – with the State Office of Public Health in the hands of the Catholic army sector – and those bodies responsible for social welfare (with the Ministry of Employment under Falangist Party control). This is a key element in understanding the health policy developed throughout the Franco period, as well as the foundation on which the current health system is based, and its problems for which solutions have yet to be found. In this sense, the fundamental reason for the mass construction of healthcare residences by those responsible for the Compulsory Health Insurance was not the absence of health centres in our country, but the Falangist Party's need to effectively establish itself among the working masses as part of the so-called National Syndicalist Revolution. Its rivalry with the Catholic army sector in healthcare matters, which manifested itself in the rejection of both the healthcare work carried out by National Public Health and the related legislation passed by the Ministry of the Interior, brought about an unnecessary duplication of expenditure on health, and healthcare institutions. The construction of anti-tuberculosis sanatoriums by the National Anti-tuberculosis Foundation undertaken parallel to and independently of the construction of the healthcare Residences of the SOE was not in vain. These two institutions became the most 'visible' part of Francoist social policy and agents of propaganda and justification for the military rising against the democratic Republican regime.

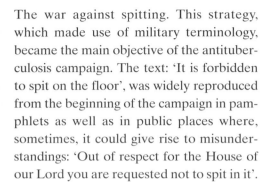

The war against spitting. This strategy, which made use of military terminology, became the main objective of the antituberculosis campaign. The text: 'It is forbidden to spit on the floor', was widely reproduced from the beginning of the campaign in pamphlets as well as in public places where, sometimes, it could give rise to misunderstandings: 'Out of respect for the House of our Lord you are requested not to spit in it'.

Figure 1: *Church in an Aragonese village at the end of the 1950s.*
Author: Dr. Agustín Serrate Torrente. Private collection, J. Molero.

Fig. 1

The crusade against 'evil'. During the Spanish post-war period the allegorical representation of Franco's crusade against communism (figure 2) coincides with the traditional image used in official publications of the National Tuberculosis Foundation (figure 3) and in the books on the popularisation of hygiene in the community ('Defend yourself', figure 4).

Figure 2: *Franco's crusade. Wall painting. Author: Reque Meruvia. Archivo Histórico Militar [Historic Military Record Office] (Madrid).*

Fig. 2

Fig. 3

Figure 3: *Información sobre la Lucha antitu-berculosa en España. Memoria correspondiente al año 1944 (1945).*
Madrid, PNA, 366 pp. Front cover.

Fig. 4

Figure 4: *Benítez Franco, Bartolomé (1942) Defiéndete. (Libro escolar de higiene). Madrid, Afrodisio Aguado, 159 pp. Illustration by J. Zubía. Front cover.*

Fig. 5

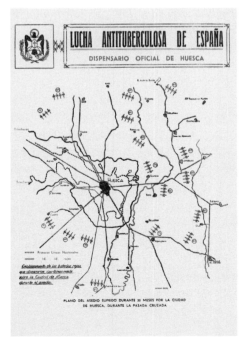

Fig. 6

Politics, war and tuberculosis. The assistance given to poor people suffering from tuberculosis in the runup to the Spanish Civil War was politically manipulated in order to avoid the victory of the Frente Popular in 1936 (figure 5: 'Against the revolution and its supporters') [See complete text in the illustration references]. In the same way, the head of the tuberculosis dispensary in Huesca had no objection to using the plan of the republican siege of the city as the front cover for its annual report (figure 6: 'Plan of the siege endured by the city of Huesca for 20 months during the last crusade'.)

Figure 5: *Pamphlet from the Acción Popular party, asking for the vote in the 1936 elections. Private collection, J. Molero.*
The text reads: Acción Popular 'Against the revolution and its supporters! 28,000 tuberculosis sufferers die in Spain every year. In 1931 there were 1,200 beds. From 1931 to 1934, this figure went up to 1,900. After a year in power, Acción Popular increased the number to 3,250 beds. Acción Popular was required to include credits in its budget in order to build eight more sanatoriums. By throwing us out, the supporters of the revolution stop the project. In order not to leave any tuberculosis sufferer without assistance, GIL ROBLES demand power. Vote for Spain! Against the revolution and its supporters!

Figure 6: *Jarne, Antonio (1939) Lucha antituberculosa de España. Dispensario oficial de Huesca. Memoria de la labor realizada en el Dispensario Antituberculoso Oficial del Estado del 4 de junio 1934 al 37 de julio 1936. Huesca, Nueva España de FET- JONS, 62 pp. Front cover.*

Fig. 7

Falangist public health and the Civil War. The sanitary responsibility of the Falangist party during the Civil War was a determining factor that contributed to the subsequent sanitary division of power. In the picture, nurses of the Women's Section of the Falange are waiting to be decorated by Franco during the Victory Parade in 1939 in Madrid.

Figure 7: *Sección Femenina de Falange Española Tradicionalista y de las JONS (ca. 1940) s.l., s.n., 316 pp. Picture from p. 289.*

At the Service of Spain and Spanish Children: Mother-and-Child Healthcare in Spain During the First Two Decades of Franco's Regime (1939-1963)

Josep Bernabeu-Mestre
Enrique Perdiguero-Gil

1. Introduction

> Thanks to the Spanish people, healthy and strong, both in body and mind, thanks to the Spanish doctor, wise, good and sensible; Alexis Carrel's terrible words will fortunately never be applied to our country: "More graves than cradles. It is thus their own fault that peoples who have broken the fundamental laws should disappear". (Bosch Marín, 1964; VI)

Aspects of the health of mothers and children in contemporary Spain have been the subject of recent summaries made by historiographers, like Esteban Rodríguez-Ocaña's *The Construction of Child's Health*. The aim of the present study is, however, to provide a more in-depth analysis of the mother-and-child healthcare programme set up by the authorities of the political regime that ruled Spain after the end of the Civil War in 1939. A brief presentation will be offered of the institutional framework within which this programme was developed, as well as of the resources available for its operation. The scientific, political and ideological premises supporting the programme will also be dealt with[1].

---

[1] The appearance of mother-and-child health protection schemes in Spain is closely linked to the establishment of social protection measures and policies during the Restoration period. In this context, the first comprehensive set of regulations on child protection was published on 17 August, 1904 (*Real Orden* – Royal Order in Council – of 10 August). Through this *Real Orden*, children under ten years of age were subject to the protection of the above-mentioned law. Protection included the children's physical and moral condition, the surveillance of children given away to mercenary breastfeeding, or those who had been granted asylum in cradle-houses, school workshops, etc, as well as anything else that could either directly or indirectly affect those children's lives from their birth until they reached the age of ten. On 24 January, 1908, the *Rules of Law on Child Protection* were passed, in the second article of which were specified the roles that had to be played by the different public bodies responsible for the protection of the youngest ones. Among these roles, emphasis was placed on protection and assistance for pregnant women as well as on the regulations for mercenary breastfeeding and its surveillance. They highlighted how convenient it was to encourage the creation of women's mutual benefit societies, free refectories for pregnant women and poor women that were breastfeeding and any other initiatives having as their aim to watch over and protect the child's life before its birth and in the first months of its life. After these early initiatives, many of which never materialised, we have to wait until the 1920s to see the first steps being taken towards the definitive institutionalisation of mother-and-child healthcare in Spain, namely the creation, in 1923, of the *Escuela Nacional de Puericultura* (National Childcare School) or the development of social insurance schemes, like the maternity insurance for working mothers of March 1929 (Decree-Law of 22 March, 1929), which, in fact, did not start until 1931.

2. The institutional framework

The political authorities set in motion various welfare, charity and health programmes after the Civil War (1936-1939) in order to solve problems related to mother-and-child healthcare. An attempt was made to coordinate them all, as we shall see, under the aegis of the *Dirección General de Sanidad* (Central Office for Health) of the *Ministerio de la Gobernación* (Ministry of the Interior). All the efforts made by the Children's Hygiene Services against infant mortality, and anything associated with it (mothers' mortality, death-at-birth rates, prenatal and pre-school hygiene), were given expression in the propaganda-oriented publications of those who, under the revealing title of *Al servicio de España y del niño español* (At the Service of Spain and Spanish Children), were in charge of showing the importance and the ideological and moral value that the victors' regime assigned to the reduction of infant mortality.

The approach to mother-and-child healthcare was based on policies that encouraged increasing birth rates while, at the same time, the hygiene argument was used in order to introduce other types of ideological and moral values.

One of the first publications in this series very clearly showed the interest behind this mother-and-child protection programme. Referring to the contents of the education being provided in *Guarderías Infantiles* (Children's Nursery Schools) and *Hogares Infantiles* (Children's Homes) set up to look after children, it said:

> In these centres, love of the mother country will constantly be instilled in the children as the supreme love, since the mother is not chosen like the wife or the children God sends us; the motherland is loved by birth like the mother, by choice like the wife and with a spirit of sacrifice for the good of our children. (Alvarez, 1939; p. 11)

Although the health authorities in Franco's regime, admitted that mother-and-child health indicators had greatly improved between 1900 and 1940 mainly as a result of improvements related to education as well as the basic living standards and healthcare – they believed that healthcare was the most important factor and the one which could cause the greatest impact (Bosch Marín et al, 1964: V-VII). The fight against mother and child mortality thus became one of the fundamental objectives (Bravo, 1954; p. 63):

> The government, eager to improve positive demographic factors as much as possible by increasing marriage and birth rates and to struggle efficiently against negative factors in matters of population, hopes to reduce mother-and-child mortality to a minimum.

Within this framework, the doctor's performance was valued above everything else and it was stated that:

> The Spanish doctor's work deserves to be known by all Spaniards; his superb work is ranked among the most important achievements of the contemporary world.
> (Bosch *et al.*, 1964; V)

The strong gender element, which, as we are going to see, prevailed in all the actions of the regime, the ideological elements of which were clearly defined, becomes obvious when it comes to the gratitude expressed for the progress achieved in the reduction of infant mortality. It is to doctors, male doctors, that:

> … for supporting and inspiring the health plans that were suitable for Spain, we owe the huge progress achieved in recent years… (Bosch *et al.*, 1964; VI)

Special mention was made of the collaboration of midwives, teachers, the thousands of women promoting healthcare in rural areas and mothers – the so-called "*colaboración femenina*" (women's collaboration) (Bosch *et al.*, 1964; VI) – although their role, and that of mothers above all, was usually expressed in negative terms:

> Women do not know how to prepare for motherhood and, needless to say, they are not only ignorant, but also do not want to learn how to bring up their children: they consider many disorders in pregnancy are physiological and would rather be attended by a poorly trained woman, with or without a qualification. This causes about 3,000 women to die in childbirth in Spain every year, and we do not have to say that free surgeries for pregnant women in Hygiene Centres have had a very low attendance if we quote the terrifying figures of 17,000 children dead at birth every year. They accept everything but being treated by competent specialists who would surely avoid these huge losses for the motherland. (Alvarez, 1939; 5)

In the fight against mother-and-child mortality, an objective that was very dear to Franco's regime, the *Ministerio de la Gobernación* – more specifically the *Servicios Centrales de Higiene Infantil de la Dirección General de Sanidad* (Central Services for Child Hygiene of the Central Office for Health) – designed guidelines concerning mother-and-child health. Action was taken by a considerable number of different state and parastate organisations, as was the case before the war (by province and town-based organisations) or was the result of the work of newly created bodies, like the *Auxilio Social* (Social Assistance) or the *Sección Femenina* (Women's Section) of the *Falange Española Tradicionalista* (the Spanish Traditionalist Falangist Movement).

The main action plans set up by the *Servicios de Higiene Infantil* were the following (Bravo, 1954; pp. 5-13):

1. The fight against the main causes of child mortality.

2. The fight against child kala-azar.

3. The fight against nutritional disorders in breastfeeding babies.

4. Campaigns to vaccinate against diphtheria[2], tuberculosis (by the B.C.G.) and whooping cough[3].

5. The fight against infectious diseases.

6. Popular health education through childcare courses given to breastfeeding mothers (including diplomas for exemplary mothers) as well as other means.

From the beginning, special attention was paid to the last, with a concentration on the rural population in particular, in an attempt to adapt it to the ideological premises on which the action of the *Servicios de Higiene Infantil* were based:

> It is true that quite an intense health propaganda campaign has been carried out in our motherland during the last decades but, perhaps because we have followed to the letter the guidelines established in other countries, because we have been unaware of our people's psychology, we have not obtained the result we expected. It becomes necessary, as a fundamental condition, to undertake an adaptation, a symbiosis between the propaganda means we choose and the psychological characteristics of our race, among which giving a good example occupies a place of honour. (Yturriaga, 1943; 1984)

In fact, the structure of the *Servicios de Higiene Infantil* was directly derived from the initiatives that were set in motion during the Second Republic (1931-1936 and until 1939 in those areas the legitimate Republican Government kept under control during the Civil War).

---

[2] Decree of 11 November, 1943 by which anti-diphtheria vaccination is declared compulsory. Order of 3 January, 1946 in which is established the official model for the certificate needed for anti-diphtheria vaccination. Order of April 1950 (Ministry of Education) regarding the presentation of schoolchildren for the official anti-diphtheria vaccination certificate.

[3] Order of 28 February, 1950 about the fight against tuberculosis in Primary Education Schools. Order of 8 November, 1950 (National Ministry of Education) by which is arranged the acknowledgement and practice of tuberculin tests in schoolchildren in national schools and primary education teaching centres.

Indeed, although Spanish healthcare had progressively achieved a considerable degree of maturity[4] during the first decades of the 20th century, it was with the arrival of the Second Republic (1931) that all this renewing activity materialised more clearly.

On 13 December, 1931, a decree was published for the creation of the *Sección de Higiene Infantil* (Child Hygiene Section). This was dependent on the *Inspección General de Instituciones Sanitarias* (General Inspection for Health Institutions) and its objective was none other than "fighting against child mortality and aspects related to it". It mobilised departments of mother mortality, death-at-birth mortality and prenatal as well as preschool hygiene. Furthermore, through a Ministry Order of 30 May, 1932, *Servicios de Higiene Infantil* were created in all the *Institutos Provinciales de Higiene* (Provincial Hygiene Institutes). They had to include surgeries for both prenatal hygiene and hygiene for breastfeeding babies as well as school hygiene[5].

Figure 1: *The cover of a book describing the services against infant mortality in Valencia, published immediately after the Civil War in Spain.*

---

[4] The enactment of the *Instrucción General de Sanidad* (General Directive for Health) in 1904 made it possible to set out the principles of a considerable number of the initiatives related to health policies that were going to be introduced. The second important boost would derive from the enactment, in 1925, of the *Estatuto y Reglamento de Sanidad Provincial* (Statute and Regulation for Healthcare in Provinces (Royal Decrees of 20 March and 20 October, 1925)). These rules made it possible '*to design a unified organisation of the different healthcare structures that had been appearing ever since the enactment of the Instruction of 1904*'.

[5] Moreover, a Ministry Order of 11 August, 1932, allowed the creation, through the corresponding budgetary provision, of mobile Child Hygiene Dispensaries. Through an Order of 31, 1933, mobile dispensaries were established in Burgos, Ávila, Segovia and Teruel.
On the other hand, in the autumn of 1931, along with the *Sección de Higiene Infantil*, the *Dirección General de Sanidad* set in motion the sections of *Higiene Social y Propaganda* (Section for Social Hygiene and Propaganda) and of *Higiene de la Alimentación* (Section for Food Hygiene). Both sections, among other functions, had to deal with issues related to mother-and-child health. In April 1933, for example, the *Sección de Higiene Social y Propaganda* developed, among other projects, a programme designed to promote breastfeeding (with the motto 'The best way to avoid mortality among newborn babies is breastfeeding by the mother') and another to highlight the importance of medical supervision ('If you can't breastfeed your newborn baby, consult your doctor before starting to bottlefeed').
Finally, we should mention the initiative on the part of the government of the Second Republic to improve rural healthcare and hygiene through the creation and operation of the *Centros Secundarios* and *Centros Rurales de Higiene* (District and Rural Health Centres; Ministry Order of 22 April, 1932). These institutions, coordinated by the *Institutos Provinciales de Higiene*, were going to play a fundamental role in the improved health of Spaniards in the 1930s.

But, as previously pointed out, the responsibility for the management of mother-and-child healthcare did not exclusively lie with these *Servicios de Higiene Infantil*, either central or peripheral, dependent on the *Sanidad Nacional* (Central Office of Health) and inherited from the Republic. (Table 1) On the contrary, there was a considerable diversity of organisations that were assigned tasks related to mother-and-child healthcare[6], including private initiatives.

Therefore, in a province like Barcelona shortly after the end of the Civil War, there were mother-and-child healthcare services that were dependent on various organisations: *Sanidad Nacional*, the Town Council, *Auxilio Social, Sección Femenina, Junta Provincial de Protección de Menores, Juntas Locales de Protección de Menores* (Town Boards for the protection of Minors), the *Instituto Nacional de Previsión* (National Insurance Institute), the Faculty of Medicine, the *Patronato de Lucha contra la Mortalidad Infantil* (Board for the Fight against Child Mortality), the *Instituto de Puericultura Integral* (Institute for Integral Childcare) and the *Inspección Médico-Escolar* (Medical-School Inspection) (Antecedentes..., 1942; pp. 10-11).

This situation continued over the years (see Table 2, in which are presented these organisations along with some of the resources and the services delivered). At the end of the period under consideration, this multiplicity of initiatives continued to exist, and charity institutions, such as the *Auxilio Social* (which became an autonomous body), still maintained an important infrastructure.

The *Law of Child and Mother Healthcare* of July 12th, 1941, was an attempt to overcome the problems arising from the scattering of resources[7] and established the need to

---

[6] The multiplicity of institutions and organisations was also reflected in the diversity of budgetary sources that had to support actions related to mother-and-child health (Article 24 from the Law on Child and Mother Health of 12 July, 1941):

a) The amounts in the state budget allocated to Childcare, Child Hygiene, School Hygiene and Maternology;

b) The contribution of the *Juntas Provinciales de Protección de Menores* (Provincial Boards for the Protection of Minors);

c) The contribution of *Mancomunidades Sanitarias* (Provincial Health Boards) and *Institutos Provinciales de Sanidad* (Provincial Health Institutes);

d) The amounts coming from the *Fondo de Protección Benéfico-social* (Charity and Welfare Protection Fund) for the establishment and installation of mother-and-child healthcare facilities).

[7] At the height of the Civil War, on the pro-coup side, the authorities of the government of Burgos had tried to coordinate all the childcare and maternology institutions with the aim of making their work more efficient, counting on the advice provided by the state's specific organisations: 'The Inspecciones Provinciales de Sanidad del Estado, through the Servicios de Higiene Infantil, will keep watch and offer advice to all kinds of Institutions related to mother-and-child protection and assistance as far as health matters are concerned.' (Ministry Order of 17 October, 1938 and Circular of 11 March, 1939).

coordinate those resources. To obtain coordination, a *Plan General de Sanidad Maternal e Infantil* (General Plan for Mother and Child Health Care) had to be established
which, in turn, had to approved by the *Ministerio de la Gobernación*. The effects of the
Plan General would be extended to the services dependent on *Sanidad Nacional*, to
local administrations, to national delegations of *Falange Española Tradicionalista y de
las Juntas de Ofensiva Nacional Sindicalista* (Spanish Traditionalist Falangist Movement
and of the Committees for the Syndicalist National Offensive, hereafter *Falange*)[8] and
to the *Juntas de Protección de Menores*.

In fact, the Law, in its article number 32, recognised some institutions as officially
cooperating with the State's functions, namely: services and establishments of Town
Halls, those in charge of Maternity Insurance (and, eventually, those in charge of the
Seguro Obligatorio de Enfermedad (Compulsory Health Insurance)), the National
Delegation of *Falange*, the *Obra de Protección a la Madre y al Niño de Auxilio Social*
(Social Help Society for Mother and Child Protection) and the *Sección Femenina* of
Falange, particularly its *Obra de la Hermandad de la Ciudad y el Campo* (Society for
City and Country Brotherhood).

The Law not only declared the obligation to teach Child Hygiene both at Teacher
Training Schools and Primary Schools, but also envisaged the introduction of a School
Medical Service to be organised through an agreement between the *Ministerio de
Gobernación* and that of *Educación Nacional* (National Education) with the collabo-
ration of the *Frente de Juventudes* (Youth Section) of *Falange*.

All these objectives were progressively achieved during the years that concern us in
this paper (see Tables 1 and 2).

The *Servicios de Higiene Infantil*, which were dependent on *Sanidad Nacional*, had a
dispensary-centred structure (with childcare and maternity surgeries) with provision
for tertiary services (centres established in the capital cities of provinces or in towns
having populations over 100,000 inhabitants), secondary services (those based in
municipalities that were the head of an administrative area) and primary services
(centres operating in rural areas). In 1962, these services had 298 doctors specialising
in childcare as well as maternologists with different time-commitments, 91 assistant
nurses specialising in childcare and 43 midwives (Personal…, 1962). Furthermore,
there was hospital medical assistance through Emergency Maternity and Pediatrics

---

[8] This party (also called the Movement) was the only one Franco created during the Civil War. It was
the result of the union of three different organisations, all of them opposed to left-wing parties.

Centres that had slowly appeared ever since the enactment of the Ministry Order of 20 December, 1941 (Bosch, 1943; Bosch, 1951).

Along with these services and centres, one must take into account the initiatives oriented towards maternity and childhood protection that were progressively developed after the introduction of Maternity Insurance. Administered by the *Instituto Nacional de Previsión* (the body responsible for the management of Social Insurance in Spain), Maternity Insurance (*General Regulations on Compulsory Medical Insurance*, Royal Decree of 29 January, 1930) guaranteed insured women medical assistance in pregnancy and at childbirth. It guaranteed, moreover, the resources needed for the woman to be able to have leave from work before and after childbirth, and encouraged the creation and maintenance of *Obras de Protección a la Maternidad y a la Infancia* (Societies for the Protection of Maternity and Childhood).

As years went by, and thanks to the financial surpluses of the Insurance, the *Obra Maternal e Infantil* (O.M.I - Mother and Child Society) was created with the aim of carrying out healthcare for expectant mothers and childcare for the children of women benefitting from these services.

In 1942, it was decided that the benefits from the O.M.I. should be extended to the wives and children of all workers included in the *Régimen de Subsidios Familiares* (Family Benefit Scheme).

In order to carry out the tasks assigned to the O.M.I, a network of Maternity and Childcare Centres was set up[9]. Trained doctors were put in charge of them, preference being given to those with the diploma of specialist in childcare. In 1948 the O.M.I became part of the Compulsory Health Insurance. Halfway through the 1950s, the number of childcare dispensaries organised by the O.M.I totalled 185, and 99 were dedicated to maternology. The number of maternologists and pediatricians or doctors specialising in childcare involved in this assistance scheme grew to 600 and 1,000 respectively (Bosch *et al.*, 1964; pp. 11-12; Bravo, 1954; p. 7).

In June 1953, an agreement was signed between the *Dirección General de Sanidad* and the *Dirección General de Previsión*, which meant that Emergency Maternal and Pediatric Centres could be used by people covered by the Compulsory Health Insurance. At the same time, a decision was made to give priority to hospital assistance, which would complete the task carried out by maternology and pediatrics

---

[9] During the early years, some dispensaries belonging to the O.M.I were set up, and agreements were made with others (Rodríguez-Ocaña, 1995, p. 25).

dispensaries, a stage that was already considered superseded (Bosch, 1951; 9). This all happened despite the efforts to persuade the population to allow assistance at child-birth (Alvarez, 1939; p. 9) in a context that, despite being medicalised, also had all the negative connotations of charity medical hospital assistance, especially as in Maternity Hospitals.

That same year the regulations for Emergency Maternity and Pediatric Centres were passed through an Order of 21 September, 1953. Thus, in 1954, there were 78 of these centres unevenly scattered throughout Spain: while some provinces had only one, others had more than ten (Bravo, 1954; pp. 130-131). Nevertheless, their real work, involving doctors specialising in childcare, maternologists, midwives and nurses specialising in childcare, has as yet not been highlighted by historiography.

When referring to hospitals, we must also bear in mind the *Clínicas de Prematuros* (Surgeries for Premature Babies), which were set up by the *Dirección General de Sanidad* with the help of other organisations that provided the premises: town halls, provincial governments, savings banks, National Health Insurance, faculties of medicine, etc. UNICEF also collaborated in their establishment. (Bosch *et al.*, 1964; p. 11)

In this respect, *The Law on Grounds for National Health* of November 25th, 1944 reinforced the coordinating role of the *Dirección General de Sanidad*. In Ground 14, dedicated to Mother and Child Health, the above mentioned *Dirección* was entrusted with the coordination and surveillance of the existing Maternology and Childcare Institutions, whatever their nature. As its main novelty, the Law envisaged the introduction of a 'health notebook' (in which important health information would be recorded) to be owned by every Spaniard from birth until they reached fifteen years of age.

3. The professionals in mother-and-child healthcare

In addition to the assistance that could be provided by the professionals in medicine and other professions that were ancillary to it, in particular midwives and visiting nurses[10], we must emphasise the role of those who received their education and training within the framework of the National Childcare School.

---

[10] With reference to the human resources that contributed to the development of mother-and-child healthcare, as well as the National Childcare School, we must highlight the role of the National Health School, of the frustrated project for a School of Health and Public Assistance Nurses, which was transformed into the School of Female Health Instructors in 1939, and of a whole series of professionals who proliferated in the early 1940s (e.g., nurses of *Falange*, social visiting nurses, social help nurses, school hygiene nurses, etc.).

Although there were antecedents, such as the proposal in 1910 for the creation of a National Maternology and Childcare Institute, it would be in 1923 (Royal Order in Council of May 23rd) that the plan for creating a teaching centre for the training of professionals responsible for mother and child health would be realised[11].

After an initial stage, which had a provisional character, a modification of the School Regulations was approved by means of a Decree on 16 July, 1932. Through this the body of teachers as well as the resources assigned to the school were consolidated and enlarged. In keeping with the modern trends of child hygiene, the following reforms were put forward: on the one hand, the development of its performance under the threefold aspect of a technical and professionally-oriented school, a child hygiene institute and a centre for scientific research; on the other hand, as long as the needs of the country did not demand a larger variety in the teaching syllabus, the school was to issue titles of Doctors specialising in Childcare, Visiting Nurses specialising in Childcare, Midwives specialising in Childcare and Child Carers.

Once the Civil War had finished, the National Childcare School became a fundamental instrument for health policy developed by the new regime as far as initiatives relating to child hygiene were concerned. This was shown in the speeches at the opening session of the year 1941-42 (Escuela Nacional de Puericultura en el curso 1941-1942, 1942; pp. 23-37):

> It is necessary to undertake the task of a moral and material reorganisation of the Spanish people, which is in need of a real cultural and health policy which, with the help of doctors and teachers, can eliminate all the germs that sicken the mind and the health of a magnificent, probably unique, human material.

---

[11] However, they would have to wait until 1925 (Royal Decree of 16 November, 1925) for the establishment of the school's Provisional Regulations, which determined the kind of teaching for each year's courses. And it would not be until February 1926 (Royal Order in Council of 12 February, 1926) that 14 senior teachers to the school were appointed (it was an honorary unpaid job). The opening of the first course was planned for October 1926.
The Royal Decree of 16 November, 1925, which developed the Provisional Regulations of the National Childcare School, also provided for the creation of Provincial Childcare Schools. As long as its resources allowed it, the National Childcare School could establish subsidiary teaching centres in Spanish provinces. The only condition it had to abide by to set up these centres was to achieve the maximum benefits in the interests of children. That was the case, for example, with a Royal Order in Council of 22 July, 1927, which authorised the installation of Valencia's Provincial Childcare School in the premises of the Maternal School in that city. In this respect, an Order in Council of 4 December, 1929 urged provincial governments to give financial support to Provincial Childcare Schools.

The National Childcare School, under the ideological and doctrinal guidelines that we have just explained, and with the losses pursuant on fratricidal conflict, kept on working with the same organisation as in the 1930s until new Regulations were approved on 16 June, 1947. The new rules, which resulted from the legal framework established by the *Law on Grounds of National Health and the Law on the Organisation of the Spanish University*, established two teaching degrees: the degree for doctors (Title of Doctor specialising in Childcare and Diploma of Doctor specialising in Childcare) and women's degrees. Among the latter, a distinction was made between two groups, namely, that of Childcare Nurses, Childcare Teachers, Childcare Midwives and women with the diploma of Childcare Specialist and that of Assistant Childcare Nurses. Also, after the reforms introduced in 1947, new Department Schools were increasingly created in various capital cities of provinces as well as in other important towns. Thus, in 1949, there were Provincial Childcare Schools in 14 provinces, eight of them with an annexed surgery for newborn babies (Bosch *et al.*, 1949; pp. 4-5).

Along with the training of all these professionals, the Regulations of 1947 entrusted the National Childcare School with other functions, such as the organisation of special education courses, encouraging studies and research related to matters like prenatal hygiene, child mortality or feeding of newborn babies, or teaching lower social classes (particularly the mothers) the fundamental notions of child hygiene.

4. Indoctrinating the female population

The importance assigned to the teaching of childcare, as referred to above, had already become evident through the Ministry Order of 20 December, 1941, by which a regulation was made for the teaching of childcare to breastfeeding mothers. Mothers' lack of education in health matters, and especially in all the aspects related to childcare, was considered by the health and political authorities as the main cause of their children's sickness and death, as we have already pointed out. As was stated by the head of the *Sección Femenina of Falange* (Escuela Nacional de Puericultura en el curso 1941-1942, 1942: p. 34):

> The only task assigned to women as regards the Motherland, is looking after the home. We are going to teach them to look after their children, because it is unforgivable that so many children, who are God's servants and future soldiers for Spain, should die as a result of ignorance. This programme is thus in accordance with the Leader's slogan 'Save children's lives through the education of mothers', accurately pointed out in reference to the health programme during Franco's speech, on December 31st, 1939, Year of Victory.

Thus, the *Sección Femenina* channelled the teaching of its doctrine through Training Services. But the 'training' of women undertaken was no more and no less than instilling in them a national-sindicalist behaviour pattern based on the axiomatic principles of the Motherland, such as 'unity of destiny', the Catholic religion 'as a moral doctrine' and childcare 'as a duty' (Gallego, 1983; p. 82)[12]. Following these guidelines, child hygiene could not be conceived differently:

> We fight for our Religion and for our Motherland. In the same way that we cannot conceive that a mother should not know and consequently cannot teach Cathechism to her children, the Motherland is built, not only by giving birth to many children, but by bringing them up with the teaching of modern knowledge, which if followed, and without having to do anything else, would make child mortality figures go down considerably. (Alvarez, 1939; p. 6)

Childcare dispensaries, through doctors' advice and visits at home by female health instructors and visiting nurses, would become the fundamental weapon to fight against 'health ignorance'. During the first five days of each month, the authorities imposed the compulsory organisation in all childcare and pediatric dispensaries (state-dependent or not) of brief courses consisting of five lectures and two practical sessions[13] (Bravo, 1954; pp. 78-81).

The number of mothers that were allowed to attend each of these courses was limited to 20. Enrollment was free and attendance was compulsory – participation in these elementary childcare courses was a condition for receiving the benefits of child assistance and charity societies. Furthermore, the mothers that made the greatest progress while following the courses were awarded the title of 'Exemplary Mother' (Bosch *et al.*, 1954; p. 14).

The education of mothers as described above was complemented by the use of other kinds of resources: radio programmes, publicity posters, etc. (Yturriaga, 1943; pp. 90-97).

Concerning this work, one must specially bear in mind the contribution of female health education volunteers from the *Sección Femenina* who, having received training, taught childcare to the rural population. The *Sección Femenina* also set up childcare

---

[12] For a general overview of this matter, see the book by Roca i Girona (1996).

[13] The lectures dealt with general childcare topics, but paid special attention to feeding (breast-feeding and weaning), to the correction of mistakes in the care of healthy and ill children (e.g., to teaching that there is no such thing as tooth and dribble illnesses), and to making sure mothers knew about the programme of health propaganda entitled *At the Service of Spain and Spanish Children: what Spain does for Mothers and Children.*

dispensaries in those rural centres that lacked public establishments, e.g., up to 43 dispensaries were set up in 1954. Mid-way through the 1950s, the so-called *Cátedras Ambulantes* (Travelling Chairs) were extended throughout the rural areas. They had several aims including the teaching of basic literacy, the fight against child mortality, hygiene and health and social education campaigns, household training and rules for cohabitation (Sánchez, 1990; pp. 40-41).

Figure 2: *Health visitor showing mothers how to wash a baby in the 1950s, probably in the building of the women's section of the Falange.*

This organisation generally affected all Spanish women through the training it gave to the country's young women so that they could play their role in the *Servicio Social* (Social Service). This meant that women had to take part in a compulsory, unpaid, assistance delivery scheme, which included the teaching of childcare basics. It's characteristics of work exploitation and social control have been highlighted by several female scholars (Gallego, 1983; pp. 91-98; Sánchez, 90; pp. 35-42). Thus, an attempt was made to achieve a real 'acculturation' of the female population regarding their role in society and childcare teaching became a central element of this[14].

The different publications issued by the *Sección Femenina* show this side of *Falange*'s female arm, especially the often re-issued *Post-birth Childcare Notions,* a summary of the 'Lessons in Childcare and Hygiene for Courses in Education in the Rural Areas'. These 'lessons' followed the habitual pattern in which childcare teaching was presented as a permanent fight against ignorance, superstition and tradition. On every page the task of health eduaction volunteers was seen as that of a person who had to enter a cultural group that was completely alien and whose beliefs, all of them wrong, had to be modified:

> What numerous women cannot, do not know or do not want to say: their confused wishes, their secret sorrows, their stifled woes, their tribulations, their superstitious fears, their suffering, their forebodings. All those pains that accumulate or can be accumulated in a corner of a woman's soul or body, and more so in those of a mother but which she would never

---

[14] On childcare as a 'moral doctrine of class', see Boltanski's monograph (1974).

expose in front of a doctor, you can know these, Health Education Volunteer for the Rural Areas. If in your task, if with your words, if with your condition as a woman, you can approach the woman whose fear concentrates the anguish in her soul.

Acclimatise your feelings to her heart; from one woman to another, carry out your task as a Health Education Volunteer. (Lecciones, 1945; p. 16)

5. Conclusions

We will end by highlighting some of the most problematic aspects of the health programme we have tried to analyse.

First we should emphasise the diversity of institutions and organisations that had responsibilities related to mother-and-child healthcare. Such a scattered scheme brought about coordination problems and made it difficult to optimise resources that were insufficient and, in general, badly distributed.

Secondly, we must refer to the influence exerted by the introduction of the *Seguro Obligatorio de Enfermedad (S.O.E.* – Compulsory Health Insurance) in the development and setting in motion of the programme we have been dealing with. The extension of the benefits of medical assistance to the child population (achieved by the Compulsory Health Insurance) made less necessary many of the assistance institutions (both dispensaries and hospitals) created by the *Dirección General de Sanidad* or dependent on it.

This gave rise to an approach in which the medicalisation of mother-and-child healthcare prevailed to the detriment of a 'childcare' discourse which emphasised aspects related to prevention and health promotion for the youngest.

Anyway, from 1963 onwards, before the real take-off of the *Seguro Obligatorio de Enfermedad* – in its capacity as *Seguridad Social* (Social Security) – the services belonging to the *Sanidad Nacional* probably played a role in the medicalisation of mother-and-child healthcare through Emergency Maternal and Pediatric Centres. Their real role among the rural population still remains to be studied in more detail.

Thus, as years went by, there was a consolidation of the separation between the group of assistance functions oriented towards solving illness among the child population (assumed by the Compulsory Health Insurance) and the functions related to prevention, that continued to be the domain of the *Sanidad Nacional* through the staff and institutions (*Delegaciones Provinciales de Sanidad*) dependent on the *Dirección General de Sanidad.*

Finally, we must draw attention to the ideological and political objectives that accompanied the Spanish health system beyond any scientific contents and premises, an objective that can be summarised as 'At the service of Spain and Spanish Children!' Following an antimalthusian and pro-birth approach, they insisted on the woman's role as mother, while simultaneously taking advantage of the programme to spread political and ideological messages. For example, when it came to regulating childcare teaching to mothers, in the short courses that the Dispensaries had to carry out, they did not fail to point out that in the diploma-giving ceremony, "… a talk will be given to mothers on their children's moral, religious and patriotic formation…" (Order of 20 December, 1941). All this without forgetting social control mechanisms implied by some of the initiatives that were put into practice (provisions assigned, educations campaigns).

Table 1

Mother-and-child Health in Spain during the early years of Franco's Regime (1939-1963)
Childcare Services directly dependent on the Central Office for Health around 1954
(Bosch *et al.*, 1964)

Childcare and Maternology Dispensaries	Human Resources and the Roles they Played
62 Childcare Tertiary Dispensaries and 62 Maternolgy Tertiary Dispensaries (Provincial capital cities)	Childcare doctors and health workers qualified in childcare
91 Childcare Dispensaries in District Health Centres and 91 Maternology Dispensaries	Childcare doctors and health workers qualified in childcare
200 Childcare Dispensaries and 200 Maternology Dispensaries in Primary Health Centres (in rural areas)	Town Doctors
1 National Childcare School and 14 Provincial Childcare Schools	Training in childcare for doctors, teachers, matrons, nurses, childcarers, auxiliary nurses, and a introductory childcare course for women and basic courses on 'How to be an Exemplary Mother' Special knowledge spreading courses for rural Childcare doctors and courses organised by the *Obra de Perfeccionamiento Sanitario de España* (Society for Health Improvement in Spain)
80 Emergency Maternal and Pediatric Centres	Cottage hospitals, having between 8 and 10 beds, situated in small towns dedicated to difficult births, serious illnesses in newlyborns in order to make these benefits accessible to those inhabitants who could not reach city hospitals
11 Surgeries for newlyborns	In certain large cities a ward was added that permitted the hospitalisation of newlyborns
8 Surgeries for Premature Babies	

Table 2

Mother-and-child Health in Spain during the early years of Franco's Regime (1939-1963)
Childcare Services not directly dependent on the Central Office for Health around 1954
(Bravo, 1954)

Services	Resources
Social Help. This organisation belonged to and was financially subsidised by Official Charity. Its action was oriented towards the poor	Social Assistance for Mother and Child, 40 Maternology Centres, 8 Maternity Houses, 40 Refectories for Pregnant and Breastfeeding Mothers, 165 Child Nourishment Centres (type Milk depots), 2 Cradle Houses (newlyborns), 28 Child Homes (3-10 years of age), 70 School Homes (10-14 years of age), 36 Mother Centres and Child nursery Schools, 556 Child Refectories, 1 Nursing home, 3 Antitrachomatous homes, 1 Antitrico-phyticum home, 1 Sanatorium for Child Tuberculosis
Higher Council and Provincial Board for protection of Minors	Child Social Assistance Centres (childcare services and dispensaries in several important cities), 111 Child Centres: Orphanages, Milk Depots, Surgeries, Nurseries, Child Homes
Sección Femenina of Falange	Preventive campaigns (especially against dyptheria) Propaganda and Education Campaigns about Childcare by female health education volunteers – more than 3,000 in the whole Spanish national territory. 1 Childcare Travelling Chair. Other institutions: 4 Prevention Centres, 30 Rural Health Centres, 15 Childcare Dispensaries

Town Halls, Provincial Governments and Charity Health Foundations (Red Cross, etc)	Paediatric and Childcare services. Provincial charity organisations (46 orphanages for new-born children and 14 Childcare Surgeries). Town charity organisations (60 dispensaries for sick children and milk depots – nourishment for poor children)
Compulsory Health Insurance (S.O.E.)	8 Maternal Residences. 185 Childcare and paediatric out-patient centres. 99 maternal out-patient centres.
Mother and Child Society (Obra Maternal e Infantil)	185 Childcare Dispensaries and 99 Maternology Dispensaries. 1,000 childcare doctors and 600 maternologists

Bibliography

Álvarez, Romero E., *Higiene Infantil e Instructoras de Sanidad*, Valladolid, Jefatura del Servicio Nacional de Sanidad (Publicaciones Al Servicio de España y del niño español), 1939.

Antecedentes para una plan nacional de obras de Puericultura y Maternología, Madrid, Dirección General de Sanidad (Publicaciones Al Servicio de España y del niño español), 1942.

Boltanski, L. *Puericultura y moral de clase*, Barcelona, Laia, 1974.

Bosch, Marín J., *El Hospital Infantil y Maternal en España*, Madrid, Dirección General de Sanidad (Publicaciones Al Servicio de España y del niño español), 1951.

Bosch, Marín J., Otero M. Blanco, J.Mª Mingo de Benito, Sánchez del Peral E. Bravo, *La Puericultura en la Sanidad Nacional*, Servicios de Sanidad Infantil y Maternal, Dirección General de Sanidad (Publicaciones Al Servicio de España y del niño español), 1949.

Bosch, Marín J., Otero M. Blanco, J.Mª. Mingo, *Puericultura Social.* 4ª ed., Madrid, Gráficas González, 1964.

Bravo, Sánchez del Peral E., *Organización y Legislación de los Servicios de Sanidad Infantil y Maternal en España*, Madrid, Dirección General de Sanidad (Publicaciones Al Servicio de España y del niño español), 1954.

Carasa, P., "La revolución nacional-asistencial durante el primer franquismo (1936-1940)", *Historia Contemporánea*, 1997, 16, pp. 89-140.

Censo-fichero de Centros y Personal de los Servicios de Sanidad Materno-Infantil en España, Madrid, Dirección General de Sanidad (Publicaciones Al Servicio de España y del niño español), 1963.

(La) Escuela Nacional de Puericultura en el curso 1941-42, Madrid, Dirección General de Sanidad (Publicaciones Al Servicio de España y del niño español), 1942.

Gallego, Méndez MªT., *Mujer, Falange y franquismo*, Madrid, Taurus, 1983.

Lecciones de Puericultura e Higiene para cursos de divulgadoras sanitario-rurales, Madrid, Sección Femenina de F.E.T. y J.O.N.S., 1945.

Nociones de Puericultura Postnatal, Madrid, Sucesores de Rivadeneyra, 1944.

Orduña, Prada M., *El auxilio social (1936-1940). La etapa fundacional y los primeros años,* Madrid, Escuela Libre, 1996.

Personal Materno-Infantil en la Sanidad Nacional Española, Madrid, Dirección General de Sanidad (Publicaciones Al Servicio de España y del niño español), 1962.

Programas de Sanidad Nacional para sus enseñanzas de Puericultura, Maternología e Higiene Escolar, Madrid, Dirección General de Sanidad (Publicaciones Al Servicio de España y del niño español), 1944.

Resumen legislativo del año 1942, Madrid, Dirección General de Sanidad (Publicaciones Al Servicio de España y del niño español), 1942.

Roca i Girona, J., *De la pureza a la maternidad: la construcción del género femenino en la postguerra española,* Madrid, Ministerio de Educación y Ciencia, Dirección General de Bellas Artes, 1996.

Rodríguez-Ocaña, E., *La construcción de la salud infantil, Ciencia, medicina y educación en la transición de la mortalidad en España. IV Congreso de la Asociación de Demografía Histórica,* País Vasco, Septiembre 1995.

Sánchez López, R., *Mujer española, una sombra de destino en lo universal. Trayectoria histórica de Sección Femenina de Falange (1934-1977),* Murcia, Universidad de Murcia, 1990.

Yturriaga, González-Jurado E., "Plan de propaganda sanitaria maternal e infantil", *in Estudios oficiales de la Primera Reunión anual de Médicos Puericultores del Estado,* Dirección General de Sanidad (Publicaciones 'Al Servicio de España y del niño español'), 1943, pp. 83-108.

The Politics of Public Health in the State-Managed Scheme of Healthcare in Spain (1940-1990)

Esteban Rodríguez-Ocaña

1. Introduction

This paper offers a broad view of the evolution of Public Health in Spain from the end of the Civil War to the present day. It aims to show how the relationships between science and politics do not occur in set patterns, but rather that the particular context of each situation obliges us to study its peculiarities. In our contemporary society, science holds a prominent position, underpinning many political tasks, such as health administration, and providing a rationale for specific corps of functionaries, such as public health officials. The science of public health has encountered changing patterns of political consent during the period of our review in Spain, a time that, after a long prodromic period (from the 1860s to the 1920s), can be described as the epoch of the rise, fall and resurrection of Public Health as a professional domain in the public sphere [1].

In the last third of the 19th century, the growth of health administration started at the municipal and state levels, and was dominated by a view of population-level health. It took several forms, from the quarantine stations at the inland borders and sea harbours to the scientific management of spas and health control of prostitutes, from chemical and toxicological laboratories for food testing to microbiology laboratories to diagnose and prevent the spread of infectious diseases. The formative period of a state structure for Public Health can be placed in the first 25 years of the 20th century. It included the ephemeral existence of a state agency for Public Health (1899-1904: *Dirección General de Sanidad*, or National Health Department, NHD), a central piece of legislation, the *Royal Decree on General Instruction for Public Health* (1904), the establishment of provincial and municipal health officers, the reopening of the NHD (1922), and its closure with the new *Rules for Public Health of the Provinces*, issued in 1925, which validated the provincial Institutes of Public Health as technical centres of public health administration. The agreement reached in 1922 with the International

---

[1] P. Marset, E. Rodríguez-Ocaña and J.M. Sáez, *La Salud Pública en España*, in F. Martínez Navarro *et al.*, *Salud Pública*, Madrid, MacGraw-Hill Interamericana, 1998, pp. 25-47.

Health Board of the Rockefeller Foundation gave a definite push forward to the steady development of public health that lasted until 1957, despite the war (1936-39)[2].

The first section of this overview deals with the question: how did the Republican and Francoist administrations maintain continuity in the sphere of public health. In the second section, I will describe the decline of public health in favor of an all-encompassing scheme of social health insurance, presided over by an immediately productive understanding of health and sustained by the spread of hospital-based medical care. In the third section I analyse the new flowering of the doctrines of public health in the context of the return to democracy, and describe the crucial merging of scientific concepts and political strategies of the left. To conclude, I offer some reflections about the ambiguous relations between science and politics in our time, in the light of these particular endeavours.

2. The post-war health crisis: the triumph of social medicine

From 1939 on, as a direct outcome of the three-year long civil war, there was a rise in the morbidity and mortality rates due to smallpox, diphtheria, typhus and malaria, among other infectious causes of death. These had been reduced during the previous 40 years. Moreover, hunger became a family companion for Spaniards and a serious epidemic of lathyrism broke out in some provinces because of the widespread use of flour made from a kind of almond (*harina de almortas*). In fact, the proportional death toll from infectious diseases increased during the first three years after the war, to peak at 35% of all deaths. The rate of infant mortality, 148 per 1,000, increased to the levels of 1923[3]. Endemic malaria, well under control by 1936, increased after 1937

---

[2] Rodríguez-Ocaña, "The Making of the Spanish Public Health Administration during the First Third of the Twentieth Century", *Quaderni internazionale di Storia della Medicina e la Sanità*, 1994, 3 (1), pp. 49-65; E. Rodríguez-Ocaña, J. Bernabeu and J.L. Barona, "La Fundación Rockefeller y España, 1914-1936. Un acuerdo para la modernización científica y sanitaria", in J.L. García, J.M. Moreno, G. Ruiz (eds.) *Estudios de historia de las técnicas, la arqueología industrial y las ciencias*, Salamanca, Consejería de Cultura de la Junta de Castilla y León, 1998, vol. 2, pp. 531-539; E. Rodríguez Ocaña, "Foreign Expertise, Political Pragmatism and Professional Elite. The Rockefeller Foundation in Spain 1919-1939", Studies in History and Philosophy of Biological and Biomedical Sciences, 2000, 31 (3), pp. 447-461.

[3] I. Jiménez Lucena, "El tifus exantemático en la postguerra española (1939-1943). El uso de una enfermedad colectiva en la legitimación del Nuevo Estado", *Dynamis*, 1994, 14, pp. 185-198, p. 188. Jiménez has made her calculations with data from the Movimiento natural de la población de España for 1939-41, considered the best source for mortality data in Spain (F. Martínez Navarro, "Algunos problemas en la reconstrucción de las series históricas de las estadísticas demografico-sanitarias", in *Estadísticas demografico-sanitarias. I Encuentro Marcelino Pascua, Madrid, Instituto de Salud Carlos III*, 1992, pp. 79-112, quote from p. 92).

and caused a catastrophic number of deaths in 1942-43. These figures reflected a considerable backslide from the successful level attained by the anti-malaria campaign put into practice in 1916-20 in different regions of Spain. This had received financial support – and praise – from the Rockefeller Foundation during the ten years before Franco's uprising[4].

This health crisis, triggered by a mixture of several morbid conditions, was not well studied or explained at the time. The political stage after Franco's victory, with its exaltation of the military, a complete lack of civil rights, and a strenuous campaign of self-propaganda, made serious investigation of the causes of these problems an impossible undertaking.

During the war, health matters on the rebel side had been under military control and this was continued in the following years, in the absence of a new civil organisation of the public health administration, along the main lines that presided during the Republican period. The victory of the fascist uprising, however, meant a purge of the public administration that affected 25% of the functionaries in the health sector, a much smaller proportion than in other collectives such as teachers, for example[5].

We know that by the end of 1942 and in March 1943 several meetings of health officers were held to exchange opinions and data about the situation. These encounters were not given any publicity at the time. The official view on the epidemics ran parallel to the authoritarian ideology of the victors: it was considered a problem of law and order, almost like a continuation of the war (by other means) against Communism and International Masonry. In April 1943, an agreement to create a new National Council of Public Health was reached, the institution that was to serve, in the words of the Minister of Interior Blas Pérez González, as "the General Staff in order to restore the disrupted public health order". From that moment on, action was taken against epidemics[6].

---

[4] E. Luengo, "Organización actual de la lucha antipalúdica en España", in G. Pittaluga *et al.* *Paludismo*, Madrid, Ediciones Morata, 1944, pp. 829-840; C. Rico Avello, "La epidemia de paludismo de la postguerra", *Revista de Sanidad e Higiene Pública*, 1950, 24, pp. 701-737; L. Clemente Fuentes, *El paludismo en la provincia de Cáceres*, Salamanca, Institución Cultural El Brocense, 1992; J. Bernabeu, "Cultura, ciencia y política. La lucha antipalúdica de la Cataluña de la mancomunidad, 1914-1925", *Medicina e Historia*, 1997, n° 73.

[5] P. Marset, J.M. Sáez and F. Martínez Navarro, "La Salud Pública durante el franquismo", *Dynamis*, 1995, 15, pp. 211-250.

[6] "La Sanidad española en el último decenio. Discurso de Ministro de Gobernación, Blas Pérez González, a preguntas de dos procuradores en Cortes", *Revista de Sanidad e Higiene Pública*, 1950, 24, pp. 469-489.

Isabel Jiménez Lucena, from the University of Malaga, has focused her sharp, lucid vision on one of the relevant components of the convulsions of the time, namely the typhus epidemics. As she sees it, the campaign against typhus served as a powerful weapon for the legitimation of the state born of the Civil War and the German-Italian intervention[7].

According to her studies, the epidemics started in 1939, but did not cause alarm until April 1941. In cities like Granada, Seville and Madrid, typhus outbreaks were consciously hidden or given less importance than they deserved, in order to avoid difficulties with foreign countries and political damage domestically[8]. Once the extent of the epidemics could no longer be hidden, a campaign of blame was run against Republicans, who were held responsible for all evils. Material cleansing was identified with ideological purity, within the realm of the current repression against the Reds. Franco's regime claimed for itself the virtue of creating a clean and healthy country, and as typhus was linked to dirt (the spread of the disease depended on lice), it followed that the disease had its origin in 'proletarian filthiness' peculiar to the popular classes, the enemies of the New State.

Therefore physical and moral contagions were identified, and the fight against the 'green louse' (the popular name of *Pediculus vestimenti*) became transmuted into a struggle against the 'red louse'[9]. This explains the repressive tone that we detect in advice on how to combat the epidemic, as shown by this example from the popular press:

> On the occasion of the present health problems… public authorities carry out a praiseworthy campaign: we must cooperate with them in the undertaking already begun with aid to the poor (and to be continued with those who attend relief canteens or kitchens, schools, poorhouses, etc). To focus on those cases brought to the fore with the collaboration of the public, and to denounce those unclean people who are a risk to their neighbors as well as to themselves and their families[10].

---

[7] I. Jiménez Lucena, *El tifus en la Málaga de la postguerra. Un estudio historicomédico en torno a una enfermedad colectiva*, Málaga, Universidad, 1990. I. Jiménez Lucena, "El tifus exantemático…", note 3.

[8] According to the Head of the National Health Department (Director general de Sanidad), Dr. Palanca, in Semana médica española, 1941, as quoted by Jiménez Lucena, *El tifus en Málaga…* (note 7), p. 66.

[9] In the words of Palanca, *Las epidemias de la posguerra. Discurso leído en la solemne sesión celebrada el día 28 de marzo de 1943 en la Real Academia de Medicina de Madrid*, Madrid, Instituto de España, 1943. But, at the same time, in a book directed to the scientific international community, he claimed that: "all that could annoy those social groups that suffered from this disgraceful illness, was suppressed by my authority". Prologue to G. Clavero del Campo and F. Pérez Gallardo, *Técnicas de laboratorio en el tifus exantemático*, Madrid, DGS, 1943, p. 10.

[10] "Divulgación sanitaria. SUR (Málaga) 25 abril 1941", quoted by Jiménez Lucena, *El tifus en Málaga…* (note 7), p. 47.

In addition to the absence of freedom and the spread of hunger and disease, the popular classes were also victims of a repressive, revengeful view of health matters by the political authorities. It is no wonder that they responded with widespread passive resistance. Thus, systematic home visits by public health nurses or auxiliary nurses, often from the Women's Section (*Sección Femenina*) of the Fascist party, were unsuccessful. In the city of Malaga, for example, 13.5% of the families visited were absent for the second visit; this rose to 47.7% on the third visit [11]. In Madrid, from 2,000 homes to be visited in a programme designed by the Area of Nutrition of the Provincial Department of Health in 1941, the door was opened at only 728 (36%). The final report, signed by Carlos Jiménez Díaz, stated that: "Most families behave in a frankly hostile manner, and, in general, they did not help us to obtain reliable data… The general attitude of the families could be said to be one of distrust" [12].

Studies by Jorge Molero on the fate of the campaigns against tuberculosis (another of the morbid conditions exacerbated by post-war scarcities) show the implementation of a conception of the population as immature, and hence unable to take responsibility for its own health [13].

The Phalangist ideas of medicine emphasised the political and moral sides of medical activities. This group held a view of diseases that went well beyond the material, and understood them as "the logical consequence of a world sunk in spiritual crisis" [14]. The struggle between Fascist ideals and decadent, worldwide materialism were to be dealt with with reference to health through the substitution at the personal level of a 'professional' strategy with a 'missionary' approach; that is, physicians ought to serve the state's interests, at the service of the Empire to come [15]. This conception was to materialise as a series of institutions, at first pedagogically dependent on the state (to guarantee the triumph of such assumptions) until eventually they would attain autonomy.

---

[11] *Ibid.*, p. 83.

[12] Carlos Jiménez Díaz, "Memoria sobre el estado nutritivo de la población madrileña (1941-1943)", prólogo de J.L. Peset, *Estudios de Historia social*, 1978, n° 5, pp. 401-465, quote from pp. 402-3.

[13] J. Molero-Mesa, "Enfermedad y previsión social en España durante el primer franquismo (1936-1951). El frustrado seguro obligatorio contra la tuberculosis", *Dynamis,* 1994, 14, pp. 199-225; J. Molero-Mesa, "Clase obrera, medicina y estado en la España del siglo XX. Bases sociopolíticas de las campañas antituberculosas entre 1889 y 1950", in J. Castellanos *et al.* (eds.) *La medicina en el siglo XX. Estudios históricos sobre medicina, sociedad y estado*, Málaga, SEHM, 1998, pp. 221-228.

[14] Alfonso de la Fuente Chaos, the national secretary of Public Health of the Spanish Falange (FET-JONS), and national Director of the 'Labourist foundation of July 18' (Obra sindical 18 de Julio) in 1942, quoted by Jiménez Lucena, *El tifus en Málaga…* (note 7), p. 29.

[15] Jiménez Lucena, *El tifus en Málaga…* (note 7), pp. 59-60.

Apparently this was a position contrary to what they called 'Marxist statism', put in practice during the Republic. But in practice, words and ideology concealed a struggle to hold the organisation of public health hostage between two political sectors among the victors: the Phalangists, who during the war had developed a friendly society active in healthcare, called the Labourist Foundation of July 18 (*Obra Sindical 18 de Julio*, the date of the beginning of the insurrection), and the 'military faction', closer to traditional conservative and Catholic politicians, which gained control of health matters during the war, and kept it for a considerable period.

The delay in building up a new permanent organisation for health affairs after 1939 was due to the hidden battle within the core of the Francoist regime. The solution came with the slow eclipse of the Phalangist group in the wake of the defeat of the Axis powers in World War II. A certain echo of this can be found within the reports on *Health Perspectives in Spain*, read before the Second National Meeting of Health Officers held in Barcelona in April 1947. The Phalangist ideals were clearly bankrupt, since the most complete report advocated increased salaries for all physicians. Moreover, since there was clear awareness of the epidemiological changes that followed the decline of acute infectious diseases, new domains for public health intervention were sought in the sphere of illnesses that accompanied urban and industrial development[16].

The conservative control of health matters was secured by the permanent ascription of the National Health Department to the Ministry of the Interior and by the appointment of José Alberto Palanca y Martínez-Fortún (1888-1973) as head of the Department. Palanca was Professor of Hygiene, a former member of the Republican Parliament through the CEDA (the powerful right-wing political party of that period), and an active military officer during the days of Primo de Rivera's dictatorship and during the Civil War. The Provincial Health Institutes formed the core of the Health Department, directed as of 30 September 1939 by provincial Chiefs (previously called Inspectors). These institutes included the preventive and social healthcare activities set down in the Republican legislation of 1932 and, as a new feature, held control of the health professions (from physicians to nurses and midwifes) in the rural areas. (Figure 1.)

As a matter of fact, their task was mostly a continuation along Republican-style lines and, between 1926 and 1957, we find a period, unbroken by the war, of strengthening

---

[16] E. Bardají López, J. Fernández Turégano, C. Laguna and B. Benítez Franco, *Ponencia general. Perspectivas de la sanidad en España, II Reunión Nacional de Sanitarios Españoles. Barcelona, abril de 1947*, Madrid, Imp. Sáez, 1947.

of the profession of Public Health in the public domain. At that time, pre-war Spanish fellows of the Rockefeller Foundation were predominant (Palanca being one of them) and established a model of comprehensive, preventive and medical care for the rural population, similar to the American model of health centres. Microbiology became a compulsory subject in pre-graduate medical studies and the National School

Figure 1: *Map of Spain at the end of 1949 showing the geographical distribution of the Provincial Health Institutes (created in 1925) and the Secondary Health Centers (created in 1932) of the National Health Department.*

of Public Health offered regular specialist training. A single corps of public health officers was also formed and the separate health campaigns carried out by private charities and municipal councils were brought together under the National Health Department and enjoyed significant success and maximum political relevance during the post-war years.

The Francoist dream of an Empire was translated into measures to encourage large families, including medical advice for pregnant women, medical care for deliveries and medical counseling on child-raising, as well as school hygiene. The missionary style of social medicine, with its campaigns for popular health education through visiting nurses, was favoured by the authoritarian government [17]. The pure aim of preserving the health of the population ranked second in the official search for legitimation by the Fascist party. Thus, action on rural health was supplemented by the work of the Women's Section of the *Falange* under a direct mandate from the Chief of State in 1940 [18]. It was carried out by a volunteer corps, which grew to 7,000 female members during its first seven years of existence. After a basic course that included training in maternal and child welfare, preventive medicine, social law, political orientation and religion, the volunteers were sent to towns and villages on missions of inspection,

---

[17] E. Rodríguez-Ocaña and J. Molero-Mesa, "La cruzada por la salud. Las campañas sanitarias del primer tercio del siglo veinte en la construcción de la cultura de la salud", in L. Montiel (ed.) *La Salud en el Estado de Bienestar. Análisis histórico*, Madrid, Editorial Complutense, 1993, pp. 133-148; J. Molero-Mesa, "Clase obrera, medicina y estado…" (note 13).

[18] R. Sánchez López, *Mujer española, una sombra de destino en lo universal. Trayectoria histórica de la Sección Femenina de Falange, 1934-1977*, Universidad de Murcia, Murcia, 1990.

Núm. 4.—Instituto Provincial de Sanidad. Servicio de Higiene Infantil.

Figure 2: *School children being examined in the Provincial Health Institute of Almeria in 1951. At the same time, practical training as 'child hygiene attendants' (auxiliares de puericultura) for women of the Phalangist Women's Section can be seen.*

vaccination, delivery of medications and clothing, and basic public health training. Their role was of a key importance in the campaign against nutritional disorders run by the Department of Public Health between 1941 and 1946, when volunteers made more than one and half million home visits[19]. In 1947 it established quite an effective programme of mobile training sessions in maternal and child welfare and health in the provinces of Castille, which was subsequently extended to all other provinces[20]. Moreover, in 1941, the Women's Section of the *Falange* was given an important position on the staff of the newly opened School for Public Health Nurses, dependent on the NHD[21]. (Figure 2)

From 1940 to 1962, a new central organisation known as the National Agency for Social Aid was created as a delegation of the Francoist Party (or *National Movement*). This also held a relevant position in welfare programmes for infants[22]. Welfare programmes, health education and prevention, particularly in the mother-and-infant domain, were thus heavily marked by political commitment in favour of strengthening the authoritarian government. These preventive campaigns, in any case, served as a means to acquaint the population with the medical profession. (Figure 3)

[19] J. Bosch Marín, *El niño español en el siglo XX*, Madrid, Gráficas González, 1947, p. 106; M.T. Gallego Méndez, *Mujer, Falange y fraquismo*, Madrid, Taurus, 1983, pp. 124-126; M.I. Pastor y Homs, *La educación femenina en la post-guerra (1939-1945). El caso de Mallorca*, Madrid, Ministerio de Cultura, 1984, pp. 54-69 y pp. 119-120.

[20] Sánchez López, *Mujer española...* (note 18), p. 42.

[21] J. Bernabeu and E. Gascón, "De visitadoras a instructoras. La Enfermería de Salud Pública durante el primer franquismo", in J. Castellanos *et al.* (eds.) *La medicina en el siglo XX. Estudios históricos sobre medicina, sociedad y estado*, Málaga, SEHM, 1998, pp. 167-172.

[22] J. López Cano, "La Obra Nacional de Auxilio Social. Evolución, situación y perspectivas", in *Problemas fundamentales de Beneficencia y asistencia social*, Madrid, Ministerio de Gobernación, 1967, pp. 91-114; Pastor y Homs *La educación femenina...* (note 19); A.M. Mata Lara, "Control social y vida cotidiana de la mujer en la España de Franco", in D. Ramos Palomo (ed.) *Femenino plural. Palabra y memoria de mujeres*, Málaga, Universidad de Málaga, 1994, pp. 221-232.

The Phalangist sector of the government held in its grasp the Labour Ministry, in which health matters had been included between 1932 and 1936, although they failed at first to recover these former areas of responsibility. From this position they pushed forward the implementation of planned social reform prepared by the National Insurance Institute *(Instituto Nacional de Previsión*, INP) during the 1930s, through the creation of a com-

pulsory scheme of health insurance for workers, which was based on the German model and started in 1942. This scheme grew from its actual implementation in 1944 to become the most impressive public agency for medical care: it started granting coverage to barely 10% of the population, and by 1968 covered 44% of the population. It also ran an extensive network of general, obstetrics and pediatrics, and orthopedics hospitals. From this stronghold, the Phalangist political family withstood all attempts to control healthcare activities by the National Public Health Department, backed by the *Public Health Law* enacted by the Ministry of the Interior in 1944. The law reinforced the territorial and hierarchical model of health centres as well as their mixed remit of prevention and care.

Figure 3: *Poster made by the Propaganda Section of the National Health Department (1949) that reads: 'It isn't disease that kills, it's Ignorance. Put the health of your son in the hands of a child hygiene doctor.'*

The impressive money-collecting system, set up by the insurance scheme, together with the control of epidemics, brought about the triumph of the insurance scheme and the banishment of the model of Social Medicine (integrating healthcare and prevention in a popular educational background) built during the previous 30 years. The general mortality rate fell below 10 per 1,000 in 1952 and by 1953 infectious diseases were no longer the main cause of death. A little later, medical specialists in tuberculosis (from the National Agency against Tuberculosis, *Patronato Nacional Antituberculoso*) as well as specialists in child hygiene (*Puericultura*) from the National Health Department became the first specialists in heart and chest diseases, and childhood diseases exclusively concerned with actual care and rehabilitation to be hired by the INP. And as early as 1942, a corps of Phalangist Nurses was created by law and immediately entered into conflict with the Public Health Nurses of the NHD. The former found an easy way to participate as 'social visiting nurses' in the new insurance-based scheme of care.

3. From compulsory health insurance to social security: the decline of social medicine

The *1944 Public Health Law* was never really enforced in full; almost nobody outside the Ministry of the Interior accepted the pre-eminence of the National Health Department, and neither the services nor the goals of the health insurance scheme were adequately coordinated. Public health officials, for their part, in the atmosphere of the lack of accountability imposed by the authoritarian regime, showed no genuine interest in enforcing its own rules. For example, by law, the Provincial Councils of Public Health, the organs of direction and coordination of health matters at the provincial level, were to meet monthly. In the province of Almeria (the only one studied so far), in the 17 years after 1944, the Council met only seven times [23]. Thus, the identity of Public Health became confused during the 1960s and 1970s, as the traditional Spanish term *sanidad pública* that served to identify public health came to denote only the hospital-centred, medical care activities of the social insurance scheme.

The birth of an extensive system of social insurance, especially during the period from 1883 to 1889, followed a fierce, long-lasting ideological war within the dominant elites *and* within the workers' organisations, as well as between these two collectives. Implementation of the social insurance system was nevertheless subordinated to political and economical conjunctures, which it helped to define [24].

Social reform in Spain aimed to make room for violence-free social relationships, as a way to build a neutral state able to instigate cooperation between classes. Reform itself became embodied in new state agencies, such as the Institute for Social Reform (*Instituto de Reformas Sociales*) and the Ministry of Labour; in protective legislation for workers, such as the 1900 law for compensation of work accidents, the 1919 law of work contracts, and others; and in several insurance schemes organised and managed by the National Insurance Institute (INP). The initially voluntary schemes (retirement in 1908), later became compulsory (compulsory retirement insurance since 1919; maternity insurance since 1931; accident insurance since 1932). During Primo de Rivera's

[23] P. Marín Martínez, *La Jefatura Provincial de Sanidad de Almería (1940-1983)*, Tesis de doctorado, Universidad de Granada, 1994.

[24] M.D. Gómez Molleda (ed.) *Los Seguros Sociales en la España del siglo XX*, 3 vols., Madrid, Ministerio de Trabajo, 1988; *Historia de la acción social pública en España. Beneficencia y previsión*, Madrid, Ministerio de Asuntos sociales, 1990; R. Huertas, *Organización sanitaria y crisis social en España*, Madrid, FIM, 1995.

dictatorship (1923-1930), the party elites and the Socialist trade unions (PSOE and UGT) became involved in the activities of the INP; this helped to support certain policies during the Republic (1931-36).

The triumph of Francoism brought radical changes. After the war, all workers' associations were prohibited and their property was confiscated. Bureaucracy at the INP supplanted all attempts at autonomous participation by workers and swept away most friendship societies[25]. At the same time, workers' representation was supplanted by state-organised phoney unions (so-called vertical unions, because they merged workers, managers and company owners into a single organisation) and a single political party, created from the artificial combination of pre-war authentic Fascists, conservatives and ultra-Catholic groups.

Surprisingly, though, the implementation of planned social measures was not halted for long. The social insurance program was extended with the addition of compulsory health insurance (1942), disability and old age benefits (1947), and unemployment benefits (1961), unified from 1963 on into a rough system of Social Security. The 'roughness' derived from its multiplicity of managerial organs and intense internal conflicts. In 25 years it granted coverage to 44% of the Spanish population. The increasing recruitment of physicians outstripped the rise in the population covered by social insurance. In 1958 more than 63% of Spanish physicians worked for the state-run health insurance programmes, two-thirds being general practitioners. In all provinces, except Madrid and Valencia, more than half of the doctors were employed by the state; in 32 out of 51 provinces, this proportion was more than 70%.

Political centralisation after the war put an end to autonomous initiatives in Catalonia, which had developed actively since 1907 except during Primo de Rivera's military regime. The new healthcare agency managed by the INP did not include pre-existing municipal health services and, as a result, most of the latter vanished. Besides, the population of most towns in Spain was not large enough to sustain a full programme of health services: the population census in more than 60% of municipalities totaled fewer than 1,000 inhabitants[26].

The new agency was structured as a network of centres for outpatient diagnosis and treatment (*ambulatorios*) established in cities, and an extensive system of hospital care,

---

[25] Ana M. Guillén Rodríguez, *Políticas de reforma sanitaria en España. De la Restauración a la Democracia*, Madrid, Fundación Juan March, 1996.

[26] R. Manzanera, J.R. Villalbí, A. Navarro and R. Armengol, "La salud pública ante las reformas del sistema sanitario", *Gaceta Sanitaria*, 1996, 10 (57), pp. 299-310.

Figure 4: *The General Hospital (Residencia sanitaria) built by the National Health Insurance in Almeria, at the time of its opening in 1956.*

with at least one hospital in each provincial capital. The former Secondary or District Health Centres administered by the NHD disappeared; the Primary Health Centres in the villages turned into Doctors' Homes. Continuous technological advances, the success of the hospital-centred model of healthcare, and the great advances in chemical therapeutics won the public's trust[27]. In fact, as noted above, the words *sanidad pública*, used to designate the public health services, came to represent the Social Security medical services, identifying health with a clinical, hospital-based type of care.

The INP undertook a National Plan of Equipment to create 16,000 hospital beds distributed among 67 'residences' (a new name for general hospitals), plus 62 full ambulatory centres for diagnosis and another 144 smaller centres[28]. From 1963 on, compulsory health insurance for workers was known as Social Security, a Spanish model of the welfare state. This change did not solve any of the endemic problems with the organisation of healthcare. It preserved the multiplicity of managerial centers and kept the focus exclusively on the curative care, hence the great drive to build large hospitals. Construction was particularly rapid between 1965 and 1974, not only in terms of new centres but also through the enlargement of older ones and the creation of specialist centres for obstetric and pediatrics, or for orthopedics. The administrative union of these special centres with an all-purpose general hospital gave birth to the so-called Health Care Cities (*Ciudades Sanitarias*). (Figure 4)

The projected number of hospital beds was reached around 1968, although distributed among fewer centres – one general hospital in each provincial capital and in eight other cities (Mieres, Ponferrada, Gijón, Puertollano, Jerez de la Frontera, Santa Cruz

[27] F. Martínez, "El modelo sanitario español", in *Primeras Jornadas de Debate sobre Sanidad Pública*, Madrid, FADSP, 1982, vol. 2, pp. 99-107; V. Ortún and A. Segura, "España: democracia, crisis económica y política sanitaria", *Revista de Sanidad e Higiene Pública*, 1983, 57, pp. 603-626; E. Nájera Morrondo, M. Cortés Majó and C. García Gil, "La reorientación del sistema sanitario. Necesidad del enfoque epidemiológico", *Revisiones en Salud Pública*, 1989, 1, pp. 15-30.
[28] Orders of 19 February 1945 and 26 February 1947.

de la Palma, Mahón y Calatayud). But the number of outpatient clinics (*ambulatorios*), on the contrary, greatly surpassed original plans, although their slow, bureaucracy-laden administration triggered widespread disgust among users.

Hospitals belonging to the health insurance or the social security system have been extraordinarily active. In the mid 1960s, when coverage was provided for around 40% of the population, more than half of all deliveries in Spain took place in such centres[29]. In 1980, although they had only 27% of all hospital beds, they cared for 73% of inpatients[30].

The programme did not end with the construction of new spaces for medical care activities – it had a deeper aim: its organisers wanted to create 'new scenarios for social propaganda and schooling in civics'[31]. Thus hospitals became the substitutes of the health campaigns of the 1930s and 1940s, which in broad terms were designated as tools for moral indroctination to win the favour of the working classes. Furthermore, the situation in Spain reflected a general theme in the Western medical world, as shown in recent studies. This was the extension of what can be called an 'industrial imperative' to the realm of massive medical care, linking ideas of industrial efficiency, laboratory and high-tech medicine, and horizontal and vertical specialisation[32].

4. The democratic transition: public health ideals and political constraints

So far we have shown the weakening of the administration of public health, the loss of municipal responsibility for services and the coming to the fore of the aims of 'health repair' linked to productivist criteria for understanding health.

Franco's death in 1975 allowed the peaceful substitution of the authoritarian regime by a democratic one to begin. Political opposition to Francoism had reached massive dimensions during the previous 20 years and, together with political demands, a new life for Public Health was called for, as well as substantial changes in the structure, strategy and functioning of the Social Security system.

[29] *Informe sociológico sobre la situación social de España, 1970*, Madrid, FOESSA, 1970, p. 819.

[30] J. De Miguel, *La Salud Pública del futuro*, Madrid, Ariel, 1985, p. 91.

[31] *I Asamblea del I.N.P.*, Madrid, INP, 1953, p. 46, and its Conclusion number 3.

[32] Barbara Bridgman Perkins, "Shaping Institution-Based Specialism: Early Twentieth-Century Economic Organization of Medicine", *Social History of Medicine,* 1997, 10, pp. 419-435; S. Sturdy and R. Cooter, "Science, Scientific Management and the Transformation of Medicine in England", *History of Science*, 1998, 36, pp. 421-466.

At that moment, and amid the largest demonstrations in history against Francoism and its heirs, a new 'health crisis' appeared, one that did not reflect the classic postulates of an epidemic. On the contrary, the health crisis of the 1970s was a showcase for the overall crisis of the welfare state, in which three layers can be distinguished: a financial crisis, a crisis of rationality, and a crisis of legitimation[33].

The financial crisis of the Western states in the 1970s was exacerbated in Spain by the bureaucratic inheritance of Francoist structures. As a result, the social security system suffered greatly between 1976 and 1982, when retirement pensions grew by 16%, disability allowances by 42%, and health costs rose by 87% (between 1975 and 1985), while the number of persons receiving unemployment benefits rose by 900%. On the international scene, Spain's level of social protection was traditionally far below that of most other European countries. For example, by 1980 Germany's public expenditure on social protection was 10% higher and spending on health 2% higher than in Spain. At the same time, spending in Ireland was 5% higher on social protection and 1.5% higher on health[34].

The public health system, divided into several administrations, was generally thought of as a fine example of inefficacy and inefficiency, since it did not help improve health and costs kept rising. External and even internal evaluation devices were absent. Moreover, there was a crisis in the sources of legitimation of the health system that affected all levels: civic associations protested against bureaucracy and lack of consideration of patients' rights, as well as against notorious cases of fraud, and health professional groups demanded new relationships between doctors, nurses and technicians, aimed at diminishing the power of physicians. These latter, for their part, protested mainly against the managerial class. Strong feelings against a perceived 'dictatorship of doctors' spread among the lay population. (Figure 5)

In this context, and together with proposals for political change, attempts were made to win favour for the development of Public Health. The conclusions of the First

---

[33] P. Rosanvallon, "Les trois crises de l'État-providence", *Aujourd-hui*, 1982, 52, pp. 29-40; F.J. Elola Somoza, *Crisis y reforma de la asistencia sanitaria pública en España (1983-1990)*, Madrid, FIS, 1991; F.J. Elola, "La evaluación de la reforma sanitaria, una base necesaria para reformas futuras", *Rev. San. Hig. Pub.*, 1991, 65, pp. 285-297. The same idea, albeit with a different terminology, is defended by V. Ortún, "Los elementos de la crisis de la asistencia sanitaria", in F. Antoñanzas and J. Pérez-Campanero (eds.) *La reforma del sistema sanitario*, Madrid, FEDEA y Ediciones Mundi-Prensa, 1992, pp. 53-67.

[34] On the effects of the economic shortages, see R. Belenes Juárez, "La limitación presupuestaria del INSALUD y la gestión de los servicios sanitarios", *Gaceta Sanitaria*, 1988, 2 (5), pp. 101-111.

Workshop of the Corps of Physicians of the National Public Health Department, held in December 1976, defended the need to include the right to health among the fundamental rights of people[35]. The participants expressed their will to collaborate in a wide-ranging transformation of the public health system, helping to implement a "new model based upon the development in the community of integral medical care" under a socialised and de-centralised National Health Service. Between 1979 and 1981 the Spanish Society for Epidemiology was created as an organic manifestation of the New Public Health[36]. This association shared the aforementioned basic assumptions and helped to elaborate on and to disseminate them, hence lending a strategic foundation to the reform under way. The NHS label meant universality, equality, solidarity and community participation. The organisation of Primary Health Care, according to WHO-UNICEF principles developed at the Conference of Alma-

Figure 5: *The front cover of the popular weekly* Cambio *16 of 27 August 1978 stated: 'Social Security: corruption and ruin. White gowns robbers'. This was to announce that its leading article dealt with the 'crisis in the health sector' while picturing people's disgust and reluctance towards physicians.*

Ata, was to be the key instrument in their implementation. This constellation of basic assumptions was accepted and defended by the broad left, the Communists and the Socialists parties, the new trade unions and other civic associations – and sustained the policy-making process once the Spanish Socialist Workers' Party (PSOE) won the general elections in 1983. The alliance between the social and political left, and the public health profession justified the phrase of 'public health reform' used by authors such as Irigoyen to denote the first phase of political change in the health system led by the PSOE[37].

---

[35] "Jornadas del Cuerpo Médico de Sanidad Nacional. Conclusiones de la reunión celebrada los días 1, 2 y 3 de diciembre en el Centro de Demostración Sanitaria de Talavera de la Reina (Toledo)", *Revista de Sanidad e Higiene Pública*, 1977, 51, pp. 1347-1349.

[36] A. Segura, "La fundación de la SEE", *SEEnota*, 1998.

[37] J. Irigoyen, *La crisis del sistema sanitario en España. Una interpretación sociológica*, Granada, Universidad, 1996.

Article 43.1 of the present Spanish Constitution guarantees every citizen the right to the protection of health. The perceived consequences of such a statement led to a fierce battle at the time the Constitution was being written: right-wing parties understood it as an attempt to expropriate the (private) market of health services in favour of total collectivisation – an echo of the exaggerated fears of medical and entrepreneurial associations during the time of the Republic[38]. We might wonder whether the right to the protection of health was not included among other fundamental rights in the First Chapter of the Constitution because of this perception and associated acute concerns.

Social pressure from the left and the confusion that pervaded governing elites meant that during the initial period of the transition between 1977 and 1983, directed by the Union of the Democratic Center (UCD), no clear strategy for change could be formulated. The main novelty was the establishment of a Health Ministry, actually a Ministry for Labor, Social Security and Health, which did very little to alleviate conflicts. In fact, economic problems monopolised the attention of the successive ministers. The perpetuation of unsolved inherited problems facilitated the aforementioned alliance and fueled its arguments[39].

The first stage of real political reform in the health system was between 1983 and 1990, under the direction of the PSOE. The first Socialist government stated publicly that the right to health was foremost among civil rights, since its necessary fulfillment was a prerequisite for the exercise of all other rights[40]. The Constitution's mandate to 'protect health' was understood as the need to promote health, to prevent disease, to cure and to achieve social rehabilitation. These goals were to be attained by a National Health System (SNS, *Sistema Nacional de Salud*) The word 'system' was thought more suitable than 'service', since the new structure of the state, as a sort of federation of autonomous regions, meant that the political administration of public services was to be devolved to the different autonomous governments[41].

---

[38] E. Martínez Quintero, "Organizaciones obreras y patronales ante el seguro social de enfermedad", in R. Huertas and R. Campos (eds.) *Medicina social y clase obrera en España*, Madrid, FIM, II, pp. 527-554; E. Rodríguez Ocaña, "La asistencia médica colectiva en España hasta 1936", in *Historia de la acción social pública en España. Beneficencia y previsión*, Madrid, Ministerio de Asuntos Sociales, 1990, pp. 321-359; M.I. Porras Gallo, "Los médicos y la prensa frente al seguro de enfermedad en la primavera de 1934… ", in J. Castellanos *et al.* (eds.) *La medicina en el siglo XX. Estudios históricos sobre medicina, sociedad y estado*, Málaga, SEHM, 1998, pp. 183-192.

[39] Ortún and Segura, note 27.

[40] P.P. Mansilla Izquierdo, *Reforma sanitaria. Fundamentos para un análisis*, Madrid, MSYC, 1986; *Ministerio de Sanidad y Consumo 1982-1986. Resumen de realizaciones*, Madrid, MSYC, 1986; P.P. Mansilla Izquierdo (ed.) *La Sanidad española 1982-1986. Crónica del cambio. 1ª etapa*, Madrid, MSYC, 1986.

[41] Mansilla, *Reforma sanitaria…* note 40, p. 24.

The SNS was born with the adoption of law 14/1986, known as *the General Law of Public Health,* on 14 April 1986. Three basic principles formed its core: a new organisation of the primary care sector, to give way to community participation and emphasis on inter-sectorial policies[42]. Surprisingly, the officials in charge of the Health Department in 1986 didn't themselves understand properly what this involved. Pedro Pablo Mansilla, counselor to Health Minister Lluch, wrote that "the promotion of health", as a central concept of reform, appeared prominently in Socialist programmes, but was scarcely translated into positive actions because it was "a new idea"[43]. This difficulty in transcending rhetoric might account for the short term in office (one-and-a-half years) of Enrique Nájera – the key person in the revitalisation of Spanish Public Health in these years – as Head of the General Directorate of Public Health (1983 to 1985).

The socialist reform did not achieve its original aims, which were pragmatically moulded in response to day-to-day problems and unexpected situations, one of the most important being the inequalities that had appeared between regions. Thus, the last 15 years have seen a 'perpetual health reform', and no end can be foreseen in the short term. This process was reinforced through the Parliamentary Commission (1990-91) created to analyse and evaluate the endeavors of the SNS. The Commission produced a Final Report, under the direction of Fernando Abril, a former Minister in UCD governments. The *Abril Report* marks the beginning of a second stage in contemporary health reform in Spain, aimed at implementing an entrepreneurial-like concept of health administration.

A critical analysis of this first stage of health reform has been provided by a number of professional, political and social associations, such as the Federation of Associations for the Defence of the Public System of Health, a leftist group, as well as by scholars, such as Francisco Javier Elola and Juan Irigoyen[44]. I would like to emphasise their similarities below.

All opinions note a mixture of achievements and failures, of successes and unresolved deficiencies, and all offer an assessment of new, unforeseen problems. First, it is a common opinion that costs have been held under a certain degree of control through budgetary cuts, but not because of any improvement in efficiency. The management structure has nevertheless been reinforced and there is agreement on the emphasis given to the ascent of a new managerial class, which has evidently benefited from the distribution of intramural power within the system.

---

[42] Nájera, Cortés and García Gil, note 27.

[43] Mansilla (ed.) *La Sanidad española…*, note 40.

[44] Elola, *Crisis y reforma…*, note 33; J. Irigoyen, *La crisis del sistema…* note 37.

A second, clear feature concerns the new primary healthcare service that has developed slowly (and is not yet fully in place in the larger cities). Little attention has been paid to self-evaluation of this new level of care and there has been little or no community participation. The definition of patients as 'clients' or 'consumers' has paralleled increments in demand and fueled unjustified expectations from the public.

Hospital reform has also failed in the domain of efficiency, while exacerbating serious tensions within the various professional collectives involved in healthcare. This source of stress even led to a series of strikes against the reforms, notably the 1987 physicians' strike.

The SNS has guaranteed the universal availability of professional care, now a fact for 99% of the population. In addition, the state has increased its financial contribution and is now the main sponsor of the system. But political decentralisation has produced a contradictory model of the SNS, which is split into regional units that differ openly in structure, practice and financing. Although local councils have been given responsibility for several aspects of public health that break from the proposed, unified model, the municipal level of health administration has disappeared and a new centralism, this time at the regional level, has taken its place.

Irigoyen calls the initial phase of reforms a "stage of enlightened despotism". For him, this public health-oriented reform was derived from theories produced by international expert groups and was implemented through the action of a minority, which did not take local conditions sufficiently into account. This critical stance disregards the developments in the doctrine of the scientific domain of Public Health, which is denigrated as mere 'ideology'. In my opinion, there are sounder explanations for the failures, namely the contradictions between inherited structures and work habits, and new health aims[45]. This legacy required its own goals, in terms of improved care, whereas the new theoretical discourse was linked to a concept of integral health, emphasising horizontal or inter-sectorial policies. The 'medical system' reacted against a 'health system' and since public health targets had a weaker institutional basis, they could easily be left aside.

Another important negative feature of the reform has been its markedly managerial character, which gave more power to the technostructure (managerial teams) than to professional groups, workers' unions and doctors' syndicates, while at the same time forgetting the people. During the early years of Socialist government, the most serious

---

[45] J.I. Elorrieta Pérez de Diego and J. García Herrera, "El nuevo enfoque de la Salud Pública. Estrategias para su implementación", *Gaceta Sanitaria,* 1991, 5 (23), pp. 93-97.

accusation was that the original aims of reform had been abandoned for economic reasons, i.e, the preoccupation with holding rising costs in check above any further consideration. Some tried to explain this by the persistence into the 1980s of the social security institutions created by Franco's government[46]. Within the old model of social security, changes have historically occurred by the enrolment of a narrow elitist circle, since free association and workers' participation were banned during the decades of authoritarian government. Therefore, important changes in the economic development of the country have fueled the expansion of the social security system, but have left its bureaucratic structure untouched for the most part. A particular feature to add to this picture is the professional inadequacy of the managers, traditionally poorly trained both in medicine or public health, and in economic and organisational matters. As a consequence, it is easily forgotten that the rationality of the system has to be sound not only in terms of money, but also in terms of health. The same weakness has led to another unpleasant feature: the close relationship between the managerial corps and the government, such that political alternatives cannot be separated from managerial decisions and vice versa. As a result, they are praised or discredited together depending on the results.

The question of community participation stands at the core of the paradoxes and shortcomings of contemporary health reform. Conceptually, as I have said, this was one of the major assets of reform. For many, it was also to be the touchstone in health policies of *change*, the diffuse hope for a better society after the death of Franco, which the PSOE used as one of its most successful slogans. From the end of the 1970s, several unregulated local initiatives arose, based upon the militant voluntarism of teams of young health professionals, as for example in Montanchez (1978-79). According to its organisers, this one-year-long experience was the most successful of all attempts in the field, since they achieved a genuine people's movement concerned with health problems that, at the same time, carried out a political campaign against the municipal council. This political commitment was perhaps at the root of the movement's success. By the beginning of the 1980s several teaching health centres (as in Novelda, Cambre, the Cartuja Barrio of Granada and other places) had tried to organise Neighbourhood Health Councils. These served mainly as a meeting place for health centre staff and local representatives, sometimes with the uncompromising presence of other public administrations. The Neighbourhood Health Councils aimed to obtain the cooperation of the local population in professionals' initiatives by showing concern for wider problems of the neighbourhood.

---

[46] Guillén, *Políticas de reforma...* (nº 25). A.M. Guillén, "Un siglo de previsión social en España", *AYER*, 1997, nº 25, pp. 151-178.

Two kinds of problems arose from these experiences, one being the diversity of local contexts, and the other, the lack of support from municipal or higher administrations. The plans for reform made in Andalucia (one of the strongholds of the Socialists) in 1984-90 established as one of its four main targets: community participation through the Health Councils in the control and management of neighbourhood's health services'. However, not one practical proposal was conceived to place community representatives on the Board of Administration[47]. As a matter of fact, as late as 1995, Andalucia was among the few autonomous regions that still lacked a legislative framework for the Health Councils created by the *General Public Health Law* of 1986. The 1986 Law declared citizen's participation a right and ordered the creation of a General Health Council for each autonomous region as well as one in each of the several healthcare administration zones into which the regions were divided. At this zonal level, detailed participation is regulated in an indirect way, through municipal councils. The functions of both types of health councils are strictly bureaucratic, the public administrations hold the majority of votes and the councils lack any decision-making capacity. By the end of the 1990s, seven regions had implemented these rules through the creation of Local Health Councils, with representatives from the municipal councils, primary health teams, workers' unions, employers' and civic associations.

At the central level, directives encouraging participation have only gradually disappeared. In the *Criterios de actuación del INSALUD para el bienio 1989-90* (Madrid, Ministerio de Sanidad y Consumo, 1989), which set down the guidelines for action by the National Health Institute, the last of several stated goals was the forging of a strategy to increase the level of social participation in the services. This included the development of schemes in local areas, the promotion of civic associations involved with health problems and the dissemination of information. The same *Criterios* for the following two years (1991-92) devoted two full pages to explaining the contents of the major aims (i.e. development of primary health care, internal coordination of health services, hospital reform and incentives for professionals), but did not refer to community participation at all, except for a general statement about "reinforcing the participation of social agents"[48]. As Mansilla noted some years earlier, it seems that nobody knew how to transform an ambitious declaration into a valid instrument of work.

---

[47] M. López Serrato and J.I. Martínez Millán, *La reforma sanitaria en la atención primaria, 1984-1990*; Sevilla, Junta de Andalucía, Consejería de Salud y Consumo, 1985.

[48] *Criterios de actuación del INSALUD para el bienio 1991-92*, Madrid, Mº de Sanidad y Consumo, 1991.

By 1990 the actual experiences of participation through Neighbourhood (or zone) Health Councils had produced a sensation of failure[49]. The lack of success can be explained in multiple ways. Some emphasise the coarseness of the theoretically unsophisticated model, others point to the political and professional resistance to accepting true participation of the people in so far as it implies a loss or at least a certain sharing of power, while there are still those who focus on the persisting ideology of 'reparative medicine'. The prestigious *Handbook of Primary Health Care*, edited by Martín Zurro and Cano Pérez and first published in 1986 (now in its fourth edition) commented on the problem of community participation in the chapter *Primary Care Directed Toward the Community* in its first two editions[50]. The main arguments were presented in two major themes: the community as "object" (followed by a description of "community health diagnosis") and the community as "subject". The inadequacy of the Health Councils had been pointed out in 1986, although they were defended as consulting bodies. A suggestion was made to implement the person of "health agents". In fact, there was no detailed analysis on a nationwide level; the authors kept a certain distance, citing studies from other countries as if they were afraid to produce original ideas. A notable feature, however, was the call for health centre staff to prevent the self-interested manipulation of participative mechanisms, which should remain linked to the needs of the population. The authors believed that without this effort on the part of staff members, the health centres would be unable to serve their function of improving the quality of life for the user population.

The 1994 edition of the same *Handbook* devotes a whole chapter to this problem, in the opening section on "Concepts". The purpose of this material seems to be to strengthen the theoretical foundation of this problem[51]. Two of the three authors are the same as in previous editions. The contents seem more soundly developed: the

---

[49] A. Botejara Sanz and R. Cordero Torres, "Participación comunitaria", in *La Sanidad española a debate*, Madrid, FADSP, 1990, pp. 279-287; A. Delgado and L.A. López Fernández, "La participación comunitaria: una revisión necesaria", *Atención Primaria*, 1992, 9 (8), pp. 457-459; I. Antón *et al.*, "Los Consejos de Salud", *Atención Primaria*, 1992, 9 (8), pp. 410-411; E. Ramos García, A. Sánchez Moreno and P. Marset Campos, "Paradojas y posibilidades de la Participación Comunitaria en Atención Primaria de Salud (I). Problemas históricos y conceptuales", *Atención Primaria*, 1992, 9 (6), pp. 334-336.

[50] L. De la Revilla Ahumada, A. Delgado Sánchez and L.A. López Fernández, "Atención Primaria orientada a la comunidad", in A. Martín Zurro and F. Cano Pérez (eds.) *Manual de Atención Primaria. Organización y pautas de atención en la consulta*, 1st ed., Barcelona, Ediciones DOYMA, 1986, pp. 62-80.

[51] L. De la Revilla Ahumada, D. Siles Román and L.A. López Fernández, "La participación comunitaria", in A. Martín Zurro and F. Cano Pérez (eds.), *Atención Primaria. Concepto, organización y práctica clínica*, 3.rd ed., Barcelona, Moby/ DOYMA Libros, 1994, pp. 95-107.

chapter starts by explaining two key concepts (those of "community" and "participation") and points out the complexity of interests, networks of relationships and needs at the community level. This new approach goes beyond the identification of the community with administrative zones. The text also emphasises the low level of formal associationism in Spanish society. The concept of participation is defined within the more general framework of social actions for health. Participation implies formal devices fueled by the health services and in some way supervised by them. Showing the influence of modern sociological and anthropological studies on their thinking, the authors discuss the inescapable plurality of options in each local context, warn against strict formalisation, and emphasise the importance of using and developing all possible bridges with people without rejecting any of them. Among these options are the local health councils themselves, regular meetings with civic associations, the establishment of a complaints service, the use of questionnaires to evaluate client satisfaction, the creation of self-help groups and the establishment of relations with other local programmes.

Figure 6: *This drawing by Loriga, published in* El Médico. Profesión y Humanidades *(14 Mars 1982, p. 38) depicts the deep fear and concern of doctors in the face of the rising campaign for 'Patients' Rights'.*

The idea has been spread that the lack of general implementation of the people's participation in the new Primary Health Care scheme leads to a perception among professionals that this goal was not worth striving for, or, conversely, that the difficulties of its implementation are proof of its purely ideological character[52]. In my opinion, this view favours the enemies of public health, such as medical associations, which aim mainly to guarantee professional autonomy. This position could be shaken by the avalanche of 'community rights'; in fact, physicians are still devoting considerable energy to defending themselves against the 'rights of patients'. Should we reject public health theories on the grounds of being 'ideological' and uncritically embrace the

---

[52] J. Irigoyen, "La Participación comunitaria", in *La crisis del sistema sanitario...*, note 37, pp. 143-225.

'business administration mentality', defended by the new criteria of the health reform as if this were created in a political and ideological vacuum? In the *Abril Report* (1991) the only mention of people's participation is found in connection with payment for services. This type of reform apparently emulates the British under Thatcher, but consciously neglects that participation was one of its main rhetorical bases and a live concern, reflected in the professional interests of several networks within the WHO and the Council of Europe[53]. The growing presence of neo-liberal forces and thinking, reflected in the victory of the conservatives in the 1996 general elections in Spain, has spread to the health scenario, and new formulations attempt to frame new concepts of social life including health policies. (Figure 6)

5. Conclusion

Public health doctrines and practices have been used by diverse political forces and governments for their own sake, i.e. to gain the public's favour, to help consolidate a post-war situation or to win votes. But it is difficult to see how 'purely' scientific aims are developed. In fact, are there any 'pure' scientific aims? The policies of Republican Public Health were substantially maintained by Franco's followers, although with a change in administrative postholders. The most serious health crisis of the 1940s was faced by emphasising the military traits of public health officials and practices, features closest to the government in power. Years after, progressive politicians and movements upheld the ideals of the New Public Health in their aims to build a new society in the wake of Franco's death and the political bankruptcy of the administrations in the late 1970s. There, the emancipating significance of health was emphasised, as was 'community participation', an expression of the new democracy.

In both cases, science was used to frame a political world. Under Franco, the initial strength was lost and the alliance between public health and politics showed itself to be a dead-end. However, in the democratic transition, even though the subordination of health policies to a broader political context has obscured a debate on strategy put forward for Public Health in the late 1970s, the result has been an increasing level of complexity within the scientific field itself. In the 1940s, public knowledge was simply unwanted and made impossible by the State. In the 1990s, there is a danger that public opinion will be shut out of any debate on the fundamental questions of health, such as community participation, which has been left in the hands of a closed cabinet of

---

[53] T. Milewa, J. Valentine and M. Calnan, "Managerialism and Active Citizenship in Britain's Reformed Health Service. Power and Community in an Era of Decentralisation", *Soc. Sci. Med.*, 1998, 47 (4), pp. 507-517.

experts. This reticence can be blamed on a fear of public participation and 'active citizenship' in the current climate of an evolving democracy in Spain[54].

Acknowledgements

This paper was funded by Project PB97-0782-C03-01 (Dirección General de Enseñanza Superior e Investigación Científica, Ministerio de Educación y Cultura). It would have not been possible without the generous help of a number of good friends, who have provided information and essential printed sources. I particularly thank Porfirio Marín, Isabel del Cura, Jorge Molero, Maribel Porras, Ana Delgado, Angélica Fajardo and Guillermo Olagüe. Francisco O'Valle helped with the original presentation given in Barcelona. Karen Shashok helped revise the English translation.

---

[54] E. Ramos García, A. Sánchez Moreno and P. Marset Campos, "Paradojas y posibilidades de la Participación Comunitaria en Atención Primaria de Salud (II). Alternativas críticas y emancipatorias", *Atención Primaria*, 1992, 9 (7), pp. 398-400.

Eastern Europe

The War on Cancer and the Cold War: A Soviet Case
Nikolai Krementsov

1. Introduction

Soviet medicine always proudly acknowledged its dependence on the politics of the first socialist state. It presented its achievements (both real and imaginary) as a direct result of implementing the policies designed by the leadership of the Communist Party to benefit the people's health. A careful historical analysis, however, shows that the interrelations between politics and medicine in the Soviet Union were far from this simplistic presentation.

This article describes two cases, very similar, yet very different. Both cases are related to the invention of a new anti-cancer treatment and involve a tangled skein of connections between four players: inventors, party officials, the public (including practising doctors), and the medical establishment. These cases are separated by a decade and thus allow us to see and analyse the dynamics of medical policies and the impact of various social, political, and cultural factors on their formulation and implementation in the Soviet Union.

2. The KR affair, 1946-1951

'KR' stands for two scientists – a microbiologist, Nina Kliueva, and her husband, a cytologist, Grigorii Roskin[1]. On March 13, 1946, Kliueva, a corresponding member of the recently established USSR Academy of Medical Sciences, presented a report to the academy's governing body (its presidium). She summarised the results of 15 years of research into the antagonism between Trypanosoma cruzi (a South American protozoan that causes the deadly Chagas disease) and transplanted tumors, research initiated

---

[1] For a detailed analysis of the KR affair, see Nikolai Krementsov, *The Cure: Cancer, Culture, and the Cold War* (in press).

in the early 1930s by Professor Roskin of Moscow University[2]. She announced that they had developed a preparation (later named, after its inventors, 'KR') on the basis of Trypanosoma, which was presented as an anti-cancer antibiotic and had been tried against a variety of malignant tumors in mice[3].

Kliueva's report aroused much interest among the presidium's members and they agreed to provide assistance in conducting further experiments and clinical trials with the promising cure[4]. On the next day, information about Kliueva's report and the presidium's decisions appeared on the pages of major newspapers[5]. One day later, Kliueva and Roskin petitioned a member of the Politburo, and Secretary of the Central Committee of the Communist Party, Stalin's chief-ideologist Andrei Zhdanov, for help in developing KR. On April 3, the Central Committee Secretariat instructed the Minister of Public Health "to take necessary measures and report [back] to the Central Committee about the results"[6]. Following these instructions, the minister issued several orders aimed at providing Kliueva and Roskin with funds, assistants and equipment.

Kliueva and Roskin's work received extraordinary publicity. At the end of April, Moscow Radio broadcast a long interview with Kliueva in its regular programme, *Weekly News*. In mid-May, the newspaper *Medical Worker* published another interview[7]. At the end of May, the popular magazine *Ogonek* published a long article about KR, supplemented with several photographs of the happy couple at work and

---

[2] Gr. Roskin und E. Exempliarskaia, "Protozoeninfektion und experimenteller Krebs. I. Mitteilung", *Zeitschrift fur Krebsforschung*, 1931, Bd. 34, SS. 628-645; Gr. Roskin and K. Romanova, "Action des Toxines sur le Cancer Experimental", *Acta Cancrologica*, 1935, vol. 1, no. 4, pp. 323-234; also G. Roskin and K. Romanova, "Untersuchung uber de Einwirkung der Prozoentoxine auf die Zellen maligner geschwulste", *Zeitschrift fur Krebsforschung*, 1936, Bd. 44, SS. 375-383.

[3] An abridged version of the report was soon published in the academy's bulletin. See N. Kliueva, "Puti Bioterapii Raka", *Vestnik Akademii Meditsinskikh Nauk SSSR*, 1946, no. 2-3, pp. 44-53. Unfortunately, the complete text of the report has been removed from the stenographic records of the session kept at the academy's archive. See the State Archive of Russian Federation (hereafter GARF), f. r9120, op. 2, d. 145.

[4] The Scientific Archive of the Russian Academy of Medical Sciences (hereafter NA RAMN), f. 9120, op. 3, d. 110, ll. 62-63.

[5] See "V Akademii Meditsinskikh Nauk", *Izvestiia*, 14 March 1946, p. 3; "Opyty Bioterapii Zlokachestvennykh Opukholei", *Trud*, 14 March 1946, p. 4. See "V Akademii Meditsinskikh Nauk", *Izvestiia*, 14 March 1946, p. 3; "Opyty Bioterapii Zlokachestvennykh Opukholei", *Trud*, 14 March 1946, p. 4.

[6] The Russian Center for Preservation and Study of the Documents of Recent History (hereafter RTsKhIDNI), f. 17, op. 116, d. 256, l. 13.

[7] See "Bioterapiia Raka. Beseda s N.G. Kliuevoi", *Meditsinskii Rabotnik*, 16 May 1946, p. 3.

at home[8]. In June, the newspaper *Moscow Bolshevik* published yet another article about the new preparation[9]. All the publications cast Kliueva and Roskin's work as an outstanding achievement of Soviet science in the fight against cancer. The inventors, however, were worried. As Roskin noted in his letter to an American colleague: "It is not our fault, but now our experiments have got into the newspapers, and Professor Kliueva and I greatly fear that we will be perceived as charlatans who promise 'miracle cures' by mysterious preparations to the terminally ill"[10].

KR research also aroused the interest of the American medical community and American government officials: in June 1946, the US Ambassador Walter B. Smith visited their laboratory and suggested organising a collaborative Soviet-American project to study KR[11]. Kliueva and Roskin's work triggered an active exchange of scientific delegations and medical information between the Soviet Union and the United States. In early November, one of the top officials of the Academy of Medical Sciences, Vasilii Parin, went to the United States as a guest of the US Surgeon General "to make an extensive inspection tour of US hospitals and 12 main cancer research centers"[12]. With the blessing of Viacheslav Molotov (a member of the Politburo and Soviet foreign minister), Parin presented a manuscript of Kliueva and Roskin's book entitled *The Biotherapy of Malignant Tumors* to the US National Cancer Institute for translation into English, as a way to ascertain Soviet priority in developing the cancer cure. A group of American researchers was preparing to go "to Moscow to consult with Professors Kliueva and Roskin regarding their announced treatment of cancer with extracts of trypanosomes"[13]. In turn, Kliueva and Roskin were invited to go to the United States in September 1947 to present their findings at the International Cancer Congress in St. Louis.

[8] See E. Finn, "Pozhiratel' Rakovykh Kletok. Novyi Sovetskii Preparat 'KR'", *Ogonek*, 1946, no. 19 (May), pp. 4-5.

[9] See Boris Neiman, "Preparat 'KR'", *Moskovskii Bol'shevik*, 9 June 1946, p. 3.

[10] G. Roskin to M. Shear, April 28, 1946. Murray Shear Papers, Box 21, "KR", in the National Library of Medicine (Bethesda, MD).

[11] I was able to find several accounts of the visit: one is Smith's report to the State Department (the US National Archives, 812. 1 Cancer); another is a letter of June 28 by the Soviet journalist Emil' Finn to a deputy-minister of foreign affairs and head of TASS, Solomon Lozovskii (RTsKhIDNI, f. 17, op. 121, d. 620, ll. 1-2); yet another is Kliueva and Roskin's report to the Central Committee written some seven months later (RTsKhIDNI, f. 17, op. 121, d. 620, ll. 68-71).

[12] "Cultural Relations: US-USSR", *Department of State Bulletin*, 1949, vol. 20, no. 509, pp. 403-417, cit. on p. 408.

[13] The Archive of the Russian Foreign Policy (hereafter, AVPR), f. 192, op. 13, papka 99, d. 47, l. 126.

Kliueva and Roskin used this American interest to solicit support for their research from the highest Soviet officials: in mid-November they again appealed to Zhdanov, claiming that the Ministry of Public Health was too slow in providing promised assistance[14]. The response was immediate. In the atmosphere of fierce scientific competition inspired by the American atomic monopoly, the Politburo apparently considered KR "a kind of biological atomic bomb"[15]. In December 1946 Stalin signed a special decree to provide Kliueva and Roskin with almost unlimited resources for their research[16]. The Politburo also lavished numerous rewards on the inventors: their work was even nominated for the highest Soviet award – a Stalin prize.

Just a few months later, however, with the dawning of the Cold War in the late spring of 1947, Stalin and Zhdanov used the exchange of materials between Soviet and American cancer specialists to stage a show trial, the "Honour Court", for Kliueva and Roskin[17]. The scientists were accused of a "lack of patriotism" and "servility to the West"[18]. The trial ended with a verdict of "public reprimand" for the accused and marked the beginning of a broad ideological campaign designed to inculcate the Soviet intelligentsia, and particularly scientists, with "patriotic spirit"[19]. The campaign resulted in establishing the Iron Curtain between Soviet and Western science: unsurprisingly, no American scientists went to the USSR to work with KR and Kliueva and Roskin were not allowed to go to St. Louis to take part in the International Cancer Congress.

Furthermore, as a part of this 'patriotic' campaign, the Central Committee disseminated the carefully edited records of the Honour Court proceedings to all the party cells throughout the country[20] and instructed the local apparatchiki to hold meetings of party members to discuss the unpatriotic behavior of Kliueva and Roskin. The Politburo also arranged for the production of two plays and a movie, which portrayed the 'Kliueva-Roskin affair' and were shown in all theatres and cinemas.

---

[14] See RTsKhIDNI, f. 77, op. 3, d. 148, ll. 6-7.

[15] This is a quotation from a letter sent to the Central Committee by a journalist who covered Kliueva and Roskin's work. See RTsKhIDNI, f. 17, op. 121, d. 620, l. 2.

[16] See GARF, f. r8009, op. 1, d. 547, ll. 263-264.

[17] Parin, who had actually transferred the manuscript of Kliueva and Roskin's book to Americans, was arrested as an American spy.

[18] For the stenographic records of the court's sittings see GARF, f. 8009, op. 1, dd. 624-626.

[19] For the details of this campaign see Nikolai Krementsov, "The 'KR Affair': Soviet Science on the Threshold of the Cold War", *History and Philosophy of Life Sciences,* 1995, vol. 17, no. 3, pp. 419-446.

[20] See RTsKhIDNI, f. 17, op. 122, d. 258, ll. 1-25. The party instructions were recently reprinted in V.D. Esakov and E.S. Levina, "Delo 'KR' (Iz Istorii Gonenii na Sovetskuiu Intelligentsiiu)", *Kentavr,* 1994, no. 2, pp. 54-69; no. 3, pp. 96-118.

Despite this countrywide denunciation, Kliueva and Roskin were allowed to continue and expand their search for a cancer cure – the Politburo commanded that a huge, top-secret institute devoted solely to the research and development of KR be built in Moscow. The institute became the country's best-equipped cancer research facility and, for four years, its staff worked at production techniques and conducted extensive laboratory research and clinical trials using the trypanosome preparation.

However, the top officials of the Academy of Medical Sciences were both envious and dubious. During these four years, with the participation of several well-known oncologists (and particularly, a specialist in chemical carcinogens called Leon Shabad), they thoroughly inspected the KR research three times[21]. The inspectors became convinced that the preparation was useless and insistently tried to seize control over the institute. Kliueva and Roskin successfully defended their work with the support of their party patrons (particularly, the former Minister of Defence and member of the Politburo, Kliment Voroshilov, who supervised medical problems). It was only in October 1951, prompted by the medical establishment, that the Politburo decided to abandon this line of research[22]. Kliueva and Roskin were fired. The academy seized their institute and appointed an old party hand, orthopedist Nikolai Blokhin, to head it.

3. The Kachugin affair

On August 4, 1957, a Leningrad newspaper, *Leningradskaia Pravda*, published an article that described a new anti-cancer treatment developed by a certain A.T. Kachugin, who suggested using cadmium iodinate and semicarbazide chloride (a chemical produced from urea) as a cancer cure. The author, a journalist, described the miraculous recovery of a patient treated by Kachugin's preparations and blamed local oncologists and the city health authorities for insufficient attention to the new prospective cure, calling for its wide testing in laboratory and clinic. He stated that "The time when heretics-discoverers were burnt at the stake has passed", and that now it is time to "provide all the necessary assistance to those who invent something new in every field, be it medicine, technology, or agriculture"[23].

---

[21] The first commission came in October 1947 (see GARF, f. r9120, op. 2, d. 183, 237 ll.); the second in December 1948 (see GARF, f. r9120, op. 2, dd. 569-570); the third in May 1950 (see NA RAMN, f. 15, op. 1, dd. 4-5).

[22] For the Politburo decision see RTsKhIDNI, f. 17, op. 3, d. 1091, ll. 25, pp. 190-191.

[23] V. Ermolaev, "Istoriia Bolezni No 10355", *Leningradskaia Pravda*, August 4, 1957, p. 3.

A year later, on November 27, 1958, the same newspaper carried another article on the same subject. Signed by three doctors who had tried Kachugin's preparations on incurable patients in the out-patient unit of the Academy of Sciences, the article bore a telling title, "A Recurrence of Oppression in Medical Science", and described the negative attitude of the Leningrad Health Department towards the new treatment[24].

On October 11, 1960, the official newspaper of the Ministry of Public Health, *Medical Worker*, published yet another article entitled "To Defend the Patients against Charlatans". This article was signed by a head of a department at the Institute of the Pathology and Experimental Therapy of Cancer (as Kliueva and Roskin's former institute was now called). The author stated that Kachugin's preparations had been tested in several clinics in Moscow and had not only showed no curative effect, but had even had some harmful consequences for the patients. The article accused Kachugin of extorting money from patients and of making money "from the terminally ill and the tears of their relatives"[25].

A week later, Kachugin responded with a letter to a Secretary of the Central Committee, Ivan Kozlov. He complained that the article in *Medical Worker* was incorrect and that the Leningrad health authorities had prohibited using his preparations in clinical practice. He asked the Central Committee for help. The party bosses intervened and forwarded Kachugin's letter to Nikolai Blokhin, the director of Kliueva and Roskin's former institute, who by that time had become the president of the Medical Academy. The academy apparatus (with the participation of Kliueva and Roskin's nemesis, Leon Shabad) prepared a response to the Central Committee, stating that Kachugin's claims were unsubstantiated. Perhaps to simply keep the inventor quiet, Blokhin informed Kachugin that he was ready to examine any patients who had been treated with cadmium iodinate and semicarbazide chloride[26].

In late 1960, Blokhin did indeed go to Leningrad and paid a visit to the out-patient unit of the Academy of Sciences, where a group of doctors continued using Kachugin's technique. In January 1961, he reported the results of his examination to the presidium. Blokhin was unconvinced, but he decided to proceed with caution. He suggested that the staff of his own institute and the staff of the Leningrad Oncology Institute tested

---

[24] M. Volokhonskaia, N. Voronko, and S. Vysheslavtsev, "Retsidiv Arakcheevshchiny v Meditsinskoi Nauke", *Leningradskaia Pravda*, November 27, 1958, p. 3.

[25] E.G. Kudimova, "Ogradit' Bol'nykh ot Sharlatanov", *Meditsinskii Rabotnik*, October 11, 1960, p. 3.

[26] See, NA RAMN, f. 9120, op. 2, d. 3397, ll. 14-18.

Kachugin's preparations[27]. The testing reportedly proved the technique worthless and the academy, through the Ministry of Public Health, forbade its usage.

In response, Kachugin solicited the support of several well-known writers and journalists who sent letters to the Central Committee and to its General Secretary, Nikita Khrushchev, personally accusing the medical establishment of ignoring the invention and of hiding the cure from the patients. As a result of the Central Committee intervention, on March 22, 1961, the Ministry of Public Health issued an order (no. 129) that commanded the Academy of Medical Sciences to organise another round of trials in Moscow and Leningrad. A year later, on April 22, 1962, a special commission of the Ministry of Public Health headed by a deputy minister, I.G. Kochergin, went to Leningrad to inspect the trials conducted at a local hospital. The commission left unconvinced. In early May, a special meeting of the Academy of Medical Sciences discussed the results of the trials conducted at Blokhin's institute[28]. All those present unanimously agreed that Kachugin's technique was, at best, useless. On May 24, 1962, the Ministry of Public Health issued a new order (no 259) that again forbade using Kachugin's preparations in clinical practice.

The inventor again appealed to his public supporters for help. A few days later, nine writers and journalists again sent a letter to the Central Committee, this time accusing Blokhin and Kochergin personally of "the deliberate distortion of facts and 'strangling' of the new anti-cancer treatment". They quoted letters from various doctors who had used Kachugin's preparations in their practices and had found them effective.

The Central Committee intervened again. Yet, this time it took a somewhat unexpected form. On August 1, 1962, the Central Committee newspaper *Pravda* devoted its entire second page to the issue of Kachugin's preparations. It published, side by side, the letter from Kachugin's public supporters[29] and an answer from the Academy of Medical Sciences signed by 15 of its most influential academicians[30]. The academicians stated that Kachugin's preparations were useless and called on the letter writers to let professionals judge the efficacy of medical preparations.

---

[27] See NA RAMN, f. 9120, op. 1, d. 3703, ll. 83-91.

[28] For stenographic records of these discussions, see NA RAMN, f. 9120, op. 1, d. 3931, ll. 1-60.

[29] Vera Ketlinskaia, N. Grudnina, I. Karakoz, A. Khrashonovskii, D. Granin, Iu. German, M. Lanskoi, S. Drabkina, and Kh. Vares, "V Prezidium TsK KPSS", *Pravda*, August 1, 1962, p. 2.

[30] A. Bakulev, N. Blokhin, V. Vasilenko, A. Vishnevskii, I. Davydovskii, N. Zhukov-Verezhnikov, P. Kupriianov, V. Parin, B. Petrovskii, A. Savitskii, A. Serebrov, R. Kavetskii, I. Kochergin, L. Larionov, I. Tager, and A. Novikov, "Otvet na Pis'mo Gruppy Pisatelei i Zhurnallistov", *Pravda*, August 1, 1962, p. 2.

What was most important is that the publication opened with a short note entitled "From the Central Committee", which announced that the party apparatus "does not consider it possible to take upon itself the role of an arbiter in testing new medical treatments". It stated that "only medical scientists can judge the correctness of particular medical techniques", and concluded that "attempts at administrative decisions in science cannot be useful and, as is well known, in our country's recent past, such attempts led to unjust accusations against certain scientists and doctors and to their being discredited"[31]. As a result of this affair, Kachugin's preparations were abandoned, and the inventor himself was brought before a criminal court for "unlawful medical practice".

4. Medicine and politics

The dynamics and outcomes of both cases illustrate that Soviet medical policies were formulated and implemented as a result of a tangled skein of interactions between four different players: inventors, party officials, the public (including practising doctors) and the medical establishment, each of which pursued their own goals and interests, and deployed all means at their disposal.

There are many similarities between the two cases. In both cases, the oncological establishment perceived the inventors (and supporters) of new preparations as outsiders and fiercely defended its own turf, not only from the inventors, but also from interference by party officials and the public. The inventors attempted to employ the existing power structure (the supreme authority of the Central Committee) to overcome the hostility of their opponents. In both cases, party officials exercised their power to lend initial support to the inventors.

However, there are many important differences between the two cases. The differences were derived from profound changes in Soviet domestic and foreign policies initiated by Stalin's death on March 5, 1953.

The KR affair developed during the late 1940s to early 1950s. This was at the height of Stalin's regime, with its militant nationalism on the domestic scene and strict isolationism on the international one, generated by the growing Cold War. A fierce scientific and technological competition with the United States spurred on by the American atomic monopoly made science a strategic priority for the Soviet political authorities. During this period, the Politburo lavished almost unlimited resources on scientific research and

---

[31] V TsK KPSS, *Pravda*, August 1, 1962, p. 2.

development. Yet, the political authorities tightly controlled science-policy decision making, defining not only the institutional, but also the intellectual development of Soviet science and medicine in an attempt, as Stalin put it, "not only to catch up with, but also soon overtake the achievements of science abroad"[32].

The Kachugin case unfolded under entirely different circumstances. After a short struggle within the Politburo, which followed Stalin's death, one of his lieutenants, Nikita Khrushchev, inherited Stalin's mantle. Three years later, in February 1956, at the 20th congress of the Communist Party, Khrushchev delivered his famous 'secret speech', which opened a broad campaign against the "consequences of Stalin's cult of personality". This campaign became known as the 'Thaw' and dramatically affected both domestic and international policies of the Soviet Union, lifting Cold War isolationism and nationalism. Furthermore, the enormous resources that the Soviet government had invested into scientific development during the 1950s paid off. Soviet science did catch up with and even overtook 'the achievements of science abroad': the Soviet Union had developed its own nuclear arsenal, sent the first sputnik into orbit around Earth and sent the first man into space.

These profound differences in the political, ideological, and cultural landscape defined the different dynamics of the interactions between all groups involved in both cases and the different roles they played in each of them.

The medical establishment initially endorsed and publicised KR research to promote its own institutional agenda, using KR as a lever to increase the importance of oncology in the eyes of party bosses and to restore its institutional base decimated by the war[33]. When party officials provided Kliueva and Roskin with almost unlimited resources, the establishment first tried to seize control over the promising preparation and the well-equipped cancer research institution, and then banished KR research. On the other hand, from the start, the establishment considered Kachugin's techniques useless and deployed all available means to suppress it. However, in this case,

---

[32] Vestnik AN SSSR, 1946, no. 2, p. 11.

[33] World War II virtually destroyed Soviet oncology as a discipline. The majority of oncological institutions in the USSR were located in Leningrad and the Ukraine, and these two regions suffered most during the war: Leningrad was besieged and the Ukraine was occupied by the Nazis for almost three years. Even the institutions located far from the battlefield were converted into military hospitals and stopped any oncological work. Publication of literature in oncology decreased ten-fold as compared with the pre-war period. In the immediate post-war years, the restoration of their institutional base became a major preoccupation of Soviet oncologists, and they used every occasion to call the attention of party bosses to the pitiful conditions of their discipline and to extract additional resources. KR proved very useful in this respect.

the establishment had to struggle against new opponents – the public, including practising doctors, who dealt with cancer patients not in central hospitals and research
institutions, but in local clinics.

The public played different roles in the two cases. In the KR affair, the public was simply a passive audience for the performances staged by the Central Committee: first the
publicity campaign in the press, then the Honour Court, the 'patriotic campaign' based
on the Honour Court and then the plays and the movie portraying the KR affair. The
inventors themselves were reluctant to talk to the media, but had no choice[34]. After initial publicity prompted by the medical establishment and the party apparatus, KR
research was made top-secret and practising doctors were excluded from testing KR.
The public was mobilised by party officials not to having a say in regard to medical
policies, but to condemning 'the lack of patriotism'. Interestingly, in the two plays and
the film that portrayed the KR affair to the public, the essence of Kliueva and Roskin's
work – their search for a cancer cure – was replaced by other medical problems.

In the Kachugin case, the public was mobilised by the inventor and organised an
intense campaign against the medical establishment. Yet, the party officials repri-
manded the public and ascertained the authority of the medical establishment over
the issues of medical research and treatment. Interestingly, in accord with the general
policy of de-Stalinisation, both the party bosses and the public made references to the
past – the oppressive regime of Stalin's epoch – but the aims of such references were
different. Writers, journalists, and practising doctors referred to the administrative
dictate of the party-state apparatus, which denied the public any influence in the formulation and implementation of medical policies. They considered the medical establishment to be a part of that oppressive apparatus and demanded a right to participate
in medical policy-making. The party bosses also referred to the past administrative
fiat, but in their pronouncements, it denied the medical establishment its right to control medical policies. The party bosses recognised the right of medical officials, but
again denied the right of the public.

The attitude of party officials towards the two cases clearly differed and these differences derived, in part, from profound changes in Soviet foreign policy. In the late
1940s, the party apparatus exercised its power over the medical establishment without
encumbrance. The growing competition with the United States for the super-power
status stimulated the Politburo to endorse a wide-scale 'fight against cancer'. The

---

[34] Actually, their contacts with the press were forced by an attempt to steal their discovery by a
colleague, who told the media that it was he who had discovered the cure. For details, see
Nikolai Krementsov, "The Cure".

American interest in KR prompted the party bosses to support KR research for five years, despite the growing opposition of the medical establishment and even despite the countrywide denunciation of the inventors as 'un-patriotic'. The abandonment of KR research in late 1951 resulted mainly from the inventors' reluctance to share control over resources with the medical establishment and the establishment's skill in playing intricate bureaucratic games with the party apparatus. Being unable to seize control of Kliueva-Roskin's institute directly, the medical establishment managed to convince the party apparatus to establish a new Institute of the Pathology and Experimental Therapy of Cancer and to make Kliueva-Roskin's institute a part of it, using the importance of cancer research in the eyes of party bosses, and KR research in particular, as a justification for organising the new, bigger institute.

In the Kachugin case, party officials, at first, exercised their authority in medical policy making, forcing the medical establishment to test Kachugin's inventions repeatedly, but, in the end, publicly relegated this authority to the establishment. One of the reasons for this unique situation was the growing influence of the Soviet oncological establishment on the international scene, manifested at the 8th International Cancer Congress held in Moscow in July 1962, just a few weeks before the Central Committee pronouncement on Kachugin's case. This congress was one of the first international scientific forums convened in the Soviet Union since the mid-1930s. According to Soviet practice, its organisation was impossible without the Central Committee's blessing. The party bosses permitted, and lavishly financed, the congress as a means to demonstrate Soviet advances in science and medicine to the world. Nikolai Blokhin, who organised and presided over the congress, skillfully employed its success to assert the medical establishment's authority over the issues of medical policies. Characteristically, the "Answer to the Letter of a Group of Writers and Journalists" contained a special reference to the International Congress as a very important instrument in solving "cancer problems".

The confrontation between the medical establishment and the other groups – inventors, party bosses, and the public – was based not only on the establishment's desire to protect its own turf, but also on the differences between the 'images' of cancer upheld by the 'professionals' and the 'outsiders'. The outsiders shared a particular 'image' of cancer: all of them considered cancer as a disease that was basically incurable by existing methods. They often saw the diagnosis of cancer as a death sentence. In the article published in 1958 by *Leningradskaia Pravda* practising doctors noted: "We observed a successful use of [Kachugin's] therapy on incurable patients, i.e., when all other methods had proved ineffective" [35]. Similarly, in their letter to the Central Committee, writers and

---

[35] M. Volokhonskaia, N. Voronko, and S. Vysheslavtsev, "Retsidiv Arakcheevshchiny v Meditsinskoi Nauke", *Leningradskaia Pravda*, November 27, 1958, p. 3.

journalists emphasised that Kachugin's technique was effective in "the treatment of incurable patients who had been rejected by official oncology experts as hopeless"[36]. The outsiders wanted to believe that cancer could be cured and believed in finding the cure.

The professionals, on the other hand, held a much more sophisticated view of cancer, considering it as a group of diseases that differ drastically in their origin, development and prognosis, although having certain similarities in appearance. The professionals did not believe in the cure. They believed that each form of cancerous diseases might require a specific treatment and in their answer to writers and journalists they listed a number of preparations that proved effective in the chemotherapy of certain particular forms of cancer. The professionals were well aware of the absence of preparations effective against the most common forms – lung, breast, and stomach cancers – and in their public pronouncements put more emphasis on the prevention than the therapy of cancer. This can be easily seen in posters published by the Ministry of Public Health from the late 1940s to the 1960s. It is worth noting that the posters published in the 1940s actually announce that cancer is curable and even provide photographs of people who 'had been cured of cancer', while the 1960s posters speak almost exclusively of prevention (see Figures 1-7).

Thus, the relationship between medicine and politics in the Soviet Union during the first two decades of the Cold War was affected and mediated by a complex skein of connections between different groups and individuals, who pursued their own, often conflicting, interests. All these players operated within a particular institutional, political, and cultural landscape that changed over time in accord with general foreign and domestic policies, and all of them used these changes to gain advantage for their own agendas.

---

[36] Vera Ketlinskaia, N. Grudnina, I. Karakoz, A. Khrashonovskii, D. Granin, Iu. German, M. Lanskoi, S. Drabkina, and Kh. Vares, "V Prezidium TsK KPSS", *Pravda*, August 1, 1962, p. 2.

Fig. 1

Fig. 2

Fig. 3

Figure 1: *Cancer is curable, if the treatment is started early. When cancer spreads through the body, it is difficult to cure it. (Published in 1946)* Courtesy of the Museum of the History of Medicine in Moscow.

Figure 2: *We have been cured of cancer. When cancer is suspected, go to a doctor immediately. (Published in 1949)* Courtesy of the Museum of the History of Medicine in Moscow.

Figure 3: *At the first signs of disease, go to a doctor. Don't lose time. The earlier the treatment begins, the easier it is to cure the disease. (Published in 1959)* Courtesy of the Museum of the History of Medicine in Moscow.

Fig. 4

Fig. 5

Fig. 6

Figure 4: *Cancer can be prevented. Go regularly, two times a year, for a medical check-up. (Published in 1961)* Courtesy of the Museum of the History of Medicine in Moscow.

Figure 5: *Don't guess: Cancer? No? Cancer. If you are in doubt, go to a doctor. The earlier a disease is recognised, the easier it is to cure it. (Published in 1965)* Courtesy of the Museum of the History of Medicine in Moscow.

Figure 6: *Don't wait for thunder to clap. Even cancer is curable at an early stage, if you get to a doctor in time. (Published in 1968)* Courtesy of the Museum of the History of Medicine in Moscow.

Figure 7: *Time is valuable. Go for a medical prophylactic check-up (Published in 1968).* Courtesy of the Museum of the History of Medicine in Moscow.

Fig. 7

The Organisation of Public Health in Russia since 1945: a Survey of Archival Resources

Lyubov G. Gurjeva

The Russian health care system has undergone dramatic changes since 1945. While there is a good record of official documents and decisions pertaining to Soviet public health policies[1], there has been little analysis of the development and expansion of the Soviet welfare system after World War II and its dramatic transformations in the 1990s from an historical and comparative perspective. An understanding of the health care system based exclusively on official publications hinders credible analysis of the changes from a highly centralised to a loosely regulated system, from a closed to an open economy, from a scarce supply of cheap pharmaceuticals to the proliferation of expensive brand names. As official publications present outcomes of discussions and embody intended consequences of policies, they do not give historians enough clues for studies of controversies, reception of policies, their unintended consequences and practices more generally[2]. Russian archives hold a wide range of sources that can help historians create more nuanced and, hence, more credible and powerful accounts of the Russian public health system. This can be achieved by bringing personalities, discussions and contradictions back into the history of public health.

The aim of this paper is to explore the holdings of Russian national archives with a view to exploring the possibilities for new studies in the history of public health. This is an opportune moment for such an project. A number of new reference publications and guides to Russian archives have recently appeared; at the same time, health services and the welfare system more generally have not received any special treatment[3]. First detailed studies of

---

[1] For Soviet documents see for instance *Zabota partii i pravitel'stva o blage naroda: sbornik dokumentov, oktiabr' 1964-1973*, Moscow, Politizdat, 1974. Russian health legislation is available on-line: http://www.chat.ru/~medical_site/zakon/zakon.htm

[2] For an example of a history based on official publicatons see E. Chazov *et al.* (eds.), *70 let sovetskogo zdravookhraneniya 1917-1987*, Moscow, Meditsina, 1987.

[3] *See Kratkyi putevoditel'. Fondy i kollectsii, sobrannyie tsentralnym partiinym arkhivom*, Moscow, Blagovest, 1993; *Federalnye arkhivy Rossii i ikh nauchno-spravochnyi apparat*, Moscow, Redaktsionno-izdatelskii otdel federalnykh arkhivov, 1994; Patricia K. Grimsted (ed.), *Archives of Russia: A Directory and Bibliographic Guide to Holdings in Moscow and St Petersburg*, Armonk, NY, and London: M.E. Sharpe Publishers, 2000. Unfortunately, some reference publications have such small imprints that they become rare books in the year of their publication, e.g. *Gosudarstvennye khranilishcha dokumentov byvshego arkhivnogo fonda KPSS*, Novosibirsk, Sibirskii Khronograph, 1998, 500 copies. A good bibliography of reference publications can be found via the home page the Centre for the Study of Russia and the Soviet Union, http://www.rus-archive.org

various aspects of the post-war Soviet health system are nevertheless being undertaken[4]. I hope this discussion will be useful to those engaged in the history of public health internationally as well as to students of Russian medical history.

This survey is limited to five specific issues, each issue being discussed in relation to one or more collections of documents. The first section deals with the general organisation of public health, which is discussed in relation to the holdings of the former archives of the Communist Party. In the second section, I look at the materials of the State Archive of the Russian Federation relating to child and maternal health. In the third section I propose various ways in which the documents from the archives of the Government and the Communist Party can be used for writing a history of patients. In the fourth section, I discuss possible historical uses of images of healthy childhood from various poster collections. Section five introduces Russian Internet resources and raises the question of their significance for medical history. I conclude by raising some questions as to the possibilities offered by the reviewed sources and their limitations.

1. Public health in the former archives of the Communist Party

In the early 1990s, in the wake of the attempted coup in August 1991, the rules and principles of access to Russian archives were revised. The 1993 law proclaimed openness and equal access to archives for individuals and organisations. This legislation has been important for the historical profession and society at large, as part of the process of democratisation. The new legislation publicised the right to information and incorporated it into the legal system. However, the scale of practical changes induced by the new legislation has often been exaggerated, especially outside Russia. In fact, the new legislation has not affected admission procedures in most archives (e.g. State Archive of the Russian Federation and the Archive of the Academy of Sciences). At the same time, there are several archives which have been nationalised and genuinely opened to researchers since 1991, notably, the two archives holding the documents created by the Communist Party of the Soviet Union (CPSU) and the archives of local Party organisations. The decreed transfer of the CPSU documents to the National Archival Fund has been riddled with political and technical problems. Nevertheless, the process of declassification and political changes prompting it have created a paradoxical relaxation

---

[4] E.g. Chris Burton, "The Patient as Participant in the Late Stalinist Health System" and Lyubov Gurjeva, "Pressure Differentials: Patients' Lobbying for Barotherapy in 1950s-1970s", papers read at the 1999 National Convention of the American Association for the Advancement of Slavonic Studies, 18-21 November 1999, St. Louis, Missouri, USA.

of the thirty-year rule in regard to the Communist Party[5]. A number of documents created by the apparatus of the Party up to 1984 are now accessible to researchers. Availability of such recent documents creates unique opportunities for research into contemporary history. For comparison, the latest Ministry of Health papers publicly available at the State Archive date back to 1969[6]. Given the Party control of every branch of the economy, the former Party archives hold documents which are relevant not only to political historians, but also to researchers in various other disciplines, including medical history.

The records of the central organs of the Communist Party are divided between three archives. The majority of pre-1953 documents are located in the Russian State Archive of Socio-Political History, the majority of the later documents are in the Russian State Archive for Contemporary History, and the papers of the Party supreme body, the Politbureau of the Central Committee, are part of the President's Archive.

Russian State Archive of Socio-Political History (RSASPH)

Central organs of the Party had special departments for co-ordinating work in industry, agriculture, transport and personnel policy. Health care, together with other elements of the so-called "non-productive sphere", such as science, education and art, was overseen by the Propaganda Department. Consequently, documents relevant to the post-war history of public health are mostly among the papers of this Department (*opis* 125, 132). Employees of the Technical Secretariat of the Organisational Bureau (*opis* 121), however, also dealt with several matters of health care. During the early post-war years technical matters included correspondence with local bodies on the maintenance of military hospitals and the rehabilitation of invalids, rehabilitation and further development of medical institutions, the expansion of the Academy of Medical Sciences and the founding of medical schools. In 1946 and 1947 the Technical Secretariat dealt with the Klueva and Roskin affair over the alleged invention of cancer cures, discussed by Krementsov in this volume.

The majority of the Party papers available to the public were created by the party apparatus, i.e. by the administrative staff, rather than elected officials. These papers

---

[5] According to the 1992 regulations, records should be open for research thirty years after their creation unless they contain state or other kinds of secrets defined by law, or information on the private lives of individuals; in the latter case the records are subject to the seventy-five year closure rule.

[6] For the permission to see later papers one needs to apply to the Ministry of Health.

include information for members of the CC, drafts of documents to be approved by the CC along with briefs and resolutions for local Party authorities and ministries related to specific CC resolutions. These papers give a good idea of what processes were routinely controlled by the Party and what specific issues were deliberated by the CC at any given time. Members of the apparatus processed reports and letters received by the CC, conducted research and collected information upon requests of CC members. The documents of the apparatus, thus, include requests and resolutions of Politbureau members and signatures of those Secretaries of the CC who had read the documents. These documents do not include resolutions and minutes of the Politbureau meetings, where the most important decisions were taken. Politbureau papers were separated from the rest of the Party documents and are now part of the President's Archive[7]. Another component of publicly available Party documents are resolutions of the Party bodies, such as Congresses and CC Plenary Meetings, which contain both guidelines for the ministries and all other administrative bodies as well as their proposals for inclusion into future Party resolutions.

Russian State Archive for Contemporary History (RSACH)

Papers deposited at the Russian State Archive for Contemporary History (RSACH) are divided into several collections by source. Of the collections which have been declassified, Central Committee papers are most relevant to issues of health care. During the 1950s health services, medical education and research were controlled by the General Department (*obshchii otdel*) of the CC; in 1962 they were charged to the newly created Ideological Department created by merging the Propaganda Department with the Department of Science, Higher Education and Culture. CC controlled the management of the following aspects of health care: research and development, medical education, epidemics and emergencies, medical industry, statistical reports, international activities and patients' complaints. According to the source of initial enquiry, CC papers can be divided into two categories: reports solicited by Secretaries of the Central Committee, and reports on enquiries received from outside the Party.

As the CC was close to the centre of political power, its papers can help one evaluate the significance of health in Soviet politics. Immediately after the end of World War II, the Party was particularly concerned with the management of military hospitals and

---

[7] The President's Archive is managed by the Administration of the President but some historical materials are being gradually transferred to the Russian State Archive of Socio-Political History (RSASPH) and the Russian State Archive for Contemporary History (RSACH).

provisions for invalids. The creation of a health care sector in the science department of the CC coincides with the official end of the post-war rehabilitation in the middle of the 1950s. From this time onwards, the CC assumes a fuller control over health care and collects information on medical emergencies, such as epidemics and infant deaths.

The CC acted as a clearing house for health-related statistics. Not only did the CC receive statistical information from various sources, but its members also decided what information could be made public. Thus, in 1967, the CC acknowledged using classified information on the number of cancer patients provided by the Central Statistical Administration (CSA) and authorised the publication of data on TB morbidity and mortality[8]. The TB data and the proposal to publish them came from the Ministry of Health. The CSA agreed to the publication, but the authorisation of the CC was needed before the CSA could go ahead with the publication. The CC could also prohibit publication of certain information, and stop or restrict the circulation of the information once available to the public. In 1963, following the request of S. Kurashov, the Minister of Health, the circulation of a book containing reports on dystrophy and malnutrition of Tajik cotton farmers[9], was restricted to "authorised readers only". Thus, CC papers are a useful, if unsystematic, repository of statistical information and analytical materials which were not available in the public sphere.

Moreover, health indicators solicited and used by the CC can give us a good idea of health-care priorities of the Soviet state. Throughout the 1950s and 1960s, the main interest was in morbidity and mortality related to infectious diseases, even though by the end of the period, heart and circulation diseases became the main cause of disability. The interest of policy-makers shifted to the data pertaining to circulation disorders and cancer in the beginning of the 1970s, when they decided that infectious diseases (except flu) no longer posed a serious threat to the majority of the population. The 1974-1975 file of reports of infectious diseases was entitled "Isolated cases of infectious diseases"[10]. In the same year, cancer, preservation of the environment, biomedical and clinical equipment and medical polymers were named as the main themes for Russian-Bulgarian co-operation in health care and medical research until 1980 and, tentatively, for 1981-1990[11]. The change of health research priorities in the 1970s may have been related to the new Soviet-American co-operation initiative of

---

[8] RSACH, *fond* 5, *opis* 56, *delo* 50, pp. 275, 222-235.

[9] V.A. Serebryakov, *Pitaniye i zdorov'e kolkhoznikov yuzhnogo Tajikistana*, Dushanbe, 1962.

[10] RSACH, *fond* 5, *opis* 67, *delo* 183.

[11] RSACH, *fond* 5, *opis* 68, *delo* 600, p. 6.

1972, which followed a Soviet-American summit and a general improvement of bilateral relations. Joint research programmes were started and information was exchanged in the following areas: heart and circulation disorders, cancer, environmental hygiene, arthritis, flu and cold, and artificial heart. An American proposal to include ophthalmology was rejected by the Soviet side [12].

Documents pertinent to maternal and child health, however, are relatively few among the CC papers. This indicates that in this area management responsibility rested largely with the Ministry of Health. Documents deposited in Party archives include reports on maternal and child mortality and morbidity, reports on investigations into infant and child deaths, and some letters of complaints regarding conditions in childrens' hospitals. Interventions of Party officials into matters of health care were often caused by journalists' or patients' complaints. The collections of letters preserved in RSACH convey the impression that complaints about maternal and child health services were comparatively rare.

2. Maternal and child health at the State Archive of the Russian Federation (SARF)

The main repository of the documents of the central health administration is the State Archive of the Russian Federation (SARF)[13], formerly the Central State Archive of the October Revolution and Socialist Development. Most documents created by the Ministry of Health before 1969 are held in the *fond* (record group) No. 8009. The documents related to the manufacture of medical equipment and pharmaceuticals were transferred to the Central Archive of the National Economy in 1967 following the creation of a new ministry to supervise this branch of the economy. SARF materials are organised by administration/department that created them and by year. Hence, the structure of the Ministry of Health *fond* reflects the changing structure of the Ministry. Thus, for the years 1945 to 1947, there is a separate *opis* (collection) for cancer research and therapy. During this period a special Anti-Cancer Administration (*upravleniye*) of the Ministry was charged with improving oncological care. In 1948 this section was integrated with the Administration of Urban Therapeutic and Preventive Institutions. Whether such re-organisations were caused by or resulted in political and policy changes, are legitimate research questions.

---

[12] *Ibid.*, *fond* 5, *opis* 68, *delo* 602, p. 57.

[13] By convention, the names of Russian archives are translated with the singular "archive".

The management of maternal and child health has also undergone a number of changes during the Soviet period. The main elements of the Soviet system of maternal and child care were shaped before World War II. It appears that post-war changes in the administration of this system reflect changes in policies. In 1938 a new Department of Delivery Care (*Otdel rodovspomozheniya*) was created at the People's Commissariat of Health (the predecessor of the Ministry of Health). The Department managed maternity hospitals and women's consultation clinics (*zhenskiye konsutlatsii*), directed the work aimed at the reduction of pain during labour and controlled the implementation of the anti-abortion legislation of 1936[14]. In 1948 the Department was enlarged to the Administration, which existed until 1953 when it was amalgamated with the Administration for the Therapeutic and Preventive Care of Children to form the Administration for the Therapeutic and Preventive Care of Children and Mothers. This change reflected the new focus of child and maternal health policy: the child.

The activities of the Ministry in the area of maternal and child health between 1945 and 1952 are well reflected in a wide variety of documents including correspondence of the Ministry, papers of the commission on technological innovation, reports of inspections, and annual reports of research institutions and Moscow maternity homes, together with case notes and statistical reports. From 1952 to 1969 the documents pertinent to maternal and child health are limited to the correspondence of the Ministry, while materials of institutions, such as maternity homes and research institutes, are no longer deposited in the same *fond*.

The management of the Soviet health care in general was based on investment and expenditure indicators[15]. Most health-related reports start with the dynamics of the number of hospital beds and doctors. The area of child health is an exception. Although numbers of beds and doctors were used as indicators in this area, infant mortality was the main indicator[16]. It was the unexpected growth of infant mortality in 1974 that prompted the CPSU Central Committee to instruct the Ministry of Health to conduct an investigation into its causes[17].

---

[14] Resolution of the Central Executive Committee and the Council of People's Commissars of the USSR, 27 June 1936.

[15] Christopher M. Davis, *The Economics of the Soviet Health System: an Analytical and Historical Study, 1921-1978*, PhD dissertation, Cambridge, 1979, chapter 7.

[16] See, for instance, the resolution on infant morbidity and mortality in Aktyubinsk region of Kazakhstan, RSACH, *fond* 5, *opis* 62, *delo* 77, p. 39.

[17] RSACH, *fond* 5 *opis* 67, *delo* 179.

In the Ministry's report the causes of infant mortality are divided into "medical" and "non-medical", which included environmental conditions and material well being of parents. This analytical distinction could be explained away as an attempt of the Ministry to avoid full responsibility for the worsening demographic situation, but it could also indicate an approach to public health, which was different from the approach adopted in some Western countries, for instance, Britain. Jane Lewis criticised British Medical Officers of Health for their attempts to solve the public health problem of infant and maternal mortality at the individual level through education, and for not engaging in radical social campaigns[18]. The Soviet Ministry Report does not openly challenge the dogma of ever rising standards of living in the country, but the vague bureaucratic term "material well-being" can be read as a covert reference to the differentiation of the standards of living and cases of poverty. Various indicators and rival analyses of economic well-being were implicated in a number of policy-oriented discussions of the dynamics and composition of the Soviet population during the late 1960s and 1970s. The CPSU Central Committee (CC) often played the role of judge and moderator between ministries (Health, Economics), research institutions and the Central Statistical Agency. Consequently, reports from all these agencies, including the Ministry of Health are to be found in Party archives. Getting a post-1969 Ministry of Health report through SARF would have involved obtaining special permission from the Ministry. In some cases there is no need to undertake this procedure, because the Ministry of Health routinely sent to the CC Health and Social Security Sector copies of reports and other documents[19].

Much medical research in the Soviet Union was conducted by the Academy of Medical Sciences (founded in 1944) through its various institutes. The Ministry of Health, however, also had its research institutes. The division of labour between the Ministry and the Academy was modelled on the division of labour between the Academy of Sciences engaged in fundamental research, and research institutions coordinated by various ministries engaged in applied research[20].

---

[18] Jane Lewis, *What Price Community Medicine? The Philosophy, Practice and Politics of Public Health Since 1919*, Brighton, Wheatsheaf, 1986, and Jane Lewis, *The Politics of Motherhood: Child and Maternal Welfare in England, 1900-1939*, London, Croom Helm, 1980.

[19] On Western debates around Soviet infant mortality see Michael Ryan, "Infant Mortality in the Soviet Union", *British Medical Journal*, vol. 296, 19 March 1988, pp. 850-851; Albert Szymanski, "On the Uses of Disinformation to Legitimize the Revival of the Cold War: Health in the USSR", *International Journal of Health Services*, vol. 12, no. 3, 1982, pp. 481-496.

[20] The Academy of Science dates back to the eighteenth century and despite some transformations during the Soviet period has remained the most prestigious research institution in the land. Academies of agriculture and medicine were also created as elite research institutions. On the Soviet policies towards the Academy of Sciences, see Vera Tolz, *Russian Academicians and the Revolution: Combining Professionalism and Politics*, Basingstoke, Macmillan, 1997, chapters 1-3.

In the area of maternal and child health, one of the main research institutions was the Institute of Obstetrics and Gynaecology of the Ministry of Health[21]. Annual reports of this institute offer various cases for studying the ways in which political and ideological decisions were implemented in research. The infamous 1948 Session of the Academy of Agriculture evaluated the situation in biology and denounced scientists for idealism, pro-Western attitudes and infatuation with "big science" to the detriment of applied research aimed at solving practical problems[22]. In the aftermath of this session, the Institute revised its research programme in compliance with the demands of applicability of research results to clinical practice. In the process of this revision, some research themes were abandoned, but most topics were just reformulated. A detailed comparison of the languages of the old and new programmes would be the subject of an interesting study. The new programme, in contrast with the old, emphasised "simple and efficient" solutions and included several obligatory attacks on the "theories of Weismann-Morgan-Mendel" as well as standard quotations of Stalin and Lysenko, who was one of the protagonists of the offensive against theoretical biology. There were also conventional references to the work of Ivan Pavlov, Nobel Laureate, whose physiological work had been canonised in the Soviet Union[23]. At the same time, one can trace certain influences of Pavlov's ideas, as they were fixed in the education system, in research and midwifery practice.

The emphasis on the functions of the central nervous system can be discerned in the widely adopted practice of psychophysiological analgesia. To put it crudely, this practice was based on the idea that if the woman giving birth knows how to control pain, she will not be afraid of it, and if she is not afraid of pain, she will not suffer from it. Hence, women were supposed to be taught various ways of pain control as part of the preparation for labour.

Combination of medication for pain control was also developed in 1940s. Extensive instructions circulated to maternity hospitals and reports from Moscow maternity hospitals would be a good starting point for a study of maternity care. The materials of a disciplinary case against a gynaecologist who altered ministerial instructions at his hospital, suggest that prescribed procedures were not fulfilled uniformly[24].

---

[21] Institute of Obstetrics and Gynaecology Annual Report, 1948, SARF, *fond* 8009, *opis* 22, *delo* 170.

[22] The Russian *"bol'shaya nauka"*, literally "big science", refers to fundamental as opposed to applied research, and should not be conflated with the notion of "big science" proposed by Derek de Solla Price in 1962 with reference to the scale of research activities. See D. de Solla Price, *Little Science, Big Science*, New York, Columbia University Press, 1963.

[23] On Pavlov's work before 1917, see Daniel Todes, *Isis*, vol. 88, 1997, pp. 205-246.

[24] SARF, *fond* 8009, *opis* 22.

Other SARF collections relevant to maternal and child health include those of the Main State Sanitary Inspection (1934-1955), the State Department of Health Resorts and Sanatoria (1938-1956), the Semashko Research Institute for Social Hygiene and the Organisation of Health Care (1942-1980), the Vishnevsky Surgery Institute (1945-1972), the Executive Committee of the Red Cross and Red Crescent Societies (1918-1965) and Izvestiya newspaper (1917-1958)[25].

3. Official documents for patients' history?

Official documents are indispensable for a study of health policies and politics, but is their relevance limited to these areas? This section argues for a wider historiographic relevance of official documents by showing how such documents can be used for answering questions about the history of the public in Soviet health care. Official documents have not been used in such a way, but I believe they can help us answer questions about the history of the public in five related areas: constructions of the public in official documents, sanitary enlightenment, voices of the public, official reactions to public concerns and self-organisation of the public. These groups of questions are not mutually exclusive, but it is interesting that in the Soviet situation they have emerged at different times. In the documents of the first post-war years the public was given a passive role within the health care system, but in the 1960s it appeared as a more active agent, and in the 1970s public opinion became an impetus for policy action and professionals used public opinion for supporting their campaigns.

Constructions of the public

In the documents of the first post-war decade, such as reports of the Ministry of Health and local Party officials, and resolutions of the CC, the public features mainly in the contexts of medical emergencies. In the reports on the failure of sanitary infrastructure, such as water supply, and ensuing typhoid epidemics the public is constructed as a collective victim. Thus, cities and villages cut off from pure water supplies are forced to use contaminated river water. In the resolutions on the containment of epidemics the public is accorded a more active role. Resolutions on containing outbreaks of infectious diseases (plague, cholera) mention living conditions of affected populations and consider "sanitary enlightenment" one of the measures to counter epidemics.

---

[25] Permission from the institution that had created the records is often required for using their records deposited at the SARF.

"Sanitary enlightenment" (*sanitarnoye prosveshcheniye*)

The Soviet system of sanitary enlightenment was conceived as an interface between experts and the general public and a means of achieving the objectives of health policies. Doctors of polyclinics, women's consultation clinics and other first tier services were obliged to educate their patients as well as provide treatment and prevention. The products of the system of sanitary enlightenment, besides internal and external circulars, plans and reports, included talks, lectures, posters, films, slides, and brochures for the general public. The system included a ministry department, a research institute, local institutions (*doma*) of sanitary enlightenment with staff and affiliated lecturers, publishing infrastructure, and obligatory sections at the end of every plan and report on health care. Was the position of this section a reflection of its perceived importance? This, of course, would be too simple an interpretation. It is noteworthy, however, that the managers and professionals of the system frequently termed "people's health care" never really saw the people as a partner in health protection. In the programmes of health education, as well as in other areas, the patients, and the population more generally, were rather seen as the objects of professional work.

It is ironic that the Russian government only embraced the notion of partnership with patients and other non-governmental organisations long after the abandoning of the rhetoric of "people's health care", in the late 1990s, under severe spending pressures. But given the new interest in the co-operation between governmental and non-governmental institutions and the emphasis on community medicine, the question of the results of sanitary enlightenment is particularly pertinent today. What knowledge and skills did sanitary enlightenment promulgate? Did this organised effort shape health awareness and behaviour of Russian patients and the population more generally? Was sanitary enlightenment marginal in the activities of health professionals and irrelevant to the concerns of the public? These questions resonate with the current British debate on health visiting and on how to strike a balance between respecting the privacy of families and making sure that new parents get the help they need. Questions about the policies and practices of sanitary enlightenment can be, at least partially, answered by the study of the papers of the Ministry of Health, particularly its various plans for, and reports on, sanitary enlightenment, as well as of the materials held at the Central House of Sanitary Enlightenment, including publications and images.

Interviews with the activists of sanitary enlightenment would also be useful in undertaking such a project, particularly in exploring the attitudes of the medical professionals to sanitary enlightenment. The profession, however, can only tell half of the story of sanitary enlightenment. The other half of this story will have to come from its intended audience.

Public voices in policy-related documents

In the 1950s few voices of the public were recorded in official documents, but during the two following decades patients and the public increasingly featured in official documents, especially in the papers of the Central Committee of the Communist Party. Some citizens, especially Party members, wrote directly to the Communist Party. Another route along which people's letters reached the Party headquarters was through newspapers and journals. Critical letters, especially where investigated by journalists, constitute a reliable source. Their reliability was guaranteed by the peculiar system of checks and balances to which Soviet journalists investigating complaints were subjected[26].

The Council of Ministers decree on the regulation of sick leave payments and leaves of absence of 22 January 1955, which reduced sick leave payments, related them to the length of work for the present employer, and introduced daily payments for hospital stay, was a cause of concern and bewilderment for many citizens. The decree immediately affected people's pay, and many took to the pen to express their grievances to the Central Committee and Nikita Khrushchev, its First Secretary. The summary prepared on 6 April by A. Kabashkin, Head of the CC Letters Sector, cites 10 letters on the new decree from all over Russia and Ukraine. Two main themes of the excerpts are the injustice of the decree and its contradictions with the Soviet Constitution and the Programme of the Communist Party. Another complaint, featuring in letters from communists, was that the text of the decree had not been published and its adoption had not been justified. These communists predicted that the decree would cause popular discontent while failing to fulfil its stated goal of reducing absenteeism.

The year 1955 is significant for our analysis: it is two years after Stalin's death, but before the famous secret speech to a Party Congress in which Khrushchev denounced Stalin's crimes and the so-called cult of personality. The letters bear the marks of Stalin's cult in the form of references to his illustrious life given for the good of the Soviet people and to the dangerous activity of the enemy of the people Malenkov, Chairman of the Council of Ministers who signed the decree. But alongside the belief in the exceptional roles of good and bad leaders and calls upon Khrushchev to use his personal power and good will and set the decree right and punish Malenkov (for instance by sending him to the shop floor of a ball-bearings factory and not allowing him to take a sick leave), there are examples of legal discourse unveiling the contradictions between the January decree and the rights to free health care and to rest (according to the

---

[26] This was well explained by I. Efimov in *Bez Burzhuev,* Frankfurt/Main, Possev, 1979, pp. 21-25.

decree, time spent on sick leave reduced the regular leave entitlement). Both authors alluding to the Constitutions (of the USSR and the Russian Republic) recognise its primacy over any other legislation and call upon the CC to bring the sick leave and hospital service regulations in line with the constitution[27].

A sweeping assumption of the absence of legal culture and general passivity of the population under totalitarian and authoritarian regimes has overshadowed the history and special features of this out-of-court Soviet legal culture. Newly available CC papers give us a glimpse of letters from the public and, in some cases, allow us to trace the uses of these letters in the decision-making process. When the Ministry of Finance proposed in 1963 that the patients treated for injuries as a result of drinking and hooliganism be charged for medical services, the Ministry of Health rejected the proposal straight away, saying that the social security entitlements of such patients were already limited[28].

It is well-known to the specialists that the Soviet health services were compartmentalised into general and departmental sections, the latter including closed facilities for the elite managed by a special administration within the Ministry of Health. It is somewhat less well known that the criticism of health inequalities became a major issue in the public debate in the glasnost years, and that Yeltsin challenged the CC on the issue of their privileges while being the Head of the Moscow Party organisation. It is not known at all, however, how and when the knowledge of health care inequalities spread in the Soviet society and became a political issue. Again, the CC papers can shed light on this question. In August 1967 the CC and the Ministry of Health granted the request of the Film-Maker's Union to treat three of its distinguished members at the elite medical facilities. The request explicitly referred to the disparity between elite and general facilities and stated that the general health services could not provide adequate care for their heart conditions. In his letters, L. Kulidjanov, the First Secretary of the Union, listed the members' popular works as a justification for their special value to the nation and of the entitlement to special medical service[29]. Readers' letters quoted in the summary received from *Literaturnaya gazeta*[30] in 1974 show a widespread awareness of a deep crisis of the general health services that failed the sick and the healthy. One of the major concerns expressed in the letters is geographical inequality. Some authors demand that basic care be provided to everybody in the country as a basic right and that detailed information on health provisions for each geographic area be published.

---

[27] RSACH, *fond* 5, *opis* 30, *delo* 135, pp. 1-6.

[28] RSACH, *fond* 5, *opis* 55, *delo* 37, pp. 22-24.

[29] RSACH, *fond* 5, *opis*, 58, *delo* 41, p. 88.

[30] *Literaturnaya gazeta* (Literary Paper): weekly of the Writers' Union distinguished for its analytical commentary on a wide range of social, cultural and ethical issues in the 1970s.

The third kind of inequality increasingly evident to the population in the 1970s was the lagging behind the West. Two areas mentioned by the readers of *Literaturnaya gazeta* are transplantation surgery and the Soviet dependence on the import of medicines. The widespread perception of the crisis of the medical services is apparent from the discussions of the ways to raise extra funding for health services in the daily press and readers' letters revealing extra payments to state medical practitioners, and recourse to the services of private mainstream and alternative practitioners.

Responses to public concerns and criticisms

Soviet politicians were aware that the quality of the health services was a sensitive issue and strove to score political points on it. In 1967 the CC unsuccessfully tried to bring down the prices of medicines to mark 50 years of the Soviet State[31]. Letters from the public constituted a useful source of public opinion for the CC throughout the post-war period, but it was not until the middle of the 1970s that a large-scale campaign was justified in terms of a response to popular concerns expressed in letters. According to the report sent to the CC from *Izvestiya* national daily, in 1974 the paper received about 400 letters complaining about the health services every month. The reviews of letters received during the first six months of 1974 by *Izvesti* and *Selskaya zhizn'*[32] prompted a hearing on health services issues at the CC. Having investigated a number of complaints, the CC concluded that most of them were genuine and decreed that the Ministry of Health should prepare a plan of action for 1975 to ensure that health care institutions were better equipped, that the patients received quality services and that medical staff were better trained[33]. A special CC resolution on the development of medical industries was passed in September 1974. In the following year, the People's Control Committee checked seven thousand health care institutions across the country.

As part of a more open approach to public information at the Ministry of Health, B. Petrov, the Minister, gave a long interview to the *Literaturnaya gazeta* science correspondent in May 1974. The Ministry of Health began to commission a number of sociological surveys of patients' attitudes, satisfaction and opinions. Economists briefing the CC on the dynamics of income distribution, however, remained oblivious to the inequalities in access to non-cash benefits. They predicted a decline of income inequalities in the 1980s, ignoring differential access to education and health services. During this period of greater openness to the public, the Committee for State Security (KGB) expressed concern over sensitive health-related information being available

---

[31] RSACH, *fond* 5, *opis* 59, *delo* 50, pp. 181-194.

[32] *Selskaya zhizn'* (Rural Life): a daily paper with an emphasis on rural issues.

[33] RSACH, *fond* 5, *opis* 67, *delo* 180, p. 178.

to ideological enemies abroad[34]. Health statistics were indeed widely used in ideological warfare, but trying to disarm ideological opponents the Soviet state organs also severely limited the public debate within the country as few contributors to discussions over health care commanded relevant statistics.

Public voices featured informed discussions of mainstream medical technologies as well as homeopathy and other non-orthodox therapies, diets and systems of exercise. Some readers wrote to newspapers soliciting information on jogging, yoga and raw diet. There is an evident discrepancy between the dismissive treatment of these issues by the medical officials and the demands for and expectations of substantial arguments and detailed explanations on the part of some members of the public. Were these interests and expectations formed thanks to their education and experience of the health system or despite that? In order to answer this question researchers have to look beyond policy documents and into the education system more generally as well as into the informal communication channels and family support networks. The sociological study carried out in 1992 confirms the importance of informal relations for Russian patients: almost half of the Russian population sought informal advice from medical professionals[35].

Although archival documents cannot help us answer the question about the sources of popular knowledge and concerns, they are useful for formulating such questions. The juxtaposition of public concerns and official responses also prompts an hypothesis for the explanation of the low status of the sanitary enlightenment. This phenomenon, I propose, needs to be explored in terms of the gap between the themes of sanitary enlightenment and awareness, knowledge and interests of the public, and the gap between health propaganda, daily experience and expectations of the majority of the population. As the mediating position of some newspapers testifies, this gap was partly filled by the press which invited and occasionally aired public views and channelled them to the officials in Ministries and the Party.

(Self-)organisation of patients

We know that Russians heavily relied on family networks for their health-related needs, but is there evidence of more extensive networks and, perhaps, informal organisations of patients and the public, more generally, in the CPSU archives? There was a strong public support, mainly by patients and their relatives, of a number of medical developments, for

---

[34] RSACH, *fond* 5, *opis* 64, *delo* 125, pp. 1-3.

[35] J. Brown and N.L. Rusinova, "Lichnnye svyasi v sisteme zdravookhraneniya i 'kar'era bolezny'" (Informal Connections in Health Care System and "Sickness Career"), *Sotsiologicheskiye issledovaniya*, no. 3, 1993, pp. 30-36.

instance, the development of hyperbaric oxygen therapy in Moscow and orthopaedic surgery in Kurgan. Some of the public support for these procedures is reflected in numerous letters and reports deposited at the RSACH. It is, however, doubtful that policies were altered and public action was taken as a direct result of patients' self-organisation. It seems that medical practitioners and journalists rallied public opinion in support of medical innovation. Whether this is so or not will only become clear after further research into this subject based on a wide range of documents and interviews. It is apparent, however, that the former CPSU archives offer ample opportunity for the study of public involvement in the shaping of the Soviet health system. In this section, I have sketched out various ways in which these opportunities can be realised and raised specific questions regarding the strengths and weaknesses of sanitary enlightenment and the roles of the public in the formation and implementation of Soviet health policies.

4. Images of healthy childhood

An analysis of the means of health propaganda is just as important as the study of health policy for the understanding of the functioning of the system of public health in general and maternal and child health in particular. Posters on child health raise interesting questions regarding pictorial conventions and their interpretations, and about the relationship between health policies and health propaganda. The SARF poster collection dating back to the 1920s holds various posters published by the Soviet government. During the first two decades of the collection's existence archivists not only collected but also preserved posters by gluing them onto cardboard. Posters and slogans from the1940s and early 1950s are also numerous, but not as well preserved. The period from 1960 to 1991 is not as well represented in the collection as earlier decades. The most comprehensive part of the post-war collection is probably the collection of slogans. Covering various areas of public life, they can help locate health education and propaganda in public places. Health related posters range from safety messages to be displayed at work places to posters advertising annual mass sporting events.

Three catalogues comprehensively describe the poster collection up to the mid-1930s – a card subject catalogue with small photographic reproductions of each poster, an alphabetical catalogue of poster captions and inscriptions, and a geographical catalogue of publishers. Each poster has a number that is noted in the subject catalogue. Unfortunately, none of the catalogues can function as a finding aide, because after several relocations posters are not stored according to the original numeration. Although the majority of posters, including the most recent acquisitions of the 1980s, have a number stamped on it, posters are now loosely arranged by subject and period. Only portraits, almost exclusively pre-war, are easy to find – they are catalogued and stored separately in alphabetical order, by subject.

The importance of posters as a means of communication has not been uniform throughout Soviet history. Their importance surged in periods of national upheaval. During the first decade after the revolution, posters, leaflets and postcards were the most widespread means of education, propaganda and advertising in a largely illiterate country. Posters became very important again during the war years, in 1941-1945. Perestroika of the late 1980s generated a new demand for visual propaganda and stimulated many young artists. Most of the post-1945 period has, thus, been relatively homogenous for Soviet poster art, with an increase in professional criticism of declining standards in the late 1950s and a recovery in the 1960s[36]. From a connoisseur's point of view, the ferment of the last Soviet years more than compensates for the uniformity of the earlier Soviet period. An historical analysis, however, should pay attention to the whole period.

Post-war Soviet students of the visual arts singled out several types of posters according to their uses, such as propaganda, presentation of technical instructions and advertising. The first category was the largest and included posters depicting "communist construction", i.e. any positive aspect of Soviet life, posters relating popular scientific information and teaching aides. It is, therefore, not surprising that images of healthy children are mainly to be found on the posters of this category. Posters dealing with child care are the least numerous group featuring healthy children among the posters preserved in the SARF research library poster collection, and indeed in other collections (e.g. The Russian State Library, The British Library Slavonic Collection, Baykov Library Poster Collection, Birmingham). Children most frequently feature in political posters elaborating the theme of peace and war. Such are the 1955 poster by V. Ivanov with the caption "Children are the happiness of peace and land" featuring two parents with a baby against a rural landscape and the 1984 poster by L. Nepomnyashchy "Not for war do we raise our sons!" depicting a mother with two children in a schematic nature setting represented by the blue-green colours and the rainbow[37].

The second most numerous group of images of healthy children is to be found on the posters promoting sport and physical exercise. These posters often have the slogan "Mother, Father and Me – We are a Fit Family!" and depict a family threesome with some sports gear, either one child with two parents or the father with two children[38].

---

[36] I.A. Sviridova, *Sovetskii politicheskii plakat, nekotorye tendentsii razvitiya plakata na sovremennom etape*, Moscow, Iskusstvo, 1975, p. 88.

[37] V. Ivanov, "Deti - schast'e mira i zemli..." (Moscow: IZOGIZ, 1955), 300 000 copies, SARF Poster Collection; L. Nepomnyashchy, "Ne dlya voiny my rastim synovey!", Moscow, Plakat, 1984, 100 000 copies, Baykov Library, Birmingham. See also the book by V. Koretskii, *Tovarishch plakat. Opyt, razmyhsleniya*, Moscow, Plakat, 1978.

[38] V.M. Salauyev, "Tata, mama, ia - sportivnaya semya!", 1984, see M.I. Goncharov, *Belorusskyi politicheskyi plakat*, Minsk, Belarus', 1984, p. 137.

The unusually dynamic poster by S. Erokhin called "Family Trip to the Health Land" uses the standard three-figure composition to show a man and two children cycling with a backpack of sports equipment[39]. Posters depicting children mastering the school curriculum, reading and taking part in communist rituals complemented those promoting physical exercise. On the posters of the 1940s and 1950s, children were often accompanied by Communist Party leaders and were set against the portraits of Lenin and Stalin[40]. The prevalence of political over public health posters is probably caused by the bias of preservation. Given the political bias of poster collections, the child of the post-war Soviet poster comes across, first of all, as a symbol of peace, future, dependence and need of protection, rather than as a physical being in need of medical care. Secondly, the child is a body and spirit that needs to be exercised and strengthened by physical activity and learning, and finally, a body that needs to be cared for. But this hierarchy may be a misleading artefact of collecting and preservation.

As the post-war part of the SARF poster collection is fragmented, any conclusions based mainly on it should be considered tentative. Nevertheless, I would offer some observations concerning poster representations of child health, which can be tested and challenged by further research. Pre-war posters on child-care elicit three different attitudes towards child health. The first attitude can be called humanistic: health, especially child health, is presented in a number of early Soviet (1918-1923) posters as an absolute value and captured in metaphors like "children are flowers"[41]. "Children are the bloom of life: protect the children!" was the slogan of the first exhibit on the protection of motherhood and childhood held in Moscow in 1919. The second attitude to health can be called "rational". The "rational" attitude also made its appearance during the first Soviet decade but this motive persevered longer than the humanistic theme. Posters promulgating and justifying rational ways of child-care frequently used the traditional *lubok* style pictures with complex many-figure compositions and lengthy explanatory messages. For instance, one poster calls upon male farmers to spare their pregnant wives from hard work. The poster consisting of a series of smaller pictures with captions condemns a heavy workload for a pregnant woman in a peasant family by contrasting the man's special attitude to his mare with foal and his indifference to his pregnant wife[42]. The series of postcards by the Moscow Exhibit-Museum of

---

[39] S. Erokhin, "Vsey semioy v stranu zdorovia!", Moscow, Plakat, 1987, 120 000 copies, Baykov Library, Birmingham.

[40] I.M. Toidze, "Ozariayet stalinskaya laska budushchee nashey detvory", 1947, web site of the Lotman Institut fuer Russische und Sowjetische Kultur, access via: http://www.russianhistory.com

[41] See SARF Poster Collection, no. 957, Moscow, 1919, see also no. 682, Moscow, 1923.

[42] "Oberegaite zhenshchinu-mat..." (Leningrad: Otdel okhrany materinstva i mladenchestva NKZ, no date), SARF Poster Collection, no. 3920.

the Protection of Motherhood and Childhood published around 1924 is also executed in the *lubok* style. Issued in an edition of 50,000 copies, the cards illustrated simple and specific instructions such as "Do not forget to give the baby boiled unsweetened water in hot weather!" and "Wash your hands before touching the baby!"[43]. The tradition of postcards dedicated to health topics was established by the Society of the Cross of St. Eugenia which published more than 6,500 postcards between 1896 and 1917[44]. This work was taken over by the Red Cross and People's Commissariat of Health who popularised good child-care practices through postcards and monumental posters depicting child-care objects and procedures[45].

The third attitude to health elicited by posters is instrumental. A number of posters from about 1930 onwards present health as a means of production. These posters present physical exercise or day care centres as a means of socialist construction: exercise produces fit workers, and day care provisions allow mothers to join labour force[46]. The caption of the 1931 poster by the artist A. Borovskaya reads: "Organising day care, play grounds, industrial kitchens, canteens and mechanised laundrettes we shall create 1,000,000 new female workers!". A 1921 poster by an unknown artist praises some of the same institutions for a different reason: "Day care centres, kindergartens and public canteens will liberate the woman!". "Between 1921 and 1931 the emphasis of the slogan and the declared rationale of child care provisions shifted from the care of street and sick children and women's liberation to women's involvement in the labour force. The instrumental attitude to health dominated the posters of the two post-war decades.

Female involvement in the public sector was accelerated by the war. During and after the war, when women's work became more widespread than it was in the 1930s, improvement of child-care provisions became a means of solving another national problem, namely increasing birth rates in a number of Soviet republics, including Russia.

---

[43] The British Library Collection of Postcards, CUP410.a.25, pp. 15-18.

[44] E.D. Gribanov, *Istochniki izucheniya istorii meditsiny i zdravookhrananiya*, Moscow, TsOLIUV, 1980, pp. 11-12.

[45] E.g. "Swaddling obstructs growth", "Weighing on spring balance", Soviet Posters, 1918-1921, no. 45 and no. 46, print run 1000 copies, The British Library.

[46] "Za sotsialisticheskuyu kuznitsu zdorovia, za proletarskii park kultury i otdykha!" ("For the socialist factory of health, for the proletariat's leisure park!"), Moscow 1932, SARF Poster Collection, no. 6931; "Ukrepliaya okhranu materinstva i detstva, my pomogayem rabotnitse byt' aktivnoy stroitel'nitsey sotsialisma" ("Fortifying the protection of motherhood and childhood, we help the female worker to take an active part in socialist construction"), Moscow, Politizdat, 1930, SARF Poster Collection, no. 5448; and "Okhrana materinstva i mladenchestva uskorit vypolneniye piatiletki" ("The protection of motherhood and infancy will speed up the completion of the five-year plan"), Moscow, Politizdat, 1930, SARF Poster Collection, no. 5449.

Figure 1: *Stylised image of the Soviet family, c. 1960. Source: Health in the USSR, Soviet publication distributed abroad, c. 1960, no date.*

This was the thrust of the legislation in this sphere during the 1940s and 1950s. The Ministry of Health decided to popularise pronatalist policies and condemn abortions. 1950s posters promoting parenthood and health, like the earlier ones, appealed to the values of life and happiness. Child health is again constructed as the utmost good. In a 1960 poster encouraging blood donation, the person saved by donors' blood is a child[47]. There are, however, significant differences from earlier "humanistic" posters. Beginning in the 1940s images and slogans were increasingly standardised. Close-ups of a happy man (or couple) holding a chubby baby in his (their) strong hands and other cheerful and sporty family groups of three made their appearance among the images of the Soviet family in the 1950s to persist into the 1980s (Fig. 1)[48]. Such posters, unlike earlier ones, claimed to depict the socialist reality, rather than to embody ideals or educate. After the almost universal employment of women was achieved, the shortage of day care stopped being an obstacle to the increase in the labour force which had to be dealt with by the central government, and became a private problem of many Soviet families. Accordingly, day care facilities stopped being a theme for visual propaganda. Since the late 1950s, a rift began to widen between the experience of child care and child health of most people on the one hand, and the images of the posters which purported to depict reality, on the other[49]. While before the war one could find posters not only in public places but also in many homes, after the war posters became less common in living spaces. During the last Soviet decades the intended audience (including some archivists?) was increasingly indifferent to propaganda and advice delivered through official channels.

[47] M. Ananyev, V. Feldman, "Spasibo donoru za spasennuyu zhizn rebenka!" ("We thank the donor for saving the child's life!"), SARF Poster Collection, no number, Moscow, Red Cross Institute, 1960, 100 000 copies.

[48] E.g. V. Ivanov, "Deti - schast'e mira I zemli" ("Children are the happiness of peace and land"), Moscow, Izogiz, 1955, SARF Poster Collection, no. 10661.

[49] The prevalence of rosy clichés was characteristic of all types of posters in the 1950s, see I.A. Sviridova, *Sovetskii politicheskii plakat, nekotorye tendentsii razvitiya na sovremennom etape*, Moscow, Iskusstvo, 1975, p. 88.

The other-worldliness of Soviet posters may explain both their disrepute at home and their popularity abroad[50]. The standard image of the happy Soviet family traditionally featured in the Soviet publications on health and welfare distributed abroad. Three-figure composition and lack of detail makes the images in Figure 1 very similar to the cliché adopted in Soviet posters. In medical publications of the 1960s, such as "Health in the USSR" and "The Soviet Health Service"[51], schematic generalised images were complemented by photographs of medical facilities, hospital-born babies and chubby children (Fig. 2).

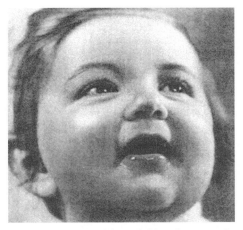

Figure 2: *A healthy child, photograph, c. 1960.*
Source: *Health in the USSR, Soviet publication distributed abroad, c. 1960, no date.*

Changes in visual health propaganda have a complex dynamic of their own, but they do reflect changes in health policy. For instance, the widespread depiction of children and babies in the company of medical professionals after the Second World War corresponds to the shift of child health policy focus from mother to child and its increasing medicalisation (Fig. 3). Graphic images of child suffering found their way onto the posters only during perestroika after the foundation of the Soviet Children's Fund, the child welfare charity. The analysis of health posters also supports broader conclusions regarding the crises of trust and signification in Soviet culture. Perestroika was an attempt to resolve this crisis by a direct appeal of the communist leadership to the people bypassing an inert bureaucracy. This drive, among other things, resulted in the publication of a number of new posters by young artists. The posters of 1988-1991 brought new themes into health propaganda and offered new perspectives on some traditional issues. In posters on alcoholism, the child had traditionally been depicted as a silent victim. Artists of the 1980s gave voice to the child suffering from parents' alcoholism and divorce. The artist I. Tarasov undermined the child-centred image of the happy family by juxtaposing the standard mother and child group with the mother's application to give up the child for adoption in the poster "I

---

[50] Cf. the Soviet military uniform, which became a fashionable youth accessory abroad, was detested by many civilian youths in the country (at least until some realised that they could make money by selling it to tourists).

[51] *The Soviet Health Service*, Moscow, Novosti Press Agency, February 1965.

give away my child"[52]. V. Kundyshev reminded the public of the absence of the family for many abandoned children and invalids, and indicated the scale of the problem by including national statistics in his composition[53]. But even during the period of glasnost, peacetime child suffering was considered extremely disturbing and the public was sometimes spared the distressing images of child disability. In one of the editions of the award-winning triptych "Compassion!" physical disability was made less prominent[54].

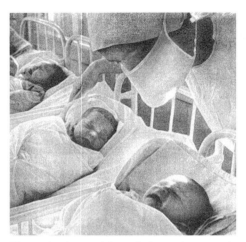

Figure 3: *Hospital-born babies, photograph, c. 1960.*
Source: Health in the USSR, Soviet publication distributed abroad, c. 1960, no date.

What is the place of images of healthy children in the Soviet public health project? Visual images seem to be completely absent from the documentation preserved by the Ministry of Health and the overseeing department of the Communist Party. Health targets were set verbally and numerically and handed down in this form to concerned officials. One of the instruments of health policy was the so-called sanitary enlightenment (*sanitarnoye prosveshcheniye*), or the dissemination of health-related information among the population. It is the work of sanitary enlightenment that was mediated by visual images. Such images, particularly on leaflets and posters, were used in specific problem areas, e.g. in locations affected by epidemics, or displayed in medical institutions and public places, such as day care centres or milk kitchens[55].

What images of child health do Soviet posters project? It is striking that all the healthy children in the posters are part of family groups. In earlier posters (until the 1950s), they

---

[52] I.A. Tarasov, "Ia otkazyvayus ot svoyego rebenka" ("I give away my child"), Moscow, Plakat, 1988, 80 000 copies, Soviet Era Posters, The British Library, no. 2032; see also the poster of the Children's Fund by the same artist, "Nash schet 707" (Account no. 707) at the web site of the Lotman Institut fuer Russische und Sowjetische Kultur accessible via http://www.russianhistory.org

[53] V. Kundyshev, "Khochu mamu" ("I want mama"), Moscow, Plakat, 1988, Soviet Era Posters, The British Library, no. 2033.

[54] "Uchastiya!" ("Compassion!"), Kharkiv, Sotsialistichna Kharkivshchina, 1988, 17 000 copies, Soviet Era Posters, British Library.

[55] Milk kitchens (*molochnye kukhni*) prepared milk mixtures for bottle feeding and provided milk products, such as sterilised milk and kefir, for families of older children.

are invariably portrayed with the mother. In the later decades, family images of two parents and one or two children become more common. The fathers are more frequently portrayed in outdoor situations and activities. After the criticism of the inappropriate painting style in the poster art of the 1950s, poster images became highly schematic. These two features, representation of children as part of family groups and lack of detail, contrast with the images in Russian advertising in the 1990s. Recent advertisements usually use photographic images. Child-consumers of goods and medical services are often portrayed without older relatives in the company of peers or medical professionals.

Photographic images became very common in posters already during the 1980s as a means to overcome the abstract clichés (which incidentally in Russian were called "poster images"). In the documentary genre of Soviet photographic illustration healthy children were most frequently portrayed in institutions and in the company of various professionals – from nursery teachers to surgeons. In the 1980s family situations also began to appear on posters and illustrations. Advertisements, as heirs of the perestroika posters, use photographic images which sometimes shock. Advertisements offering images of capitalist construction and dreams also have an affinity to earlier Soviet political posters. The complex process of poster production, however, mediates the relationship between various traditions of representation. Without an investigation of this process our understanding of the role of images in health policy would be incomplete and possibly even distorted[56].

5. The Internet: information resource or historical source?

The World Wide Web (WWW), or the Internet, is a relatively new source of information for historians. It is all the more important, then, that we try to master it and reflect on its relevance to history writing. This section provides a brief overview of health and medicine related sites on the Russian web and offers some considerations on their possible uses by historians. The main aim of this section, however, is to raise the issue of electronic sources for medical history and initiate further discussion.

There are various ways of navigating the Russian medical Internet. General search engines, such as *Aport, Rambler and Yandex* allow for simple and advanced searches and can be used for retrieving specific information. For more general searches, I would recommend classified lists such as *@Rus*, formerly *Au!*, (www.au.ru, over 900 medical

---

[56] Victoria E. Bonnell in *Iconography of Power: Soviet Political Posters under Lenin and Stalin,* Berkley, University of California Press, 1997, notes the relative paucity of sources on poster production after World War II.

sites and two annotated thematic guides), *List* (www.list.ru, over 900 medical sites) and *1000 Stars* (www.stars.ru, over 600 medical sites)[57]. Who are the main players of the Russian medical web? The largest and most frequently visited site is Russian Medical Server, supported by the Open Society Institute. Some government institutions, such as the Ministry of Health and the Russian Republican Hospital for Children also have their sites; the latter was set up with the technical support of the Russian Academy of Sciences Institute for Space Research. Advertisements of services and products dominate the medical web, but there is a fair amount of information for professionals and lay public, which is not directly related to sales. Notably, there are medical sections in all major Internet libraries. By 1999 the Russian Internet had become more reflexive, and a number of analyses of its development and prospects have appeared on- and off-line. WWW has become an increasingly important and respectable information medium. While a few years ago most sites were set up by amateurs, today most information resources are provided by professional corporations[58]. The distribution of information sources mirrors the domination of urban centres and multinational pharmaceutical companies in the off-line world. There are some strong alternative provincial information providers, but non-profit organisations are yet to consolidate their presence on the web[59].

In the area of child health, there are more sites dedicated to illness than to health. With the exception of dentistry-related sites, which usually feature happy clients, they are illustrated by various images of children in sickness and distress. "Family advisor", one of Rambler's top 20 medical sites, has an image of a sick child opening each page dedicated to an illness. These images maintain design consistency, and play varying roles in identifying conditions. While the close-up image of a girl in bed staring at the reader with her deep blue eyes does little to help the parents identify sleeplessness in their child[60], the picture of a boy with a bright pink rash on his cheeks may be helpful in identifying food allergy in a child. The overwhelming impression conveyed by this and other medical sites is that child health should not be taken for granted. The dominant style of presenting information on the web is medical. Illustrations are photographs and line drawings. The political dimension of child health is absent from advice and sales literature. Only policy documents and works of social criticism

---

[57] These data are for August 1999.

[58] Aleksandr Sherman, "Beskonechnaya gazeta: ot sredtsv massovoy informatsii k massovoy informatsionnoy srede" ("Endless Newspaper: From Mass Media to Mass Information Medium"), *Nezavisimaya gazeta*, 31 August 1999, p. 15.

[59] Evsey Weiner, "Nemeditsinskiye zametki po povodu epidemii v Oblivskoy" ("Non-Medical Notes on the Oblivskaya Epidemic"), *Russkii zhurnal*, 27 July 1999, http://russ.ru/netcult/99-07-23/vainer.htm

[60] http://home.ricor.ru/1_1/child/bess.htm

explicitly refer to child health as a morally and politically laden indicator. Romantisation of the child in the political context, which was characteristic of Soviet posters, seems to be outdated. The romantic child has not, however, altogether disappeared from the public gaze; its heir is the consuming child of the 1990s featuring in various advertisements of child-care goods on- and off-line.

For the purposes of the present analysis I would like to isolate three distinct ways in which historians can use the Internet: as a source of information, as a secondary source and as a primary source. First of all, we can use the Internet as a source of information, such as archive and library catalogues, opening hours and contact addresses. The national Library Net programme to render library catalogues accessible on-line was launched in 1997, and the State Medical Library of Russia (Moscow) expects to have its system operational by the autumn of 1999. At the moment, its on-line resources are limited to on-line versions of some printed catalogues[61] and general information and contact addresses of other medical libraries[62]. The Federal Archives Administration has undertaken a number of projects to render some guides and catalogues accessible via the Internet and CD-ROM[63]. Many medical sites listed in the above mentioned classified directories provide descriptions and contact details of a range of medical research and clinical institutions, individual doctors and various non-governmental organisations. There is a geographical bias towards Moscow, St. Petersburg, Kiev, Minsk, Russian regional centres, and towards famous provincial medical institutions, such as the Kurgan centre for orthopaedic surgery headed by Dr. Ilizarov. One can, nevertheless, search for specific institutions and groups of institutions and specialists dealing with specific subjects.

Second, we can use the Internet as a secondary source and teaching aide. The Internet offers much scope for the publication of conference papers, work in progress and student projects. Given the length of the publication process in most humanities journals and the wide academic audience, the Internet can well complement existing paper publications. The main impediment to the growth of web publications, as Jon Agar has suggested, is the weakness of peer review in this medium[64]. The ways in which medical historians use web-based information and Internet publications are not different from the ways in which other specialists may use them. It is, therefore, the third use of the Internet, namely as a primary source, which is relatively more interesting to us here.

---

[61] http://www.scsml.rssi.ru/menu.html

[62] http://www.scsml.rssi.ru/reprus.html

[63] This information is available through Chadwyck-Healey http://www.chadwyck.co.uk, Media Lingua http://www.archives.ru and Abamedia http://www.abamedia.com

[64] Jon Agar, "History of Science on the World Wide Web", in *British Journal for the History of Science*, vol. 29, 1996, pp. 223-227.

Can WWW documents be used as primary sources? Discussions of the uses of other types of sources, for instance, oral history[65], suggest that a more productive form of this question is "how can WWW documents be used as primary sources?". Researchers need to take into consideration specific features of this group of sources such as the time scale, compatibility with other sources, reliability, etc. WWW resources have a relatively short time scale and are present-oriented. The Russian Internet took off in 1996 and few sites date further back than that. The sites are frequently revised and only the latest version is accessible at any given time. Consequently, unless the site has a mailing list or one copies site contents over a period, one would not know how the site changes. Repeated surveys can be carried out by someone engaged in a project set in the present day and focussing on clearly identifiable web sites, such as the studies of medical institutions or patients' organisations. One can also use the data on the use of electronic medical libraries in conjunction with interviews and other sources in studies of popular medical practices. The use of electronic resources will be more problematic in studies going further back in time. Such studies would need to integrate electronic evidence for part of the studied period with other sources. One just cannot afford to ignore the Internet in the studies of the dynamics of medical education and popular medical practices. In these studies, the question of the uses of web sources by doctors, students and the public would be critical.

Questions of the relationship between authors and users, however, are not unique to the Internet, and many historians have resources for dealing with them. If one were to take use seriously, one cannot assume continuity in the use of any kind of source. For instance, books have not been used in the same way over the ages. The technologies of production and consumption of books have changed dramatically. The cultural value attached to the book has varied over time and differed from one place to another[66]. The problem of the Internet may seem more radical because it is a relatively new and comprehensive medium. This impression, however, may be superficial in relation to concrete research questions. Historical analogies can be drawn between the advent of the Internet and of the mass popular press. Historians have analysed the relationship between mass press and advertising, readers' letters and advice books[67]. The relationship between Internet

---

[65] Soraya de Chadarevian, "Using Interviews to Write the History of Science", in Thomas Söderqvist (ed.), *The Historiography of Contemporary Science and Technology*, Amsterdam, Harwood Academic Publishers, 1997, pp. 51-70.

[66] See for instance Robert Darnton, "Readers Respond to Rousseau: the Fabrication of the Romantic Sensitivity", in his *The Great Cat Massacre and Other Episodes in French Cultural History*, Harmondsworth, Penguin, 1985, pp. 209-249.

[67] James Curran and Jean Seaton, *Power Without Responsibility: The Press and Broadcasting in Britain*, London, Routledge, 1991.

resources and commercial sponsorship can be studied just as the connections of new advice books to the food industries in the beginning of the century. The Internet has given manufacturers new means of advertising medicines to doctors and consumers.

The new possibilities of electronic communication will enhance historians' resources for dealing with the electronic challenge. One of the advantages of web sources over traditional paper archives is that many people can have immediate access to the same source, but this accessibility, of course, raises new anxieties regarding the authenticity of sources. The Internet has a potential for on-line discussions and feedback, but how would one ascertain where this feedback was coming from? Thus, as every type of source, the Internet provides new opportunities and raises old and new questions. It is clear, however, that the Russian Internet with considerable medical resources and about 2 million users is a relevant source for medical history; moreover, the Internet cannot be ignored in a range of studies. Furthermore, historians can use their expertise in dealing with this new phenomenon.

6. How have primary sources been used?

As medical historians have hardly used the Internet, the question of the uses of primary sources is limited to more traditional paper sources. There are two ways of answering this question: first, through a review of literature, second, through the analysis of "use of document" records. I will start with the second way, and then relate the registered use of archival resources to broader issues of the historiography of Russian public health.

The former Communist Party archives carefully register each reader. Each file has a "use of document" form, and the staff make sure these forms are filled in diligently. On the basis of these forms one can trace the usage of particular files by readers. According to these forms, very few researchers have used materials relating to health care. One journalist from *Literaturnaya gazeta*, one medical doctor and one researcher from the Serbskii Psychiatric Institute studied most health-related files before declassification, during the early 1990s. They have been mostly interested in decisions pertaining to medical research and development, and the history of psychiatry. At the SARF, the use of documents is not systematically recorded. From the "use of document" forms, which were provided and used by readers, I conclude that the most popular issue in the area of maternal and child health was abortion. Both Russian and foreign readers used these data. Russian readers can be traced to the Research Institute for Obstetrics and Gynaecology. No historical academic publications using these data or the information from the former Party archives, however, have been located yet. Most likely, they appeared in newspapers, dissertations, specialised medical journals or institutes' internal publications. *Literaturnaya gazeta* has a tradition of investigating health care going back to the 1970s. Its publications may have been a more important source of health-related information for the educated public than the works of "sanitary enlightenment". An analysis of its publications would be indispensable to the study of popular health-care practices.

The number of registered users and uses is small for making conclusions. However, the very fact that it is so small tells us that national archives have not been extensively used for medical history. The present survey, however, demonstrates that Russian national archives offer rich resources for the study of the organisation of public health in general and its specific aspects, such as maternal and child health or the participation of the public in the health system. The fact that most Russian users of archives belonged to medical research institutes is corroborated by the organisational structure of the history of medicine in Russia: research is carried out and the subject is taught at medical schools, and history of medicine is a medical degree. History of medicine textbooks cover histories from antiquity to the present day[68]. Articles appear in medical journals and are usually dedicated to important anniversaries. A major institution in this area, the Semashko Institute for Social Hygiene and Organisation of Health Care, and other agencies periodically publish the lists of memorable dates in the history of medicine[69]. If the history of medicine is dominated by work celebrating important dates in the lives of important men, the history of public health suffers from the absence of personalities[70]. Whereas the history of doctors, especially medical researchers, is written with recourse to their personal papers and conceived as a process in which knowledge and practices can be negotiated, the history of public health is written with reference to official publications and statistics, and is conceived as a sequence of static structures, in which medical knowledge is taken for granted.

In the recent history of health care there are few individual actors. Subjects are mostly collective, monolithic and anonymous. This is true of most Russian- and English-language publications. At least two of the causes of this situation – limited use of archives and ideological attitudes – can be overcome today. D.V. Gorfin in his 1963 review of histories of Soviet public health noted that they best related decisions of the Communist Party and government decrees, while difficulties and different schools of

---

[68] Tatiana Sorokina, *Istoriya meditsiny*, 2nd ed., Moscow, Paims, 1994; P.E. Zabludovskii et al, *Istoriya meditsiny*, Moscow, Meditsina, 1981.

[69] A. Alieva, *Znamenatelnye daty istorii meditsiny na 1958 god*, Moscow, Medgiz, 1958; *Znamenatelnye i yubileinye daty istorii meditsiny i zdravookhraneniya*, NPO Tatarmedinform, 1994.

[70] Medical professionals also contribute to this view of public health and sanitary enlightenment, e.g. E. Chazov *et al.*, (eds.) *70 let sovetskogo zdravookhraneniya 1917-1987*, Moscow, Meditsina, 1987.

public health were not analysed[71]. Unfortunately, the latest Russian textbooks in the history of medicine also emphasise uniformity and continuities of the Soviet health care system and do not pay any attention to changes and debates within it. Thus, Tatiana Sorokina writes that the Soviet system, particularly its structure and strategy was formed during 1918[72]. Debates over specialisation of public health institutions, their role in prevention (*dispanserisatsiya*[73]) and insurance medicine, the outcomes of which determined concrete forms in which the principles of Soviet health care were implemented, are not considered[74]. English-language authors of the 1960s and 1970s highlighted some of the difficulties of Soviet public health and criticised the system from the left and from the right[75]. This literature, nevertheless, also did not address the existence of different schools and debates in Soviet public health. Only in the 1980s did Michael Ryan, a political scientist who followed closely the development of Soviet health care, introduce individual actors into the post-war Soviet health care system: they were Ministers of Health and some doctors, whose behaviour he analysed in relation to the dynamics of the medical profession. Ryan made good use of reports, interviews and analytical essays published during the first years of openness (1985-1989). Today historians can move on and use archives and overcome simplified images of Soviet and Russian public health. International comparative work is particularly important in this project, because it prompts new questions and helps overcome the effects of everyday familiarity with one's own contemporary history. Archival materials can go some way in revealing past controversies and mechanisms of decision-making. The period until 1969 is best served by archival resources, but the former Communist Party archives provide some unique documents up to 1984. They should be a starting point for an historian embarking on interviews, which, of course, can provide a more nuanced picture of events. Archives are best used in conjunction with a whole range of sources available to historians, including the Internet. They can serve as a point of reference for evaluating

---

[71] D.V. Gorfin, "Istoriographiya razvitiya sanitarnogo dela, kommunalnoy gigiyeny i gigiyeny truda", in M.I. Barsukov, ed., *Ocherki istoriogrphii rossiiskogo zdravookhraneniya*, Moskva, Meditsina, 1963.

[72] Tatiana Sorokina, *Istoriya meditsiny*, 2nd ed., Moscow, Paims, 1994, pp. 326-340.

[73] Soviet medical institution aimed at early identification of diseases, treatment and supervision of patients.

[74] Even the studies drawing on local archival materials focus on the continuity of Soviet health care and treat innovations as unproblematic. See M.I. Yarovinskii, *Zdravookhraneniye Moskvy 1581-2000*, Moscow, Meditsina, 1988.

[75] E.g. Vincente Navarro, *Social Security and Medicine in the USSR: a Marxist Critique*, Lexington, Mass., D.C. Heath and Co., 1977; and Mark G. Field, *Soviet Socialized Medicine*, New York, 1967.

public versions of past events accessible through newspaper articles and interviews and for checking dates and sequences of events, for which one cannot rely on oral history.

Acknowledgements

I am grateful to the staff of the State Archive of the Russian Federation, Slavonic Department of the British Library and Baykov Library for advice on their poster collections. I also thank Ilana Löwy for editorial advice, Mick Carpenter for help with illustrations and Vladislav Sokolov for consultations on the Russian Internet.

Tuberculosis in Poland, 1945-1995: Images of a Disease
Barbara Markiewicz

1. Introduction

An "image of disease" is a relatively well-understood concept in medicine. It is a defined as a set of clinically recognisable symptoms, which makes possible the diagnosis of a given disease and the determination of its stage. The image of a given disease is subject to geographic and historical changes: thus a disease called "syphilis" may have distinct definitions in different places and periods. The "image of disease" is often viewed as a problem internal to the medical profession. This paper does not deal, however, with the "images of disease" constructed by the medical profession. Its goal is the identification and the description of historical phenomena which belong in the main to the realm of politics, but also to that of society and culture. I share Revel's and Peter's opinion that "a disease may be (…) a privileged point of view from which one can see more clearly the real meaning of administrative mechanisms or religious practices, relations between centres of power or the society's self-image"[1]. From a methodological point of view, a chronic disease which has important social consequences, such as tuberculosis, offers an especially privileged view-point on political and socio-cultural phenomena. I treat therefore the clinical image of tuberculosis as a premise or an assumption, while the principal object of my study are the projections, the reflections, and the transformations of this image in the social consciousness, as well as in propaganda, in administrative structures, or in political action.

In the years 1945-1995 images of tuberculosis in Poland were determined by a rhetoric shaped around the central theme of "struggle". When the perceived threat of an epidemic decreased, this struggle gradually assumed a less violent form. However this way of thinking about tuberculosis continued to play a central role in the organisation of treatment and of prevention of this pathology. On the social level, this continuous sense of threat generated the "tuberculosis myth", while on the academic and administrative levels, it facilitated mystification, and justified solutions that violated the patients' personal freedom and subjectivity.

---

[1] Jacques Revel and Jean Pierre Peter, "Le Corps, l'homme malade et son histoire", in Jacques Le Goff (ed.), *Faire l'histoire*, Paris, Seuil, 1974.

During the fifty years covered by this paper, the picture of tuberculosis developed dynamically, mainly due to discoveries in the area of pharmacology (new drugs, first of all antibiotics), and medical technology. This process can be described as a shift from an image of tuberculosis as a threatening epidemic and a social disease, to one of an individual illness and a contingent event[2]. As tuberculosis – and especially pulmonary tuberculosis – started to be perceived as one among many infectious diseases, its image became increasingly blurred, losing its threatening aspect and its distinct outline, and thus its unique status, and its distinct identity in the lay social consciousness and among the experts. The aim of my paper is to take these very general reflections on changes in the image of tuberculosis as a starting point of a study focused on some of the more specific features of the genesis and the transformations of images of tuberculosis in Poland.

2. Tuberculosis in Poland 1945-1955: from cultural myth to political mystification

Tuberculosis as a political disease

The specific image of tuberculosis in Poland in the years 1945-1955 was, I propose, determined by two factors. Firstly, the very high prevalence of this pathology. Before World War II, Poland had one of highest incidence and mortality rates of tuberculosis in Europe. Moreover, the incidence of this disease greatly increased during the war. Before 1939, approximately 0,5% of the total population suffered from tuberculosis, and in 1945, just after the war approximately 5% of the population was diagnosed as having this disease[3]. Secondly, after World War II, when Poland became one of the satellite countries of the USSR, the new government attributed a high priority to the struggle against "social diseases" Tuberculosis was recognised after 1945 as the most important among these diseases. Affecting a large part of the population, it became a

---

[2] This history is most concisely illustrated by the changes in the title of the journal published since 1909, and devoted to the problem of fighting tuberculosis. It was originally entitled *Gruzlica* ("Tuberculosis"). In 1962 its title was changed to *Gruzlica i choroby pluc* ("Tuberculosis and Lung Diseases"), and in 1991 to *Polska Pneumologia i Alergologia* ("Polish Pneumology and Allergology"). According to the journal's editorial board, "the change of title was imposed by life itself and by the changing epidemiology of respiratory system diseases, i.e., decreased incidence of tuberculosis and increased incidence of neoplasms as well as of chronic pulmonary and bronchial diseases", 1991, vol. 59, no 1-2.

[3] Data concerning 1945 were established in specific conditions only by physicians, without statistical approaches. They were revised several times later. Officially it was stated that in 1945 the number of deaths caused by tuberculosis was higher than 20 per 10,000 inhabitants (in 1939 it was approximately 18, in 1946 -15.7, in 1947 - 14.1, in 1948 -12.7 and in 1949 -12.1).

problem both for the sick and for their surroundings, and it affected people's attitudes and actions. From the state's point of view, negative popular attitudes towards the new power were related, among other things, to a high prevalence of tuberculosis. Such analysis influenced in turn priorities in the assignment of public funds and shaped administrative and propaganda actions. On the other hand, the specific form of anti-tuberculosis activity was also shaped by the general structure of the political system of "really existing socialism".

Both factors, the high prevalence of the disease in Poland in the post-war era, and its perception as a political issue, played a central role in shaping the two categories used in this study to classify the materials from the years 1945-1955: myth and mystification. The linguistic proximity of the words "myth" and "mystification" may suggest some connection between these two phenomena. My intention is, however, to contrast them, and to indicate that they have distinct origins and different histories. The myth of tuberculosis was formed in the 19th century, well before the advent of "scientific medicine" and of the development of sophisticated medical technologies. Its main elements were developed in a period in which tuberculosis was a very frequent and usually incurable disease. The structure and the meaning of specific elements of the tuberculosis myth was modified by new developments in medicine. However, the most essential features of the myth survived in a fundamentally unchanged form. The "tuberculosis myth" was international, but it was updated in Poland after World War II, due to the intensification of the epidemic of this disease. On the other hand, the mystification of tuberculosis in Poland in the 1950s was a local, specific and partly contingent event.

The origins of the mythical image of tuberculosis in Poland

My reflections on the "myth of tuberculosis" are grounded in Ernst Cassirer's theory of symbolic forms. This theory provides us with a framework for the understanding of a myth and with methods for its critical study. One should bear in mind, however, that this study transposes Cassirer's ideas to a very different historical and social context [4].

---

[4] On the social and cultural history of tuberculosis in Western countries, see e.g., René and Jean Dubos, *The White Plague, Tuberculosis, Man and Society*, New Brunswick, Rutgers University Press, 1987; Linda Bryder, *Below the Magic Mountain: A Social History of Tuberculosis in Twentieth Century Britain*, Oxford, Clarendon Press, 1988; Barbara Bates, *Bargaining for Life: A Social History of Tuberculosis, 1876-1938*, Philadelphia, University of Pennsylvania Press, 1992; Barabara Rosenkrantz (ed.) *From Consumption to Tuberculosis*, New York, Garland, 1994; Sheila M. Rothma, *Living in the Shadow of Death: Tuberculosis and the Social Experience of Illness in American History*, Baltimore, Johns Hopkins University Press, 1995; Katheryn Ott, *Fevered Lives: Tuberculosis in American Culture Since the 1870s*, Cambridge, Mass., Harvard University Press, 1997.

A disease acquires its mythical form when certain concepts and images consistently ascribed to it become fixed in the general consciousness. Not all diseases acquire a mythic dimension. Such a fate awaits mainly diseases which affect a large part of the population at the same time (pestilence), or, alternatively, pathologies that always accompany mankind. Tuberculosis satisfies both these conditions. Initially recognised as a calamity that could not be overcome by medicine, it was also recognised as a widespread health problem. These particular features of tuberculosis contributed to the generation of a "myth of tuberculosis". Grounded in analogies, such a myth usually has its roots in specialised medical knowledge which is, however, deeply modified through a contact with lay concepts and images. The "myth of tuberculosis" maintained its dynamic nature, and although occasionally it came close to becoming a stereotype, it underwent numerous modifications.

Mythologisation of a disease fulfils similar functions as the mythologisation of the powers of nature. It allows for the domestication of dangerous and unavoidable phenomena and their integration into the existential sphere. However, the most significant meaning of a myth of a disease is its social dimension. The formation of a mythical picture of a given pathology facilitates the communication between patients and physicians, and between patients and persons in their immediate surroundings. Without a shared set of concepts and images which operate on various levels of social life, mobilisation against the threat of disease would be very difficult. For a myth is not only able to transmit certain amount of knowledge, but also, or rather above all, to provoke distinct emotions.

It is difficult to present the structure of the myth of tuberculosis in a short and systematic way. As Cassirer puts it, the character of a myth is a-theoretical. However, I would like to indicate its most important "conceptual" and "visual" (perceptional) elements. Both refer to the sources of the disease, its modes of transmission, its symptoms, its course, and its treatment. A clear-cut difference exists, moreover, between the ways this disease is perceived on the individual level (the image of a patient with tuberculosis) and on a global level (the image and the understanding of the disease itself). The nature of the former resembles that of an archetype, and it originates in a long-forgotten past. It can be directly connected with the Greek name of the disease, phthisein (consumption) which refers to the external symptoms of the illness. Tuberculosis was first identified on the basis of a visible "emaciation" and "wasting away" of the organism, easy to discern without specialised medical knowledge. According to the Hippocratic theory of humours the cause of consumption was a disturbed balance of four "humours", induced by "exsiccation" of phlegm. This image was partly modified through the popularisation of the new medical name of this disease, tuberculosis. This name refers to a pathological finding: the "tubercles" found during the autopsy in the lungs of the deceased. The histopathological identification of tuberculosis could not, however, be directly visualised by the patients, who had the tendency to continue to view tuberculosis mainly in terms of wasting away.

The gap between the popular image of tuberculosis and its medical picture widened with the discovery that the etiologic cause of tuberculosis is a bacterium, invisible to the naked eye, and the parallel application of X-rays (thus the art of visualising the invisible interior of the body) to the diagnosis of this illness.

Physicians occasionally oscillated between lay and expert image of tuberculosis. In "Physicians' Diaries" published in Poland in 1939, a physician from Staroleka, in the region of Poznan, Dr. Sabina Skopinska, explained that "the disease appears to me like one of the monsters that I saw on the roof of Notre Dame Cathedral in Paris. With its gloomy disposition, protruding lips, and droopy canine ears, this monster looks persistently at the world, and whoever gets into the circle of his magical sight, dies. The shocking pictures of the slow agony and the death of young consumptives whom I helplessly observed as a physician, forces me to search in my imagination pictures of these mythical monsters in order to personify somehow this terrible suffering." A clash of the popular image, the mythical picture and the medical one is described also by an anonymous physician from Warsaw: "A dangerous memento, a gloomy threat for the whole of civilised mankind. Unforgettable is this terrible impression when, for the first time, as a young student I saw this mysterious, powerful enemy in its crimson armour imprisoned under the microscope glass. So this minute rod-shaped bacillus, visible only at enormous magnification, took up the fight against the whole of mankind; it is the cause of immeasurable pain and suffering, it fills hospital wards all over the world with 'living corpses' and with patients who go through the agony of pain with no hope of getting cured"[5].

Art creatively developed the individual aspects of the myth of tuberculosis. Susan Sontag, who also uses the term "mythology of tuberculosis", points out that in the 19th century the indication and the emphasis on certain symptoms accompanying this pathology, such as the putative intensification of sexual excitability or the development of excessive sensitivity, had led to the perception of tuberculosis as a disease endowed with a specific "romantic character", and its occasional description as a "sickness of desire "[6]. Through its modification of the human form, and the promotion of the physical type of a gaunt, pale, nervous person, tuberculosis entered also the aesthetic canon of fashion. In the fine arts, tuberculosis, especially when presented by

---

[5] Pamietniki Lekarzy, ZUS, Warszawa, 1939, p. 80, p. 216.
[6] Susan Sontag, *Illness as Metaphor*, New York, 1978.

doctors in private practice (hygienists and public health experts had a somewhat different image of this disease), appears as an illness which favours the individualisation of the patient, and in particular as an element accompanying artistic creation. However, new developments in medicine influenced the artistic vision of tuberculosis too, and deprived it of its romantic veil.

Already in the19th century tuberculosis was perceived as a social phenomenon. Its sources and its propagation were linked in the lay consciousness with landscapes of overcrowded, smoky industrial cities, with poor, dark and humid lodgings, and with malnourished, gaunt workers' families. These pictures were generated mainly through political agitation and propaganda, not through a direct popularisation of medical knowledge. With the formation, in the 20th century, of the modern, pluralistic political sphere, health questions have been included in the political fight. First of all, left-wing parties (socialists of various kinds, and then communists) indicated the class character of certain epidemic diseases, shaping thus the model of tuberculosis as a social disease.

Capitalism, that is, the political system which, struggling for better profits, condemned large segments of the population to poor working and living conditions and to malnutrition, was blamed for the high prevalence of tuberculosis. Radical political propaganda associated therefore the possibility of fighting epidemic disease with the change of the political system. In Poland, this social image of tuberculosis was also established through literature. One of the classics works of Polish literature, the novel *Przedwiosnie* [Early Spring], written by Stefan Zeromski in 1924 (who himself suffered from tuberculosis), presented tuberculosis as a part of social problem in independent Poland (i.e. after 1918). In his social vision this problem could be symbolically resolved by the construction of "glass houses". The hero of another Zeromski novel, *Ludzie Bezdomni* [Homeless People] of 1899, a physician, Dr. Judym, who dedicated his life to treating the poor, became a national icon. The vision of "glass houses" was closely associated with a radical change of political system, and socially active physicians added a new set of images to the myth of tuberculosis. After the second world war, these new images influenced party activists, physicians and architects. Thus in 1945 Dr. Tadeusz Kielanowski from Lublin, in a text published by the *Dziennik Zdrowia* [Health Gazette], an official publication of the Ministry of Health, proposed constructing a special "housing estate for patients with tuberculosis", and to call it "Judymowo"[7].

Zeromski's approach was, nevertheless, exceptional. Before the Second World War literary images of tuberculosis referred mostly to individual cases of this disease. While

---

[7] *Dziennik Zdrowia* no. 9-10 (Dec. 15, 1945), p. 222; Archive of New Records, Warsaw.

tuberculosis as a social phenomenon occasionally induced feelings of protest and revolt, especially in socialist circles, the presence of a "consumptive" at home did not evoke protest or surprise. At most, he was perceived as a minor disturbance to his surroundings, because of the noise he made when coughing. The consumptive individual lived and died in a "common room" – the title of the novel by Zbigniew Unilowski (1909-1937) who, like one of the figures in this novel, died from tuberculosis in a sublet flat. The image of a patient with tuberculosis changed after the Second World War. A short story "The Lovers from Marona" (*Kochankowie z Marony*) by the well-known Polish writer, Jaroslaw Iwaszkiewicz, (1894-1980), depicts a phtisic patient as a person isolated from society and locked away in a sanatorium. This sanatorium resembles a prison more than a hospital. It is a closed space fenced with barbed wire, and which one can leave only by showing a pass at the gate or by escaping from it. Tuberculosis is presented as a major threat, a dangerous disease which can bring about the destruction of the "healthy" world. Moreover, the story's main focus, the friendship between a consumptive and a former delinquent, constructs a parallel between a medical and a social pathology. Iwaszkiewicz's story illustrates the way the individual myth of tuberculosis was superseded in post World War II Poland by the myth of this disease as a social and political phenomenon.

Mechanisms of mystification of tuberculosis in the post World War II era

In post World War II Poland official ideology conceptualised tuberculosis as a social phenomenon and a "class disease". The lay picture of tuberculosis was not transformed by this ideological shift. The pressure of the new political situation influenced, however, its scientific and medical images. The change in political conditions created new possibilities in the fight against this disease. It allowed the centralisation of financial and material resources (that is control of hospitals, convalescent houses and outpatient clinics), the introduction of methods of supervision of the sick modelled on the methods of control of populations in a totalitarian state (registered place of residence, obligation to work and assignation of workplace), and the implementation of compulsory mass examinations (x-ray examinations, vaccinations) and of treatment and rehabilitation of patients. To a certain extent at least, the large-scale introduction of anti-tuberculosis measures in the 1940s and 50s followed the ideas of socially-minded physicians, who in the 1920s and 30s stressed the need to develop a holistic approach to the problem of tuberculosis, and explained that this disease was not only a medical problem but also, and for some, mainly a political and an economical one. This trend was amplified with the accentuation of the political dimension of tuberculosis in the post-war era. In the so-called Stalinist period, that is, in the years 1949-1956, this pathology became the object of special ideological "treatment". The notion of "mystification" in the sense of a conscious formation of a false picture of tuberculosis based on the uncritical acceptance of the ideological assumption provided by the Party is especially pertinent for this period. The goal was to develop the "right" (that is, in agreement with the principles of ideology), rather than "true" knowledge about this disease. The structure of the "mystification of tuberculosis" which supported this goal was determined by the authorities. Its most important elements included:

– biological theories modelled on "Michurin's, Lysenko's and Pavlov's teachings";

– ideological principles, which took the form of a dogmatic interpretation of Marxism, in that variant codified by the "Short History of the All-Russian Bolshevik Communist Party [WKPB])";

– political guidelines of organisation of the party and the government which closely followed the Soviet Union model, and which were to conform to Stalin's authority (for example, instructions for specific public health actions were always heavily adorned with Stalin's quotations).

The guidelines drawn up by the Ministry of Health for medical researchers, issued in 1951, recommended that one "base the direction and the methods of research on Pavlov's theory, and (…) strive for its creative application in medicine." Materials published in the years 1950-1953 in the journal *Gruzlica* ("Tuberculosis"), a journal of the Polish Society of Scientific Research on Tuberculosis and of the Polish Institute of Tuberculosis, tried to develop a new theory of tuberculosis, rooted in recent achievements of Soviet science. The new, revolutionary approach to this disease was to be based on the view, obligatory at the time, of a permanent confrontation between two antagonistic world-views: the materialist and the idealist, the dialectical and the metaphysical, the scientific and the non-scientific (irrational), the progressive and the reactionary. Jozef Parnas's article "Mitchurin's evaluation of anti-tuberculosis vaccinations" attempted to interpret the history of tuberculosis in the light of these conflicting categories[8]. According to this study, the reactionary, metaphysical current in the studies on tuberculosis was to be found in the approaches of Koch, Cohn, and Virchow. These scientists accepted the "stability and invariability of bacteria species", a view which made it impossible to grasp the similarity between the tuberculosis bacillus in humans and in animals. The progressive approach in this domain was represented by the French school of Louis Pasteur, reinforced by Polish and Russian scientists who collaborated with Pasteur, such as Metchnikoff, Danysz, Vinogratzky and Gamaleja. The representatives of this school studied the "variability of viruses and bacteria under the influence of the environment". Their approach had led to the development of a vaccination with an attenuated strain of the tuberculosis bacillus,

---

[8] Jozef Parnas, "Miczurinowska ocena szczepien przeciwgruzliczych", *Gruzlica*, 1951, 19 (1).

Bacille Calmette Guerin, (BCG), through using methods similar to those developed by Mitchurin. (Mitchurin was a Russian expert on plant breeding who developed new species of plants through non-sexual hybridisation; his studies were later seen as emblematic of the "new Soviet genetics" which disregards fixed heredity, and focuses on environment-derived change, a symbol of the boundless capacity of humans to change the material world).

"The development of the BCG strain", Parnas explains, "was an outstanding confirmation of the rightness of Mitchurin's science, which stresses the decisive influence exerted by external factors on inherited traits. This important achievement teaches us that the man armed with reason and science can control pathological processes in a creative way. He can curb the virulence of the bacillus, and use its immunising features to save mankind from infectious diseases." Despite the resistance and protest of reactionary (mostly American) microbiologists who "support the principles of Morgan's metaphysical bacterial genetics", the view of Koch's bacillus as highly variable and as having distinct stages of development was revived thanks to the courageous research of Dr. Boshjan from the Institute of Experimental Veterinary Science in Moscow. He had boldly overthrown old canons and dogmas, and had proven that the tuberculosis bacillus had bacterial, viral and crystalline forms[9]. Parnas legitimated the BCG vaccination through a reference to Mitchurin's and Lysenko's studies and to Pavlov's and Speranski's theory of the reflex arc (that is, the "ideologically correct theory") and perceived this vaccination as a model of new medical science: "Mitchurin's teachings tell us that we can direct consiously the development of traits profitable for us, we can fix and magnify these traits, and so it allows us to create new forms and species… BCG vaccination, applied in agreement with the laws of Michurin's biology, creates the possibility of the developmen of hereditary immunity to tuberculosis"[10].

In 1952 the journal *Gruzlica* ("Tuberculosis") published a paper which discussed Prof. Shebanov's proposal to ground studies on tuberculosis in the application of Pavlov's theory to the area of immunology, diagnostics, therapy and prophylactics of this disease. "Tuberculosis infection, its course, and deterioration or improvement of the patient's health," Shebanov explains, "should be associated with the functioning of the nervous system". Soviet scientists used Pavlov's theory to question the previously

---

[9] The so called cyclogenic theory of bacterial growth was popular in the 1910s and 1920s, and even in the 1930s some eminent bacteriologists, such as the Frenchman, Charles Nicolle and the Pole, Rudolf Weigl, believed that some bacteria, like some parasites (e.g., the malaria plasmodium), could have several distinct life-stages. Such a belief was, however, anachronistic in the 1950s.

[10] Formal instructions for investigators issued in 1951 by the Health Ministry also proposed to base tuberculosis research on Pavlov's theories. *Official Gazette of the Ministry of Health*, 1951, no. 15, Item 152, Archive of New Records, Warsaw.

accepted ideas of primary and secondary infection and the principles of the classification of tuberculosis. A correct description of the form of tuberculosis should, they proposed,"list all the functional disorders recognised in the organism, not only the ones observed in the affected organ" Soviet scientists were aware of the fact that the development of such a radically new approach to tuberculosis was a long-term process. It was to be linked with a fight against the dogmas of Virchow, Koch, and Ehrlich, allegedly deeply rooted in physicians' minds.

Edmund Szlenkier's article "The influence of psychic factors on treatment of pulmonary tuberculosis" similarly advocated the use of the theories of Pavlov, of his collaborator Speranski, and of his follower Bykov, in order to enhance the efficacy of anti-tuberculosis therapy[11]. It proposed to use suggestion in order to stimulate the patient's will-power, and legitimated this rather unusual medical practice by the claim that, "our observations show that the functioning of the nervous system obviously exerts influence on pulmonary tuberculosis (…) We had found that psychic stimuli mediated by the central nervous system influenced the state of the patient's internal organs and induced the regression of tuberculosis lesions in the lungs of some patients". In 1954, *Gruzlica* announced the scheduled publication of a series of articles about the practical consequences of the application of Pavlov's theory to the understanding and the therapy of tuberculosis. These articles were never published. One may assume that the change of political climate in Poland following the "destalinization" which started with the 20th Congress of the Soviet Communist party (1955), abolished the obligation to produce "politically correct" scientific theories.

During the Stalinist period, the subordination of science to politics included not only theoretical issues, but practical considerations as well. The Tenth Congress of the Polish Society for Studies on Tuberculosis (Bytom, 29 August - 9 September, 1951) stressed that "for the first time in the history of the Society's Congresses, the participants often spoke about the necessity of connecting science with practice, and about the need, for health services, to follow the example of miners and steel-workers to fulfil and to go beyond the goals of the Six-Year Plan". Janina Misiewicz, the Head of the Institute of Tuberculosis, gave a lecture on "The laws of materialist dialectics as applied to the fight against tuberculosis" which outlined the ways historical and dialectical materialism should be applied to the study of tuberculosis. In the capitalist system, Misiewicz explained, the struggle against tuberculosis was mainly grounded in charity. Despite the efforts of some socially minded physicians, such policies were

---

[11] Edmund Szlenkier, "Wplyw bodzcow psychicznych na leczenie gruzlicy pluc", *Gruzlica*, 1953, 21 (5).

doomed to be inefficient. because they were conducted in a system based on the exploitation of the working class. Only a socialist system, which transformed the fight against tuberculosis, into "a social duty" of the state was able to erdicate tuberculosis. In the debate which followed this lecture, the participants proposed to establish a team for the study of historical and dialectical materialism at the Institute of Tuberculosis.

The Six-Year Plan (1951-1956), which co-ordinated the development of all the sectors of the nationalised economy, outlined the precise goals for the fight against tuberculosis in Poland. The mortality rate of tuberculosis was expected to decrease from 10.4 per 10,000 persons in 1951 to 8.0 per 10,000 in 1956. The projections of the existing trends predicted that the decrease of the mortality rate to 1.5 per 10,000 persons would be achieved around 1965. The spread of tuberculosis was attributed mainly to the poor living conditions of the workers and the peasants. The main aims of the Six-Year Plan in Poland were "the construction of the foundations of socialism", and "the improvement of the living conditions of the working masses". According to the Party's activists, the "execution of the Six-Year Plan would remove the main causes of the high prevalence of tuberculosis: malnutrition, overcrowded living quarters, poor sanitary culture, and unhealthy work conditions." The plan included precise data on the numbers of hospital beds, specialised outpatient clinics and convalescent homes set aside for the treatment of tuberculosis. It also outlined specific preventive measures. The majority of these concrete goals were not achieved, however, while the first law regulating the prevention and treatment of tuberculosis, the "Act on Tuberculosis Control", was only voted in 1959.

The struggle against tuberculosis was legitimated by ideological arguments but also, and for some, above all, by economic considerations. Tuberculosis, spokespersons of the government stressed, is a chronic disease which entails high economic costs. The catchword of the "rationalisation" of the control of tuberculosis should by understood, above all, as a call for cutting down expenses. Thus the "rationalisation of sanatorium treatment" through the introduction of aggregate sanatorium, outlined in the Six-Year Plan, aimed primarily to decrease maintenance costs. Even the rhetoric of "class policy" had its economic justification. According to the party and government authorities, in a captalist system only the "exploiters" were able to benefit from an adequate anti-tuberculosis treatment. Capitalist countries, interested above all in curing the rich, favoured thus a costly sanatorium treatment. By contrast, socialistic medicine aspired to deal in an efficient way with an important number of sick individuals. It privileged therefore the establishment of numerous specialised outpatient clinics. Some patients needed, nevertheless, to be treated in inpatient institutions, and faced the problem of shortages in sanatorium beds. According to the Ministry of Health, workers should have priority of access to treatment. Places in sanatoriums should be distributed by social committees which classified the patients according to their social origins. The same priorities were applied to antibio-therapy. In 1951, a period in which streptomycin was still a rare product, only 1/3 of tuberculosis patients in Poland could have been treated by this drug, and those were supposed to be selected according to class criteria. This practice was legitimated by abstract criteria of class justice, but, above all, by the need to treat rapidly heavy industry and mine workers who were important for the fulfilment of the Six-Year Plan. Economic considerations may explain why a well-developed network of anti-tuberculosis clinics was established in the mining region of Silesia, and why this region was also attributed 1/3 of the existing sanatorium beds. This unique combina-tion of class justice and economic efficacy was summed up on a banner carried by the Health Service employees during the demonstration of 1st May 1953: "Our goal is the prolongation of men's lives: the lives of free men, of the builders of Nowa Huta and of Warsaw, of the producers on work on co-operative and on state farms, that is, of the architects of socialism."

One should add, however, that the mystified, ideological image of tuberculosis coex-isted at that time with a "professional" image of this pathology. The latter was similar to the scientific and medical images of this disease in the West. Aware of the real threat of the epidemic of tuberculosis, the political authorities had enough common sense not to neglect well-proven methods of prevention, detection and treatment of this disease. Polish experts on tuberculosis never lost their international contacts, and their representatives (though probably only those judged "politically safe") attended international conferences and congresses. Their relative freedom contrasted with the restrictions imposed during the Stalinist period on many other groups of scientists. In parallel, professional journals dealing with tuberculosis continued to publish reviews and discussions of the most recent literature on the subject while the newest methods of treatment and newly developed drugs, such as streptomycin, were rapidly imported from the West. One may conclude that while "tuberculosis mysti-fication" was omnipresent on the discursive level, it had relatively less influence in medical practice. The mystification's main goal in the fifties was to consolidate polit-ical loyalty to the USSR. However up until the 1970s, the strong need to justify med-ical activities with a political ideology did affect in numerous direct and indirect ways the doctors' activities.

3. The structural aspects of struggle against tuberculosis in Poland

The institutional picture

The mythologisation and mystification of tuberculosis described in the previous section belongs to the domain of culture in a broad interpretation of that term. This section deals, by contrast, with concrete institutional developments which shaped the image of tuberculosis in Poland. These institutional developments reflected the needs of the new political power. They were first shaped in the years 1945-1950, and were consolidated in the 1950s and 1960s. The deeply-set inertia which characterises, as a rule, all Polish institutions, can explain why the main institutional development in the area of fight again tuberculosis remained fundamentally unchanged from the 1960s on, and why they has survived the political transformation of the regime which started in 1998. The recent reform of the Polish health care system, introduced in 1999, may, however, bring important changes to these institutions.

The new political system which was introduced in Poland and in other countries controlled by the USSR after the Second World War, had two points of reference, one positive (the model of "the only socialist country in the world"), and one negative (the "capitalist world"). The supporters of the new regime advocated revolutionary changes, grounded in a radical break with the capitalist past. Solutions and values connected with the previous system were presented as harmful, apparent or illusory, and were therefore rejected. One of the propaganda's main tasks was the "unmasking" and the revealing of the "true face" of the pre-war system. In the case of tuberculosis, propaganda mainly emphasised the elitist character of medical services and their unavailability for the poor proletarian masses. This lack of access of the poor to medical services directly reflected the essential trait of capitalism, namely, the existence of private property and of a free market which, in medicine, assumed the form of a private medical practice.

As late as the mid-1960, popular publications, such as *Mala Encyklopedia Zdrowia* ("The Little Encyclopedia of Health"), explained that private medical practice was the basis of health care in all the capitalist countries so that in all these countries health problems were deemed the citizen's private affair[12]. The consequence was that

---

[12] *Mala Encyklopedia Zrdowia PWN*, Warsaw, 1963, Bibloteka Problemow, vol. XVI.

poor persons had limited, if any, access to medical services. Socialist countries introduced, by contrast, a radically new model of health care, based on:

- The State's responsibility for it's citizens' health;

- Centralised management of health care, which was contrasted with the lack of centralisation of health services in the majority of capitalist countries;

- Planification of health care objectives for the whole nation;

- Free and easy access to all the health services, with priority given to workers in key branches of the economy (coal mining, the production of steel, heavy industry);

- A focus on prophylactics, and a close linking of medical treatment with prevention.

Striving to realise these postulates, the State tried to abolish private medical practice. This goal has never been fully achieved, and some doctors continue to see private clients. By contrast, the State could take over the control of all the hospitals and clinics, expropriating not only the private owners of such institutions but collective owners as well. For example sanatoriums and clinics operated by the Anti-Tuberculosis Society (active since 1900), the Polish Anti-Tuberculosis Union (founded in 1925) and the Polish Red Cross, were nationalised. Moreover, both the Anti-Tuberculosis Society and the Polish Anti-Tuberculosis Union ceased their activity after the war, because the fight against tuberculosis was redefined as a duty of the Socialist State. On the other hand, the Polish Phthisiatric Society (a professional association of experts in this area, founded in 1911) was not dissolved, but it was fully controlled by the State, as was the society's journal *Gruzlica* ("Tuberculosis"). The Polish Society for Studies of Tuberculosis, formally a continuation of the pre-war Society for Studies on Tuberculosis, was also allowed to function, probably mainly becuse its existence enabled Poland to continue to participate in the International Anti-Tuberculosis Union, which is an association of societies and not of State representatives. It was nevertheless closely supervised by the State. A 1951 official document which outlined the new functions of Polish Society for Studies of Tuberculosis stated that the society's activities should be based on material dialectics, and should be firmly grounded in everyday life and linked with the health needs of the working masses.

The post-1945 Polish State did not recognise the need to develop autonomous programs and services dedicated to public health. Every "service" in the Polish People's Republic was a part of the State apparatus which, in turn, served to establish and reinforce the party structure hidden in its shadow. This permanent subjugation of health needs to ideological considerations and to party directives may account for the fact that after an important initial success in the immediate post-war era, the major investment in anti-tuberculosis campaigns in Poland did not lead to marked reductions in morbidity and in mortality. After 1956, the State became aware of its inability to directly control the entire society. It legalised several kinds of private or co-operative activity, including some in the health services, allowing thus the opening of a small "public space" in this domain. The new political developments made possible the revival of organisations such as the Social Committee for the Fight against Tuberculosis and the renewed Polish Red Cross. These organisations remained under the State's and Party's control, but this control was restricted to the financial aspects of their activity, and to the supervision of their staff. Their daily activity was not supervised closely, and they were able to partly re-establish their pre-war traditions: they collected money, provided direct help for patients and their families, and organised preventive actions, for example summer camps for children from communities with a high prevalence of tuberculosis. While non-governmental organisations provided useful services, their role was marginal, and the fight against tuberculosis continued in the main to be organised in a planned and centralised way.

In the "really existing socialism", the State's administration suffered from a specific form of schizophrenia: all its structures, on every single level, were doubled by the Party's administration. In addition, every institution had its own Party unit that could influence its decisions. The Party organisations had a direct and highly visible influence in the period of the formation of the new State structure (1945-1955), but their influence became less visible after 1956, and from the 1970s on, Party structures were eager to hide in the shadow of State administration. However, the model "a person/ a citizen/ a party member", unknown in democratic countries (where the binding model is of person/citizen) continued to be seen as valid. Being a Party member defined the person and the citizen: it determined what kind of person (Soviet, socialist, backward, etc.), and what kind of citizen (conscious versus unconscious or irresponsible citizen) one was. In each institution the party members constituted a specific pressure group, described as "active members". Party members who worked in institutions dealing with tuberculosis were associated in a "tuberculosis active members group". Their task was to link more firmly the struggle against tuberculosis to general political goals. For example, in 1965, a resolution of this group explained that, "The group of tuberculosis active members is convinced that the fundamental tasks of the base-level units of the Polish United Workers' Party in anti-tuberculosis clinics should include the development of ideological education among party members as well as among individuals who do not belong to the Party." "Active members" transmitted directives from the Party authorities to particular institutions, and occasionally, especially during the early years of the communist regime in Poland, even intervened in the private lives of personnel. In critical moments, the group of "active members" was expected to support unpopular Party decisions. For instance, during the 6th Congress of the Polish United

Workers' Party in 1968, which started a political campaign against "Zionists" (in fact, an attempt to eliminate political opposition, with strong anti-Semitic accents) the group of "tuberculois active members" proclaimed its support for the Party line.

Officially, however, the Party's role was defined as "ideological guidance", while the State administration was solely responsible for the functioning of health services. Poland's health care administration was first organised in 1944, with the establishment of the Supreme Extraordinary Commissariat for the Fight Against Epidemic Diseases. In 1945, when the Ministry of Health was formed, this Extraordinary Commissariat was transformed into the Sanitary-Anti-Epidemic Department. Up to 1948, pre-war institutions like Social Insurance or Health-Fund Societies functioned independently of the Ministry of Health. The final unification of all the health services, that is, their definitive nationlisation, occurred in the years 1948-1952. In 1957, the Ministry of Health was transformed into a Ministry of Health and Social Care. In 1962, private medical practice, tolerated until that year, was abolished and physicians were officially transormed into civil servants. This move was legitimated by the need for a more rational distribution of health services. According to the decree of 3 September, 1946 which outlined the organisation of the Ministry of Health, the fight against tuberculosis was under the jurisdiction of two divisions of the Ministry. The Division of Social Medicine was responsible for hygiene, mother and child care, worker's health and the fight against "social diseases" (venereal diseases excluded), while the Sanitary-Epidemiological Division dealt with the fight against acute infectious diseases and against tuberculosis. The latter Division had two branches dedicated to tuberculosis: "Anti-Tuberculosis Action" (later transformed into an independent "Division for the Fight against Tuberculosis"), and "Institutional Anti-Tuberculosis Treatment." These two branches supervised all the institutions which treated patients having tuberculosis.

The unification of the health care system in Poland was linked with the division of the country into administrative zones and to an obligatory assignment of patients to district clinics on the basis of their residence. District clinics included separate anti-tuberculosis clinics whose main task was the preliminary detection and prevention of this disease. Each district clinic covered 3-5,000 inhabitants. District clinics were subordinated to county clinics, each covering 40-60,000 inhabitants. The Ministry's guidelines stipulated the presence of one medical specialist in this area per 60,000 inhabitants, and one specially trained nurse per 33,000 inhabitants. Only the country clinics were authorised to perform specialised diagnosis of tuberculosis, to register patients, to organise their treatment, and to find appropriate jobs for patients with tuberculosis and for convalescents. County clinics were, in turn, subordinated to departmental (wojewodztwo) clinics, which employed higher level experts. The main tasks of departmental clinics included the training of personnel employed in anti-tuberculosis clinics, the co-ordination of treatment on the department level, and the follow up of the epidemiological situation in the department. All the anti-tuberculosis clinics, and all the hospital wards specialised in the therapy of tuberculosis were subordinated to local, or regional Health Departments. Sanatoriums and preventoriums were directly subordinated to the Ministry of Health. The administrative divisions established in the 1960s were partly modified in the 1970s. While theoretically the organisation of the detection and the therapy of tuberculosis in Poland was highly rational, in fact it was far from being as transparent and homogeneous as it appears in official publications, and it became incrasingly bureaucratic.

In 1947, the government established an independent structure, the Polish Anti-Tuberculosis Institute (decree of the Council of Ministers of 28 October, 1947). Its goal was to co-ordinate the struggle against tuberculosis in Poland, and to unify all the activities of health services, from prophylactics to therapy, within the framework of a single programme. The Institute's employees worked in committees which distributed rare drugs, such as antibiotics (a task which was especilly important immediately after the war, and which was later transformed into distribution of "non-standard", and thus more expensive medication). The Institute also elaborated guidelines concerning the optimal use of the available anti-tuberculosis drugs In the initial period of its existence one of its official tasks was also to provide the ideological education of tuberculosis experts, especially in the domains of materialistic dialectics and Pavlov's theory. Since 1963 the activities of the Institute, renamed the Institute of Tuberculosis, became gradually restricted to scientific research on tuberculosis. The Institute of Tuberculosis, which still exists, has its own scientific publications: *Komunikaty* ("Cummunicates"), *Wiadomosci o Gruzlicy i o Chorobach Pluc* ("News about Tuberculosis and Pulmonary Diseases") and *Walka z Gruzlica* ("Fight Again Tuberculosis"). These publications are a valuable source of information about tuberculosis in Poland.

The legal picture

In every country, the legislator has to deal with diseases which constitute a threat to public health. The generally accepted solutions put certain obligations both on healthy individuals and on sick ones. The latter often have to be isolated from healthy persons. In democratic countries, the establishment of public health regulation is frequently complicated by the need to balance public considerations and private freedoms. By contrast, in the communist regime, health was not viewed as a private affairs of individuals. Public health issues were totally controlled by the state. Legal solutions were not negotiated in a dialogue with civil society, but were unilaterally decided by the State's administration, which did not need to worry (in principle at least) about the possibility that the population would oppose its measures. The scope of the State's intervention was limited in the main by the technical and financial difficulties of imposing the desirable solution. For example, despite the fact that the Polish state declared that everybody should have free access to the treatment of tuberculosis, this access was limited by serious shortages of health care professionals, of available hospital/ sanatorium beds, and by financial difficulties which restricted the possibilities to buy appropriate equipment and drugs [13].

The first legal act regarding tuberculosis was a 1952 law which, among other things, introduced obligatory vaccination. It was completed by a decree on obligatory BCG vaccination, issued in 1955, which made obligatory the vaccination of all new-born children, a tuberculin test and, if necessary, revaccination of children in their 2nd, 4th, 7th, 12th, 15th and 18th year of life. Failure to conform to obligatory vaccinations was punished by fines imposed on parents. The introduction of an obligatory BCG vaccination was justified mainly by economic reasons. According to calculations made by the Independent Division for the Fight against Tuberculosis of the Ministry of Health, 26,000 years of work were lost annually because of tuberculosis. The costs of tuberculosis treatment and of disabled persons were also very high. On 22 April, 1959 the Polish Parliament adopted the "Law on the Fight Against Tuberculosis", which for more than 30 years was the main legal framework for dealing with tuberculosis in Poland. This law was still viewed as valid in 1995, although many of its elements were already outdated.

The new law placed the fight against tuberculosis under the exclusive jurisdiction of the Ministry of Health. The commentary of this law explicitly stated that the organisation of the fight against tuberculosis should take into consideration the cost/benefit ratio of preventive and curative actions. The "Law on the Fight Against Tuberculosis" was divided into two parts. A general part, adopted as a resolution of the Council of Ministers, affirmed the general principles of the fight against tuberculosis, while a second part detailed the financial aspects of this law. It provided free services in the domain of prevention, diagnosis and treatment of tuberculosis, and free rehabilitation of patients with tuberculosis, of convalescents and of persons invalidated by tuberculosis. Unlike earlier resolutions, the new law did not mention a priority of treatment for the "working classes", and was overtly presented as having a universal, not a class character. This fact did not, however, contradict the regime's ideological assumptions – it even confirmed them. The "Law on the Fight Against Tuberculosis" was depicted as prefiguring the next stage of development of Polish socialism. While Poland was still

---

[13] Circular n° 1 of the Health Ministry, about the organization of health services, dated 1 May 1945, Archive of New Records, Warsaw.

at the stage of the "construction of the foundations of socialism", the new law was construed as an innovative legal act, compatible with the principles of a fully developed socialist health services, thus as a demonstration of the concrete advantages of such a regime[14].

The "Law on the Fight Against Tuberculosis" provided free treatment of tuberculosis to all who lived in Poland (i.e., not only to Polish citizens). It defined the terms "patient with tuberculosis" and "convalescent". A patient with tuberculosis was "a person suffering from pathological changes induced by an infection with tuberculosis bacilli, and who, for this reason, requires treatment, health rehabilitation or occupational rehabilitation". A "convalescent" was a person who no longer manifested clinical symptoms of tuberculosis, but required the services of an anti-tuberculosis clinic and was registered in such a clinic. The obligations laid down in the law were based on the ideological assumption of the supremacy of the common interest over the well-being of an individual, and of the unlimited power of the State over the individuals residing in its territory. For instance, an appropriate state health agency had the right to ask all the persons who lived in the national territory to undergo preventive vaccinations as well as medical examinations, and to provide information that might be helpful for diagnosing tuberculosis, to detect a source of infection or to prevent an outbreak of tuberculosis. Such an agency could also enforce isolation of the patient by putting him/her in a hospital or sanatorium, and could provide compulsory treatment of children and adolescents. Patients with tuberculosis had the legal obligation to obey the physician's indications and to inform the appropriate agency about the change of their place of residence. An anti-tuberculosis clinic was entitled to give qualified personnel from the health services the right to enter the apartments of patients and to visit their work places, "in order to collect data concerning the patients' life and work conditions as well as to provide sanitary and hygienic instruction". Certain elementary civil rights of patients were thus suspended by this law.

In order to satisfy the State's ideological assumption that work was not only an activity destined to provide a means of subsistence, but also a value in itself, a large part of the "Law on the Fight Against Tuberculosis" was dedicated to the codification of employers' duties towards patients with tuberculosis. The employer – often the State – was obliged to provide appropriate jobs for these patients (in 1959, there were approximately 390,000 patients with tuberculosis who continued to be gainfully employed),

---

[14] Jan Stopczyk and Mieczyslaw Juchniewicz, "Historia uchwaly o zwalczaniu grozlicy w Polsce", *Gruzlica* (1959), 28 (11), 1960; M. Juchniewicz, "Aktualne zadania sluzby zrowia w zwiazku z wejsciem w zycie ustawy z dnia 22 kwietnia 1960 roku o zwalczaniu gruzlicy", *Gruzlica* (1960), 29 (12).

and to organise their retraining when a change of occupation was necessary. Additional regulations, which completed the "Law on the Fight Against Tuberculosis" provided a year of sick benefits to patients who were unable to work. During this period the employer was not allowed to fire the sick employee who, if cured, was entitled to return to his/her previous work place, and if still sick, had the right to receive a disability pension. This solution was highly beneficial for the patients. On the other hand, the very real benefits provided by the Law became also a tool to reinforce its repressive character. The "Law on the Fight Against Tuberculosis" stated that a negative recommendation of the anti-tuberculosis clinic could deprive patients of their sick benefits and of other services guaranteed by the Law. It directly linked thus the material fate of tuberculosis patients with their compliance with medical instructions provided by an official institution.

The statistical picture

Data published in the Polish Statistical Yearbook indicate that the most prevalent form of tuberculosis in Poland in the years 1945-1995 was disease of the respiratory tract. Tuberculosis was twice as frequent in men, especially young men (22-40 years old), than in women. Contrary to the stereotype established in its mythologised and mystified picture, tuberculosis was a greater public health problem in rural areas than in the cities. Its prevalence was higher in the regions characterised by a low level of urbanisation and industrialisation, such as the voivodships of Lublin, Krosno or Elblag, than in highly polluted industrial towns such as Katowice or Lodz. The publication of statistical data on tuberulosis in Poland, one should stress at this point, was an activity on the borderline between medical practice, academic activity and political action. In an ideal model of public health, medical practice should provide data which are collected and processed by expert statisticians, then becoming a starting point for administrative actions. However, in communist Poland problems arose already during the collection of data, they were amplified during the processing of these data, and the final results could have been subjected to additional political manipulation.

The fate of data about tuberculosis collected during the Six-Year Plan may illustrate this point. One of the Plan's main aims was to demonstrate the efficiency of the new political power and the superiority of the socialist system over the capitalist one. The initial data which served as the basis of the Plan's previsions were modified in order to fit the final goals. Thus, since the goal was that in 1965 the number of deaths caused by tuberculosis would decrease to 1.5 per 10,000 inhabitants, original data were revised to make this goal seem more realistic. According to the corrected data, the incidence of active tuberculosis (as revealed through radioscopy), evaluated in the years 1945-1949 at 1.4%, was in fact closer to 1%. The political rhetoric of that time put the entire blame for the high incidence of tuberculosis on the previous political system. The governmental propaganda affirmed, however, that initial data on the prevalence of this disease were often exaggerated by incompetent and insufficiently educated informers, and that the image of Poland as a tuberculosis ridden country was inaccurate. In addition, circa 1950 the government's spokespersons stressed that the death rate from tuberculosis was decreasing so rapidly that in ten years it might be possible to speak about the eradication of this disease in Poland[15].

Although initially the decrease in the prevalence of tuberculosis in Poland was indeed very rapid, the disease was not easy to eliminate. In 1957, 15,000 persons died from tuberculosis in Poland. Tuberculosis was the third cause of death in Poland in that year, following cardiovascular diseases and cancer (up to 1950 tuberculosis was the second cause of death, after cardiovascular diseases)[16]. In 1960 the authorities had to admit that "tuberculosis is the most prevalent infectious disease in Poland and is the cause of approximately 5% of all deaths, and of more than a half of the deaths due to infectious diseases". At that time Poland had one of the highest death rates for tuberculosis among countries of the Eastern Bloc. There were 39.1 tuberculosis-related deaths per 100,000 inhabitants in Poland, 35 per 100,000 such deaths in Rumania, and 31 per 100,000 in Hungary. Moreover, if in the 1950s the statistics were accused of being too pessimistic, in a later period, and especially in the 1970s, they were criticised for being excessively optimistic. The under-evaluation of the prevalence of tuberculosis was attributed mainly to mistakes in the recognition of the causes of death. Between 50 and 60% of tuberculosis- associated deaths, some experts proposed, were not recognised as such because the diagnosis was not made in specialised institutions. To avoid this kind of error, the Institute of Tuberculosis bulletins checked the data provided by the Main Statistical Office by comparing them with autopsy reports, with death files in hospitals, with autopsy reports of the Department of Forensic Medicine, with case records of anti-tuberculosis clinics, with data from sanatoriums, and with interviews conducted in the dead patients' places of residence.

In the years 1945-50, the main indices of the epidemic threat of tuberculosis were based on the number of newly recorded cases as estimated on the basis of an X-ray examination and on the number of tuberculosis-related deaths. On the other hand, it was assumed that X-ray examinations detected only 10-15% of the new cases. As late as 1965, only 22% of cases of non-pulmonary tuberculosis and 40% of

---

[15] O. Buraczewski, "Zwalczanie gruzlicy w planie szesciolenim", *Gruzlica*, 1952, 20 (6).

[16] O. Buraczewski, and H. Rudzinski, "Znaczenie spoleczne raka pluc w porownaniu z gruzlica", *Gruzlica*, 1970, 38 (1).

pulmonary tuberculosis patients had their diagnosis confirmd by bacteriological or his-
tological examination. However, from 1965 on, epidemiological indices of the prevalence of tuberculosis in Poland systematically incorporated bacteriological data. They
became thus comparable to world indices and could be incuded in international comparative analyses. They could also be used to calculate the annual infection risk, estimated in 1966 at 0.7%. The indicators used in the statistical description of tuberculosis
in Poland, and which appear most frequently in the Bulletin of the Institute of
Tuberculosis were: incidence (the number of new patients), morbidity rate, confirmed
by bacteriological examinations, death rate from tuberculosis, and absence form work
induced by tuberculosis (the latter measure was seen by the health authorities as one
of the most significant statistical indices connected with this pathology). According to
data provided by the Ministry of Health, tuberculosis lead to the loss of 5,776,418 work
days in 1951 and 9,587,219 days in 1958. Until the 1970s tuberculosis was the most frequent cause of disease-related absence from work, and thus a source of significant economic losses. Polish authorities were annoyed by the fact that these losses were not
directly correlated with a decrease in the incidence of tuberculosis. For example in
1972, the expected number of work days lost because of tuberculosis should have been
3,088,095 days (a calculation made on the basis of an average of 92.3 absence days per
patient and per year), while the observed number was twice as large – 6,095,591 days,
or 182 days of absence per patient[17]. The authorities decided therefore to tighten the
control over medical decisions on the management of tuberculosis.

In the 1970s, the incidence of tuberculosis decreased significantly and this disease
ceased to be regarded as a social disease. In parallel, the incidence of cattle tuberculosis diminished too. In the 1960s the latter was a very serious veterinary problem;
15% of cattle in private farms and 40-100% of cattle in State-controlled farms suffered from this pathology. The rate of infection of cattle had dropped however to
0.5% in the late 1970s[18]. In the 1980s the incidence of human tuberculosis in Poland
continued to decrease steadily with an average rate annual decline of 10%. The disease was not eradicated, however, and the annual infection risk, evaluated in 1989 at
0.2%, was still higher than in the majority of European countries. The incidence rate
of tuberculosis increase with age, and this disease was also frequent among young
adults: more than 40% of the cases were found in the age group of 20-44. Among the
newly detected cases there was a high proportion of fibroso-cavernous pulmonary
tuberculosis. In the early 1990s public health investigations revealed that 27-37% of

[17] Janusz Birnacik, "Absencja chorobowa z powodu gruzlicy pluc w Polsce jako pomocnicze
kryterium oceny efektywnosci opanowania gruzlicy", *Gruzlica*, 1975, 43 (10).

[18] Janusz Osinski, "Stan walki z gruzlica bydla w Polsce i poszukiwanie wspolzaleznosci miedzy
gruzlica u ludzi i u zwierzat (okres 1959-1966)", *Gruzlica*, 1967, 35 (1).

the Polish population was infected with the tuberculosis bacillus, and that 4,500 patients secreted bacilli in their sputum. In 1995, the last year included in my study, the Polish Institute of Tuberculsis estimated that there were 3,736 patients suffering from "active tuberculosis" (the presence of tubercle bacilli in these individuals was confirmed in a microscopic examination), that is, an incidence of 9.7 per 100,000 citizens. The incidence of active tuberculosis, including relapses, was 41.4. Respiratory track tuberculosis was detected in 96% of the newly registered cases. The coefficient of sputum-positive patients was 23.7. However, for the first time since 1990, these indices had shown a downwards trend, perhaps a hopeful sign. Epidemiologists estimate that, assuming the continuation of an annual decrease of 10% in the incidence of tuberculosis, Poland would reach the level of European countries with the lowest annual incidence risk of tuberculosis, such as the Netherlands, in 30 to 40 years[19].

4. Treatment and prevention of tuberculosis

Chemotherapy

Treatment of tuberculosis took the form of a strategic action, in line with the "war against disease" rhetoric used in the post-war era. Therapeutic strategies were elaborated jointly by the Ministry of Health and the Institute of Tuberculosis. Treatment of tuberculosis was thus carefully planned and supervised by the central administration, an activity justified by the scarcity and the high cost of antibiotics, and by the need to elaborate therapeutic protocols to use these new drugs. The first Communication of the Institute of Tuberculosis concernig chemotheraphy (May 1950) discussed the advantages and the drawbacks of streptomycin, while the second Communication (published in September 1950) discussed the therapeutic uses of para-aminosalicylic acid (PAS). In the 1960s, when new and expensive drugs, such as ethionamide (ETA), cycloserine (CS), or pyrazinamide (PZA), were developed in the West, the Communications presented these drugs, and discussed their possible application as "substitute drugs" which could be used by patients who were allergic or intolerant to the usual (and much cheaper) anti-tuberculosis drugs. In 1965 the authorities established a list of institutions entitled to use these "substitute drugs" and fixed their rules of distribution. The Institute of Tuberculosis elaborated, in parallel, the criteria of recognition of drug-resistance, and established a list of laboratory tests necessary to fill an application for a "substitute drug".

---

[19] J. Leowski & Miler, "Gruzlica w Polsce i na swiecie – stan aktualny i przewidywany po roku 2000", *Pneumologia i Alergologia Polska*, 1991, 59, pp. 9-10.

Treatment of tuberculosis with streptomycin had begun in Poland in February 1947. Initially it was administered only to those patients who provided the drug themselves. In March 1948 (thus relatively early) the Polish State started to import streptomycin produced by the American pharmaceutical firms Merck and Pfitzer. The Ministry of Health established a Committee for the Allocation of Streptomycin for Adult Patients, composed of physicians and of officials of the Ministry. The list of the committee members was confidential. Treatment with antibiotics was conducted in the Wolski Hospital in Warsaw. Because of the initial scarcity of this drug, the doctors tried at first to administer the smallest efficient doses. Until June 1948 the drug was administered daily for 140-200 days, later for 100-120 days (10 mg /kg weight). Initially streptomycin was used to treat bronchial tuberculosis, microfocal disseminated pulmonary tuberculosis, renal and genital tuberculosis and tuberculous encephalomeningitis in children. Streptomycin was also administered to patients who were prepared for a thoracoplasty or extra pleural pneumothorax, and to patients who suffered from bilateralisation following a pneumothorax. At the end of 1949, the standard therapy with streptomycin was modified to two weekly injections of 1g for at least six weeks, with a total dose of 12-20 g per patient. In 1950s streptomycin treatment was often coupled with PAS (para-aminosalicylic acid) therapy. The usual dose of the latter drug was 0,5-1,0 g a day. From 1955 on, the standard therapy was a prolonged (6-12 months) treatment with a combination of INAH (isonicotinic acid hydrazide) and PAS.

The introduction of streptomycin in the late 1940s and early 1950s decreased by 6.5% the number of tuberculosis -related deaths (from 113.1/100 thousand deaths in 1945 to 105.8/100 thousand in 1952). The massive introduction of INAH further decreased the number of tuberculosis-induced deaths In 1952, the first year of introduction of INAH the death rate from tuberculosis was 105.8/100 thousand, and it dropped to 65.2/100 thousand in 1953. Antibiotherapy gradually transformed tuberculosis from a lethal pathology into a chronic disease requiring long-term treatment and convalescence. Patients with tuberculosis who were not cured five years after their initial diagnosis usually became disabled, while doctors discovered that some of the patiens they considered as definitively cured had relapses. Communications issued by the Institute of Tuberculosis in the 1960s explained that if six months of treatment with streptomycin INAH and PAS did not put an end to the disease, surgery was usually necssary 9-10 months later. A well co-ordinated, uninterrupted and long-term (6-12 months) treatment, the experts explained, could cure at least 90% of patients who were in early stages of tuberculosis. The success of a therapy depended however on adeqate medical care, and on the compliance of the patient. Both were sometimes unsatisfactory, and in the 1980s, the average rate of cures was 80%. The existence of an important number of patients who suffered from chronic tuberculosis led to a renewed emphasis on the development of surgical methods of treatment.

In the 1960s the group of "Phthisiatric Active Members" (that is, tuberculosis experts who were Party members) pointed to continuous shortages of drugs and to errors in the methodology of their application, and asked the central authorities for new instructions. The therapy of tuberculosis had lost in the meantime its military character. The Communicationss, formulated as orders, were replaced in the 1960s by "Indications for the functioning of health care and social care services in the area of the fight against tuberculosis" (1969) elaborated by the Department of Prophylactics and Treatment of the Institute of Tuberculosis, and signed by the Minister of Health. These "Indications" included more eneral, tactical instructions directed mainly to administrators in the health service like, for instance, general instructions concerning the distribution of substitute drugs, such as ethambuthole and capreomycin. The amended Instructions, introduced in 1974, were noteworthy for a certain liberalisation. The treatment of tuberculosis was not limited any more to specialised centres. Every physician who diagnosed a case of tuberculosis and who confirmed this diagnosis by a bacteriological test, was allowed to select appropriate drugs and to supervise the patient's therapy. Surgical treatment was still indicated, but it was limited to extreme cases only, e.g., when the patient was allergic or intolerant to drugs, or to patients who suffered from chronic cavernous tuberculosis and who remained sputum-positive after 12 months of treatment. The new instructions also stated that a further prolongation of the division of anti-tuberculosis drugs into "basic" and "substitutive" was no longer justified. However, since the indices of elimination of tuberculosis in Poland were still far behind European standards, a new explanation of this fact was formulated: "The basic cause of this unfavourable state is lack of discipline in those patients who receive treatment irregularly and cease to take their medicines too soon". Thus, the patients themselves were presented as the greatest obstacle to achieving good results in the fight against tuberculosis, a situation that was to be corrected by a better supervision of these patients.

The new system of supervision of patients with tuberculosis, the Central Register of Tuberculosis (CRT) introduced in January 1985 was introduced to improve the control of the sick. It was completed by the establishment, in 1994, of a Central Register of Child and Adolescent Tuberculosis. The Register system, which is still functioning, aims to provide a complete quantitative verification of all the newly detected cases and to facilitate the monitoring of treatment in all the patients who suffer from active tuberculosis. A year after the onset of illness, the CRT provides the first assessment of the results of the treatment, and each patient included in the Register is observed during three years. Data provided by the Register allow one to trace with greater precision the extent of tuberculosis infection and to follow regional differences in the prevalence of this disease. CRT includes all the cases of active tuberculosis confirmed by bateriological examinations. It is established on the basis of the "statistical records of patients registered in an Anti-Tuberculosis Clinic", and includes the data on drugs applied in each case, the ways they were combined, and the duration of intensive and maintenance therapy.

Inpatient health services

Temporary isolation of patients, especially of sputum-positive ones, has been and still is an important element in the treatment of tuberculosis. Tuberculosis belongs to the model of a "climatic disease" – a pathology strongly influenced by changes of the climate. The traditional treatment of tuberculosis, which involved a temporary change of place of residence and the search for "healthy" surroundings, played an important role in the myth of tuberculosis. An additional important element was the isolation of the sick in such "healthy" places. The development of new therapies of tuberculosis modified the form and the meaning of the isolation of the sick. The introduction of antibiotics and the possibility of achieving a complete cure reduced the period of isolation, and decreased the importance of sanatorium treatment. The experts proposed that the optimal period of hospitalisation was three to four months, a period sufficient to eliminate the tuberculosis bacillus from the organism, and to make the patients "sputum-negative", that is, non-infectious. In post war Poland, the treatment of tubercuosis patients was conducted in hospitals and sanatoriums and, in parallel, in institutions such as the "half sanatorium" and the "preventorium", which did not isolate the patients. A "half sanatorium" provided them with a healthy way of life and permanent medical care in their leisure time, while allowing them to work during the day. A preventorium was an institution for children seen as being in danger of developing tuberculosis and for convalescent children. It provided balanced nutrition, a healthy environment and medical supervision. A similar objective – to improve the health of individuals in danger of developing tuberculosis – was promoted by the Central Council of Trade Unions, which funded special vacations in rest-homes for such persons.

The main site for the treatment of tuberculosis in the immediate post-war era was the sanatorium. The sanatorium treated patients in different stages of the disease, and a proposal to rationalise the therapy of tuberculosis by constructing separated institutions for the treatment of specific types of this disease was never realised. Soon after the war, all the existing sanatoriums (such as a 400 bed sanatorium in Otwock, near Warsaw, built and funded with the help of Sweden) were nationalised, and new ones were opened. Besides its heuristic value, sanatorium treatment carried also a symbolic meaning: it demonstrated that the working masses were now given an access to "bourgeois" forms of therapy. In the 1950s the authorities paid special attention to the "right" (that is, working class or peasant) social origin of patients treated in sanatoriums. Ministry of Health representatives explained that it was sometimes necessary to neglect strictly medical indications of sanatorium treatment in order to preserve the right proportions of white-collar workers and blue-collar ones.

In the 1940s and 1950s "progressive physicians" argued the traditional formula of the sanatorium was in contradiction with the "ideology of the working masses" which gave priority to work, and with progressive medical theories (based on Pavlov's teachings) which linked organic pathologies with the nervous system, and therefore with social pathologies. They questioned therefore the value of a long-term physical rest connected with total idleness. In 1950, a special instruction of the Ministry of Health introduced occupational therapy – physical work, but also sports and crafts – in the sanatoriums. The main goal was therapy through work. Usually patients were not paid for their labour, though in exceptional cases they could obtain a premium or reward, intended to stimulate a positive attitude towards work. One of the most important function of sanatoriums, some authors proposed, was the restoration of the productive capacities of the patients[20].

Initially the allocation of beds in sanatoriums was centralised by the Ministry of Health. In the immediate post-war era, the increase in the number of sanatorium beds was viewed as one of the most important indices of the intensification of the fight against tuberculosis, especially as compared with the pre-war situation. The perception of the role of the sanatorium was, however, radically modified in the 1960s. In the years 1963/4, the main burden of the long-term care for patients was transferred from inpatient institutions to outpatient clinics. At the same time the government limited the number of institutions specialised in the therapy of tuberculosis, and declared that the treatment of the majority of adult patients with chronic tuberculosis was to be provided by general hospitals and all-purpose (and not exclusively anti-tuberculosis) sanatoriums. Separate inpatients institutions were destined only for new cases of tuberculosis and for sputum-positive patients, and were to be divided into surgical, preventive and maintenance sanatoriums. These modifications were justified, above all, by economic considerations. In 1965, at the meeting of the group of "Tuberculosis Active Members", the Minister of Health, R. Baranski, claimed that physicians needed to teach society that "outpatient treatment was as efficient in curing tuberculosis as hospital or sanatorium treatment". He stressed in parallel that the new approach to the therapy of tuberculosis would allow for considerable savings, permitting thus a more rational distribution of limited resources. The Health Ministry also strongly recommended avoiding the excessive and unjustified use of sanatorium or preventorium treatment.

---

[20] A. Neumann, "Terapia zajeciowa w sanatoriumach przeciwgruzliczych", *Gruzlica*, 1955, 24 (8).

The sharp decrease in the incidence of this disease from the 1970s on, and the development of new techniques for the treatment of tuberculosis, decreased the need for separate inpatient anti-tuberculosis institutions, and thus for expensive sanatorium treatment. These developments are illustrated by the table below.

Years*	Sanatoriums	Half-sanatoriums	Preventoriums
1946	48	-	28
1950	83	-	54
1955	83	12	59
1960	86	15	59
1965	85	15	56
1970	66	12	12
1975	47	11	17
1980	30	9	12
1985	25	9	11
1990	24	8	9
1996	13	5	9

*) Data from the Statistical Yearbook of the Main Statistical Office (GUS).

While in 1970 sanatoriums provided treatment to 78,472 patients, half-sanatoriums to 2611 patients and preventoriums to 28,386, in 1995 only 14,586 patients were treated in sanatoriums, 651 in half-sanatoriums and 8,129 in preventoriums.

Physicians and patients

All the material dealing with tuberculosis, including letters to editors and published memoirs and diaries of doctors were censored in communist Poland. It is therefore difficult to find out how the laws, regulations, instructions and guidelines about the prevention, the detection, and the treatment of tuberculosis were reflected in everyday medical practice. We know that the government tried to control physicians' activities and, especially in the 1950s, to adjust health care to the general model of the organisation of labour in a socialist economy: "when we consider the great achievements of planned work in the Soviet Union, we can easily see that the guidelines for the application of dialectic materialism in the health services should be inspired by the work of the great theoretician and practitioner in the domain of social life organisation, The World Leader of the Working Class and the Champion of World Peace, Joseph Stalin." The government expected the work of tuberculosis experts to follow the general guidelines of a planned economy, while conforming at the same time to principles of "socialist science" such as Pavlov's theories. The elaboration of a national plan of treatment of tuberculosis was expected above all to fulfil "social and national tasks", that is, to reduce loss of productivity due to disease by curing sick workers "in the shortest possible time" in order to allow them to return to the productive circuit[21].

Indirect evidence, such as official talks which criticised physicians, point to doctors' resistance to the ideological underpinning of tuberculosis therapy. Officials, such as the representatives of the Ministry or the Institute of Tuberculosis, frequently complained about the "conservatism" of physicians. This conservatism was manifested, inter alia, in increasing the dosage of anti-tuberculsis drugs in contradiction with official instructions, or in excessive prolongation of sick-leaves. Physicians were also often accused of prescribing sanatorium or preventorium treatment too frequently. In the 1960s they were accused of not detecting tuberculosis (its underestimation) while in the 1970s of too frequent and unjustified diagnosis of this disease (its overestimation). On the other hand, even official spokesmen occasionally recognised the limits of the State's centralised power. Thus Dr. Buraczewski from the Institute of Tuberculosis explained in 1964 that "public opinion is an underestimated power, and... may influence even the acceptance or rejection of certain treatment methods as well as legislation concerning tuberculosis"[22]. The concept of "public opinion" should be understood here, I believe, as meaning passive resistance among the physicians, because the same article refers to events such as the abandonment of pneumothorax in the treatment of tuberculosis or the rejection of the Danish BCG stain, which induced bothersome side effects. The fact that the role of doctor's opposition was noticed did not mean, however, that it begun to be respected. Its recognition was rather aimed at putting an end to situations in which differences of opinion or resistance could occur. When the patients were offered different methods of treatment by two physicians, they were inclined to accept the one which was less burdensome for them. It was important to thus eliminate such situations, and to elaborate rigid guidelines for the treatment of tuberculosis (including surgical treatment).

Until the 1970s patients with tuberculosis were not visible in public debates on this disease. In the 1950s and 1960s patients were automatically expected to observe doctors' instructions, and to be grateful for their treatment. Patients' lack of compliance was usually associated with lack of discipline and with "asocial attitudes". An "asocial patient" was defined as a "patient with an active tuberculosis who violates the estalished social and legal norms with his conscious and malicious behaviour, thus harming his environment and the society". Since the treatment was most often interrupted by the patients whose tuberculosis was linked with alcoholism, it was proposed to

---

[21] J. Stopczyk, "Plan leczenia chorego na gruzlice", *Gruzlica*, 1955, 24 (3).

[22] O. Buraczewski, "Problematyka oswiaty sanitarnej w walce z gruzlica", *Gruzlica*, 1964, 32 (7).

apply legal sanctions to such patients. Dealing with petty offences, The Adjudicative Boards, whose meetings could take place within health service institutions, were entitled to pronounce such sanctions. Patients who refused treatment could also be sent to specific anti-tuberculosis institutions with a more strict treatment regime.

However in the 1970s the opinions of patients with tuberculosis started to be investigated, mainly by psychologists and sociologists. These experts studied the patients' attitude to their treatment and the level of compliance with it, aiming at finding efficient and non-repressive ways to convince them to follow faithfully their therapy and therefore to avoid an import waste of public money.

Co-morbidity of tuberculosis and alcoholism was and, it seems, still is one of the most difficult problems in the treatment of tuberculosis in Poland[23]. Treatment has always brought poorest results in this group of patients, and the proportion of relapses was also high. At the end of the 1980s professional journals started to publish reports on the co-morbidity of tuberculosis and AIDS[24]. Patients with tuberculosis living in rural areas usually suffered from a more severe course of tuberculosis than individuals who lived in cities. Their disease was also more dangerous for the surroundings. Peasants were claimed to be characterised by "inertia, fatalism, and deeply rooted mistrust". Since their attitude hampered efforts to convince them to treat their tuberculosis, the authorities tried to promote such treatment with economic stimuli, mainly though a reduction in their obligatory contribution to the state (the obligation, for individual peasants, to give a part of their production to the State was abolished only in the 1970s)[25].

Treatment of tuberculosis also included a recommendation for adequate nutrition. This recommendation was not, as a rule, resisted by physicians or patients, probably because of its strong ties with the myth of this disease. On the other hand, the term"adequate nutrition" is culturally and historically conditioned, and the popular ideas on this subject (especially about the need to overfeed individuals with tuberculosis) had to be corrected by the expert. The patient was thus provided with information on this topic by the physician, while similar information was published in popular literature, in journals and in magazines (thus food columns in women's magazines, such as *Pzyjaciolka* ["Girl-friend"] published recipes for patients with tuberculosis). The "Little Encyclopaedia of Health" of 1963 proposed that the "daily standard value

[23] According to the Bulletin of the Institute of Tuberculosis, 13% of individuals who, in 1995, suffered from bacteriogically-confirmed tuberculosis, were alcoholic: "Gruzlica i choroby ukladu oddechowego w Polsce w roku 1995", in *Informator Instytutu Gruzlicy*.
[24] P. Krakowka, "AIDS a gruzlica", *Penumologia Polska*, 1988, 54 (1).
[25] I. Szczuka, "Gruzlica miejska i wiejska", *Pneumologie Polska*, 1987, 35 (10).

protein requirement of a patient with tuberculosis is ca. 70-80g, vegetable protein requirement, approximately 50g. Patients with tuberculosis should avoid excess of fat. A patient should receive appoximately 100g of fats per day, in the form of fresh butter (50-60g), pork fat, pork grease, oil, and approximately 5000g of carbohydrates: cereals, vegetables, sugar, fruit, jams, salads. In winter a spoonful of cod-liver oil is indicated, since it contains vitamins A and D. Overfeeding and stuffing the patient with food is a superstition; he/she should preserve normal body weight"[26].

5. Prevention of tuberculosis

BCG vaccinations were the most important method for the prevention of tuberculosis. Large scale BCG vaccination was
introduced in Poland in 1948, under the
auspices of UNICEF, and with the support of the Danish Red Cross. After the
introduction of the Anti-Tuberculosis
Law (1959), BCG vaccination became
obligatory and it covered all children up
to the age of 18. While in 1948, 20% of
new-born children were vaccinated, in
1975 the rate of vaccination was 91.1%
and in 1995, 98.1%. Despite these mass
vaccinations tuberculosis did not cease to
be dangerous, even in the vaccinated populations. One of the reasons was inadequately performed vaccination.

A BCG vaccination protects one from tuberculosis.

According to the Institute of Tuberculosis
experts, post-vaccination scars which indi-
cated that the BCG vaccination was properly executed were found in only 80% of vaccinated Polish children. In the 1980s some specialists contested the validity of the BCG
vaccination using a Brazilian bacterial strain, considered as too weak: studies conducted in the Institute of Tuberculosis revealed that the efficacy of the vaccination with
this strain was 65% and the average duration of protective action just six years. The
main method for diagnosing tuberculosis and for identifying groups with an increased
risk of infection was mass radiological examinations. In the 1940s and 1950s more than

---

[26] *Mala Encyklopedia Zdrowia PWN*, see note 12, p. 426.

40% of patients were diagnosed thanks to microradiography. Their proportion decreased to approximately 25% in the 1960s, and at the end of the 1970s to 8.8%.

Despite the initial expectations, socialism did not bring about the eradication of tuberculosis. The highly centralised State power was unable to cope with the epidemic of tuberculosis either materially or organisationally. It was not able to impose new hygienic patterns or to create new habits. The authorities strove to disguise their helplessness with highly visible actions. They multiplied conferences, meetings, resolutions, indications and instructions. When the authorities finally decided that it was not realistic to hope that the tuberculosis epidemic would disappear thanks to a universal increase of the population's standard of living, the main goal of their activity became the raising of social consciousness. Propaganda and education became central: popularisation of information concerning tuberculosis, its ways of spreading and methods of avoiding it, lectures delivered by physicians and nurses in schools and factories, large scale diffusion of booklets, posters, radio broadcasts and educational movies. One of the fundamental tasks of this educational action was to overcome superstitions, especially those connected with the myth of tuberculosis, and to counteract both the fear of tuberculosis and social indifference. Education was intended to reduce the fear of infection in healthy persons and, at the same time, "to stimulate alertness and dynamics in the social fight against tuberculosis".[27] In 1958 the Department of Methodology and Organisation of the Institute of Tuberculosis conducted a survey of the basic knowledge about tuberculosis among healthy persons and among tuberculosis patients. This survey revealed that such knowledge was partial and fragmentary.[28] The respondents were ignorant of methods of early detection of tuberculosis, tuberculin tests and vaccinations. Many of them indicated cold, poverty, or mental stress, and not bacteria, as the cause of tuberculosis. The authors of this study concluded that it reflected the shortcomings of education about tuberculosis, conducted in an irregular way, and without being adequately targeted on specific sub-populations of recipients.

In 1961 the journal *Gruzlica* ("Tuberculosis") published an outline of information and indications that were to be used in an educational initiative[29]. Entitled, "What everybody should know about tuberculosis", it remarked that:

1. Tuberculosis was caused by a bacterium, Mycobacterium tuberculosis, discovered by the scientist Robert Koch.

---

[27] O. Buraczewski, "Problematyka oswiaty sanitarnej w walce z gruzlica", *Gruzlica*, 1964, 32 (1).

[28] J. Grodecka, "Zasob wiadomosci o gruzlicy u osob z roznych grup spolecznych (na podstawie badan ankietowych w r. 1958", *Gruzlica*, 1961, 29 (7). Similar investigations were repeated in the years 1964-1966, *Gruzlica*, 1968, 35 (6).

[29] *Gruzlica*, 1961, 29 (9).

2. Tuberculosis was an infectious illness. It was spread by persons suffering from this pathology as well as by infected animals.

3. Tuberculosis could be acquired through contacts with patients suffering from this disease:
   - through using the same kitchen utensils, underwear, bed-clothes, towels, hand-kerchiefs, articles of everyday use as the sick person does;
   - through staying in the same room with a sick person. When such person spoke aloud, coughed, or spat, tubercle bacilli, found in his/her sputum, floated in tiny drops of saliva, and thus infected the surroundings and the household members.

4. Tuberculosis was spread through milk coming from cows infected with this disease. To destroy the tuberculosis bacilli in milk, it was necessary to boil it several times. One should never give unboiled milk to children.

5. BCG anti-tuberculosis vaccination was the best protection against tuberculosis. BCG vaccinations were obligatory in Poland. Vaccinations had to be repeated if the result of a tuberculin test were negative. Parents were reminded to vaccinate children against tuberculosis.

6. Cleanliness, fresh air and BCG vaccinations protected a child against tuberculosis. People were encouraged to wash their hands frequenly, to wash fruit, to keep produce clean and to air their flats, bedding and clothes frequently.

7. Tuberculosis was curable if detected early. Radiological examinations detected tuberculosis. People were told to go to radiological examinations.

8. Every person who had come into contact with a patient suffering from tuberculosis at home or at work should often go for checks in an anti-tuberculosis clinic. Children should be supervised with particular care.

9. Tuberculosis could be cured in persons who:
   - obeyed the physician's orders;
   - received systematic and uninterrupted treatment according to a physician's indications;
   - did not attempt to "cure themselves";
   - conformed to basic rules of hygiene and kept their surroundings clean;
   obeyed the instructions on how to protect other people, and especially children, against tuberculosis.

The main organism responsible (from 1957) for the diffusion of information about tuberculosis was the Social Committee for the Fight against Tuberculosis and Pulmonary Diseases. Booklets and posters published by this Committee popularised elements of the "minimal knowledge about tuberculosis". Such educational activities did promote occasional changes in social habits such as the interdiction of spitting in public places or the advocacy of the use of handkerchiefs. However, even the most intensive propaganda campaigns were not able to trigger a radical change in attitudes towards personal and environmental hygiene, the only efficient way to consciously prevent tuberculosis. Desirable attitudes in this domain need to be connected with the development of a sense of responsibility for one's own health and for one's environment.

Healthy or Happy Child: An Interplay of Politics, Health and Values

Danuta Duch-Krzystoszek

Anna Firkowska-Mankiewicz *

1. Introduction

Neumann's proposal of 1847 that "medicine is politics, done otherwise" could have been the motto of our paper written in 1987, that is, two years before the radical change of the socio-political regime in Poland. This paper, entitled "Ideology - Politics - Health: A View from Poland" attempted to analyse the reasons for the poor health status of the Polish population from a macro-social perspective[1], namely from the point of view of the dominant socialist ideology with particular political and economic priorities. Such a macro-social perspective enabled us to look at health problems as possessing a specific instrumental or bargaining value which either won or, more frequently, lost in a confrontation with other values or priorities considered important by the authorities. An analysis of a relationship between medicine and politics, taking as an example the problem of the "production of healthy children" in Poland during last 40 years, with a special emphasis on the period of early 1950s, may be used to illustrate the heuristic interest of our macro-social approach The main thesis, which we would like to document in this paper, is that under the so called "actually existing socialism" regime in Poland, the supposedly ideologically neutral question of children's health and happiness became a subject of violent ideological conflict, because of the ways it was used to demonstrate the superiority of communism over capitalism.

The early period of "actually existing socialism" in Poland is of great interest for social scientists in general and for sociologists of health and medicine in particular, because in this period all domains of social life were under pressure from communist ideology and a totalitarian political system. The domination of the ideology was summarised in the ironic expression "when reality did not correspond to the ideology, so much the worse for reality". The improvement of the health status of the population (mainly of

---

* The authors express their gratitude to Joanna Kieniewicz-Górska for her assistance and for interesting information.

[1] A. Firkowska-Mankiewicz, M.P. Czarkowski, D. Duch, A. Titkow and R. Tulli, "Ideology - politics - health: a view from Poland", *Health Promotion International*, vol. 5, no. 2, 1990, pp. 151-160.

manual workers, women and children) was viewed by the regime as an important propaganda goal, but also as an important concrete aim. The exaggerations of propaganda notwithstanding, one must accept that much was accomplished in the 1950s and early 1960s in the area of health, especially if one takes into consideration the extent of war damage in Poland and the country's difficult socio-economic situation immediately after World War II. Among the greatest achievements in the area of maternal and children's health were free access to health care for children and for pregnant women, free hospital deliveries, medical supervision of new-born babies, education of mothers about the proper care of infants and children, obligatory vaccinations free of charge, and special campaigns against rickets, tuberculosis and so called dirty-hands diseases (childhood diarrhoea). All these developments led to a drastic reduction in infant mortality, perinatal mortality of mothers, and of childrens' morbidity.

Thanks to these measures, in the years 1946-1950 infant mortality dropped more than tenfold. The dramatic improvement of health indicators in the 1940s and 1950s was an important propaganda asset for the new system. During the late 1960s, 1970s, and 1980s, when the indicators stopped improving or even occasionally started to worsen, information about this fact was treated as dangerous and it was totally or almost totally suppressed thanks to the existence of a very efficient censorship. However, notwithstanding the government's efforts to mask the absence of improvement in the population's health, it became increasingly clear that in the 1980s Poland had one of the worst health indicators in Europe. It had one of the highest infant mortality rates, a very high percentage of underweight infants, and the highest death rate resulting from contagious or parasitic diseases. Moreover, medical examination of recruits to the army revealed that only 15% of young men in this age group could be classified as totally healthy[2]. Consequently, in the 1970s and 1980s, the government put the accent on "unhealthy habits" and on the individual's responsibility for their own health, while limiting public health campaigns. At the same time, it severely restricted the circulation of information about the health status of the population.

In the 1990s, a decade of radical economic, social and political changes in Poland reveals conflicting trends in health policies, and therefore also in the "production of healthy children". On the one hand there is complete freedom of information, including on the shortcomings of the health system and the deficient health status of the population, including children. Attempts to reform the health system were, however, slow. The reform was delayed for almost ten years, and when finally implemented in 1999,

---

[2] Firkowska-Mankiewicz, *et al.*, *op. cit.*, note 1; A. Ostrowska, "Health-promoting lifestyles", *Dialogue and Universalism*, no. 9, 1998, pp. 97-110.

it was judged as being badly prepared, while the time is too short to evaluate its effects on general health indicators, inclusing those of children's health. On the other hand, the "production of healthy children" is subject to strong pressure by the Catholic church and of right wing political parties. Such pressures are reflected in the debate on abortion law, an openly political issue in Poland. This law has been modified to a less or more restrictive one with almost every change of the government, from the Solidarity government to a post-communist one and again to a post-Solidarity government. Under the latter it has been changed to the one of most restrictive laws on this practice in Europe. These legal oscillations are not without concrete effects on maternal and child health. A spectacular example is the policy on prenatal diagnosis. A major discussion in the forum of the Polish Parliament against performing prenatal diagnosis, and penalities in cases where the foetus is damaged, resulted not only in a decrease in performing amniocentesis, but also in the tendency of paediatricians and obstetricians to discourage mothers with at-risk pregnancies to have such a test, or even not to inform them of a such possibility. A very restrictive abortion law (abortion permitted only in cases of rape, of malformation of the foetus and of the risk of the mother's life) has almost totally stopped legally performed abortions: in 1980 there were 138,000 cases, while in 1998 there were only 310[3]. At the same time illegal abortions have increased and there is a growing number of abandoned new-borns. One cannot ignore, however, the positive results of the new regulation, with an increased awareness of the problem of unborn children.

Returning to the alternative presented in the title of our paper, "healthy *or* happy child", we will try to show that this alternative was not a valid one during the early communist regime in Poland. In the 1940s and 1950s, the official propaganda images implicitly assumed that a healthy child was a happy one, presenting health as the unique condition for children's happiness. In later periods, and especially in the last decade, the notion of happiness has broadened significantly, and has embraced the sphere of emotions and the one of interpersonal relations. This change is dramatically expressed in the modification of attitudes towards children's disability. Until the 1970s disabled children were totally invisible in official discourse, and handicap was not presented as a social problem – perhaps because only healthy children were seen as efficient builders of socialism in the future. From the mid-1970s until the present the idea has been more and more systematically promoted that disability is a normal aspect of life and that disabled children and families with a disabled child can and have the right to be happy, to be accepted and treated as other members of society – but with

---

[3] *Aborcja - bezpieczna, legalna, dostepna*, Warszawa, Wydawnictwo Federacji na rzecz Kobiet i Planowania Rodziny, 1999.

the necessary support. This message is slowly seeping into general public awareness. Its dissemination is strongly promoted thanks to the activity of grass-roots, non-governmental disability organisations which have been developing dynamically in Poland during the last decade. They work for full citizenship for people with disabilities, effectively using the framework of human rights and social justice. As a result we observe a slow change towards a greater acceptance of children's as well as adults' disabilities.

2. The situation of women and children in Poland

We start the discussion of our data with a short description of historical changes in the situation of women and children in Poland, which will briefly sketch the changes in the hierarchies of goals and values in this area in the last four centuries. In the 17th and the 18th century, women and children were subordinated to the rule of their husbands and fathers. Marital and parental power was usually enforced with rigidity, severity or even cruelty. Physical punishment was the more frequently recommended way of child rearing and, especially in poor rural families, also as a method of abortion (e.g. manuals for confessors recommended asking husbands whether they had beaten their pregnant wives)[4]. Children from more affluent families were often separated early from parents to be sent to a wet nurse, and thereafter to tutors or boarding schools where flogging was an everyday practice[5]. A treatise written in 1750 blamed parents, even those from noble families, for neglecting their children. Parental carelessness, the author proposed, was the main reason for the slow increase of the population in Poland. Indeed, at that time 35% of children died before the age of one year, and 65% before they had reached reproduction age[6]. There are, in parallel, isolated testimonies of a warm and caring attitude towards women and children but such attitudes, if present, depended exclusively on the good will of husband and father[7]. Patriarchal attitudes and parental tyranny persisted in the 19th and even in the early 20th century, although in some cases their practical effects were gradually attenuated by the development of affective bonds within the family. However, even deeply loved children were reared with severity and without any formal respect for their rights and autonomy, while children's happiness was not presented as a desirable educational goal. The rigidity of this education pattern was often softened by mothers.

---

[4] B. Jedynak (ed.), *Kobieta w kulturze i spoleczenstwie*, Warszawa, 1990, vol. I, pp. 12-13; J. Tazbir, *Okrucieństwo w nowozytnej Europie*, Warszawa, 1993.

[5] J. Tazbir, "Stosunek do dziecka w okresie staropolskim," in S. Golinowska, *Przemiany w warunkach życia polskich rodzin w okresie transformacji, w: Rodzina – jej funkcje przystosowawcze i ochronne*, Warszawa, PAN, Centrum Upowszechniania Nauki, 1995, pp. 155-166.

[6] K. Bartnicka, "Dziecko w świetle pamiętników i powieści polskiego oświecenia", *Rozprawy z Dziejów Oswiaty*, 1992, vol. XXXV, pp. 41-46.

[7] Tazbir, *op. cit.*, note 5, p. 165.

On the other hand, Polish women, especially those of noble descent, preserved the right to keep their dowry and their own property after their marriage. They were thus able to participate in the family's economic decisions. The nobility's ethos, which saw the members of this class as free agents, and which stipulated equality of principle between all the noble families, also protected married noblewomen who, when in conflict with their husbands, could ask their parental families for help and protection[8]. The status of Polish women paradoxically improved during the partition of Poland when the country lost its independence (1795-1918). This period brought to the fore the model of the heroic Polish Mother (Matka-Polka) who, through her educational role, held the main responsibility for the preservation of Polish national identity, language, culture and tradition. Her national duty was to devote herself to her family and motherland. Her social prestige was relatively high, but it was not tantamount to the recognition of her right for self-realisation and autonomy. Her only culturally and socially approved activity was to adequately perform the roles of wife, mother and patriot, and her elevated status was directly related to her success in these roles[9].

The collapse of an economy based on landed aristocracy and the industrialisation of Poland in the second half of the 19th century created a first wave of economic pressure for a massive entry of Polish women into the labour market. The second, and more important wave of this process took place in the aftermath of World War II. Women who were integrated into the work force faced an important increase in their duties. Communist propaganda added to the traditional model of women – the guardian of the family fire and of the motherland – another image, that of the woman as producer, proudly driving a tractor or working in a factory without, obviously, neglecting her obligations to her husband and children. Polish women accepted the burden of a double work-day. They performed all their professional and familial obligations, often even at the expenses of constant fatigue and health problems, and often viewed their exclusive responsibility for household duties as a source of pride, allowing them to maintain a self-image of "irreplaceable managers of the family's life"[10]. The "managerial matriarchy" became a source of gratification, domination and high self-esteem for many women, facilitating, on the other hand, their acceptation of the fact that women were openly discriminated against in the labour market, that they occupied less prestigious jobs and received lower salaries, and that they suffered from a highly unequal division of labour in the family[11].

---

[8] A. Titkow, "Kobiety pod presja. Proces kształtowania sie tożsamości", in A. Titkow and H. Domanski (eds.), *Co to znaczy byc kobieta w Polsce*, Warszawa, Wydawnictwo IFiS PAN, 1995, pp. 9-39, p. 12.

[9] *Ibid.*

[10] *Ibid.* p. 31.

[11] *Ibid.* See also J. Heinen, "Marginalisation économique et sociale des femmes en Pologne et en Bulgarie", *Mouvements*, no 6, 1999, pp. 84-91.

The situation of Polish women in the post World War II period reflected the double pressure of well-entrenched cultural patterns, and of dominant ideological and economic trends. In the early post-war period, when all the hands were needed to restore the economy, women were encouraged to work outside the home. The government created then a system of day care centres and kindergartens to allow them to return to their workplace at the end of their maternity leave. In the 1970s and 1980s, when the economy collapsed, the government's propaganda promoted, by contrast, a traditional family model, and encouraged women to stay at home in order to take care of their young children. In the 1990s, when a drastic change of the socio-political system led to high levels of unemployment, women were often the first to be fired in the name of the "natural division of social and family roles". The view that "a man – the father of the family – should stay employed, while a woman finds equally responsible tasks in the household and child rearing", was defended by conservative politicians and, moreover, was shared by the majority of Polish men[12]. According to recent surveys 65% of Polish men continue to view women above all as mothers and wives. By contrast, many Polish women aspire to combine professional and family roles (41% in 1978, 52% in 1989)[13]. Moreover, a survey made in 1993 revealed that more than 70% of Polish women would elect to work even if there was no economic pressure to do so[14].

In fact, however, throughout the post-war period the aspirations of women themselves were seldom taken into account. Economic and ideological considerations led to the promotion alternatively of either the 'female worker', or the 'Polish Mother', but none of these images was related to a genuine emancipation and true liberation of women. Moreover, if in the 1990s numerous conservative politicans openly declared that a woman's main task was to be a homemaker and a mother, a similar opinion was propagated in the 1950s and 1960s by many communist leaders. The communists' concern about the "production of healthy children" transformed women's health into a political category. Labor legislation, it is true, protected women. Women were not allowed to occupy jobs which could harm their reproductive capacites, pregnant women and those who had small children were given lighter tasks. It became impossible to fire a pregnant woman, and each working woman was entitled to a paid maternity leave. Many of these laws and decrees remained valid in the post-communist regime, and paradoxically, some were used in the post-communist era to discriminate against

---

[12] M. Michalik, "Spoleczno-globalne i makrostrukturalne uwarunkowania rozwoju rodziny", in Z. Tyszka (ed.), *Rodziny polskie u progu lat 90tych*, Poznan, CPBP, 1991.

[13] D. Duch-Krzystoszek, *Malzenstwo, seks, prokreacja. Analiza socjologiczna*, Warszawa, Wydawnictwo IFiS PAN, 1992; A. Titkow, *Miejsce dziecka w swiecie wartosci*, Warszawa, IFiS PAN, IS UW, 1984.

[14] *Postawy wobec pracy i aspiracje zawodowe kobiet*, Warszawa, CBOS, Research Report, 1993.

women in the labor market. For exemple, regulations which accord to mothers (but not to fathers) the right to stay home to take care of a sick child, were interpreted as marking all women as less efficient and less reliable workers.

Children maintain their elevated place in the hierarchy of cherished values. Nevertheless, the average number of children in Polish families has systematically decreased in the last twenty years, and the reproduction rates fell in the late 1990s below the level required for the replacement of generations. The Polish state does not possess a coherent family policy, while previous social welfare benefits were abolished as a consequence of the economic crisis. Maternity and family supplements were reduced to a symbolic amount of money, many public day care centres and kindergartens were closed (while private institutions which replaced them are very expensive), schools have limited or even totally suspended their social activities such as free meals for malnourished children, free medical and dental care, and the organisation of sport, culture, recreational and vacation activities for children. Statistical data indicate that families with children (especially those with more than two children) are those who suffer the most from the negative consequences of the recent political and economic changes in Poland[15]. Only recently the Polish Parliament started the long-awaited debate on a pro-family taxation system though thus far (fall, 1999) it has not introduced any pro-family decisions.

The degradation of the material conditions of life of Polish families is paralleled by an increase in the percentage of children who suffer from difficulties at school, and by a growing number of cases of parental incapacity. At the level of rhetoric everybody agrees that children and their good relationships with parents are very important. The dominant model is no more a disciplinary one, and the ideal is free and friendly relationships between parents and children. Thus while 44% of interrogated parents admit to having been beaten by their parents, only 9% recommend the physical punishment of a child. The reality tends to be more complicated: while only 9% of parents approve physical punishment as a recommended method of education, 47% believe that it is not harmful, and 23% acknowledge that they punished physically their child at least once during the last year[16].

---

[15] A. Firkowska-Mankiewicz, "Jakosc życia rodzin z dzieckiem niepełnosprawnym", *Psychologia Wychowawcza*, vol. XLII, no 2, 1999, pp. 134-145; Golinowska, *op. cit.*, note 5, pp. 51-68.

[16] Duch-Krzystoszek, *op. cit.*, note 13; *Dzieci, rodzice, pieniądze*, Warszawa, CBOS, Research Report, 1993; A. Titkow, *Spoleczno-kulturowa tozsamouswienie polskich kobiet*, Warszawa, Unpublished Research Report, 1998; *Wychowanie i opieka nad dziecmi w polskich rodzinach*, Warszawa, CBOS, Research Report, 1995.

In practice, the majority of Polish parents do not have enough time, knowledge, and parental skills to efficiently promote the development of healthy, well-adjusted, responsible and autonomous personalities for their children. A child in the 1950s and 1960s was most often perceived in an instrumental way – as a factor stabilising a marriage and giving continuity to the family, a source of parental joy and satisfaction, and a protection against loneliness, especially in old age [17] – and not as an autonomous human possessesing an intrinsic value and having specific, individualised rights. Some change can be observed, especially in families with higher socio-economic status and a higher level of education. They view children as an expression of love, a way on enriching one's life, and a source of personal joy [18]. In parallel, numerous individuals and families, especially in lower socio-economic strata, continue to hold a utilitarian view to children, presenting them as a natural goal of a marriage or a means to receive care in one's old age [19]. There is, however, a general trend to pay greater attention to the education of children, and to the fulfilment of their emotional needs. The magazine *Your Child*, discussed in this paper, played an important role in the promotion of the vision of children as autonomous human beings who have an intrinsic value of their own.

3. Images of "happy and healthy children" in the press: a case study

The material we have chosen to use to illustrate the issue of "production of healthy children" in Poland comes from a monthly magazine for parents, entitled *Your Child* (*Twoje Dziecko*). It was founded in 1951, under medical patronage (its publisher in the years 1951-1989 was PZWL-Polish Medical Publishing Agency). Until the early 1990s it was the only publication of this kind in Poland. For four decades, *Your Child* was the most influential guide for Polish parents, not only because of its large diffusion (it sold 250,000 copies of each issue) but also thanks to its close contact with its readers. Each year about 2000 of the letters send to the magazine were answered in print by a team of physicians, lawyers, and psychologists. In addition, its staff spontaneously performed counselling for parents who came directly to the magazine's office.

The magazine's language was openly didactic, though it chose a persuasive rather than a directive tone. It attempted to convince, not to present authoritative views. One

---

[17] I. Kowalska, "Historia rozwoju rodziny i jej uwarunkowania", in Golinowska, *op. cit.* note 5, pp. 115-140; Titkow, *op. cit.*, note 13.

[18] A. Kotlarska-Michalska, "Niektóre wskaźniki opieki nad malym dzieckiem realizowanej w głównych kategoriach rodzin wielkomiejskich", *Roczniki Socjologii Rodziny*, Poznan, 1990, vol.; Titkow, *op. cit.*, note 13.

[19] W. Ignatczyk, "System wartosci małzenskich preferowany przez mlodziez polską", *Problemy Rodziny*, no 3, 1993, pp. 15-19.

approach frequently used by its staff was to formulate ideas as an opinion of a mother who wished to share her experience with other mothers. A different rhetoric device was a supposed dialogue between a less informed and a better informed mother, the latter being presented as a women who listened to the specialist's advice, with excellent consequences for her child's health. The magazine also published articles presented as diaries of well-informed new mothers, in which they explained how they coped on a daily basis with health problems, hygiene and education of small children.

In the 1950s *Your Child* had a strong political bias – an evaluation which was confirmed explicitly in an interview with one the magazine's chief editors at the time. Its main message and aim was double: to help parents to rear a strong and healthy child (a goal which, for the editors, was identical to that of rearing a happy child) and to convince its readers that this aim could only be fulfilled in a socialist country. At first this ideology was transmitted in a very obtrusive way. Relatively quickly, however, the political pressure weakened and the magazine was able develop more freely its specific profile as a publication devoted partly to health issues, and partly to educational and psychological problems of children and teenagers, and of the specific difficulties of child-rearing. This relative freedom was possible thanks to the position of chief-editor who, quite exceptionally, was not a member of the Polish United Worker's Party, but whose appointment was approved by the Party's Central Committee.

The relative editorial freedom of *Your Child* has been attacked twice. In the 1970s a new director of the Polish Medical Publishing Agency who published it tried, without success, to force the members of the editorial board to become members of the Communist Party. To counter-balance this pressure, the staff members appointed a "Party Commission", composed of four carefully chosen professionals (a psychologist, a sociologist, a medical doctor and the director of the Children's Friends Association), all members of the Communist Party. This body protected the decisions of the editorial board and buffered it from political pressures from the outside. The second attack came during the time of "martial law", instated in Poland in 1981 following the increase in tension between the government and the free trade union, Solidarity. This time the magazine risked being suspended for publishing an interview with an influential opposition priest, and its staff (like all Polish journalists) was submitted to a "loyalty check". In *Your Child* this "loyalty check" was performed by a commission composed of a director of the Medical Publishing Agency, a representative of the Ministry of Health, and a delegate from the Ministry of Internal Affairs. Nobody was fired thanks to the efficient intervention of the magazine's "Party Commission". The relative independence of *Your Child* and its relative freedom to pursue an independent editorial line in the 1970s and 1980s was partly the result of the activity of well-chosen and competent advocates of the magazine, active in the "Party Commission".

The other reason was probably the authorities' belief that the magazine's profile did not threaten the dominant ideology and government policy. Moreover, in the early 1950s, when the magazine was founded, the government's initiatives could be presented as making an important contribution to the improvement of children's health, so allowing for an efficient linking of health care issues with political propaganda.

4. The value of health in communist ideology in the 1950s

Socialist ideas were developed as a critique of capitalism, in particular of the living and health conditions imposed upon the working class. It is thus is both understandable and logical that the protection of the workers' and peasants' health occupied an important place in the communist party which transformed health-related issues into a powerful propaganda argument. The claim that only socialism could provide optimal conditions for the physical and the spiritual development of the individual was used later to legitimise a new political order, and to demonstrate its superiority over capitalism. Even the bourgeois sociologists, the official propaganda claimed, were aware of the fact that socialist regimes provided optimal conditions for the preservation and improvement of man's health[20]. That granted, it must also be said that ideological attitudes towards health were as a rule dualistic, if not overtly cynical. On the one hand, the regime's spokespersons frequently declared that the most important goal of a socialist society was to insure a full development of human beings. At the same time human health was treated in a totally instrumental manner. Workers' health was presented, firstly, as an element which enabled them to fight efficiently for a new social order and, secondly, as a necessary condition for the economic development of a nation. Here is a characteristic statement:

> The communist attitude towards health is based on a Leninist principle, namely on the necessity to see the physical and mental health of working people not as their personal problem, but as *national property*. Among the many factors which affect the socio-economic progress of a society – workers' health, that is *their working capacity* – plays a major and increasingly important role (…) The death of every human organism which fails to reach working age should be seen as an irreparable loss to the collective… Hence the efforts to further lower the death rate of infants and to improve the health of children and young people[21].

---

[20] G.I. Tsaregorodtsev and A.F. Polis, *Social Problems of Medicine*, Warszawa, PZWL, 1971.
[21] *Ibid.*

A picture on the cover of the first issue of *Your Child* represents a child who is healthy and happy because, it is strongly hinted, he is living in socialist country. The political character of the journal is reflected in its editorial:

> *Your Child* is a newspaper for you, parents, but especially for *working mothers living in cities and in the country*. We want it to be your friend and to help you to rear a healthy and happy child [...] At the same time we want you to know how children live all around the world. How children live in the Soviet Union and other People's Democracies, who, under the solicitous care of parents and the state grow up to become brave strong people, and how thousands of children live in capitalist countries, and who suffer, together with their parents, from poverty, famine and exploitation.

Two official statements reproduced in that issue leave no doubt that the socialist state will take responsibility for the production of healthy children. The Minister of Health, Sztachelski, explains thus that "Child care it is not only an individual or family matter, but it is directly related to the future of our country and to the blossoming of social-ism"[22]. Hanna Slomczyñska, the Director of the Department of Care for Mother and Child in the Ministry of Health, similarly explains that "A child is not only the joy and pride of his parents, but the greatest treasure of the state. Child-rearing is above all the fulfilment of the state's most important duty, because healthy and strong youth will make possible the construction of socialism in Poland. The protection of mothers' and children's health is situated at the very top of the Six-Year Plan's priorities"[23]. Similar messages are repeated constantly throughout all the issues of the magazine which appeared in 1951. Lets look now more closely at the content of these issues.

5. The child and the socialist state – a 1951 point of view

Early issues of *Your Child* contain overt political propaganda, occasionally totally unre-lated to the problems of children. The magazine published texts on the great socialist leaders (mainly Soviet ones), on Polish – Soviet friendship, on anniversaries of political events etc. In each issue there was a section entitled "Let us remember", which invites mothers to remember dates such as the anniversary of Lenin's death or Stalin's birthday, the anniversary of the creation of the Red Army, or of the first session of the first

---

[22] *Twoje Dziecko* ("Your Child") no 1, 1951, p. 2.

[23] *Ibid.*, p. 3.

People's Government in Poland. The magazine also published photographs of socialist leaders together with children, in order to soften the leaders' public image and indicate their good will. Images of Poland's President Bierut with children, of Lenin with children, of Stalin with children, were accompanied by texts indicating the great leader's merits and his devotion to the people. Token children were also systematically shown in pictures of ceremonies and of official events.

Children's health and happiness were also integrated into a framework of political indoctrination. This indoctrination was based on two main arguments. Firstly, that healthy children are the future builders of socialism. They represent therefore the hope for the dissemination of the ideology and practice of socialism, not only in Poland but world-wide as well. And secondly, that the child's situation in socialist countries is a self-evident proof of the superiority of socialism over capitalism. The latter argument is put to the fore through a comparison of the situation of children in socialist and capitalist countries and of the lives of Polish children before Word War II and then under the People's Government. In order to illustrate the difference between poor children who live in capitalist countries, and the lucky ones who live in socialist ones, the journal used crude images. For example, it juxtaposed two pictures. In one four children are drawing something on the big blackboard. In the other, a women and a child sit amidst pots on the ground. A text explains that "Romanian children are educated in beautiful kindergartens, while – their mates in India live in a deep poverty". Another text tells the story of poor workers' children from West Germany, Italy, and France, who were invited to East Germany and Poland for summer vacations, in order to enable them to enjoy, even if briefly, the privileged situation of children of their age in socialist countries. Western governments, scared by the subversive potential of such a visit prevented, however, these children from spending their summer in Eastern Europe; some were even brutally pulled out from trains. In parallel, the magazine provided data about thousands of Polish children who spent their summer vacation in camps and colonies, an image which is sharply contrasted with the pre-war times when poor, hungry, sick children were forced to spend the entire summer in dirty and polluted towns.

The alternative between 'healthy' and 'happy' does not exist in the 1950s. The main message in Your Child's articles is that children who had the supreme luck to be born in a socialist country are always big, strong and healthy and these two conditions makes them automatically happy: *tertium non datur*. The magazine then identified the reasons why children who live in socialists countries are healthy. Firstly, they are born big, strong and healthy because their working mothers (who love their socialist country and love to work for it) know that working during pregnancy, especially outdoors, is good for their and their children's' health. Secondly, children are healthy because the state provides them with medical care free of charge. They are born in a hospital with good medical care and are vaccinated against contagious diseases. Thirdly, children are healthy because their mothers are taught by specialists (doctors, nurses, dieticians) how to feed and to protect them. Mothers are informed that their children should be breast-fed, should be given vitamin D, that even in winter they should drink fresh juice and eat fresh vegetables. Mothers are also instructed to wash their hands before preparing meals, to keep the child's environment clean, and to regularly bath their children. Fouthly, children are healthy, happy and safe because their mothers have built beautiful day care centres for them where they are left, under good qualified care, immediately after maternity leave, so enabling their mothers to return to work (mainly physical), and to build cites, to work in factories, or to drive tractors. Finally, children are healthy because Polish experts have been instructed by Soviet specialists. They can benefit therefore from the important achievements of Soviet medicine in the domain of maternal and child health care.

The 1951 issues of *Your Child* rarely evoked educational problems, reducing good parenthood or, to be precise, good motherhood, to care issues. Mothers' main task was to take good physical care of their children: they needed to wash them, to feed them correctly, to take them for walks, and to ensure that they received all the obligatory vaccines. The magazine seldom mentioned children's concrete health problems. Only occasionally it provided information about specific diseases, mainly infectious diseases or rickets. Moreover, such diseases were presented, in the main, as sad remnants of capitalism, condemned to disappear shortly. Disabilities were seldom mentioned. Children born in a socialist country had no right to be disabled, firstly, because only this system offered good medical care for mothers and children and, secondly, because only a healthy person could construct socialism. The issue of mental handicap (children who, at that time were called mongoloid or feeble-minded) turns up solely in the context of the persistence of social pathologies (mainly alcoholism), presented as the main cause of mental retardation. The magazine also seldom speaks about the family – rather a surprising absence in a publication officially dedicated to child-rearing. In the early 1950s issues of *Your Child* there is not a single photograph of a child surrounded by both of his/her parents and by siblings. Children are either depicted in a political context, as mentioned earlier, or in day care centres, kindergartens, other collective structures or, more rarely, with their mothers. The fathers are almost totally absent. When a man (not necessary a father) is shown, he usually has a secondary role only. In all the 1951 issues there are only 18 photographs of men, mainly politicians or soldiers, and among them only two pictures representing a man who accompanies a child. Child care is thus unambiguously presented as divided, in an unspecified proportion, between mothers and specialised institutions.

6. The magazine's evolution from the 1950s to the late 1980s

October 1956 was a decisive date in post-war Poland – the end of the Stalinist period and the beginning of the rule of Wladyslaw Gomułka, which lasted until December, 1970. The regime remained, in the main, totalitarian, that is, it maintained the priority of political and ideological considerations in all domains of life[24]. However, magazines such as *Your Child* did not serve any longer as sites of direct and obvious propaganda by the regime. From 1957 on it seldom published programmatic texts, pictures of great communist leaders, or articles on political issues, while events such as the International Woman's Day, or the International Day of the Child were presented as good reasons for a happy celebration of the "socialist approach to human beings". At the same time, and especially during and immediately after the 'Polish October', editorials in the magazine mentioned "the period of errors and deviations" (a code name for the Stalinist era), the absence of close relations between the party leadership and the people, the need to rehabilitate the victims of the previous political period, deficient planning of the economy, which did not take human needs sufficiently into account, and the specific plight of mothers of small children. The latter theme included criticisms of low income, of a poor distribution system which induced shortages of food and of clothes in the shops, and of the insufficient number of day care centres and kindergartens. A typical article, published in October 1956, compared politicians to short-sighed parents who see only positive, and not negative signs of development in their child: they notice that the child is growing up, not that s/he is threatened by a deficiency disease.

In the later years of the Gomulka period, with the stabilisation of the new regime, direct political allusions disappeared from *Your Child*. The magazine continues to maintain a mainly apolitical line to this day. The sole exception was the support of the new "pro-family" orientation introduced in the early 1970s, with the beginning of Gierek's rule (Gierek headed the Polish Government between 1970 and 1981). The level of income of the population increased greatly in the early 1970s. At the same time the state introduced free medical insurance for peasants, and abolished the difference in health insurance regimes between physical and white collar workers. During this period women's waged work, seen as absolutely necessary for the state in the 1940s and 1950s, was seen as optional. In 1972 a resolution of the VI Congress of the Polish Communist Party explained that "women's employment, and the need to conciliate working hours with the important educational tasks of women, is a problematic issue".

---

[24] Firkowska-Mankiewicz *et al.*, *op. cit.*, note 1.

Women were therefore strongly encouraged to benefit from a three-year long, unpaid, "education leave" at the end of their paid maternity leave[25]. In parallel, the party proposed to facilitate early retirement in women-dominated occupations, the introduction of one free Saturday per month (until then, all workers were employed six days a week) and the development of services in the countryside. A *Your Child* article, commenting on this resolution, praised decisions which facilitated women's tasks as mother and as homemaker, and allowed her a better possibility to combine her duties as a worker and as a mother. The new law, the article proposed, could also facilitate the involvement of grandmothers in the care of their grandchildren.

In the early 1970s men were not presented as either co-responsible for family life or as co-educators of their children. Fathers mentioned in *Your Child* articles of that era were as a rule presented in the traditional roles of a 'model' for boys, and an 'object of admiration' for girls. In parallel, woman's role as homemaker was glorified in a style reminiscent of the 1950s Western 'feminine mystique' (frequently vilified in the West in the 1970s…). Mothers were presented as being responsible for the presence of a good atmosphere in their home, for the right behaviour of their spouses, and for the appropriate education of their sons. "A mother", an article published in *Your Child* explains, "brings warm feelings and understanding into the life of her son. She helps him to fulfil his goal to became a man like his father is, and she is his main support and guide in the difficult pathway which will lead him to adult manhood"[26]. "A man's feelings towards his children", another article explains, "depend mainly on the attitude of his wife. A woman needs to be warm, patient, understanding, and to have a good sense of humour in order to create a pleasant atmosphere in the family. Thanks to her efforts, the house becomes a true haven for her husband"[27]. The overall impression of the official attitudes to women during the communist period is of instrumentation of their role. The party viewed itself as entitled to decide what women really wanted. In the 1950s, when their labour force was seen as important to the state, women were asked to contribute to the "construction of socialism" by working outside the home, and in particular by taking "men's jobs". In the 1970s, when their work was no longer needed by the state, they were encouraged to view homemaking and child care as women's role and as their true vocation in life.

The first articles indicating a more substantial role for the father appeared in *Your Child* in the 1980s. Fathers were then encouraged to assist at their child's birth, to help

---

[25] *Twoje Dziecko* ("Your Child"), March 1972.
[26] *Twoje Dziecko* ("Your Child"), June 1972.
[27] *Twoje Dziecko* ("Your Child"), September 1972.

their wives to take care of the new-born babies, and later to be actively involved in child-rearing. At the same time, the magazine significantly increased the number of photographs which showed fathers with their children, and those of entire families. The new focus on the paternal role did not, however, modify the presentation of women as holding the main responsibility for the psychological well-being of the family and for the education of children. In the 1980s, the general trend was to move away from the public towards the private and the intimate; accordingly, woman's role as homemaker and as a mother acquired an even greater importance. Several articles published in *Your Child* at this time openly promoted the idea that women should give priority to their duties as mothers over their professional tasks. This trend was prolonged in the early 1990s. Facing the rise of unemployment following the collapse of the communist regime, some economists openly favoured solutions grounded in a gender-specific division of labour: "One should fix clear-cut rules, according to which, in a family with children, the man should be granted a waged labour, while the woman-mother should be responsible for household duties and for children's' education. The maintenance of this natural division of roles is an appropriate solution for the reduction in the number of available jobs"[28].

•••

Let now return to the main subjects discussed in the magazine in this period, namely the health and education of children. From its very inception *Your Child* was engaged in major campaigns against diseases (rickets, tuberculosis and other infectious diseases) and promoted health and hygiene: vaccinations, systematic health controls of pregnant women, newly-borns and small children, and appropriate feeding regimes. This trend continued in the 1960s and 1970s. Probably the most important health campaign, and one conducted practically without interruption in the magazine's 50 years of existence, was the energetic promotion of breast-feeding.

From the earlier to the most recent issues of *Your Child* breast-feeding was presented as having a highly beneficial effect on the child's health and well-being. In the 1950s and 1960s, when the state accentuated the importance of women's professional work, the magazine simultaneously strongly promoted breast-feeding, and gave advice on how to collect the mother's milk to be used during her absence. At the same time, *Your Child* propagated a rigid model of feeding babies, and strict adherence to pre-determined hours. In the 1970s, the articles on this subject de-dramatised the issue of rapid loss of milk by the mother, and explained that maternal milk could be readily

---

[28] Michalik, *op. cit.*, note 12, p. 158.

replaced by its substitutes. However, in the 1980s, and especially in the 1990s, the magazine again launched an energetic campaign in favour of breast feeding, this time, on child demand, without proposing strict feeding hours. This campaign was conducted under the slogan "food (mother's milk) and love". At the end of the 1980s and the beginning of the 1990s the journal conducted a spectacular and highly effective initiative entitled, "to give birth in human conditions". This programme helped bring about significant improvements in obstetric clinics and encouraged mothers to demand more respect for their rights as human beings and as patients. One of its consequences was propaganda in favour of home births.

However, the articles published in *Your Child* in this period were not limited to discussing the physical well-being of children. One of the consequence of the magazine's new sensibility to broader health issues was the visibility of handicap, and especially of mental handicap. The problem of children with disabilities first appeared in *Your Child* in the 1960s. At that time, self-help groups fighting for education and support for their intellectually disabled children were spontaneously created, thanks to the determination of the parents of such children. For many years these self-help groups were the only independent parents' movement in socialist countries. In the 1970s the magazine started to present more systematically and objectively the problems of children with disabilities. Articles on this topic, published under the heading "they are among us", argued that disabled children not only had right to be among us but that they and their families also had the right to happiness and to our respect and necessary support.

Other articles displayed, in parallel, a constant concern about children's education and psychological well being, the ways their personality develops within their family, and their adjustment to life in society. Professional psychological guidance provided by the magazine's experts aimed both at helping parents deal with educational problems and at working for the improvement of parental skills and the promotion of a happy family life (for example, a long series of articles on marital conflicts). Texts analysing the role of grandmothers initially presented them simply as temporary caregivers, for example, when parents were working. Articles published in the 1970s and 1980s stressed, by contrast, that parents and grandparents have different, and distinct tasks, which should not be confused. Another 1980s innovation was the publication of articles on legal problems related to family life such as divorce and alimony, mistreatment of children by family members, or denial of paternity.

To sum up, the main change in the 1960s, 1970s and 1980s was the disappearance of the 1950s identification of a healthy child with a happy child, and its replacement by a more complicated perception of all the elements which may affect the harmonious development of a child.

Danuta Duch-Krzystoszek - Anna Firkowska-Mankiewicz

7. Your Child in the post-communist era

In 1989, following the disappearance of the magazine's original publisher, the editorial board of *Your Child* managed to convince the publishers of the prestigious journal *Res Publica* to 'adopt' *Your Child*, a decision which turned out to be highly profitable for the new publishers. Regardless of the fact that in the 1990s *Your Child* has lost its monopolistic position in the market (three other magazines for parents, sponsored by foreign editors, are now sold in Poland) it continues to be a commercial success, and 150,000 copies are sold every month. Unlike its competitors which imitate Western publications, *Your Child* has remained a totally Polish enterprise. It acquired, however, a new, more modern image: bigger volume (from 16 pages during 1951-1989 to 100 and more pages later on), numerous glossy photos and – *signum temporis* – numerous advertisements.

If one compares the 1950s issues of *Your Child* with those of the 1990s, the main difference, besides the obvious difference in the external 'look' of the journal, is the totally apolitical character of the current magazine. It is true that, once the early 'militant' period of the communist regime was over, the editorial board of *Your Child* was able to achieve a relative freedom from political and ideological pressures, thanks to its wise use of social techniques. Its relative autonomy reflected also the fact that this magazine almost never engaged in open anti-regime activities, and presented itself exclusively as a competent and tactful guide for parents, whose only aim was to help them to improve their children's health and psychological well-being. The magazine still deals mainly with health issues, defined, however, in a broad sense which includes psychosomatic and psychological determinants of health and illness.

In the 1990s the magazine *Your Child* is a well balanced publication, resilient to superficial, unverified methods of medical or psychological intervention and to the pressures of advertising companies. While publicity is crucial to the magazine's survival, *Your Child* supervises the quality of the advertisements its accepts: the products they promote need to conform to the journal's editorial policy and philosophy. For example, the journal advocates breast feeding, so that all publicity for baby food has to include the statement that the best food for infants is their mother's milk. It also refuses to publish publicity for alcohol and for tobacco products. The magazine's present policy also calls attention to the problem of the child as consumer. Advertising today is a very powerful agent creating unhealthy behaviour, especially among children and teenagers, creating tension between a 'happy' young consumer and current ideas about children's health. Up until now *Your Child* has effectively defended its readers from an alternative 'happy but not necessarily healthy' child, refraining from advertising cigarettes, alcohol, sweets and unhealthy food. But for how long?

Drinking as a Political Act: Images of Alcoholism in Polish Literature, 1956-89

Olga Amsterdamska

Polish literature – just like the Polish population – appears to be soaked in alcohol. The literary omnipresence of drinking, however, is not a mere reflection of the less-than-sober Polish reality of the post-war era of real socialism. Instead, alcohol functions as a polysemic trope which writers have put to 101 uses. Literary drinking constructs shared but often implicit cultural meanings, creates and undermines recognizable metaphors and symbols, confers social and individual identity to a variety of characters, or – used as a plotting device – unlocks the complexities of political and social life under the communist regime.

In the social science jargon of contemporary Poland, alcoholism appears as a "social pathology"; in the anti-alcoholic discourse of the Catholic Church, it is a worrisome sign of "moral disintegration which can result in the biological decline of the Nation"; in the eyes of doctors and psychiatrists, it is likely to be regarded as a disease or a psychiatric disorder, an underlying cause of other medical problems. No such unequivocal reductions, however, are possible when we examine the polyvalent significance of drinking in literary works of the Polish writers. It is this multiplicity of meanings that renders the analysis of drinking in literature interesting from the point of view of public health. For while I would not like to suggest that any individual Pole has ever been driven to drink by political considerations, or that the literary meanings and uses of alcohol are either a direct reflection or unique creators of sociocultural attitudes and beliefs, they do point to the complexities and ambivalences in the cultural understanding and explanation of alcoholism. In other words, just as the heterogeneous literary constructions of alcohol use and abuse do not create a single, unequivocal or even coherent "image" of alcoholism, so also the lay constructions of drunkenness and alcoholism constitute a patchwork of significances, a rich and multivocal repertoire of explanatory, justificatory and critical images, which the public health exhortations to "drink in moderation" or warnings that "alcohol kills" do not even begin to address.

Polish literature is of course not unique in its use of drinking as a symbol, metaphor, or literary device. The drinking habits of all manner of fictional characters signal much about their social class, ethnic, regional or national identities to the readers of French, English or American novels. Immoderate drinking as portrayed by Scott

Fitzgerald or Hemingway is used to reveal the character's psychological make-up, unconscious drives and desires, or attitudes to the social world. Drunkenness can be used to unmask the fragility or meaninglessness of social conventions, anomie, or social hypocrisy. As an element of the carnivalesque, drinking can turn the world upside down by suspending "all its hierarchical structure and all the forms of terror, reverence, piety and etiquette."[1]

The cultural meanings of many of the images of drinking that appear in post-war Polish literature fit well into these more universal categories, even if they acquire a specific local color. In the worlds created by some Polish writers, however, alcohol consumption assumes also a set of distinctly political meanings: it represents the sociopolitical world of "real socialism," lays bare its corruption and demoralization, posits its insoluble dilemmas, exposes the fictional naïveté of the propaganda world of the happy worker and peasant striving for a better future, and opposes a powerless (and drunk) "average Pole" to a powerful (and drunk) apparatchik. Polish literary drinking exposes and reaffirms the ambivalences of liberty, equality, and fraternity *à la polonaise*. In a single move, the bottle of Vodka Vistula portrayed on the cover of a 1980s oppositional novel represents a trusted means of preserving the existing social order and a symbolic Molotov-cocktail exploding the myths of the socialist realist paradise.

The politics of alcoholism in socialist Poland were thus embedded not only in the infamous police-operated "sobering stations," in the politically expedient anti-alcoholic campaigns, or in the economics of the alcohol trade, but also in the exploration of drinking as a parody of and a metaphor for Polish sociopolitical reality in the works of such writers as Marek Hłasko, Marek Nowakowski, Kazimierz Orłoś, and Tadeusz Konwicki. All four of these writers explored everyday life in socialist Poland. All of them, in one or another period of their activity, encountered difficulties with censorship, and many of the works I will be discussing had, prior to 1989, been only published abroad or in the so-called "second circuit" or samizdat. Whatever their other literary or aesthetic merits, they were understood and judged as political statements and associated with the opposition to the official culture of People's Poland. Though all of these writers were born in the 1930s, their literary debuts came in different periods: Konwicki began his publishing career already in 1945 (though the novel I will consider here – A *Minor Apocalypse* – dates from 1979). Nowakowski and Hłasko published their first works in the mid-1950s and were closely associated with the October thaw, de-Stalinization, and the turn away from the socialist realist canon of

---

[1] Bakhtin, *Problems…*, pp. 122-23.

the early 1950s. Despite the general relaxation of censorship in Poland in this period, Hłasko encountered publishing difficulties, and in 1958 he left Poland for good. He died in Germany in 1969. Nowakowski continued to work in Poland, but in the 1970s and 80s, he was publishing abroad and in the underground publishing houses. Orłoś's first publications date from the 1960s, but the novels we will examine here date from 1970 and 1985 – and neither of them appeared in the official publishing houses. Three of these authors – Orłoś, Konwicki, and Nowakowski – were associated with *Zapis*, the first independent (underground) literary magazine that began publication in 1976.

•••

Alcohol was, of course, present in Polish literature long before it came to symbolize the problems of real socialism. The images of drunken peasants in late nineteenth century novels, or Witkiewicz's promotion of drugs and alcohol as superior ways of viewing perverted reality, or Tuwim's celebration of drinking folklore and its elaborate language share little, however, with the metaphor of the "drunken motherland"[2] in which the general alcoholic excess sums up all the wrongs of the social and political reality. Initially, however, it was the government and its public health propaganda rather than the writers that defined drinking in political terms.

In 1955, one of the early signs of the coming post-Stalinist thaw was the publication of Adam Ważyk's *Poem for Adults*.[3] Ważyk's 16-part poetic cycle confronts the less-than-perfect reality of post-war reconstruction with the official party propaganda, which attributed all remaining Polish imperfections to politically inspired sabotage. In the official version of reality, drunkenness is just such a political problem, and Ważyk ironically contrasts the anti-alcoholic campaign – a poster which equates vodka with enemy diversion – with the gray and mundane reality of a train station buffet where young men travelling to build the new socialist "steel works" in Nowa Huta encounter a pretty and bored rather than evil barmaid, Miss Jadzia, who serves them vodka.

> At a train station buffet
> Miss Jadzia serves at the bar
> So pretty when she yawns
> So pretty when she pours
> WATCH OUT! THE ENEMY TEMPTS YOU WITH VODKA!

---

[2] Wierzyński, "Stabilizacj," p. 28.
[3] Ważyk, "Poemat dla Dorosłych," pp. 143-52.

You'll surely get poisoned here
Miss Jadzia will take off your shoes
So pretty when she yawns
So pretty when she pours
WATCH OUT! THE ENEMY TEMPTS YOU WITH VODKA!

Don't go to Nowa Huta, young man,
The poison will get you en route
May the national fish in you stomach
And the serpentine poster protect you:
WATCH OUT! THE ENEMY TEMPTS YOU WITH VODKA![4]

If the pretty barmaid can hardly make it as "the enemy", the villains remain unmentionable. It is only by implication that Ważyk points his finger at those responsible for "the great socialist enterprises" of the steel works in Nowa Huta, where thousands of dislocated peasant-workers had to show their devotion to the ideals of socialism by engaging in Stakhanovite feats of overproduction while living in substandard conditions, liberated from their families and the social constraints of their villages.

In Ważyk's indictment of Stalinism, the cardinal political problem is not the struggle with an ideological foe, as the authorities suggest, nor the political system itself, as later oppositional writers intimate, but the gap between the verbiage of the revolution and everyday reality. The official discourse on alcoholism serves here as just one example of the incongruity of the world and the word.[5]

---

[4] Ważyk, "Poemat dla Dorosłych," part 6, pp. 146-47.

[5] Ważyk thematizes the disparity between reality and its official representation also when the explicit connection with alcohol is absent:
"The dreamer Fourier had charmingly predicted
that lemonade will fill our seas.
And doesn't it?
They drink sea water,
called –
lemonade!
And secretly return home
to vomit.
Vomit. (Ważyk, "Poemat dla Dorosłych," part 12, p. 149.)
And in another poem from 1956, "It's Alcohol that Demoralizes Youth," Ważyk returns to the irrelevance of propaganda, using yet again the anti-alcoholic campaign as a synecdoche: "Parrots strangled in knotted ties are singing. People are hoarse like a travelling cinema, a magical poster whispers in a tram, that alcohol, alcohol is the cause..." (Ważyk, "To Alkohol Demoralizuje Młodzież," p. 157.)

While Ważyk satirizes the official politicization of vodka which was omnipresent in the anti-drinking campaigns of Stalinist Poland, prose writers of the 1956 "new wave", such as Hłasko and Nowakowski, can be read as embroidering on the official idea that drinking, drunkenness, and alcoholism have political meanings. But the "enemy" which alcohol helps them to identify is a reverse image of the enemy presented in the public health propaganda. In the process, the literary meanings and uses of alcohol multiply.

Hłasko's two novellas, *The Eighth Day of the Week* and *The Graveyard* (as well as many of his short stories I will not discuss here) are a rich store of such meanings of drinking.[6] Drinking functions there not just as a motif, but as an essential element of the plot.

As we learn in the first sentence of *The Graveyard*, its protagonist, middle-aged party activist Franciszek Kowalski, "drank vodka extremely rarely and only on extraordinary occasions; he never drank in excess of what he could hold, and never had to be told later by others what he had talked about and how he had behaved."[7] Franciszek makes an exception when he accidentally meets an old friend, a comrade from the wartime underground, and decides to celebrate with a glass of vodka. The glass stretches into a liter, and Franciszek is drunk when he starts making his way home. He sings, gets into a joking squabble with some workers standing on a bus stop, and after accidentally accusing a policemen of drunkenness gets arrested and taken to a police-run sobering station. A one-time drinking binge has gotten him into jail, and as Franciszek does not remember what he said to the police when he was angry about being arrested, he cannot answer the accusation that he expressed some antigovernment feelings. He is released the next morning, but as he attempts to deal with his "error" in manner that his party morality dictates to him, he discovers the hypocrisy of his party bosses (who are willing to use their influence to protect him, but throw him out of the party and the job when he attempts to deal with his problem in an honest and open manner), the priority of political expediency over family considerations (once he is declared a traitor, his son as well as the fiancé of his daughter walk away), the terrible fates and disappointments of his buddies from the underground, and so on. At the end of the novel, Franciszek is a homeless, lonely drunk, free of his political illusions. The assurances of the policeman who reveals to him that he had said nothing objectionable on that first evening when he was arrested are by now irrelevant. Even if "the truth has turned out to be even stupider than [he] suspected,"[8] he was wiser now. And now he

---

[6] Both novellas have been translated into English: Hłasko, *The Graveyard*, and *The Eighth Day of the Week*. I cite here from the original Polish editions; all translations are my own.

[7] Hłasko, "Cmentarze," p. 97.

[8] Hłasko, "Cmentarze," p. 237.

could honestly answer the policeman's question – no, he does not like it here... And that, of course, lands him in jail again.

Seemingly, in Hłasko's version of the education of a naive believer, alcohol is only a literary device – it is after all not alcohol, but sober attempts to deal with police intervention that open the protagonists' eyes to the political reality of Stalinism. And yet, the political significance of drinking in Hłasko's novel is more complex. To begin with, just like kings' jesters and fools, drunks are expected by everyone to be telling the truth.[9] The ancient assumption of *in vino veritas* has now been taken up by the police state. No matter how emphatically Franciszek denies that whatever he supposedly shouted while drunk was not what he really believes – his drunk pronouncements are taken by the policemen, by his cell-mates met in the sobering station, by his party superiors, and even by his son, as expressions of his deeply held, even if soberly and strategically concealed, opinions. As the sergeant at the police station assures Franciszek, "what a sober man has in his heart, the drunk one has on his tongue."[10]

In *The Graveyard*, it is not "an enemy that tempts you with vodka" but vodka that reveals the enemy within you. And while Hłasko maintains his ironic distance from this popular idea, vodka eventually does render Franciszek free of political constraint, and therefore, truthful. As a party member, he was naive and all too willing to close his eyes to what was happening in his factory; as a drunk, he can diagnose clearly what is wrong: "every tyranny ends more or less like a woman's beauty: the more magnificent the facade, the more rot inside, the prettier the dress, the more squalid the body; the more talk about strength and loyalty, the more terror and the weaker those who rule."[11]

And not only does alcohol dissolve Franciszek's delusions, it also makes him no longer afraid. To be a drunk is to have the freedom others are denied:

> "Each of us thinks he has done nothing", he said. "Each one of us, one way or another, thinks, he is innocent. But a moment comes, when others begin to have power over us, and then it no longer matters what we think about ourselves and what's important is only what they think about us". He sighed and turned on his side. "Thank God," he said, "that I am

---

[9] Bakhtin discusses the history of this association of drink, food and ability to speak the truth in his discussion of literary imagery of banquets: "The banquet with its variations was the best milieu for absolutely fearless and gay truth. Bread and wine disperse fear and liberate the word... Wine liberates from fear and sanctimoniousness" (Bakhtin, *Rabelais and His World*, pp. 287-88).

[10] Hłasko, "Cmentarze," p. 126.

[11] Hłasko, "Cmentarze," p. 235.

only a drunkard. This is the only thing that gives me some insurance; if someone will think something about me, it will be just that one thing."[12]

In his novella, Hłasko seems to present a choice facing Poles: you can live a lie, be a swine and a puppet, or you can be a drunk. This is the lesson Franciszek takes from his visits to his various colleagues from the wartime communist underground – only one of whom, the heavily drinking Painter, sees the failure of the ideals he fought for. This claim and variations upon it are rehearsed also in other works by Hłasko, as well as in some stories by Nowakowski.

A different version of this impossible choice is most explicitly – though only as an aside – stated in another of Hłasko's novellas, *The Eighth Day of the Week*. It is spoken by a nameless drunk at one of the many bars where much of the action of the novella takes place: "I am leaving this place. In this country one can only be a drunkard or a hero. Normal people have nothing to do here. Adieu."[13] Heroes are presumably those who can somehow maintain their integrity in world in which integrity can only get you hurt. The protagonists of Hłasko's *Eighth Day of the Week* are not able to do so.

To be only slightly unfair, Hłasko's novella can be read as an explanation of how housing shortage leads to alcoholism: in the cramped living arrangements of contemporary Poland, a young woman, Agnieszka, who has not yet abandoned the hope of transcending the limited world of her parents and neighbors, cannot find a place where she and her lover can meet. Nameless drunks accost her and her lover on the streets; a drunken friend frustrates their date by failing to vacate an apartment. As Agnieszka's search for privacy is continually frustrated, she herself turns to drink, goes to bed with a stranger accidentally encountered in a bar, and – having compromised her "pure love" and abandoned her illusions – breaks up with her lover. The theme of pure feelings degraded and devalued by everyday reality – in which alcohol now appears as a cause rather than a response to degradation – is repeated in the story of Agnieszka's disillusioned brother, who drinks immoderately and continuously while hopelessly waiting for a decision of a married woman he loves. She decides not to leave her husband when she discovers her lover drinks. And – if the message were not yet clear enough – it is repeated in a subplot in which another young man, a lodger in the apartment Agnieszka shares with her quarrelling parents and brother, does manage to get together with his girl only because he does not know – or chooses not to know – about her recent drunken infidelity. Or, as Agnieszka's drunken brother explains to her:

---

[12] Hłasko, "Cmentarze," p. 117.
[13] Hłasko, "Ósmy Dzień Tygodnia," p. 24.

"This is the twentieth century, Agnieszka: Isolde lives in a bordello, while Tristan drinks with pimps on a street corner. Today, people have no time for great passions: they get up in the morning, sip their soups in dairy bars, crowd in the trams, buy cheap furniture on installment, quarrel with conductors over five cents, and so on."[14]

In Hłasko's story alcohol mediates and marks the distinction between "real" and "ersatz" passions in a setting in which, literally and figuratively, there is no place for authenticity and people drink to forget (or is it forge?) their illusions. Alcohol anesthetizes, makes the fake appear real and renders reality fake. In all these respects alcohol is a response to the indefinite problems of the time. But while Hłasko does not openly associate alcohol with authenticity, it is precisely while drunk that the protagonists are best able to diagnose their own situations. While drunk, Agnieszka's brother mercilessly analyzes the world around him, the ins and outs of intoxication, and his own personal and political failure. And, it also while drunk that Agnieszka defines her "ideal of life without illusions and myths":

– "You are doing your master's?"
– "In philosophy. An occupation which consists in infallible explanation of life phenomena. Comical, isn't it? And you?"
– "A journalist. An occupation which consists in writing complete and honest truth. Comical, isn't it? Among the three of us, it's Elzbieta who is the best placed. Simply a whore. An occupation without miracles and illusions."
– "It's not an occupation," said Agnieszka. She smiled. "It's a morality. Uncamouflaged whore is the highest morality achievable by today's woman."[15]

In the structure of his novella, Hłasko uses drinking to raise universal "existential" and psychological issues and relates it only loosely to the specific social and political conditions, but the drunk characters in Hłasko's novella also comment on the specific significance of alcohol in Poland. We are not told whether the hypocrisies of journalism or philosophy are specific to mid-century Poland, but it is clear that the significance of vodka is. As Agnieszka's brother imagines an appropriate icon for Poland, drinking becomes a national trait:

– "Jeanne d'Arc represents France," said Piotr. "The Americans would like the Statute of Liberty to represent their democracy. Russia has been imagined as a bear. And Poland?"
[…]

---

[14] Hłasko, *ibid.*, p. 25.
[15] Hłasko, *ibid.*, p. 84.

> – "I think about it sometimes," he said. "You know?" – he pointed to the drunks –, "Such a guy in a cheapo suit for 600 zloty. Slightly drunk. In an enormous waiting room. Without a schedule of arrivals and departures. And to make the image complete, in his left hand he could hold "The King Spirit" [Polish romantic poem]. In the right had, a bottle, for balance."[16]

The drinking of Agnieszka's brother also has a local political dimension, for he drinks not only to forget his disappointments in love but also to forget his political past:

> – "Explain to me, how one is to forget the past, what one lived by, how one acted towards others?"...
> – "But you did nothing wrong."
> – "I had no power. I had only fanaticism. I was a swine within my own small reach. I tried as hard as I could. That also means something. It's easier to cleanse off the big mistakes, than the petty nasty things one did, I swear. I was a party secretary at my own university. I expelled guys from the university only because they had an aunt in Pernambuco or because their great-grandfather was a tsarist spy. I tried as hard as I could, believe me. And now I want to know: where am I? Am I a swine or a hero?"...
> – "You won't discover it here in the bar. Besides, there is always the idea – wise and just."
> – "That's true. But it is the weakness of every wise idea that fools try to realize it."
> – "It's all words", said Agnieszka. "[...] You're looking for excuses to drink...."[17]

Grzegorz's unanswered question as to whether he is a swine or a hero contains an unspoken third term, not included in his dichotomy – for rather than being either a swine or a hero, he can choose to be a drunkard who stands outside the normal moral and political choices. "A drunk in Poland is treated as a case apart, drunkenness is a new, special morality. Because every one knows that when a man drinks, something is bothering him."[18]

Though authenticity is not to be found in Agnieszka's and Grzegorz's world, drinking does offer Hłasko's protagonists fraternity and equality, which, even if they are not altogether genuine, surpass those which can be found in the sober world. And so, not only do "drunks hug each other," "shout, sing, call each other names, drink bruderschaft, exchange kisses and handshakes,"[19] but it is only over vodka that Agnieszka's

---

[16] Hłasko, *ibid.*, p. 79.

[17] Hłasko, *ibid.*, p. 60.

[18] Hłasko, *ibid.*, p. 27.

[19] Hłasko, *ibid.*, p. 22.

brother is able to talk honestly to his old-time friend and now political opponent. Vodka, like tiredness, is the one thing that unites the Poles.[20] Over vodka fraternity is possible and political differences cease to matter, even if they re-emerge only a few hours later when the two ex-friends meet in the office of the secret police.

Just as drinking creates fraternity, so also vodka can work as a social equalizer. And even though there are clear differences between "the downtown inns where the elite is having fun, and those establishments where petty bureaucrats bring their vodka in briefcases and open it under the table,"[21] late in the night these differences cease to matter because everyone – whether educated, powerful, and well-off or poor and marginalized – comes together to finish off their drinking in a sleazy "giant barrack," where usually peasants who bring vegetables to town come to drink:

> There was a crowd by the buffet; an atmosphere of a joyous dawn. A tall, man with salt and pepper hair and a lofty face, dressed in a well-fitting suit English wool, was slapping the shoulder of a young man who looked like a beginning cutthroat. The tall man spoke loudly:
> – "I am just a regular fellow. From Wola. Before the war I would go to Cinema Roxy.
>   I liked cowboy movies. One could see them in Wola. You know Stasiek Malinowski?"
> – "No," replied the fellow wrinkling his low forehead.
>   The grayish man beamed.
> – "You see. You see. God, those were terrible times! There was hunger. There was poverty.
>   No way to find a job…" With a grand gesture he raised his hand.
> – "Madam!" he said to the barmaid. "Princess! A round for everybody. On my account.
>   We will all drink to the workers' Wola." He turned to the young man. "I am Andrzej, and you?"
> – "Kazik."
>   The grayish man clapped his hands.
> – "Give me a kiss." He handed a glass to the young man. "Your health, Kazik. And to Wola."[22]

And thus, alcohol achieves what the ideology and practice of socialism failed to bring about: it bridges the enormous social distance between a well-dressed architect and a local cutthroat from the workers' part of town. And even if the equality thus brought about is certainly temporary, it is, nonetheless, more genuine than its ritualistic invocation in the toast to the "workers' Wola."

---

[20] Hłasko, *ibid.*, p. 59.

[21] Hłasko, *ibid.*, p. 56.

[22] Hłasko, *ibid.*, pp. 62-63.

In the post-1956 literature of "small realism" the theme of drinking as the basis of fraternity – or if one prefers, as the lowest common denominator of sociability – in an anomic society returns almost compulsively. It is, for example, omnipresent in the short stories of Nowakowski, who since the mid-50s has composed vignettes of contemporary life not only on the criminal margins of Polish society but also in the working class, bureaucratic, and "small business" milieus living, usually, on the outskirts of Warsaw and attempting to "manage" (whether just to make ends meet or actually to "make it big") in their banal and sordid environment.[23] While much of the drinking that goes on in Nowakowski's stories seems to be just as meaningless, pointless, and normatively neutral as any other activity that his bored and resigned characters routinely engage in, no social occasion seems ever to be complete without large quantities of alcohol, and those few who do not drink are portrayed as outcasts – heartless, calculating, and ultimately alone in their financial success and social failure. In the short story "The Head", for example, the protagonist cannot be trusted because although he was "excellent as a host, cordial, exchanging a kind word with everyone, and offering food; himself, he took only small sips, and would never get drunk. He did not like vodka, cold-blooded skunk."[24]

This does not mean, however, that the fraternity created by drinking is a lasting or a real one. Often enough, it is just as instrumental or strategic as other social relations in Nowakowski's Poland. Vodka can accidentally bring together people who belong to different social worlds before they float away yet again into their separate lives, and it allows for fellowship because only while drunk can they jointly express their frustrations, or their feelings of enslavement and failure. After a long day of drinking, the employees of an underground warehouse and a restaurant serving foreigners "greedily sipped the last remains of cognac in their glasses. Each one for a different reason. The manager Czesiek did it because of nostalgia and sadness difficult to express; Kichawa, the director of the nightclub, because of his wonderful Parisian memories. Spuchalak and Kolos drank to the barmaid, Olka Zwierz."[25] In "Hades," as one of the characters explains, vodka is "the deafener" – "if you don't drink the entire order in your head falls apart and one piece knocks against another. You don't know what fits with what... But once you drink something..."[26]

---

[23] See, for example, Nowakowski's stories in such collections as *Zapis, Gdzie Jest Droga na Walne?* or *Benek Kwiaciarz.*

[24] Nowakowski, *Zapis*, pp. 26-35, p. 31.

[25] Nowakowski, "Hades," p. 294.

[26] *Ibid.*, p. 262.

But if Nowakowski's disappointed and demoralized characters drink out of power-lessness and lack of control over their own dismal lives, and drink to mute their disappointments, drinking also gives them insight into their miserable condition and occasionally a sense of power and freedom they do not have in their sober lives.

In "One Day in Europe,"[27] as in many of Nowakowski's stories, drinking begins early in the day and continues well into the night as a motley group of buddies and acquaintances moves from a hotel cafe to its bar and then to a restaurant, a veterans' club brimming with war veterans, officers of the security police, partisans, and party faithful. A middle-aged writer gets carried along with the generally dissolute company, and takes part in the drinking and in the pointless chatter seemingly without a will of his own. As one vodka follows another, his mood changes from easy conviviality to aggressive disdain for the surrounding crowd. It is only when he is thoroughly drunk that he stages a minor political provocation by first initiating an anti-Semitic conversation, and then, after hearing his companions warm up to the subject, getting up to toast "the health and prosperity of the Polish officer Menachem Begin." And as he explains, "Why a toast for Begin! I don't care a fig for Begin. But nothing I hate more than this damn unanimity about everything. I do not want to belong to this choir. That's why it was Begin."[28] In Nowakowski's story, alcohol returns an individual voice to his narrator-protagonist-alter ego, and frees him both from the constraints of the pretended political consensus and from the etiquette of drunken fellowship. At the same time, however, the consumed vodka frees him the responsibility for his own voice. Once drunk, he is no longer accountable. As his friend explains to the Club's manager ready to detain him for the "provocation": "Comrade, the man is simply tired and got mixed up [...] One shouts all sorts of things when drunk."[29] In Hłasko's Poland of the early 1950s, when the regime still seemed to want to discipline souls and not only behavior, even an accusation of having shouted something against the state when drunk was enough to ruin a life. In Nowakowski's Poland of the 1970s, when enforcement of ideological conformity gave way to the enforcement of political indifference, shouting "all sorts of things when drunk" is grudgingly tolerated. Just as in the 1950s, the drunken pronouncements are taken to reveal what a person really thinks, only now the powers-that-be no longer care what one thinks, as long as one's behavior and words conform to their demands. But if so, it is not surprising that to the inebriated, but perceptive protagonist, even the drunken ability to speak the truth does not change the sense of failure:

---

[27] Nowakowski, "Jeden Dzień w Europie," pp. 7-57.

[28] *Ibid.*, p. 51.

[29] *Ibid.*, p. 52.

I still had so much to say. To myself. To others. The need to throw up everything. Infinite stream of words. […] And it was impossible to say. Once spoken, it immediately became anemic, unimportant. Missed. The broken wings of my literature. The trampled bird, that beats its wings against the ground. So much grief, anger, hatred. So much about literature. I also thought of the authorities, that trample and dirty literature. […] Empty words multiply like worms. […]

– "I am a loser," I said. And I did not want to be alone in this loss, so I added, "We are all losers."[30]

In Nowakowski's stories from the 1970s and 80s, just as in the novels of Orłoś and Konwicki, it is no longer only the losers, the misfits, or those too weak to oppose the regime while sober, that drink compulsively. The drunken party apparatchiks, prosecutors, and government officials seem to be subject to the same enslavement to alcohol, though their drinking is usually presented as a mark of unfettered freedom. While the drinking of the "common man" is portrayed as a response to an unsatisfactory social reality, a "deafener", or a futile means of achieving freedom, fraternity, and equality, the drinking of the party bosses serves as a mark of virtually uncontrolled power. Those in power drink because they are free to do so, and can enjoy alcoholic excess with impunity. In Nowakowski's "Two Days with the Angel"[31] the alcoholic and insatiable local prosecutor Angel lords it over his subordinates, his clients, and the Europeanized attorney from Warsaw. He fails to appear in court, buys illegal moonshine, and makes arbitrary decisions with the assurance of an absolute ruler. It is not clear why Angel drinks, but he surely does it with abandon, and has the power to impose alcohol on others less eager to indulge. To Angel and those like him, alcohol is not only a sign of power, but also a means of extending freedom from all constraint and creating fraternity which would otherwise be politically and socially unthinkable.

In Orłoś's *Magical Den*[32] the virtually unrestrained power of the members of the party and government elite in a small provincial town is signaled as much by their freedom to organize drunken orgies as by their ability to engage in black market trade, build public toilets on the private lot of a poor carpenter, use public funds for their own profit, or order arbitrary arrests. They seem always able to shift responsibility away from themselves, to transform one drunken reality into another one more advantageous to them. When a drunken party secretary runs over a pedestrian postman, the

---

[30] *Ibid.*

[31] Nowakowski, "Dwa Dni z Aniołem," pp. 58-99.

[32] Orłoś, *Cudowna Melina.*

official account blames the postman for causing the accident while drunk. In these local party circles, drinking is the sine qua non of membership, and the chairman of the local government, the single "honest" man occupying an important position in the town, is perceived as a "stranger" and an "outsider" precisely because he does not drink. As he complains to his friend "drink, one has to drink. Only then you're one of them. And I don't drink."[33]

In the world of *The Magical Den* the privileges of drunkenness are, however, not equally distributed. The license to be drunk does not extend to those who want to expose the local corruption: the chairman and his fatally alcoholic friend, who pretends to be a reporter working for a Warsaw newspaper and whose snooping around makes the local elite profoundly uncomfortable. In the end, the attempt to expose the party bosses fails precisely because of the pretended-reporter's inability to stay away from alcohol.

While in Hłasko's world, becoming a drunk was the third way, open to those Poles who were too honest to accede to the corrupt world and yet too weak, too alone, and too disillusioned to oppose it soberly; Nowakowski's and Orłoś's portrayals of the drunken elites alongside the drunken masses present drinking not as an option, but as virtually the only way of life. The focus is no longer on the difference between those who do and those who do not turn to vodka, but rather on the manner in which social and political inequalities are expressed in distinct patterns of drinking. And thus, those "on top" not only consume different kinds of alcohol and do so in different places than those on the bottom of the social ladder, but their indulgence has few unpleasant consequences beyond the fact that it leads to a hangover and stimulates a craving for more alcohol.

Such use of drinking as a metaphor for the entire Polish social and political reality seems to achieve its grotesque culmination in two novels written in the last decade of the communist regime: Konwicki's *Minor Apocalypse*[34] and Orłoś's *The Depot*.[35]

Just like in Hłasko's *The Graveyard*, in Orłoś's 1983 novella *The Depot*, drinking and the institutions associated with it serve as central elements of the plot. In both works the manner in which drinking is being dealt with by the political authorities serves as a literary device for deconstructing the sociopolitical reality of communist Poland. But the differences between the two novellas are telling. Whereas Hłasko tells the story of an honest man who falls but in the process comes to understand better the world in which he lives, Orłoś's story is an account of how those who have fallen try

---

[33] *Ibid.*, p. 154.

[34] Konwicki, *Mała Apokalipsa*. For the English translation see *A Minor Apocalypse*.

[35] Orłoś, *Przechowalnia*.

jointly to reform the world which mistreats them, and in the process free themselves, if only temporarily, from their enslavement to drink.

Józef Kamieniak, one of the protagonists of *The Depot*, bears some similarity to Franciszek Kowalski, the ill-fated hero of *The Graveyard*. Both maintain an ideological commitment to communism and both are defeated by drinking and the cunning world of communist officialdom. Orłoś's hero, Kamieniak, also known as "Marx," is a former official in a local government who has lost his position and has been abandoned by his family because of his drinking. When the story begins, Kamieniak, who has just received his monthly pension, promptly goes drinking, and eventually finds himself detained by the police and transferred to the sobering station, known in the local slang as "the depot." At the station, Kamieniak encounters its thoroughly drunk and debauched employees, gets beaten up, and has his remaining money stolen by the staff which operates the depot as a business venture and regularly robs its unwilling clients. While the grim and mechanically ideological police guardians of Franciszek Kowalski seemed to be mostly interested in what he says (and in scaring him to enforce unanimity), the alcoholic managers, nurses, and doctors who "take care" of Józef Kamieniak are mostly interested in what he has – since what he has can be stolen.

Since Kamieniak's treatment at the depot is by no means unique, the story he tells his fellow-drunkards after his release generates much sympathy and a joint decision on the part of the "antisocial element" (otherwise known as the local drunks) to protest their systematic mistreatment and the robbery which take place at the depot. The protest takes the form of a manifesto and of a boycott of the local drinking holes and liquor stores. As the sudden sobriety in the town cuts off the flow of income for the employees of the depot, the protest generates much concern in the local party and government circles, and the initially successful action fails when the authorities arrange to bring into town a contingent of drunks from a neighboring city. Their solidarity broken, the drunks return to the bars, while the leaders of the anti-socialist disturbances land in prison.

In Orłoś's tale of the heroic revolt of the drunks, the world of those who drink with impunity encounters the world of those for whom drinking is an expression of powerlessness. The confrontation of these two drunken worlds, a confrontation in which the victory of those already in power seems never to be really in question, serves as a rather transparent, if ironic, metaphor for the grand Polish political confrontations of the early 1980s.

Alcoholism is no longer either a consequence of political disappointment or a perverse manner of achieving the liberty, equality, and fraternity denied in the sober world. Instead, drunkenness in its many avatars diagnoses the disease of the entire society: of those on top as well as those on the bottom, of the rulers, the ruled, and those who now come together to revolt against the existing order. In the days and in the aftermath of Solidarity, it turns out that the revolt of the powerless drunks need not be an individual endeavor…

The metaphor of a "drunken motherland" was, as we have already seen, not new in the late 1970s. Hłasko called on it in 1956, Wierzyński used it in a 1968 poem, and the expression "drunken Poland" had, by the 70s and 80s, become something of a banality. The grotesque Poland of the future portrayed in Konwicki's *A Minor Apocalypse* seems to be a literary embodiment and specification of this idea. The novel, which narrates the last day in the life of an oppositional writer who has been asked by his fellow dissidents to set himself on fire in a gesture of symbolic protest, never fails to remind us that everybody in this half-Polish, half-Soviet Warsaw remains perpetually drunk. In addition to signaling the constant presence of unidentified drunk passers-by and onlookers, the wandering writer encounters drunk milk carriers, drunk dissidents, drunk plumbers, black marketeers, party bosses, mothers taking their babies for a walk, artists, movie directors, policemen and secret service agents, cloakroom attendants, intellectuals, cooks, retired party activists and newly rich on the make, doctors on duty in the hospital and their patients, musicians, demonstrators, priests, and elderly gurus of the opposition… But if in this rendition of the Polish landscape, drunkenness appears as one of the many signs of the general disintegration and malaise, alcohol is also the one inalienable right,[36] the basis of all sociability, and the only common denominator in a society in which even political opposition seems to be cut from the same cloth as the rest of society and its regime. Against this drunken background, the only remedy for the protagonist's perpetual hangover (which, incidentally, seems to occur also without drinking) appears to be the staging of a symbolic self-immolation. In Konwicki's novel, there is no longer a distinction to be made between sobriety and drunkenness, between the drunkenness of those on top and those on the bottom of society, or between reality and illusion.

In the worlds created by the Polish writers, drinking and the social arrangements for dealing with alcoholism became multipurpose ideological and political symbols. Their precise meaning was changing in tandem with the political circumstances in post-1956 Poland and paralleled political and social changes in society and in the structure and ideology of the political opposition which moved from the idea of internal party reform (revisionism) to the notion of a civil society and solidarity as a mode of seemingly hopeless resistance.

Drinking was continuously portrayed as a "normal" response to abnormal conditions, and given the politicization of all aspects of everyday life, alcohol became a tool for

---

[36] Konwicki, *Mała Apokalipsa*, p. 204.

revealing the truth behind the distortions of the official reality. At the same time, the literary portrayals of alcohol and immoderate drinking followed the changes in the political situation in Poland and changes in the nature of political opposition. In Ważyk's and Hłasko's attempts to capture the distortions of Stalinism, alcohol is a used mainly to contrast the world of propaganda with the world of everyday life, reflecting in its crooked mirror also the official public health propaganda which presented excessive drinking as a form of political diversion. In Nowakowski's stories alcohol is "a deafener." It's indulged in by everyone, for it creates an illusion of freedom, equality, and fraternity in a society in which "making it" by whatever means and at whatever price is the only concern. And while alcohol frees one from convention and political constraint, such freedom is now also meaningless and illusory. Nowakowski's uses of alcoholic imagery provide an ironic comment on Gomułka's years of "little stabilization". But the same irony is also an unwitting commentary on the official anti-alcholic propaganda which in the 1960s and 70s pursued its cause by telling people how expensive and financially ruinous for a family an alcohol habit can be. In the novels of the late 1970s and early 80s, alcoholic excess changed its meaning yet again. It became yet another element of the grotesque status quo and it reflected the apparent impotence of those who supported the system and benefited from it, as well as of those who opposed it.

As Polish writers explored the literary potential of alcohol, drinking ceased to be an issue in its own right and became a multivocal symbol and symptom of a sick political reality. It remained immune from any of the various "scientific" or "medical" interpretations of alcoholism and did its work as a reverse mirror image of the no less politicized images of alcoholism peddled by the public health authorities.

Bibliography

Bakhtin, Mikhail, *Problems of Dostoevsky's Poetics*, trans. Caryl Emerson, Minneapolis, University of Minnesota Press, 1984.

· Bakhtin, Mikhail, *Rabelais and His World*, trans. Helene Isvolsky, Cambridge, Massachusetts Institute of Technology Press, 1968.

Hłasko, Marek, "Cmentarze," in *Ósmy Dzień Tygodnia. Cmentarze*, in *Dzieła Zebrane*, Warsaw, Da Capo, 1994 [orig. 1958].

Hłasko, Marek, *The Eighth Day of the Week*, trans. Norbert Guterman, New York, E.P. Dutton, 1958.

Hłasko, Marek, *The Graveyard*, trans. Norbert Guterman, New York, E.P. Dutton, 1959.

Hłasko, Marek, "Ósmy Dzień Tygodnia," in *Ósmy Dzień Tygodnia. Cmentarze*, in *Dzieła Zebrane*, Warsaw, Da Capo, 1994 [orig. 1957].

Konwicki, Tadeusz, *Mała Apokalipsa*, Warsaw, Niezależna Oficyna Wydawnicza Nowa, 1997 [orig. 1979].

Konwicki, Tadeusz, *A Minor Apocalypse*, trans. Richard Lourie, New York, Aventura, 1984.

Nowakowski, Marek, *Benek Kwiaciarz*, Warsaw, Czytelnik, 1961.

Nowakowski, Marek, "Dwa Dni z Aniołem", in *Dwa Dni z Aniołem*, Paris, Instytut Literacki, 1984, pp. 58-99.

Nowakowski, Marek, *Gdzie Jest Droga na Walne?* Warsaw, Państwowy Instytut Wydawniczy, 1979.

Nowakowski, Marek, "Hades," in *Fortuna Liliputa*, Warsaw, Wydawnictwo Alfa, 1997 [orig. 1978], pp. 243-304.

Nowakowski, Marek, "Jeden Dzień w Europie," in *Dwa Dni z Aniołem*, Paris, Instytut Literacki, 1984, pp. 7-57.

Nowakowski, Marek, *Zapis*, Warsaw, Państwowy Instytut Wydawniczy, 1965.

Orłoś, Kazimierz, *Cudowna Melina*, Paris, Instytut Literacki, 1973.

Orłoś, Kazimierz, *Przechowalni*a, London, Puls Publications, 1985.

Ważyk, Adam, "To Alkohol Demoralizuje Mlodzież," in *Wiersze i Poematy*, Warsaw, Państwowy Instytut Wydawniczy, 1957, p. 157.

Ważyk, Adam, "Poemat dla Dorosłych," in *Wiersze i Poematy*, Warsaw, Państwowy Instytut Wydawniczy, 1957, pp. 143-52.

Wierzyński, Kazimierz, "Stabilizacja," in *Czarny Polonez,* Paris, Instytut Literacki, 1968, p. 28.

Community and Individual Changes in Propaganda against Alcoholism in Poland from 1945 to the 1990s

Justyna Laskowska-Otwinowska

Alcohol abuse appeared in Poland immediately after the generalisation of the technology for the distillation of vodka. Previously, Poles drank mainly beer and honey-alcohol. The higher social strata – the aristocracy, the royal court and the upper clergy – also imported wine and tokai, primarily from regions of the Kingdom of Hungary, which had multiple trade relations with Poland stimulated by the fact that the royal families in these two countries were related. The introduction of a stronger alcohol into a society not previously acquainted with the use of such alcohol, almost automatically leads to addiction; one may recall the spread of alcoholism among the Indians of North America, or among the Mongols during the dominance of the Soviet Union. Poland was not an exception to this rule, and already centuries ago the problem of excessive alcohol consumption had ethical and political connotations.

From the very beginning, propaganda against alcoholism contained an ethical element. The Catholic church led the initiatives against alcohol abuse. The Church identified alcoholism above all with the sin of drunkenness. It appears, along with the sin of gluttony and other excesses, against the virtue of abstinence, especially important during the numerous periods of fasting. One may add that Poland was characterised by a great frequency of fast days (significantly higher than in the neighbouring Catholic countries). This high frequency of fast days may be connected with a specific traditional culture, characterised by an especially widespread cult of the Virgin and the saints, and by numerous Church holidays which, according to ethnographers' analyses, were superimposed on sacred days of cults of pagan origin. In parallel, alcohol was used in Poland to underline the importance of lay ceremonies: births and deaths, weddings, the construction of new houses, the opening of work facilities, initial stages of longer trips, and even commercial activities like trading, taking on new employees, and the end of a seasonal work, such as work in the fields. Such festive uses of alcohol have deep roots. Anthropologists explain that intoxicating substances (in Europe, mainly alcohol) are used as "road signs" indicating that at the given moment one is in contact with the sacred. Moreover, the intoxicating effect of alcohol is supposed to facilitate contacts with the sacred sphere. Reflecting on the genesis of the widespread excessive use of alcohol in Poland, we should take into account the high frequency of periods when everyday life events are made sacred in Poland. Seen in this light, the ethical element of the anti-alcohol propaganda of the Church takes on a multi-level dimension. It becomes associated with Polish culture – the culture of many fasts and numerous celebrations – not only in a formal way, but in a very concrete way as well.

The consumption of alcohol in Poland was also influenced by the country's economic conditions. Poland was an agricultural country almost up to World War II, densely populated, strongly differentiated in its social structure and in the distribution of material possessions. Polish agriculture was strongly stratified socially: huge land properties contrasted with a great number of poor households, and an important number of 'peasants without land' who had very limited opportunities to find employment in industry. An agricultural economy is especially sensitive to weather conditions. While the 'huge famines' remembered by Polish people are usually associated with World War II, many regions suffered each year from pre-harvests-periods of hunger induced by the exhaustion of reserves of food from the previous season[1].

Even outside hunger periods, food consumption was strictly regulated among the poor, the average farmers, and occasionally even among the affluent ones who respected local custom and a stringent standard of thriftiness. A sumptuous life style was especially ostracised among the Polish peasants, and no one dared to break this rule. Current studies conducted by nutritionists on the calorific content of peasants' meals indicate that such meals, even when relatively copious, often did not have a fully satisfactory nutritional value. Nutritionists also show that alcohol was a popular element of these meals. It was only by adding the calorific value of the alcohol consumed to a given meal that we obtain the energetic value of food needed by the organism during intensive work. I propose therefore that consumption of alcohol was a rationally justified (if not always conscious) way to supplement a calorific deficiency, and a true necessity for people constantly exposed to malnutrition. Drinking seems to have been the only way to survive for individuals who were often faced with hunger, and an acceptable way to cope with nutritional deficits. Until the mid-nineteenth century, alcohol frequently appears in the menus of charitable organisations, such as hospitals and hospices for the poor, as a supplement for calorie-deficienct meals. Similarly, administrators of labour colonies and saved money through decreasing the food rations of prisoners and deliberately substituting food by alcohol. Statistics given by nutritionists about the caloric intake in the Polish countryside thus shed new light

---

[1] J. Szetylla (ed.) *Nędza i dostatek na ziemiach polskich od średniowiecza do XX xieku,* Warszawa, Wyd. Semper, 1992.

on the problem of alcoholism in Poland and indicate a new way for viewing this problem, i.e. not only simply as a national defect (a Pole means a drunk), but also as a possible strategy for survival.

The economic and/or cultural justification for alcohol consumption notwithstanding, excessive drinking caused anxiety because of its great popularity. Alcohol abuse was not limited to the poorest strata of the population: it undoubtedly had the character of a national plague. As a result, a variety of arguments were used to fight alcoholism. Poland, a country torn for centuries by political and social unrest, is characterised by its ability to constantly adjust explanations and discourses to a current social and political orientation. Such explanations were often highly persuasive, especially in the absence of contradictory information. Thus, for example Mary Douglas proposes that the Polish rural population was conditioned to alcohol consumption by the landowners, a plausible but inexact statement[2]. It is true that in a feudal economy peasants were occasionally obliged to purchase certain amounts of alcohol in distilleries belonging to the landowners for whom they worked. However, this example is limited both in time and in its geographic extent, and cannot be used as a generally valid explanation.

If one takes a close look at the history of anti-alcohol propaganda in Poland, it is easy to notice how the argumentation changes together with changes in the economic and political situation. One wave of explanations follows another. The persons indicated as guilty of popularising alcoholism in Poland are (in chronological order): in the 18th century, the Jews, owners of inns and enemies of Christianity; in the 19th century, the enemies of the nation, that is, the "partitioning countries" (Russia, Austria and Prussia, which divided Poland among themselves at the end of 18th century); in the years 1918-1939, "foreign capital", set against the renewal of the Polish state after years of partitioning and, alternatively, Polish capitalists who were enemies of the proletariat; during the Second World War, the German occupant; after 1945, again capitalists, degenerated clergy, rich peasants, foreign spies and saboteurs – all enemies of socialism and of the Soviet Union; finally – in independent propaganda diffused during the 'Solidarity' period – the enemies of the Polish nation. One may conclude that in periods which followed a major political disaster, such as the partitioning of the country, foreign occupation, or other events which put Poland's independence at risk (such as the tensions around the independent trade union 'Solidarity' in the years 1980-1981), patriotic argumentation ("alcoholism induced by Poland's enemies") comes to the fore. By

---

[2] Mary Douglas (ed.), *Constructive Drinking: Perspectives on Drink from Anthropology*, Cambridge, Cambridge University Press, 1988.

contrast, in periods of economic unrest or political transition – the formation of independent Poland (1918-1939), of the Polish Popular Republic (PRL) (1944-1989), the economic transformation after the fall of communism (from 1989 on) – social arguments ("popular alcoholism encouraged by specific social strata") predominate.

One concept remains, however, everpresent in anti-alcohol propaganda in Poland: the anxiety for the family in which someone (almost always the father) is an alcoholic. The woman, or a mother-alcoholic appears rarely in anti-alcohol propaganda. Even in anti-alcohol propaganda used during the communist period the main figure is the drinking man, and drinking among young persons is discussed more often than drinking among women. This absence of women may be related to the specific place of women in Polish culture. Women hold an especially high position in this culture for many reasons, from religious (the central place of the cult of the Holy Virgin), through political (mothers were represented as the protectors of the nation), to economic (the mother is seen as the representative of her family's heritage). In such a context, the subject of the drinking woman was, to a large extent, a taboo. It was easier to describe a woman as a victim of somebody else's alcoholism than as a victim of her own addiction. Only in the 1990s has the propaganda openly discussed the specific issue of women's alcoholism and pointed, in parallel, to the existence of alcohol abuse not only among teenagers, but also among children.

•••

An analysis of anti-alcohol propaganda between 1945 and 1998, indicates a shift from arguments which refer to the community to arguments addressed directly to the individual. After the Second World War propaganda against alcoholism in Poland was closely correlated with the general propaganda of the state. An additional, and relatively marginal dimension, was the fight against the private, illegal distillation of liquor, grounded both in economic and sanitary arguments ("illicit distillers of liquor poison people and steal money from the State")[3]. The use of propaganda against alcoholism for state purposes was in all probability a result of a general tendency to unify all forms of social and even private life, typical of totalitarian states. This tendency to homogenise official discourse and practices had a significant influence on the perception of alcohol propaganda by Polish society. Memoirs of the activists of the anti-alcohol movement reveal the existence of strong social antagonism towards their activity, which

---

[3] *Walczymy z Alkoholizmem* ("We Fight against Alcoholism") Broszura Komendy Głównej Powszechnej Organizacji Służby Zdrowia w Polsce, 1950, p. 5.

probably can be at least partly explained by the generalised resistance to official propaganda, whatever its subject. The word propaganda has, by itself, a negative meaning in the Polish language. Moreover, communist propaganda used arguments which were so simplistic and exaggerated, and which were so incongruent with reality, that they almost automatically provoked a reflex of rejection.

Anti-alcohol propaganda had several stages. The 1950s were a period of almost romantic idealisation. The anti-alcohol propaganda of that era was mainly based on talks, especially in work places ('classical' lectures and 'chatty talks' supposedly grounded in a free exchange with the public, but in fact planned ahead of time with activists, who were present in the audience and asked pre-prepared questions), and on the diffusion of written and visual materials: leaflets, posters, and banners with anti-alcohol slogans.

All the talks, publications and leaflets of that period promoted "the creation of a new man" who had "high moral standards", was "creative", and had the "right class consciousness", who was "solidly rooted in Polish reality" and was "full of enthusiasm, and unconditionally devoted to the Polish People's Republic". This unusual creature was "called into being for the great revolutionary purpose of building a new political system". To make this happen, urges Dorota Kluszynska, new slogans were needed to maintain a socialist militant, who was already an activist in an anti-alcohol movement before the Second World War, active in the anti-alcohol movement after World War II. One of them promoted abstention from alcoholic drinks, because "alcoholics are not interested in social life and they do not participate in the great task of reconstruction of our country". Kluszynska's leaflet uses military terms and is characteristically entitled: "Let's Win the Battle against Alcoholism!"[4] It urges that one fight alcoholism "in the name of the love of our country, in the name of the reconstruction of Poland, in the name of peace". According to the author the task can only be achieved collectively, through showing the beauty, and the nobility of participation "in a great campaign of rebuilding our lives on a new basis". A person who has the right attitude and the right level of enthusiasm about the crucial task of the construction of socialism, views drinking as a waste of workers' time and health, and therefore as a serious offence. We were, however, invited to believe that "when the capitalism is defeated, alcoholism will no longer exist."[5]

---

[4] Danuta Kluszynska, *Walkę z alkoholizmem wygramy! Zarys problematyki walki z alkoholizmem*, Warszawa, Wyd. Nowe Zycie, 1950.

[5] *Ibid.*, p. 4.

In parallel, in the 1950s the propaganda argued that the true source of alcoholism in Poland was "a disgraceful pre-Second World War heritage". Alcoholism was the direct result of the inducement of the masses to heavy drinking by the landowners, the rich peasants, the money-lenders and finally the clergy[6]. This trend continued during the Second World War, when the Germans, helped by the same "oppressors" and "enemies of the people" continued to promote heavy drinking. Popular lectures on alcoholism often started by attempts to demonstrate that drunkenness was a "social failure" and a "weapon in the hands of enemies of the working class. Since it is generally known that the capitalists have deliberately promoted heavy drinking among the workers, those who continue to drink are ignorant and stupid, and therefore are unable to prepare themselves for a struggle against capitalism"[7].

The main issue in propaganda in the 1950s is thus the collective responsibility for drunkenness. Drunkenness is a crime against the State: one glass of vodka equals to the loss of one working hour. A man who drinks does not fulfil his duties as a worker, and hampers the realisation of the Six Year's Plan (1950-1955). The crusade against drunkenness is at the same time a battle for the Plan, that is, a struggle for a peaceful and happy future. The anti-alcohol campaign has therefore a double goal: to save the drinking man from being devastated and becoming a social failure, but also, for some above all, the promotion of larger societal goals. A "healthy" and "aware" majority should have a decisive influence on alcoholic individuals, and should use its moral pressure to convince them to undergo a treatment.

In 1959 the Polish state voted its first anti-alcohol law. The law was far from being a very restrictive one: for example it did allow young people and even children to drink beer (up to 4,5% of alcohol by content) and it did not ban beer from the workplace. At the same time the law institutionalised the anti-alcohol movement. In the 1960s and 1970s anti-alcohol propaganda in Poland was expected to be grounded in ethical, rather than in political arguments. Guidelines for activists published in 1967 affirm that an anti-alcohol activist should avoid simplified formulas employed in the previous period. Such activists should possess, besides professional qualifications, high moral, ideological and social values. The 1967 guidelines state that an anti-alcohol lecture should start with a presentation of elementary moral norms and legal rules, then describe situations in which alcohol contributes to the violation of such rules and norms. Such a lecture should therefore shape the world view, the attitudes and the convictions of citizens. One of the leading activists of the anti-alcohol movement, Jan

[6] Danuta Kluszynska, *Jak szlachta rozpijała chlopow*, Warszawa, Dom Slowa Polskiego, 1951.
[7] Danuta Kluszynska, *Wódka jest wrogiem rodziny*, Warszawa, RWS Prasa, 1950, p. 2.

Falewicz, proposed to follow the insights of Vladimir Illitch Lenin, "one of the greatest experts in sociological techniques of influencing people of our times", and of other Soviet specialists who were aware of economic and class differences among the persons to whom propaganda was directed, and to modulate the anti-alcohol message according to the audience to which it was directed.

The most successful methods to fight alcoholism, Falewicz explained, were:

1. mass education;

2. facilitation, that is, economical and administrative measures which combine propaganda with policies;

3. individual persuasion through direct contact;

4. manipulation, that is propaganda which is diffused without the consent or knowledge of the individual.[8]

In order to achieve maximum efficacy, not only state institutions, but also schools, the army, the Party, and other social organisations (youth organisations, clubs, trade unions, local unions, and circuits of commercial distribution) should be involved in the propaganda work. "In some circles we should not underestimate the influence of the Church", he added. The author drew attention to the "negative propaganda" of the 1950s (very general and schematic anti-alcohol slogans, occasionally naming and shaming individuals guilty of alcoholism) which, he said, was not only inefficient, but occasionally had a "boomerang" effect. It was therefore important to introduce new slogans and arguments. One-sided arguments (alcohol is invariably harmful) could be used in well disposed circles, or, alternatively, in poorly educated ones. Neutral arguments (presentation of arguments both for and against drinking) could be used in circles less favourably disposed and/or better educated ones.

Falewicz proposes also to graduate one's arguments, starting with the weakest argument, and ending with the strongest one. Anti-alcohol propaganda, he explained, should provoke uneasiness rather than anxiety or fear, and should present anti-alcohol activists as psychologists, friends and advisers. He stresses the role of the media in anti-alcohol propaganda. Documentary movies, short films, satirical films, cartoons and experimental movies were efficient tools of anti-alcohol propaganda, and he proposed to organise festivals of specialised propaganda movies. On the other hand, the

---

[8] Jan K. Falewicz, *Problemy propagandy przeciwalkoholowej*, Warsawa, SKP, RSW Prasa - Ruch, 1966.

presence of vodka in popular films, Falewicz notes, had the opposite effect: it would be good if "one of the celebrities refused to drink vodka on the screen". The press could print anti-alcohol messages, while literary works by authors such as Hans Fallada, Marek Hlasko, John Belleycorn or John Steinbeck could be used to illustrate the destructive effects of alcohol. The main emphasis, however, ought to be put on the use of radio (which, at that time, was more popular than television, cinema or the printed press) as a major tool of anti-alcohol propaganda.

The 1980s, a period which followed the suppression of the 'Solidarnosc' movement, were characterised as years of "general social and national apathy". Some individuals maintained a clandestine political activity, but many Poles viewed all forms social activity as senseless. The generalised feeling of the lack of purpose led to a passive boycott of all the government's decisions and a partial paralysis of all official activities. Paradoxically, the restrictions imposed by martial law (promulgated in 1981) went hand in hand with a certain liberalisation. Both are reflected in a typical leaflet, "A History of Alcoholism and the Fight Against it", by K. Moczarski[9]. Moczarski openly complains about the weakening of the anti-alcohol movement. In the 1980s there were only thirty thousand members of the government-sponsored movement. A similar process can be observed in the anti-alcohol movement run by the Church. Nevertheless, Moczarski views the Church as the only possible hope for the anti-alcohol campaign. He describes the long record of the clergy's achievements in fighting alcoholism, from the sixteenth century (Gregoire from Sanoka) to modern priests such as Father Padacz. He concludes by explaining that in a period when there was a crisis of authority, we should turn to the preserved tradition. Moczarski's brochure had a nationalist orientation. Everybody who was a patriot (no matter which political organisation he belonged to) is presented as rational, moral and wise. The main argument is that all Poles should work together to eliminate alcoholism because this was "our duty to the Nation, religion, the Church, society and to decent human behaviour"[10].

•••

Alcoholism continues to be a tragic problem in post-communist Poland. The authors of current anti-alcohol propaganda stress that paradoxically, the fall of the communist system, associated at first with hopes of disappearances of many social pathologies, aggravated the excess of alcohol consumption. A 1993 leaflet states that, "alcohol consumption in Poland has completely escaped the State's control". In 1992 the average

---

[9] K. Moczarski, *Historia alkoholizmu i walki z nim*, Warszawa, SKP, 1983. See also, Jan K. Falewicz, *Walka o trzeźwość narodu*, Warszawa, Wydawnictwo Prawnicze, 1982; Jan K. Falewicz, *Alkoholowe ABC, Zielona Góra*, Warszawa, SKP, 1985.

[10] *Ibid.*, p. 8.

consumption of alcoholic drinks exceeded 10 litres of pure 100% alcohol per capita, reaching thus the highest recorded level in the history of Poland. Beer consumption increased three times, while the consumption of alcoholic drinks increased by 28%. About 2-3 million persons abuse alcohol, 1 million require detoxification treatment, and 4 to 6 million persons live in families with an alcohol problem. More than 80% of elementary school children had already had contact with alcohol, 16% of elementary school pupils occasionally get drunk, and 7.5% systematically come to school after drinking alcohol. The average age of initiation to the use of alcohol has decreased to 12 years. About 20% of children from alcoholic families require a psychologist's care[11].

In the 1990s organisations which deal with alcoholism were decentralised, and the burden of anti-alcohol propaganda was shifted to local authorities thorough a bill that combines the attribution of local licences to sell alcohol with the development of activities aiming at the prevention of alcoholism. The number of anti-alcohol activists further decreased in the 1990s. There are now only a few thousand of such activists in Poland, and they mainly propose therapies based on medical and psychological help. In addition, in Poland there are numerous self-help groups of alcoholics – Alcoholic Anonymous, Al.-Anon, Alateen, ACA (Adult Children of Alcoholics), and the Church's Crusade for Freeing Man – modelled on similar groups in western Europe and the USA. Recent approaches to alcoholism (of both the activists and the self-help movement) are grounded in the treatment of this phenomenon as a disease, in widening the range of therapeutic methods, and in the individualisation of diagnosis and of therapy of alcoholism. Contemporary propaganda against alcoholism occasionally evokes social issues: one publication explained thus that alcoholism, which "discourages a necessary initiative and dynamism" is particularly dangerous in a period when the Polish political system is being radically transformed. Such argumentation is, however, exceptional. As a rule, anti-alcohol propaganda is addressed to the individual. Based on the praise of the instinct of self-preservation and of free will, it focuses on the balance of individual costs and benefits. The abuse of alcohol, recent publications explain, leads to cynicism, callousness, opportunism, the disappearance of an esteem for higher values, vulgarisation of the language, brutality, and the lowering of one's standards of living. Publications which deal with alcoholism, activists affirm, should avoid platitudes about the society and nation and a moralising or a militant tone. They should develop instead arguments touching the value systems of each person, and should propose practical ways of dealing with a concrete and highly individualised problem.

---

[11] M. Jasinska, *Alkoholizm-Bibliografia*, Warsawa, SKP, 1993; Jan K. Falewicz, *ABC problemów alkoholowych*, Warszawa, PARPA, 1993.

Recent publications indicate a shift in argumentation, from an anti-alcohol propaganda which is directed at the masses and focused on collective responsibilities, to an individual-oriented approach, centred on particular difficulties of a specific person, and aiming at the improvement of that person's well-being. The change is so dramatic that, especially if one takes into account the pejorative meaning of the term propaganda in Polish, it is legitimate to ask whether the anti-alcohol activity of the 1990s can still be viewed as propaganda, or should rather be described as a banal offer by the market.

Stop drinking, come with us to build a better future.

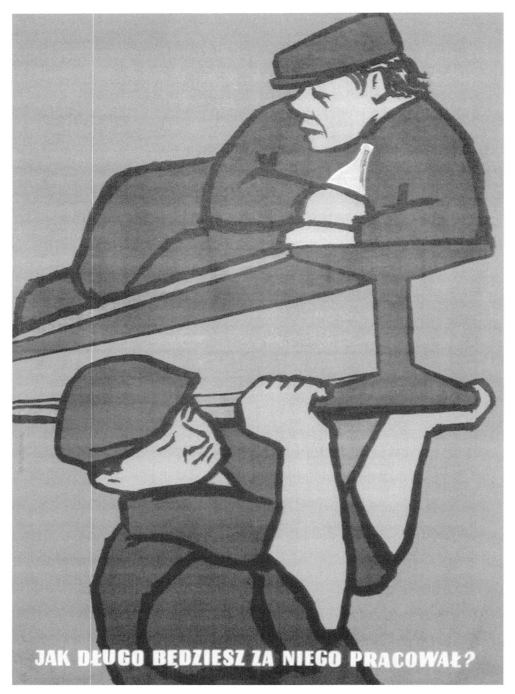

How long are you going to work for him?

The 1950s

Citizens, be tough!

It was suuuch fun…!

You must stop this once and for all.

Sobriety is a soldier's special duty.

Even if you do not drink much… this is what you are losing
(after a month – a shirt, after half a year – a watch, after a
year – a camera, after several years – a motorcycle).

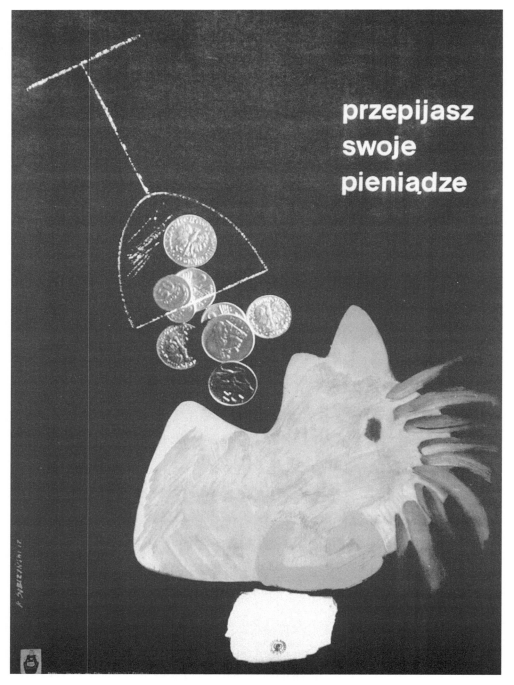

You are wasting your money.

The 1970s

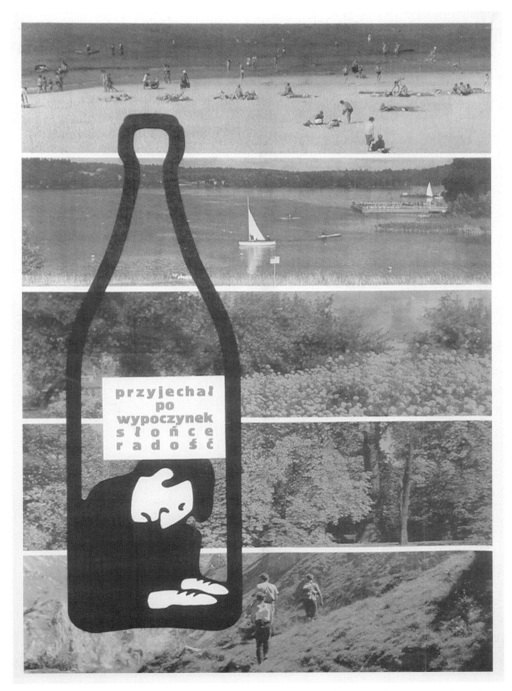

He came for rest, sun, happiness.

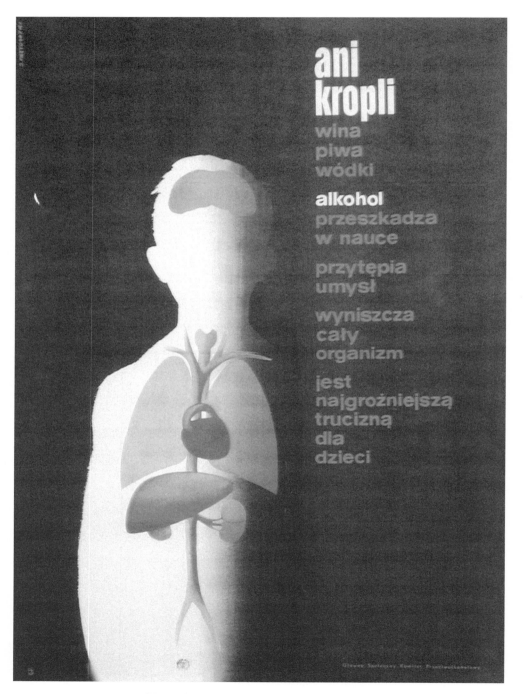

Not a single drop of wine, beer, or vodka. Alcohol disturbs learning, dulls the mind, destroys the organism. It is the worst poison for children.

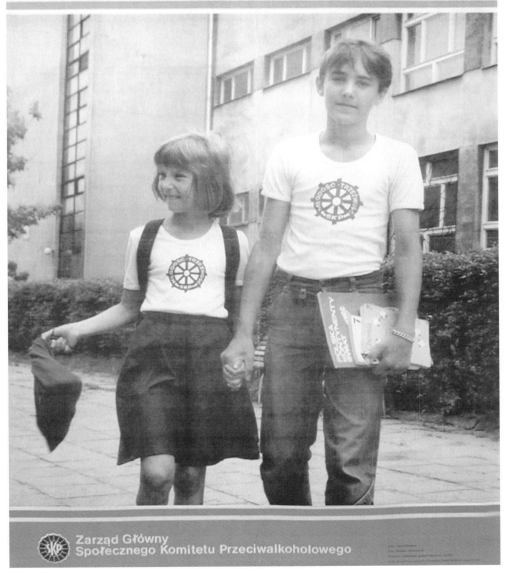

Our school is participating in the competition "youth and sobriety".

With Jesus and Mary towards sobriety: The XXIst week of prayers for the sobriety of the Nation, February 17-23, 1988.

Czy jesteś na tyle mężczyzną, aby powiedzieć sobie ,,dość'' we właściwym momencie? Jeżeli chcemy się napić, pijmy rozsądnie.

Are you man enough to be able to stop at the right moment?
If we want to drink, let's drink reasonably.

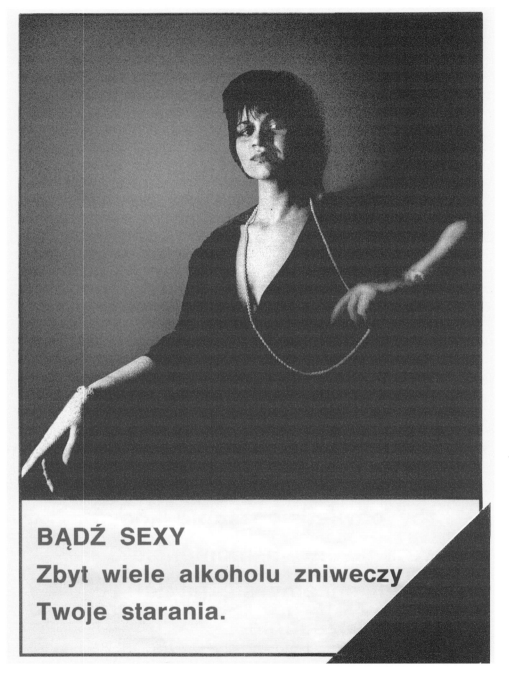

BĄDŹ SEXY
Zbyt wiele alkoholu zniweczy
Twoje starania.

Be sexy. Too much alcohol will undermine your efforts.

The Medicalised Sobering Stations:
A History of a Unique Soviet Practice

Sergei Orlov

During the last four decades it has been practically impossible to find in the former Soviet Union a person who was not acquainted with the meaning of the term 'vytrzvi-tel', the 'medicalised sobering station' for drunken persons. This term was first introduced in the 1930s. In the next twenty years such sobering stations were banalized, and became firmly integrated into the fabric of daily life in the Soviet Union. Notwithstanding all the deep political and economical changes in today's Russia, 'sobering stations' remain in the country's life and consciousness.

The 'medicalised sobering stations' played an important role in both the official and the non-official Soviet culture. Nevertheless this term does not appear in general encyclopaedic dictionaries or in specialised encyclopaedias, such as the Medical or the Law Encyclopaedia. This absence reflects the fact that while the sobering stations are a well known social phenomenon in Russia, their official existence is rarely acknowledged openly. The rare documents on this topic, published either by official research institutions or the Ministry of the Internal Affairs, are usually comments on the official instructions and rules. Moreover, an important portion of the information related to the sobering stations is still viewed as a state secret. Hence the relative ignorance of this phenomenon in the West. For example, some Western publications associate the activity of the Soviet "Society for the Struggle for Sobriety" exclusively with the 'perestroika' period, disregarding the length and the importance of institutionalised efforts to fight alcoholism in the Soviet Union and the unique form taken by these efforts.

The main goal of this paper is to discuss three related questions: the history of the sobering stations in the Soviet Union, the stations' relations with the state and with other public organisations, and the function and internal structure of these stations.

From the mid-seventeenth century on, the Russian state taxed and supervised the production and the sale of alcohol. In the 1895 the State introduced a 'Wine monopoly'. For two hundred years – from the XVIII century until the first decade of the XX century – methods of administrative control of drunken persons in public places remained essentially unchanged. The main controlling mechanism was the isolation of the drunk. According to paragraph 256 of the Police Regulations of 1782, a drunken person should be kept in the police division for 24 hours "on bread and water" until completely sober, and chronic alcoholics were to be kept in special 'correction houses' until they were reformed.

The situation was radically changed after the October Revolution of 1917. The Bolshevik Government inherited the so called 'prohibition law' of 18 July, 1914. From the first post- revolution days the struggle against alcoholism was associated with class struggle. In December 1917 the government appointed I.F. Vydzan as Commissar for the struggle against drunkenness. During the Civil War and so-called period of War Communism alcohol was absolutely prohibited. This prohibition was legislated in two acts – in the Decree of the Council of People's Commissars of December 19, 1919, and in the Plan for the Electrification of Russia. Both stated that drunkenness was a crime which could be punished by several months in prison. The political rhetoric of the time associated drinking with the desire to return to a capitalist regime, and with the obstruction of the construction of communism. Such views continued to guide the Soviet authorities' attitude towards alcoholism for many years, and were reflected in official language. Even in the first years of the New Economic Policy (NEP) (a liberalisation of the state's control over the economy, introduced at the end of 1921), the attitude towards drinking did not change. The production of alcohol continued to be severely restricted. For example during the last six months of 1922 and the first two months of 1923, only 3 717,5 litters of pure spirit were (officially) distilled in the Soviet Union. This alcohol was destined exclusively for persons who worked under difficult conditions, especially those who worked in an extremely cold climate.

During the early years of the Soviet regime, alcoholism was not perceived as a permanent social problem but as an unfortunate heritage of the capitalist past, which would necessarily disappear in the new regime. Nevertheless, it was seen, in the main, as a medical problem, if moderate, and as criminal issue, if extreme, but not as a question which had to be treated by a unique combination of medical and repressive action. Thus, one of the first Soviet official regulations related to administrative pressure on drunken persons, issued on 17 December, 1925 by the People's Commissars of Justice and of Internal Affairs and the Procurator of the Republic, discussed only drunken behaviour in public places. Persons who disturbed the public order by inappropriate behaviour when drunken, these regulations stated, should be jailed and put in isolated cells. The governmental directive made no mention at all of the possibility of medical assistance to drunken individuals administered under the militia's supervision.

The Addiction Section of the Moscow Public Health Department was created in 1923. Its beginnings were very modest: one doctor and one nurse. Seven years later there were similar prophylactic centres in practically every area of the town. The system of medical assistance to persons addicted to alcohol was not homogenised, and there were great disparities between towns and between regions. In the 1930s Moscow had numerous and very active addiction sections, while at the same time Leningrad had only six regional 'narcologists' (addiction experts). The militia's participation in the activities of these sections was initially reserved to special occasions. Its role was codified in instructions "On forced treatment of the persons, who are socially dangerous and do not want to be given appropriate treatment" (of 7 April, 1927) and "On application of forced treatment to alcoholics who are socially dangerous" (of 24 April, 1927). The official position – criminalization of drunken behaviour and its assimilation to other types of disorderly conduct – failed nevertheless to deal in an efficient way with the issue of drunkenness in public places.

One of the demands made during the election campaign for the Moscow City Council of 1927-1928 was the opening of sobering stations in the city, in order to solve the chronic problem of drunken persons in the streets. The Moscow campaign was successful. The first medicalised sobering station was opened in 1928 on Kosaya street in the Moscow neighbourhood Krasnaya Presnja. It was the result of a joint initiative of the Regional Committee of the Communist Party, the Regional Council of the People's Deputies, the Regional Department of the Militia and the Regional Department of Public Health. This initiative was also supported by the trade unions. The station was financed by the Regional Soviet and by the factories situated in the Presnja. A special article about this pioneering initiative was published in the Communist Party newspaper *Pravda*, and the information was seen as sufficiently important to be reproduced in the Russian emigrant press in the West. This station was relatively small. It had 20 beds and, as a rule, all of them were occupied. In addition to the bedrooms, the station had a medical consulting room, a bathroom, and two rooms for the personnel. It employed 10 persons: medical attendants, male nurses and militia men. The militia men's tasks included the general keeping of order and the transport of drunken individuals to the station. Cold showers, baths, oxygen ventilation of lungs and massage were used to accelerate sobering. If necessary, patients were immobilised by tying them down. The maximum length of stay at the station was 24 hours. The persons who were interned in the station had to pay for their stay. The price of medical assistance was 3 or 5 rubles, and it varied according to the social status of the station's occupant.

A second sobering station was opened in Moscow at the end of 1929. It had 20 beds and employed 21 persons. In many ways these early sobering stations were similar to 'narcological services' in hospitals which dealt with addicted persons. They can be viewed of as a bigger version of these services. The main difference was that sobering stations, unlike hospital wards, had close co-operation with the militia as their permanent feature. An idyllic description of the second Moscow station, published in the journal *Sobriety and Culture*, praised this initiative, and recommended its generalisation. It also proposed transforming church buildings into sobering stations for the workers, in the framework of an anti-alcoholic campaign under the slogan: "Kill God and vodka". The first 5-years plan (1930-1935) officially adopted the concept of sobering stations, and the People's Commissariat of Public Health included in its plans a project to open 800 sobering beds. The Society for the Struggle with Alcoholism saw this goal as much too modest, and insisted on the need to organise 200 stations of 30 beds each.

The sobering stations were initially viewed as the first level of medical intervention against alcoholism. The work of these stations, their advocates proposed, should be co-ordinated, and should be integrated with other medical actions destined to fight addiction to alcohol. The impossibility of realising such a goal became obvious in the early 1930s. The purely medical component of the anti-alcohol campaign was then eliminated, and was gradually replaced by an increased emphasis on the dissuasive and the repressive tasks of sobering stations. This change of orientation was legitimised by political reasons: "too much was said about the alcohol's influence on kidneys, liver or the spleen", the party officials explained, "but nothing was said about its influence on the construction of socialism". The organisation of the first medical sobering station in Leningrad (opened the 14 November, 1931, in Marat's street, following a resolution of Leningrad's Council of the Deputies of the People "On the regulation of sobering stations", voted the same day), reflected the turn towards a more repressive role for sobering stations. Among the 44 members of the station's staff there were seven militia men, one doctor, one doctor's assistant and 22 male nurses. The only task of the militia men on the station's staff was to keep order within the station; drunken individuals were transported to the station by the city's militia men.

The Leningrad station was placed under the control of the General Department of the Leningrad Regional Board of Workers and Peasant Militia. The Department had issued a special document, "Temporary General Instructions for the First Medical Sobering Station" (regulations of 14/11/31) which defined the norms for the stations" staff and the standardised form of administrative, medical and financial documents. These documents became later a model for the organisation of other sobering stations, and they constituted a base for subsequent regional legislative acts. State legislation was, by contrast, determined by the 'Regulations' issued in 1932 by the Peoples' Commissariat of Public Health in co-ordination with the Main Management of Militia. The main parameters of the structure and the functioning of sobering stations were thus determined in the years 1931-1932. They remained practically unchanged during the next 25 years. The only important transformation took place in 1940 when all existing sobering stations were definitively brought under the jurisdiction of the People's Commissariat of Internal Affairs, thus efficiently centralising control over these stations.

Between 1945 and 1955 there weren't any signs that the government or the Party paid special attention to sobering stations. This may be partly explained by the fact that during this period the Ministry of Internal Affairs underwent a series of structural reforms which kept its officials busy, and partly by the relative stability of the consumption of alcohol in the Soviet Union. However, in 1956 the Minister of Internal Affairs issued "New Regulations for the Medical Sobering Stations", which included an "Instruction on Medical Assistance for the Person Brought to the Sobering Stations". According to the 1956 regulations, the Council of People's Deputies placed the medical sobering stations under the responsibility of two departments of the Ministry of Internal Affairs. The general direction of the stations was the responsibility of the department for the Management and Protection of Public Order, while medical assistance was the responsibility of the department of Medical Management. These documents were later modified in 1970 and in 1985 by special decrees of the Minister. The 1985 decree was issued in co-ordination with several other Ministries. In the intervals between the Ministry decrees, regulations and instructions concerning sobering stations were occasionally adjusted by special directives issues by the Ministry.

According to the 1956 instructions, the organisation of the staff of a sobering station, and the rank of its director, depended on the number of beds at the station. Stations with more than ten beds were directed by a 'registering inspector', those with more than 20 beds, by a 'deputy commander', and those with more than 30 beds, by a 'platoon commander'. If there were more than three stations in the town, the medical assistance group at one of them could hire a full-time physician. In 1978 'groups for prophylactic action' were integrated into the stations' organisation, and regulations issued in 1986 decreed that every station should have an 'inspector of the prophylactic room', who supervised the state of the station's clients. Stations with more that 30 beds were to have a second inspector. The inspector's activities were directly controlled by the station's director. All the personnel of a sobering station, the new instructions stipulated, should be trained to recognise pathologies which may induce symptoms similar to those of drunkenness (heart attack, attack of epilepsy, etc.) and if persons suffering from one of these pathologies were brought to the station, the staff should be able to give appropriate first aid assistance before the patient was transferred to a hospital. Although the new instructions gave a greater importance to medical treatment of patients, the sobering stations continued to be under the jurisdiction of the Management and Protection of Public Order of the Ministry of Internal Affairs, and remained under the supervision of divisional inspectors of militia.

The work of sobering stations was co-ordinated with the one of different state and non-state structures and institutions. Its general orientation was provided by decrees of the Central Committee of the Communist Party, of the Supreme Council of People's Deputies and of the Council of Ministers of the Soviet Union. These institutions determined the main goals and means of the anti-alcohol prophylactic actions. The concrete details of daily work in the stations were regulated by directives issued by the Ministry of Internal Affairs. The sobering stations – a semi-prophylactic, semi-repressive structure – were connected permanently with different levels of organisation of the Communist Party and of the Trade Unions, from the town or region level to local units, such as workplace party cells, local party committees, and base units of the trade union organisation. Each person brought to the sobering station had to pay a fine. These fines were collected by the Administrative Commission of the Council of People's Deputies. The administrations of factories and of other workplaces played an important role in the co-ordination of the repressive action of sobering stations. The stations notified the workplace of each person brought to be sobered up in the station. The workplace was obliged to answer the station's message rapidly and to provide precise information about their reaction to their employee's drunkenness, the disciplining measures undertaken against that person, and the steps taken in each case to prevent a repetition of such incidents. One of the main functions of the stations' senior staff was the analysis of data provided by inmates' workplaces, and the elaboration of methodical and practical recommendations stemming form these data. The efficacy of both the prophylactic and the repressive functions of the stations was evaluated on the basis of permanent contacts with the workplaces and with various organisations.

In the late 1950s and the early 1960s, official ideology promoted the central role of non-governmental and non-Party organisations, such as comradely courts, volunteer public order squads, womens' councils, and house councils, in protecting public order. The construction of communism was presented in official propaganda as a processes of the disappearance of the state, a process during which non-governmental organisations would gradually replace the official state's institutions. The main 'civil' organisations having direct links with sobering stations were the 'volunteer public order squads' and 'comradely courts'. According to official documents, 'volunteer public order squads' were at first organised through a "spontaneous working masses initiative" at Leningrad's biggest factories in November 1958. In fact, this 'spontaneous' process was tightly controlled by the Party. The movement to form similar squads rapidly spread all over the Soviet Union with the Party's active help. In March 1959 it became official through a special decree of the Central Committee of the CPSU and of the Council of Ministers of the USSR, "On Working People's Participation in the Preservation of Law and Public Order in the Country". From 1959 until the late 1980s the 'volunteer public order squads' assisted the sobering stations' personnel in transporting drunken individuals from public places to the station. The squad's members were also allowed to bring such persons to the station on their own initiative, and 1-2% of the individuals who stayed at sobering stations were brought there by members of 'public order squads'.

In the late 1950s the participation of members of the 'volunteer public order squads' in the sobering station's work had one positive effect: the incorporation of some medical students and medical personnel into mobile patrol groups which picked up drunken individuals on the streets. The militiamen working with the station's staff usual lacked even elementary paramedical education and were not sufficiently trained in first aid techniques. They were therefore unable to deal in an efficient way with the increasingly frequent – and very dangerous – cases of intoxication by so-called 'liquids with alcohol content' (methyl alcohol, industrial alcohol and the like). The presence of volunteers with medical and para-medical training increased the efficacy of primary diagnostic and first aid assistance given at the stations, and improved the quality of care of dangerously intoxicated persons. 'Comradely courts' were organised at workplaces (factories, offices), house councils, collective farms and at other institutions. One of their tasks was the organisation of a reaction to the information, provided by the sobering stations, about drunken behaviour of workers or inhabitants. All such cases were discussed at the open sessions. The court's 'verdicts' took the form of recommendations addressed to the workplace's administration or to local and civil authorities. The 'courts' proposed an appropriate reaction to each case of drunkenness: public blame, public reprimand, or a recommendation to use administrative means to influence the person's behaviour.

In the 1960s and 70s the practical orientation of the activity of sobering stations was shaped to a great extent by their relations with the medical organisations. At this time there was a growing tendency to play down the straightforward, militia-based repression of the drunk and to give priority to a repressive form of medical assistance. This trend was partly rooted in an increased tendency to treat drunkenness as a form of social atavism, associated with the survival of capitalism, an interpretation strengthened during the Cold War years. In parallel, the tendency to privilege the medicalized repression of drunkenness might also have been related to the important increase in the consumption of alcohol in the Soviet Union. Until the 1970s medical statistics included only data on chronic alcoholism. Data on the number of persons repeatedly brought to sobering stations, collected by the militia, were thus probably a more exact reflection of changing patterns of alcohol consumption in the Soviet Union. The growth in the number of 'frequently drunken persons' was extremely rapid: from 273,000 in 1960 to 2,500,000 in 1970. This important increase led to the development of a new system of forced treatment of drunkenness: the Medicalized Labour Preventoriums. The first 'Preventoriums' were organised in Kazakhstan in the 1960s. In the 1970s this form of forced treatment of alcoholics became universally adopted in the Soviet Union. It was legitimised by two Decrees of the Supreme Council Presidium, published in 1972 and 1974.

The development of Medicalized Labour Preventoriums was effectively the last step in the construction of a system of a repressive medicalized response to the growing alcoholisation of the society. In some of its more formal aspects, this system was similar to the early 1930s projects. However this similarity was merely superficial. While both the original plans for 'medical sobering stations' and the projects for 'medicalized labour preventoriums' stressed the medical aspects of dealing with drunkenness, in the latter model medical aid was a secondary and derivative measure accompanying the main goal of 'preventoriums': the forced isolation of alcoholics from society. In parallel, the new trend toward the isolation of alcoholics and their 're-education' through forced labour was reflected directly in the activity of sobering stations. During the 1970s and 1980s these stations were gradually transformed from institutions dedicated to the specific task of sobering up the drunk, to organisms whose main goal was to identify chronic alcoholics. The medical assistance provided by the sobering station was accordingly minimised, and the main goal of each station was redefined as the registration and selection of potential patients for different levels of forced treatment.

The treatment in 'preventoriums' was conducted on an impressive scale. In 1985, at the beginning of the last Soviet anti-alcohol campaign, the country had 236 'preventoriums' which 'treated' 202,000 patients; at the peak of the campaign there were 329 'preventoriums' and 249,000 patients. In the years 1990-1991, during the declining phase of this campaign, there were still 272 'preventoriums' and 112,000 patients.

Cumulative data on the activity of institutions who dealt with alcoholics in the Soviet Union from the early 1970s to the early 1990s reveal that these institutions treated more then 4,3 million individuals on a permanent basis, among them approximately 500,000 women. The activity of the sobering stations in the 1970s and 1980s reflected the important rise in alcoholism in the Soviet Union. Approximately 6 million drunken individuals, (among them 128,000 women) were brought to these stations in the year 1987 alone. (One may add that the percentage of women is higher among chronic alcoholics than among individuals brought to sobering stations, because women who abuse alcohol tend to drink at home rather than in public places). The important increase in the volume of activity of the sobering stations made it practically impossible to maintain even a minimal level of medical assistance, strengthening even more the repressive tradition of these institutions. At the same time, the consumption of alcohol continued to increase.

In the early 1990s there was a wide-spread feeling that the existing system of dealing with the problem of alcoholism – developed by the Soviet Regime – was grossly inadequate. This feeling was reflected in the decree of the Supreme Council of the Russian Federation "On the Discharge of Persons from the Medical Labour Preventoriums for Chronic Alcoholics", of 28 February, 1991. In 1992, the Government of the Russian Federation published a decree (no. 282, of 4 May, 1992) on the abrogation of the state monopoly over alcohol. A year later the President of Russia published a decree (no. 918, of 11 June, 1993) on the restoration of the state monopoly for producing and selling alcohol. The state system for ensuring this monopoly was organised by the decree of the Council of Ministers of the Government of the Russian Federation issued two months later (no. 279). These decrees notwithstanding, in the 1990s the government's control over the production and sales of alcohol was very partial. One of the consequences of the chaotic state of the market was the increase in number of individuals poisoned by falsified alcoholic beverages, and therefore in the number of drunken persons in need of specialised medical assistance. The personnel at sobering stations were practically alone in handling such medical emergencies. The situation was aggravated by the tendency of the sobering stations' personnel to continue a repressive policy, due to the scarcity of hospital departments able to deal with alcohol-related problems, and the de facto collapse of the system of forced treatment of alcoholism.

In the 1990s, the fate of sobering stations became a topic of dispute between the Ministry of Internal Affairs and the Ministry of Public Health. In some regions the supervision of these stations was transferred from the militia to medical organisations. The results of such transfers were mainly positive. The new law of the Russian Federation "On the Militia" (of 18 April, 1991) clearly indicated that medical sobering stations must be headed by some other state structure, not by militia. Propositions in this direction were developed in a special decree of the Government of the Russian Federation of 17 September, 1992. Following this legislation, the Minister of Internal Affairs ordered the sobering stations to be placed under the jurisdiction of the Ministry of Public Health. The transfer was, however, paralysed by the absence of appropriate regulations. The Ministry of Public Health reacted aggressively to what it perceived as purposeful sabotage of the new arrangements, and its spokesman declared that "the attempts by the Ministry of Internal Affairs to impose upon the public health organisations (…) and its reluctance to abandon the supervision of the medical sobering stations are unlawful and harm departmental interests". The only way to overcome such blockages, still present in 1998, is probably the development, on the regional level, of new forms of collaboration between the militia and the medical authorities. Such attempts were made in the St-Petersburg region, where a collaboration was successfully established among the Department of Internal Affairs of St.-Petersburg and the Leningrad Region, the Committee of Public Health of the St.-Petersburg Administration and the Committee of Public Health of the Leningrad Region. Thanks to this co-operation, medical assistance provided by the sobering stations was reorganised, and was modelled on first aid medical stations. The new arrangement put the accent on the medical component of the sobering stations and limited the importance of the repressive role without, however, making it disappear completely.

Alcoholism continues to be a major social problem in Russia. Moreover, it is seen as the leading cause of the recent dramatic decrease in life expectancy in Russia, especially for men. One may predict therefore that the long career of Russian "medicalized sobering stations" will probably not come to an end in the near future.

Round Table:
Policies of Health in Europe:
Past Experiences and Perspectives
for the XXI Century

Barbara Gutmann Rosenkrantz

It is difficult to turn away from the rich and detailed papers and discussion of this conference and to pursue the schematic generalizations of a concluding Round Table. Nonetheless, we can and should differentiate significant phases in the history of 20th century public policy with regard to the prevention of disease and the promotion of health. For much of this century, metaphors identified with themes of war and conquest link the victories of laboratory science, the collaboration of international health efforts and the disease outbreaks that followed in the wake of social disorder and misery. Yet ironically, for the first time in human experience, epidemic outbreaks were not seen as the inescapable lot of man, but rather as a consequence of malfeasance and adversity. While public health policies of the 19th century were generated in response to epidemics, the 20th century is largely characterized by regulatory measures intended to prevent the eruption of dangerous diseases. Three constituencies – public officials, medical scientists and urban populations – framed the transfer of knowledge and experience into policy and practice. Over the century the past development of efficient prophylaxis has depended in part on the growth of social and scientific resources. Strategies for preventing and curtailing the impact of dread disease were tied to political cultures that authorized the identification of specific dangers and decreed intervention through regulation. My contribution to the concluding session is a brief historical review to locate the responsible authorities and their points of view as their influence waxed and waned.

This history is grounded in 19th century responses to epidemic outbreaks of cholera and other water-borne contagions. These pestilences dramatically exposed differences between the victims and those who escaped death, leading to the conclusion that survival was the result of careful personal behavior as much as particular circumstance. Explanations of the causes of fevers had for centuries called attention to the dangers of foul air and water, but there was little opportunity to systematically identify factors that encouraged survival. Urban life provided more circumstances for drawing lessons from comparison as well as greater reliance on public resources for social welfare. Regulation gained authority and public action in times of fear spawned the conviction that epidemics were the result of negligence as well as ignorance. At the end of the 19th century Henrik Ibsen portrayed the complications of intervention in his play, *An Enemy of the People* (1882) when Dr. Stockmann, a public health official, exposes contamination of the local Baths that leading citizens expected to be a source of tourism and local wealth. Despite threats by his brother the mayor and other investors in the Baths, Dr. Stockmann steadfastly resists temptations to withhold the bad news. Although the play was published in the year that the bacillus causing typhoid was identified, there is little reason to believe that Ibsen perceived the potential for moral dilemmas in this scientific milestone. It is more likely that science was not the empowering force it shortly became and that the Norwegian playwright instead reflected on the difficulties of upright citizens when the corruption of public life was a familiar source of tension.

The shift from reliance on personal behavior to support for regulations that made the state responsible for the health of the public required a new and more powerful political infrastructure as well as secure knowledge about the specific causes of epidemic outbreaks. Highlights in the chronology of scientific discovery marking the resolution of conflicts about the causes of dangerous disease are the backbone of a triumphalist history of public health. On the other hand, the social factors that made it possible to transform scientific knowledge into public policy are more difficult to identify. Despite increasingly complete collections of vital data that documented the significance of age, sex, income and residence of populations, European statesmen committed to promoting public health in the interest of national strength faced two kinds of problems; first, how to isolate and identify the critical variables of differences in mortality, and equally important, how to gain popular support for interventions. Louis Pasteur and Robert Koch, who are usually identified with discovering the germs of contagions that eventually empowered 20th century public health, cited the social barriers to deploying this knowledge as obstacles to the control of contagion. Enactment of public health law, enforcement of regulation, and provision of the social institutions and scientific practices designed to protect the health of populations were dependent on changes in the political climate that generally accompanied industrialization and on the growth of government resources, as well as on new scientific knowledge. Battle is a frequent metaphor used in recalling these engagements, they were characterized, however, as much by stealth and persistence as by force.

At the end of the 20th century we can identify two trends in public health policy that followed this groundwork, one aimed at social circumstance the other at personal behavior. In both cases the foundation of public health policy rested on determining the factors that differentiated between resistance and susceptibility to disease. Earlier, attention had focused on sources of contamination, for example the quality and quantity of public water supplies affecting both the comfort and health of urban populations. This made way for large scale civic investment in natural resources, but the responsibility of public health for water supplies was cast in a general framework rather than related to specific disease. During the past 100 years, however, the sciences of bacteriology, immunology and epidemiology shaped the salient information on which public health policy rested. The authority of this information was gauged by its relevance to both health authorities and the general public. Both professional and popular support of stringent measures to protect the public from dangerous diseases

Barbara Gutmann Rosenkrantz

required health policies and practices that fit into a larger framework of knowledge and experience.

For much of the century European nations oriented their public health policies around recognition of the unequal impact of contagious diseases on the lower classes and the young. The general misery connected with two world wars separated by two bruising decades of economic depression underscored this association. In this context, the practical tools of bacteriology and immunology offered opportunities for powerful public health interventions through diagnostic and preventive services that were expected to dull the impact of poor living and working conditions. Support for public institutions and scientifically approved standards of personal hygiene were incorporated in measures that effectively protected individuals who were without the resources for protecting themselves. By mid-century all European nations had laws that authorized public health services that were intended to assure a common standard. Differences in national history and resources inevitably shaped, and in some cases seriously compromised, these intentions.

Epidemiologic history was also shaped by international events affecting the scientific and social underpinnings of public health policies. The eradication of smallpox was a testimony to the power of international collaboration, and on a national scale eliminated need for smallpox immunization. Immunization against the contagious diseases of childhood became a mainstay of most public health programs, but in the poorest nations neither funds nor the infrastructure required were in place to combat diseases primarily affecting children. And tuberculosis, the scourge of industrializing nations, had a resurgence in wartime that was boosted by poverty and forced migration, as was AIDS, a new pandemic for which no scientific treatment or immunization was known.

Epidemiologic statistics implicated both social resources and individual behavior, but public health authorities were inadequately equipped to mount a response. In the absence of clear cut prophylaxis for diseases that were once believed to be under control neither scientific nor popular support was adequate for effective interventions. Unlike the earlier years of the century, when the impact of differences in social circumstance could be confined through "magic bullets" of immunization, control was now reoriented, implicating, as in 19th century epidemics, personal behavior, impotence where there was little 20th century public health science. Neither national nor international public health organizations had the finances and infrastructure to meet this challenge. Under these conditions it is not surprising that questions were raised about the efficacy of public health policy. The fringe benefits of social rehabilitation were not as obvious as when measles and polio were prevalent and when the battle against these diseases of childhood was widely supported in wealthy nations. Public

health scientists in all fields were challenged by many new questions but were
apparently incompetent when it came to
working out and explaining the moral and
epidemiologic liabilities of neglect to public health across social and national
boundaries. Despite important successes
and many skilled and devoted warriors,
public health stalwarts lost some of their
bravado and took refuge in telling war
stories from the past.

'Brief encounter, GREAT DANGER!
Disease threatens!'.
An East German poster, 1946.

Esteban Rodríguez-Ocaña

The phrase "Policies of Health" is somewhat misleading in a historical perspective, since what we have had, at least until the declarations of Alma Ata (1978), have been some kind of "Policies faced with Disease". And in countries such as Spain, where the public health profession is mostly a specialised field within medicine, the abuse of the "health" label might even contribute to extend medical imperialism.

After the WHO conventions of Alma Ata and Ottawa there exists a professional commitment to promote health policies. I would say that this is *the* peculiarity of recent public health with its emphasis on the adoption of cross-sectorial policies aimed at the promotion of health, stemming from a view of health as a result of the interaction of diverse conditions (environment, population, genetic load, social organization, medical care, and so on).

A major problem, though, refers to the position to be reached by public kealth experts in order to achieve such aims. Recent Spanish experiences, which I tried to explain in contribution to this volume, show the mirage of the un-written arrangement which has presided over recent public health practices: PH officers collaborate with the general action of the government, through the efficient administration of health care facilities, and the government is persuaded to undertake coordinated initiatives intended to achieve the health goals (but which do not). Others papers read in this conference have also shown that "health" has not been a value by itself in most countries. On the contrary, it has been employed as an instrument of political or social values, like the unity of race, Fascist "Empire" or the building of Socialism.

The *Supreme Presidium*, so to speak, of health policies has been historically occupied by a *troika*, Morality being given a seat between Science and the State. Change in any of these domains will indeed produce changes in health politics.

Scientific innovations depending on new technologies, shifts of paradigms, and the like, are reflected – after a while – in the design of health policies, shaping new aims and methods. In the realm of science it seems to me that the great change coming is to cope with the outgrowth of genetics and biotechnology. If we accept the romantic statement that *Nature imitates Art* we should worry a lot about the world of pre-destination that we are about to enter, depicted in recent science-fiction novels and films.

Morality comes always with a mirror and a yardstick; it both compares and punishes. The moral construction reflects a world suited to the need for the reproduction of any given society. Transnational studies and comparisons such as those that have taken place during this conference show that industrial societies require very similar moral traits in their citizenship, independently of whichever cultural diversities we might find.

A change in moral values is probably linked to deeper transformations in social, economic and power-sharing structures. I declare myself unable to trace a pattern for such changes nowadays.

And so we come to the state. The political ground for democracy requires a growing compromise from the people; oligarchic transnational plutocracy strives to keep citizens away. In this sphere I would say that the challenge is to share the benefits of affluent societies with the rest of the world. That is, to make real the goals of universality, solidarity, equality and community participation on a world-wide basis. The concept of health, today and tomorrow, appears necessary and simultaneously as an individual, social and universal condition for the development of humankind.

Virginia Berridge

The presentation mentioned that in the UK public health had a higher profile for the Labour government, and a Minister for Public Health had been appointed for the first time. It drew out five themes relevant to more distant history which were apparent in the more recent history.

1. Issues of law, regulation and health are being brought together at the local level

The post war focus, in particular since the 1970s, on lifestyle and risk is being modified with an emphasis on safety.

The term 'community safety' is used across a range of recent policy documents, for both crime and health concerns. The local emphasis and the stress on cross boundary working in these documents has echoes of the 1970s, when similar issues were in play.

The notion of the environment is being brought back into public health, although in rather a different way from 19th century environmentalism. The workplace and public space are both foci of the new environmental public health. Law, regulation and health are intermingled with a more punitive turn is some areas e.g. drug testing.

2. Inequality is back on the agenda

A few years back, inequality could not be talked about.Now it is back as 'social exclusion' (previously 'variations in health'). But for public health one trend is for it to be treated in a medicalised way e.g. NRT on prescription. How does this issue vary across Europe?

3. The nature of internationalism

This remains an important force within public health. The WHO continues to be an important force, and the EU is now a key player in developing an international/ European health ethos e.g. over tobacco/drugs.

The developing country dimension of health issues is increasingly important e.g. AIDS and the Third World; smoking and developing countries. There are parallels here with the situation with opium at the end of the 19th century.

Virginia Berridge

4. Public health and primary care

In the British context, the tension between public health and the general practitioner has been significant. Both have laid claim to similar territory. Now in the UK there is a 'primary care led NHS'. The general practitioner seems to be the focus of local health intervention through the new primary care commissioning groups. So where does this leave public health – whose practitioners are also involved at the local level through the new Health Improvement Programmes?

5. New scientific alliances

Epidemiology has been the dominant technical tool of public health in the post war period. But increasingly it is under stress, and new alliances with biomedicine and with genetics are developing. The dominant scientific paradigm for public health is changing, with echoes of the hereditarian 1890s as well as the 1990s.

372

Klim McPherson

The theme for this meeting seems to be 'Medicine is politics, done otherwise' which you take as your starting point. However we talk now of public health, which is very much broader than medicine, and right now I believe we are at an important historical and crucial watershed for public health. Public health concerns populations not individuals, it is concerned for the long term well-being of those populations (where any short term beneficial consequences of successful public health policy are rare). These differences of breadth and long-termism between medicine and public health are real and are becoming more important in the determination of what is successful public health strategy. No longer is the tendency to medicalise public health strategy necessarily the best strategy, and this really has been the dominant theme for so long. This is not to say that medicine is not important in public health, often it is vital, but that it really has very different constraints, expectations and purpose from those of public health.

Public health unlike medicine is not demand (or illness) led and public health therefore really is dominantly political, although it is clearly scientific. This is unlike medicine which is dominantly scientific and hence strives, mostly successfully, to be apolitical. Public health strategy has to be a matter of public policy because it often satisfies no immediate perceived need for individuals, while medicine inevitably responds to manifest and immediate individual need. In so far as public health issues can be wrapped in medical clothes appropriately then a 'medical' response might be appropriate, but increasingly this is becoming more and more difficult and, most importantly, inappropriate. Primary prevention is a crucial case in point where frankly medicine *per se* has nothing to offer except in so far as the phenomenon being prevented is often, but not always, a disease. But, I believe, that dominant connection has now run its course. Nonetheless we do witness now a clear struggle for legitimacy in primary prevention with pharmaceuticals, for example, attempting to medicalise almost every aspect of intrinsically problematic behavioral or political strategies.

An example which symbolises the essential dilemma in modern public health is the strategic attempt to diminish the burden from prostate cancer, largely, of course, a disease of elderly men. Because the plausibility of therapeutic advantages of early treatment for cancer is accepted *primie facie*, so the idea that diagnosing prostate cancer earlier rather that later must be beneficial does not, it seems, need to be proven. Hence men with (or indeed without) mild and essentially benign symptoms associated with urination can easily be persuaded that a simple test will enable an earlier diagnosis of cancer, if present. This may possibly save their lives, just like the early detection of breast cancer can do for women. However most of the pressure for this course of action comes from clinical medicine and a natural concern that anybody has about getting cancer. (Urology clinics are where prostate cancer patients end up and where the burden of this disease is perceived most starkly of course.) However there is very little doubt that widespread prostate cancer screening would, and maybe is, leading to a public health disaster for elderly men.

The reason is that the test itself (the PSA test or digital rectal examination) is not particularly specific for detecting harmful cancer and identifies many false positives. Much of prostate cancer is relatively benign and essentially harmless, in the sense that men will survive their life span with such cancers without symptoms. No test can yet tell which cancer is which, and furthermore there is evidence that early treatments serves no useful purpose in the malignant version anyway. Thus the screening of men with legitimate concerns will yield widespread incontinence, infertility and impotence induced by unnecessary surgery and very little, if any, benefit from improved treatment of prostate cancer. The trouble here is that many men with 'cancer' detected have every reason to be extremely grateful, notwithstanding these awful side effects, since they cannot know whether their 'cancer' was benign or not, nor whether the treatment was beneficial as a consequence of earlier diagnosis. All they can see is that the awful operation has saved them from instant death from cancer. And if they live for a long time after radical surgery then obviously that is the reason, but many of them would have lived with cancer undetected for a long time anyway

However, of course should they die from cancer that will attributed to the fact that their test was not done early enough, so the notion which justifies screening and the policy is a clear winner. As Frank Dobson remarked at a dinner the other day; he felt for those interested in the prevention of illness since those that benefit from their concerns, in this case the thousands of men spared invasive surgery which would probably be useless and harmful, do not know that they benefit. This compared with the few who appear to suffer; those that die from prostate cancer who could have been cured by earlier diagnosis. There may be no such people in reality, but there will certainly be many, in present circumstance of the medicalisation of public health, who can reasonably see themselves in that position, given particularly the commercial interests in selling such 'prevention' tests. Such a strategy has the other predominant virtue of the medicalisation of public health – its implicit, and successful emphasis on blaming the victim. However, its usefulness to men is devoid of any evidence in its favour whatsoever.

There are other examples such as this, where the medicalisation of public health is heavily disadvantageous but where the evidence base is somewhat sophisticated and holds little sway against arguments of intrinsic medical plausibility for the individual. This is what makes public health political, as well as currently seeming to require a certain explicit de-medicalisation, in the clear interests of the public's health.

Hence the watershed in public health requires that it asserts itself as a discipline and an intellectual enterprise in its own right and takes the true responsibility for the health and wellbeing of the public on the shirt tails of nobody. The notion of population health is complex and poorly explored relative to the complexities of individual health. Yet it is clear that the benefits from a more successful public health policy are, in principle, much greater now than any possible benefit from a greater understanding of individual health.

But these benefits have to be reliably and sensibly portrayed. The idea is not simply to prevent death or illness, but to prevent premature and unwanted death and illness. Coronary heart disease is, of course, one of the better ways of departing from the developed world particularly, if sudden and unexpected. But a coronary event aged 62 is usually a very bad idea, since it is likely to involve surgery and medicines and severe interruption to one's life. If fatal, the loss felt by one's closest relatives is likely to be profound, whereas such things are to be expected at around age 82. The point here is that serious coronary events before age 70 are eminently preventable, as social class 1 people in the UK have already demonstrated, as well as in America and in Australia. People simply moderate their diet, quit cigarettes and exercise in a sensible and acceptable fashion and their risk essentially disappears. Nobody knows what happens if Western populations eat in a such a manner to reduce cholesterol levels to those experienced in the Far East or in Africa. Whether it is possible to do so easily in large numbers is untested, but the consequences are quite exciting and dramatic to predict, given what we know about the epidemiology of this disease in these various cultures. Coronary heart disease, now the biggest killer could become quite rare as far as we know.

But let us in public health, again be wary. Randomised trials of population interventions to reduce cholesterol by dietary means have failed, in aggregate, to have any significant impact. But this is not surprising, inevitably measured in the short term, among such perfectly healthy individuals for whom only radical and permanent dietary changes will importantly affect serum cholesterol, then in the longer term. Hence, it is argued, such a strategy is worthless and only drugs which reduce cholesterol can have any effect. Short termism appears more attractive and, of course, many commercial interests can benefit enormously. What we do not know is whether a sensible and comprehensive food policy, affecting price and availability, might not have a dramatic and relatively painless effect on the burden of premature coronary disease in Western communities.

Take another example, that of nicotine. The drug regulation agencies throughout the World are there to protect the health of the public when exposed to therapeutic medicines. The notion is that such preparations should be demonstrated to offer a net benefit and to safeguard the public from unexpected disasters such a Thalidomide. These agencies are the ultimate and entirely legitimate manifestations of what are disparagingly referred to by neo-liberals as the 'Nanny State'. But ensuring that the medical prescription is as safe as could be expected, and disallowing those that might cause more harm than good in aggregate, is a serious and complicated business that any civilized community has a right to expect of its expert governance. The fact that any individual could make a personal balance on the basis of his or her utilities that countered the particular recommendation obviously does not, in general, allow such individuals to ignore the ruling of the regulating agency. And this a perfectly normal part of healthy life, not to be abused of course.

Now nicotine replacement therapy is given, like any other medicine, very close attention and is only licensed in particular delivery systems (chewing gum for example), in particular packs and under particular prescriptive constraints. This, notwithstanding the fact that nicotine delivery systems in the most unsafe and ludicrous packaging and marketing milieu are still allowed almost completely uncontrolled in any corner shop. This has to be, of course, out of respect for those already addicted to these lethal products.

Thus young children still now routinely become addicted to nicotine at a time in their lives when cigarettes are hardly harmful at all and when demonstrating independence of spirit is absolutely vital to most of them. When all that begins to wear thin, quitting is by then really problematic at precisely the time when continuing to smoke will seriously jeopardize their life chances. It is a strange paradox that young children are not allowed nicotine replacement therapy until they can demonstrate addiction to cigarettes.

Either nicotine is a drug in its most common delivery system, whose safety matters to people, or it is not, and herein lies another essential dilemma for public health. The regulating agencies could take the obvious step and include nicotine as a drug, which it is, and subsume the substance as a medicine. They could then, under existing legislation, only license products delivering less than a certain amount. Then a system would be in place whereby the addictive nature of cigarettes (which is what eventually kills, by inducing long term smoking), could be gradually and sensibly controlled, with due respect for those already addicted. Teenagers could then more easily quit, if they wanted, before harm starts to be done – after age 25 roughly. The idea that the manufacturers will voluntarily agree to reduce nicotine delivery is just silly, as it is clearly in direct violation of their commercial interest. But their profits and the premature deaths of 50% of addicted smokers is otherwise guaranteed.

Now the medicine regulating infrastructure clearly saves lives and harm and is an essential part of any public health structure. John Snow removed the pump handle before he knew precisely why so many died of cholera while using the Broad Street pump. That was a clinical reflex to overwhelming short term evidence and a massive immediate disease burden. The equivalent now is nicotine, animal fat and epidemiological research into the prevention of prostate cancer. At the moment the first two are clear but fail to be implemented ! That is because the evidence base is not so stark, and in part this is because the evidence comes from long term observation alone. Public health needs to take the bull by the horns. The nanny state is a real red herring – attracting teenagers to lethal addiction is what we all would despise as enabling easy and cheap diets that cause coronary disease. Much better to enable easy, cheap, varied and attractive diets that don't.

Information Note

This conference was organised in the framework of a series of initiatives taken by the European Commission in order to stimulate reflection and debate on science and technology on a European scale, focusing attention on subjects related to historical, cultural, ethical and social aspects of science and technology.

The originality of these initiatives Conferences, when compared with other initiatives in this field, was to address the questions dealt with specifically within their European dimension: attention was concentrated on the particularity of the situation in the field concerned in Europe in comparison with other parts of the world; the differences between European countries and regions; the aspects related to the process of building Europe; the needs and possibilities of collaboration at European level, etc.

The conferences organised in this framework have put together a broad spectrum of people from different horizons: historians, sociologists, philosophers, specialists in "science studies", researchers in natural and exact sciences as well as in social sciences and humanities, people in charge of research and policy-decision makers, representatives from the industrial and entrepreneurial world and citizens' associations, etc. Organised by national or European institutions, each conference drew together between 100 and 200 people. The proceedings were systematically published and broadly disseminated.

Agenda

1994

Title	Place	Date	Organisation
"Scientific Expertise in European Public Policy Debate"	London	14 - 15 September 1994	London School of Economics and Political Science
"Science and Languages in Europe"	Paris	14 - 16 November 1994	Ecole des Hautes Etudes en Sciences Sociales – Centre Alexandre Koyré
"Science and Power: the Historical Foundations of Research Policies in Europe"	Firenze	8 - 10 December 1994	Istituto e Museo di Storia della Scienza
"Science, Philosophy and the History of Sciences in Europe"	Paris	9 - 10 December 1994	Association Diderot
"Science in School and the Future of Scientific Culture in Europe"	Lisboa	14 - 15 December 1994	Instituto de Prospectiva

1995

Title	Place	Date	Organisation
"History of European Scientific and Technological Cooperation"	Firenze	9 - 11 November 1995	European University Institute
"Science, Law and Ethics in Europe"	Paris	8 - 9 December 1995	Association Diderot

1996

Title	Place	Date	Organisation
"The Future of Postgraduate Education in Europe"	Firenze	17 - 18 June 1996	European University Institute
"Images and Science Education in Europe"	Paris	3 - 4 October 1996	CNRS Images/Media FEMIS

1997

Title	Place	Date	Organisation
"Industrial History and Technological Development in Europe"	London	20 - 21 March 1997	The Newcomen Society
"Interdisciplinarity and the Organisation of Knowledge in Europe"	Cambridge	24 - 26 September 1997	Academia Europaea

Title	Place	Date	Organisation
"Sciences, Myths and Religions in Europe"	Royaumont	13- 14 October 1997	Association Diderot
"Science and Technology Awareness in Europe: New Insights"	Roma	20- 21 November 1997	Hypothesis
"European Science and Scientists between Freedom and Responsibility"	Amsterdam	2 - 3 December 1997	Royal Netherlands Academy of Arts and Sciences/ALLEA

1998

Title	Place	Date	Organisation
"Writing and Science in Europe"	Nice	12- 14 March 1998	Association Anaïs
"Electronic Communication and Research in Europe"	Darmstadt	15 - 17 April 1998	Academia Europaea
"History of Science and Technology in Education and Training in Europe"	Strasbourg	25 - 26 June 1998	Université Louis Pasteur/ALLEA
"Images of Disease. Science, Public Policy and Health in Post-war Europe"	Barcelona	25 - 28 November 1998	Maison des Sciences de l'Homme

1999

Title	Place	Date	Organisation
"Cultural Identities and Natural Sciences in Europe"	Bologna	16-17 April 1999	Association Transcultura

European Commission

Images of Disease

Luxembourg: Office for Official Publications of the European Communities

2001 – 382 pp. — 17 x 24 cm

ISBN 92-894-1146-5

Price (excluding VAT) in Luxembourg: EUR 18.50